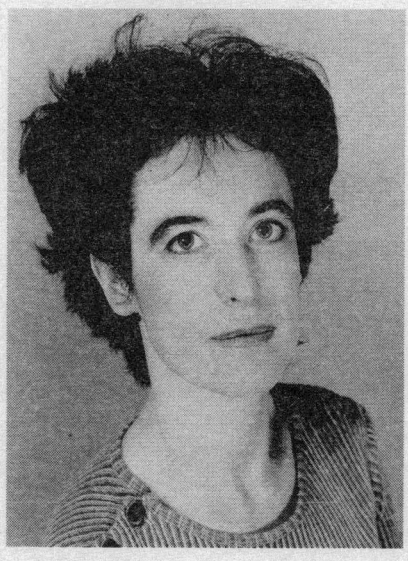

Helena Drysdale is the author of three other highly acclaimed travel books: *Alone Through China and Tibet, Dancing with the Dead* and *Looking for George*, which was shortlisted for the *Esquire*/Apple/ Waterstone's Non-Fiction Award and the J. R. Ackerley Award for Auto- biography. She currently lives in London.

HELENA DRYSDALE

MOTHER TONGUES

Travels through Tribal Europe

PICADOR

First published 2001 by Picador

This edition published 2002 by Picador
an imprint of Pan Macmillan Ltd
Pan Macmillan, 20 New Wharf Road, London N1 9RR
Basingstoke and Oxford
Associated companies throughout the world
www.panmacmillan.com

ISBN 0 330 37281 5

3 5 7 9 8 6 4 2

A CIP catalogue record for this book is available from
the British Library.

Phototypeset by Intype London Ltd
Printed and bound in Great Britain by
Mackays of Chatham plc, Chatham, Kent

www.helenadrysdale.com

'I pass, like night, from land to land;
I have strange power of speech;
That moment that his face I see,
I know the man that must hear me:
To him my tale I teach.'

SAMUEL TAYLOR COLERIDGE
'The Rime of the Ancient Mariner', Part VII

'And yet they think that their homes shall continue for ever:
and that their dwelling places shall endure from one generation
to another; and call the lands after their own names.'

PSALMS XLIX 11

'I who have stood dumb
When your betraying sisters,
Cauled in tar,
Wept by the railings,

Who would connive
In civilised outrage
Yet understand the exact
And tribal, intimate revenge.'

SEAMUS HEANEY
'Punishment', from North

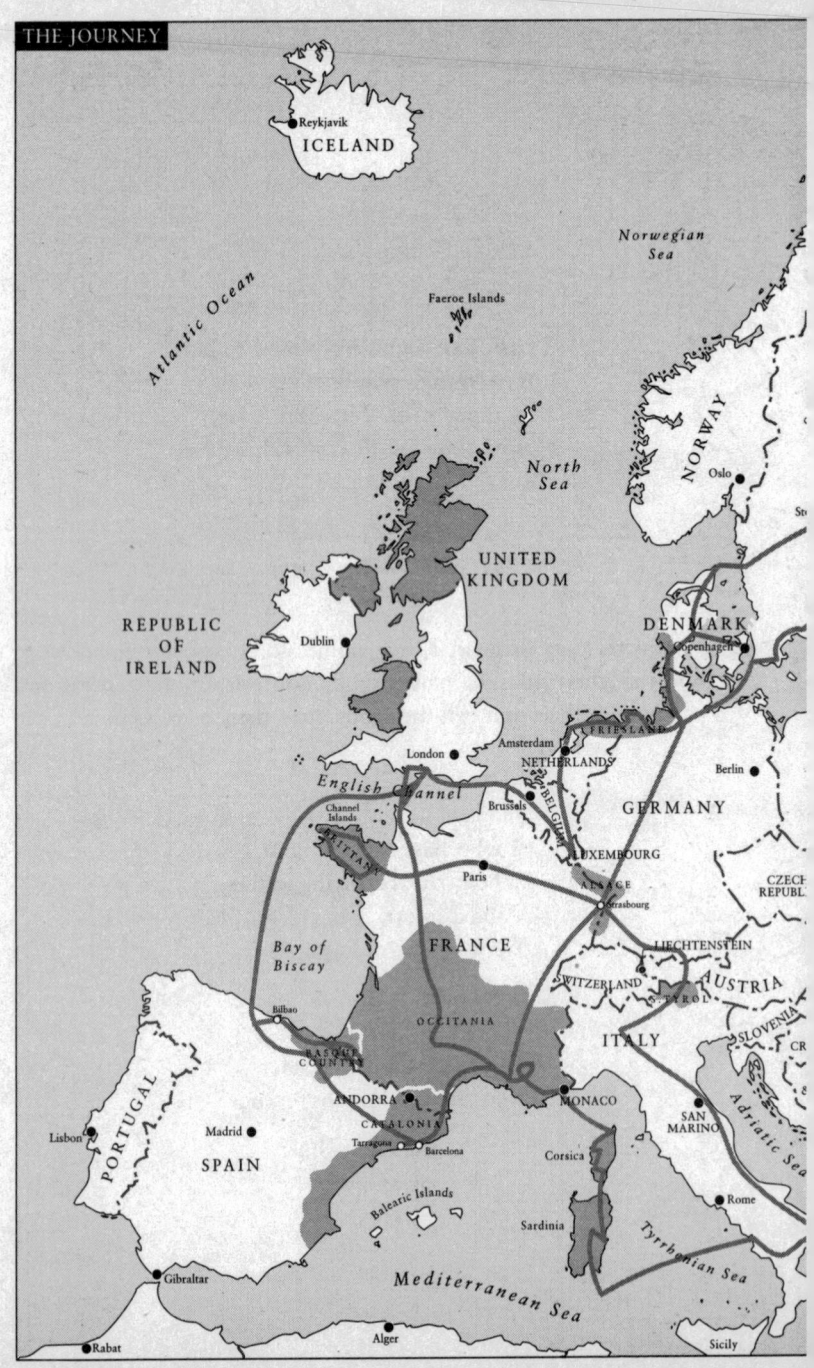

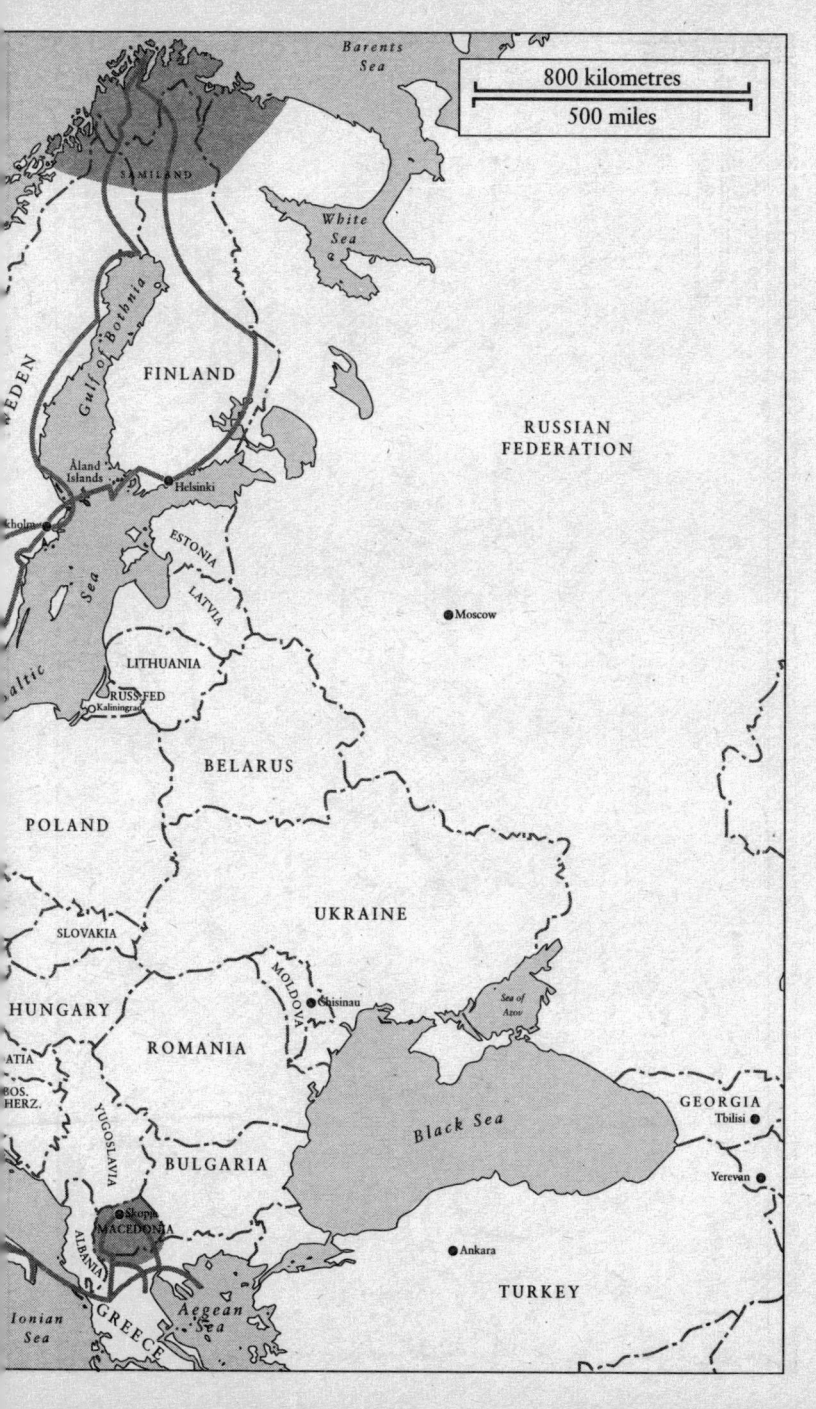

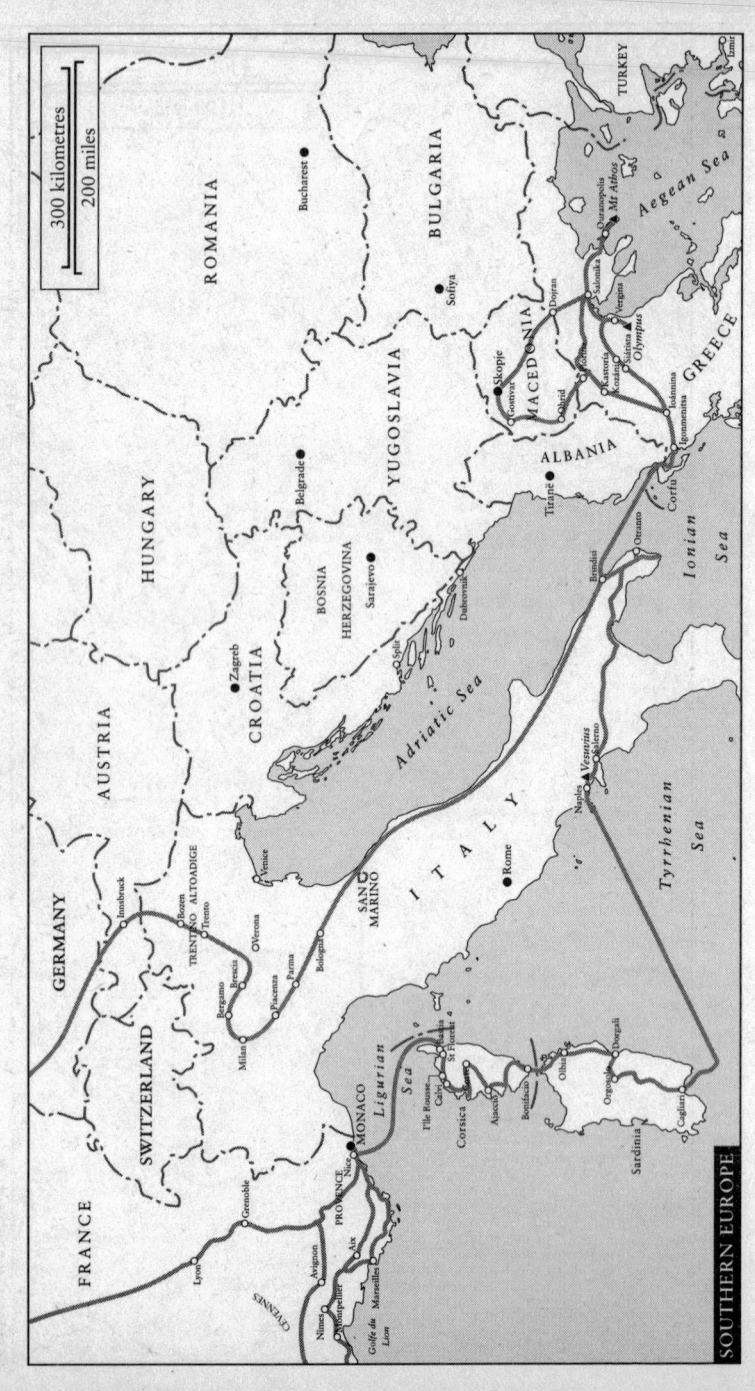

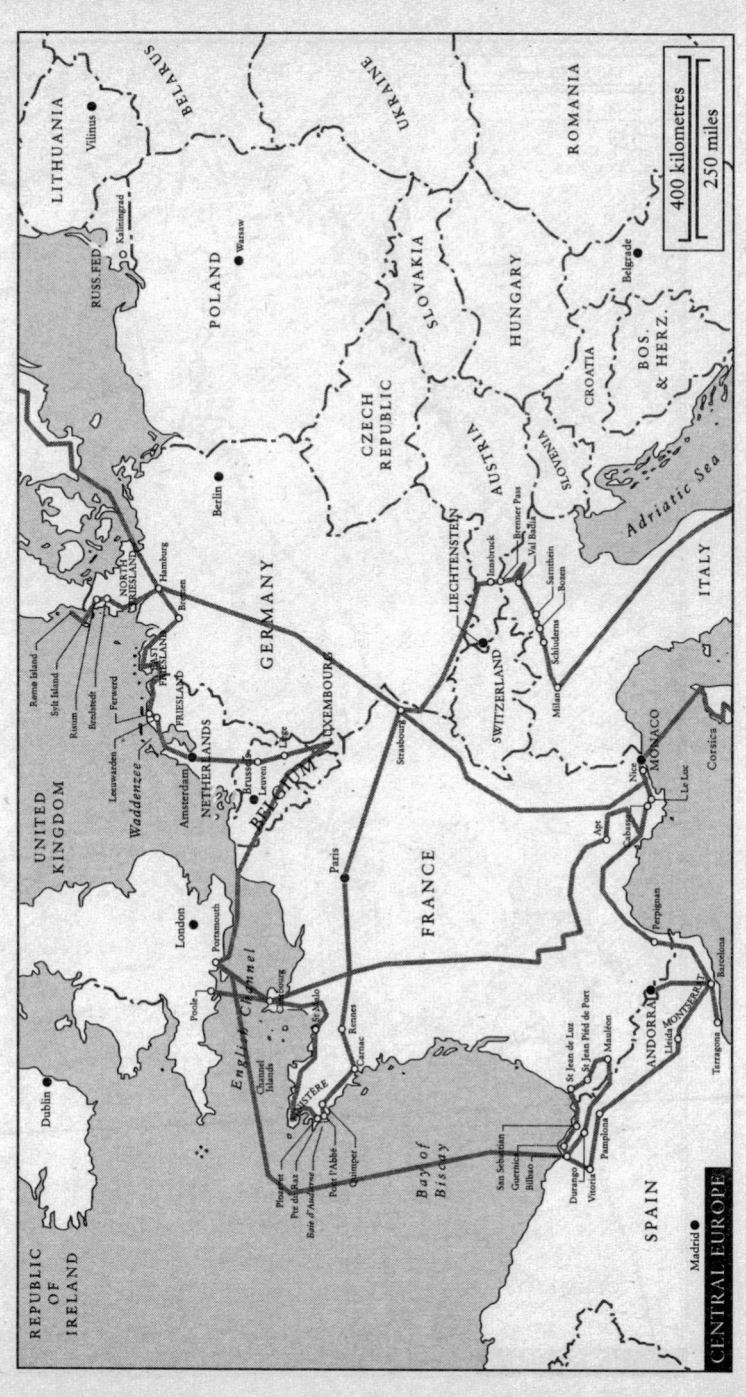

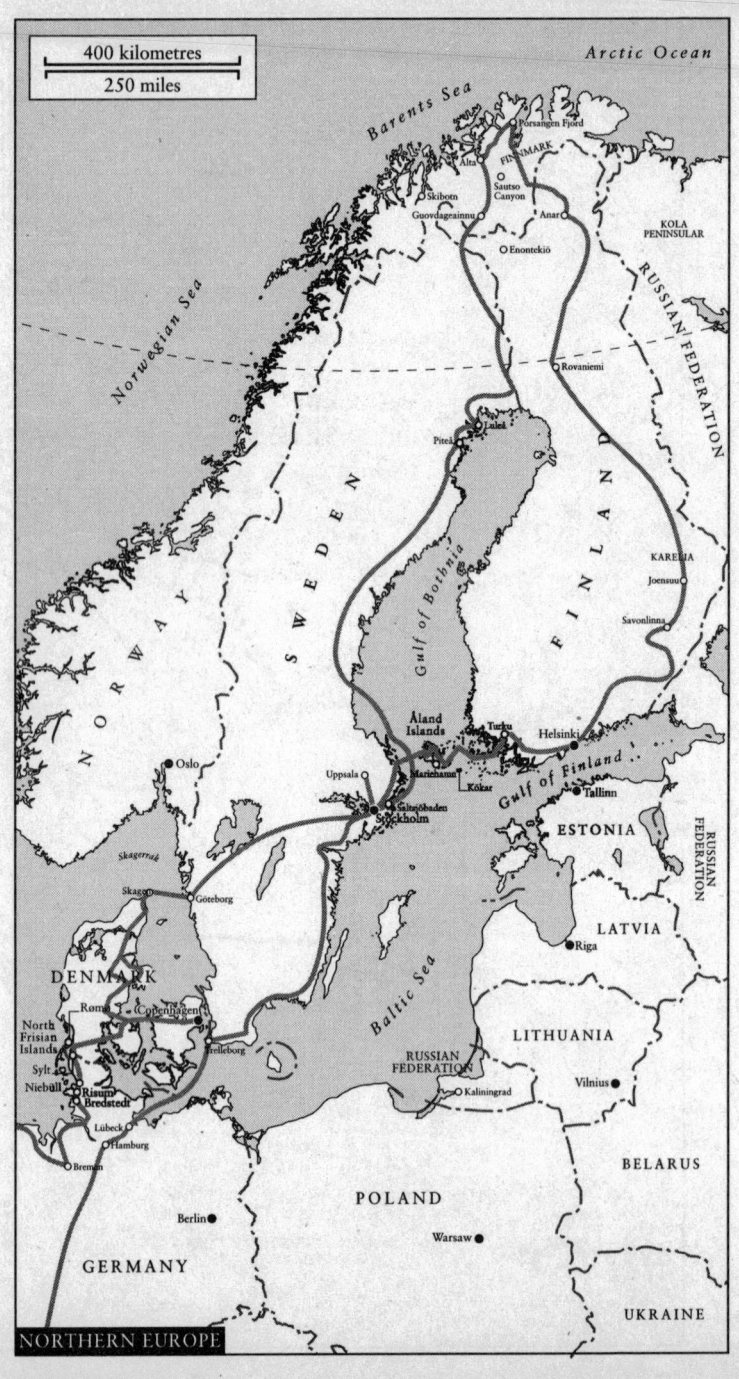

400 kilometres
250 miles

Arctic Ocean

Barents Sea

Pörsangen Fjord

Alta
FINNMARK
Skibotn
Sautso
Canyon
Guovdageainnu
Anar
Enontekiö

KOLA
PENINSULAR

RUSSIAN FEDERATION

Rovaniemi

Norwegian Sea

N O R W A Y

S W E D E N

Piteå
Luleå

Gulf of Bothnia

F I N L A N D

KARELIA
Joensuu

Savonlinna

Åland
Islands
Turku
Helsinki

Oslo

Uppsala
Mariehamn
Kökar
Gulf of Finland
Tallinn

Saltsjöbaden
Stockholm

ESTONIA
RUSSIAN
FEDERATION

Skagerrak

Skagen
Göteborg

LATVIA
Riga

Baltic Sea

DENMARK
Rømø
Copenhagen

LITHUANIA

North
Frisian
Islands
Trelleborg

RUSSIAN
FEDERATION

Sylt
Niebüll
Risum
Bredstedt

Kaliningrad

Vilnius

Lübeck
Hamburg
Bremen

BELARUS

POLAND

Berlin

Warsaw

GERMANY

UKRAINE

NORTHERN EUROPE

Contents

Acknowledgements

Our journey was intended to encompass the EU as it stood in 1996–7. That meant all Western Europe plus Finland, but minus Norway, Switzerland, Liechtenstein, Iceland, the Channel Islands, and other off-shore dependencies. In the end the story took us beyond our boundary into Norway and Macedonia, but shortage of space prevented me from including in the book the Irish, Welsh, Scots, Luxembourgois, Sorbs, or Galicians. I also had to cut out Romanies and Jews, on the grounds that I was investigating speakers of languages who were rooted to a place, and the relationships between them and that place. Apologies to them and other speakers of non-state languages who have been excluded. They will have to wait for another volume.

There are so many people to thank. Before we had even embarked, we were already indebted to Rosamund Pomeroy, who helped us buy the Mob, and to Nick Charrington, who showed Richard how to keep it running.

Then there were those who welcomed us with open arms, and allowed us to turn our Mob into a mobile guest suite. For Tallulah and Xanthe these visits were like little trips home. In France our kind friends were Peter and Jenny Alliott, Tim and Adrienne Maguire, Phippi Richmond and Nick Wood, Matthew and the late Johanne Drysdale, Lauraine and Serge Lecrinier, Sophie and Jean François, Corine and Laurent Loubatières, and Roland and Babette Bec; in Sweden Alf and Ann-Sofie Westelius; in Finland Harry and Jaana Charrington; in Denmark Alan and Collette Havsteen-Mikkelsen, and Ulla and Eigil Hoydal; in Barcelona Charlotte Faber and John Marais; in Italy the Winspeare family, and Francesca Patrizi and Oberto dal Pozzo; in South Tyrol and Innsbruck Johannes and Cecily Trapp; in Greece Angelos Katsaounis; in Wales Margaret Greenwood, Mansel and Caroline Kedward, the Earl and Countess Lloyd George, Maryllin and Raphael Maklouf, and Michael and Jill Griffith; finally in Scotland Andrew and Mary Gladstone. A huge thank you to them all.

Some of these, and other useful contacts, were provided by Rosie Boycott, Martin and Frances Caiger Smith, and Alan Watson.

I am deeply indebted to those who helped in the writing of *Mother Tongues*. The following read and commented on all or parts of the manuscript: Dr Durk Gorter, of the Mercator-Education Network for Lesser-Used languages, and a professor of linguistics at the University of Amsterdam; Professor Larry Trask, Professor of Linguistics in the School of Cognitive and Computing Sciences at the University of Sussex; and Nicholas Ostler, President of the Foundation for Endangered Languages. Obviously, any errors that have sneaked through are my own.

I am grateful to the poet Christopher Reid for sending me Seamus Heaney's poem 'Punishment'; to Oana Lungescu – European extraordinaire – for the Catalan translation; to Hans-Christian Søborg, Director of the Alta Museum, for the nineteenth-century Sami poem; to Martin Leeburn for crucial Basque information; to the European Bureau for Lesser Used Languages for providing what material they had; to Luke Hughes for the Cavalli-Sforza connection; and to Nicholas Crane for that crucial plural.

I would also like to thank Vicki Ingle at Cadogan Guides who provided Cadogan Guides to almost every country in Western Europe. These witty and well-informed guidebooks were the best companions we could have had. I am also grateful to the K. Blundell Trust for a generous grant.

I am grateful to Faber and Faber for permission to quote from 'Punishment' from *North* by Seamus Heaney, published by Faber and Faber in 1975.

Thanks also to the editorial team at Picador – Peter Straus, Richard Milner and Becky Senior – and to my agent Derek Johns, always patient, always encouraging. Thanks too to orthopaedic physician Dr Clifford Harley, who (for free) kept my back going as long as necessary.

Last, but not least, undying gratitude to Richard, Tallulah and Xanthe, for coming too. This book is for them.

Note on the text
The language of toponyms is an emotive political issue in Europe. Throughout the book I have used generally recognized toponyms for internationally known places (Bilbao for example, rather than the Basque Bilbo), but have reverted to local toponyms for smaller places.

Searching for the Sautso Canyon

The door swung shut behind me. I stood on a slick of granite, sniffing the mist. On the back of each wet molecule rode smells of the tundra: damp, peat bogs, moss, an underwhiff of dung. I breathed deeper. Around me spread fells, vast mountains flattened over millennia by ice and, in late July, still snow-patched. There was no horizon; my wilderness was without limits, it simply dissolved.

Then from the mist a herd of reindeer materialized, ghostly at first. They were nervous creatures with tangled antlers, some very young, their white tails eagerly erect. They ignored me and trotted past, pausing to nuzzle through moss, and away, back into the mist.

The door slammed open. Tallulah screamed, 'Don't go! Please don't go!' Richard tumbled after her. She bucked in his arms, writhing, face swollen, tear-wet hair spiked all over her head. 'Please don't go! *Please!*'

I hesitated.

'Just *go*, go on. Leave now. I'll be fine.'

I could hear Xanthe howling in her cot.

'Go *on*! Just enjoy it!'

Resolute, I put up my hood and strode away. It was eight o'clock in the evening.

Somewhere ahead of me a fissure split the earth. Here a beautiful salmon river, the Alta, plunged into the Sautso Canyon, the deepest canyon in northern Europe. I could neither hear it nor see it, but I knew it was there. Red paint splashed on to intermittent rocks marked the route, so I didn't bother to take the compass. Besides, up in the Arctic the magnetic forces of the North Pole do peculiar things to compasses, pulling them this way and that, making them lie.

The stress of departure faded. I began to exult at the empty expanse. I had found my escape valve. Now, as far as I could see, and much further, there was nobody. Just a wide open place circled with cloud. I had the same secret pleasure as if I were out in a stolen dawn, with everyone else asleep; but this was a stolen night – night and yet not night, for it was light as midday.

My rustling waterproofs blocked the sounds, so I took them off, despite the drizzle. Now I heard the wind, grunts of deer, and above them the single lonely cry of a golden plover.

I squelched through seeping black quagmires past black crow-berries and black-berried junipers, past stands of tortured birch. Then out into heather. It coated tumuli of peat whose cores were locked in permafrost. Here and there the bedrock broke the surface, like the earth's bones poking up from some geological cemetery, their gleaming shafts freckled with lichen.

The upthrusting penis-shaped rocks would have been *sieidi* to the Sami – sacrificial sites, imbued with primeval powers. Some Arctic rocks still bear traces of the fish fat that was smeared on them to bring good fortune to fishing.

This was the open-steppe tundra through which Neanderthal man hunted and scavenged, using his sturdy limbs to drag the frozen carcass of some Pleistocene mammoth back to his cave. He squatted at his fire to defrost it and tear it apart with his massive teeth. His skull was so thick and helmet-like it could protect his head from the cold; his huge nose warmed the air before it reached his brain. His brain was large, but he probably still communicated in grunts. It is possible that he had no language.

At some time during the ice ages, 40,000 to 30,000 years ago, the lumpen Neanderthal was replaced by someone more like myself, Palaeolithic man. Seasonal glaciers still covered the North in a band, their southerly limit crossing from the middle of Wales to the southern foothills of the Alps. The land looked like this. My view was his view. I felt the thrill of being in touch with my own pre-history.

Instead of ranging freely like Neanderthal man, Palaeolithic man understood the migratory nature of the herds he lived off. He built settlements across their seasonal trails. He built traps, and lines of cairns that converged like funnels to drive the herds over cliffs. And what he liked best was reindeer. Archaeologists found that in the Dordogne caves, where we began our own journey three months earlier, almost all the 'faunal assemblages' were reindeer remains. Reindeer bones and antlers were crafted into tools and sculpted into beautiful objects, and reindeer skin and furs were worn as clothes.

As the air warmed and the last ice caps retreated, forests grew. Reindeer were pushed north and north again in search of open pasture, until they reached the top of the world and could go no further. Man followed.

I noticed the herd to my right. These were not wild reindeer, which have died out; these were herded by their Sami owners, following ancient grazing routes. I'd seen a Sami map that marked their routes in red, like thread veins. They'd been following those veins for thousands of years.

One mid-sized male was frisking about, still white in his winter coat, but shedding it; tufts of white hairs dotted my route. I pocketed some for Tallulah, to add to the collection of bones and shells and peculiar seeds that littered her toy box.

I circled a grey-green tarn edged with reeds with tops of fluffy cotton. Tallulah had a clump of reed cotton that she said was for cleaning Xanthe's bum. Little ones! I felt guilty about leaving Richard with them; he would have loved this. But it was my turn. I had appointed myself monitor of our brief moments of solitude.

I reached a waterfall. Veils of snowmelt, trailing dripping strands of icicles, tumbled into a gorge that fed the Alta. Although the paint-splashed rocks had disappeared, I followed this tributary down, scrunching across a patch of dirty old snow. The path narrowed into a birch wood and dropped towards the canyon; I heard a hollow booming, but couldn't see the river for the trees. On the opposite bank an emptiness of birch and scrub – silver squiggles against a russet ground – mirrored what I could not see vertically below.

Then I reached the edge.

Land plunged each side to swooshing grey water, and between, as if waiting for something, hovered two grey clouds. It was grand, marvellous. Every summer for eighteen thousand years, since the ice left, that gorge had been booming, those clouds waiting. For what? For nothing. Just for themselves.

Pleistocene or Neolithic time meant nothing. This was the beginning and end of time. It was a mystery I could not even begin to fathom, on the northernmost rim of the world.

The hated Alta Dam lay upstream, out of sight. Here, during the 1980s, a battle over land and fishing rights was fought between the Sami and the Norwegian government. A gulf had divided them. It was why I had come. The government had proposed to dam the Alta to construct a hydroelectric power plant. The fishing would be destroyed, and vast tracts of precious reindeer grazing land would be flooded. For centuries the Sami had lost land to mines, timber companies and dams, but this was one dam too many. The Sami protested against the relentless encroachment on their territory, but to deaf ears. So for the first time the Sami fought back. There were demonstrations, hunger strikes, mass arrests, and tragedy when a photographer, attempting to destroy the dam approach bridge, was blown up by his own bomb.

They lost: the dam was built. But in unexpected ways they won. Alta became a catalyst. It was not just that the government reduced the scale of the dam and flooded less land; it was that the plight of the Sami became an international issue. They were joined by environmentalists. Their profile rose. They showed that they were capable of getting together across international frontiers and standing up for themselves. They frightened the government with their nascent violence. The most crucial result was that in Norway and Finland (and later in Sweden) laws were passed which at last recognized Sami as a separate national language. After centuries of deliberate assimilation, at last the Sami would see their children legally taught at school in Sami. They would see their towns and villages up on signposts in their own ancient Sami names. By rescuing their language from oblivion, the Sami were saving their very identity, their sense of themselves as a people. Without their language, they would be lost. This was not ancient history; this was in 1992.

Mosquitoes were biting; I couldn't linger. Backtracking to the waterfall, the red-splashed rocks reappeared and I realized that earlier I had taken the wrong path. I had seen the canyon, but not the deepest part. That lay beyond the waterfall. I crossed its head by leaping from rock to rock.

The deer came by. I had the unsettling sensation of being watched. Maybe Sami herders and their dogs were camped in some hideaway.

Until eighteenth-century missionaries committed auto-da-fé on the shamans and their painted magic drums, a Sami *noaidi* could put his ear to his drum while drumming and listen to its speech by following the movement of his drumstick; with the help of those he encountered on the way – mountains, reindeer, bears, birds, gods, tents, flies, whose images were painted on his drum – he could assist the transmigration of the soul; in a state of ecstasy he could travel into realms of the dead or the future. He sang of his journey to the land of spirits. He could also 'travel' into the landscape around him, using the drumstick as a compass to track the herd during migrations or to find the way through barren wilds. The *noaidi* was like a wanderer, listening to the song, as if listening to the heartbeat of life, and following it, as if following an invisible path.

I stood and listened, half expecting to hear some *noaidi* drumbeat. Instead I heard my own breathing, seeping streams, and beneath these sounds a deep monotone, almost like the drone of a bagpipe. I wasn't sure what it was – perhaps water, perhaps wind – but it was always there. It had been since this landscape was created. It was the hollow sound of emptiness. As the evening wore on it grew louder.

I passed some orange peel and white tissue paper. Even here! Loathsome tourists, I cursed, prepared to defile this pristine place. Or maybe it was the herders. I had seen tracks of an off-road vehicle, probably the Sami who no longer drove sleighs but came in from the town to check on herds before heading back to the bright lights, leaving a stain behind.

More tributaries, rushing and rocky, with the canyon running parallel but invisibly over the fell. I waded through the uliginous swamp, my socks sodden. I was beginning to feel spaced out with hunger. But I had to go on. Like Ibsen's Little Eyolf who followed the Rat Woman to his death by drowning, I didn't want to go on but I had to. I had to go on because I didn't want to.

I climbed a ridge, convinced that beyond must lie the canyon, but saw only more ridges, more rivers, more cairns, more bogs. There were no final barriers. Unlike a Sami nomad I was new to this landscape and could not read it. Blue-grey clouds swung low like waves. My bumpy heather-clad horizon was like a shore between land and sky. And still that monotone.

I had been walking and wading for four hours.

I thought about those waves breaking over me, the mist closing in, about falling and hurting myself, about Tallulah crying so hysterically as I left. Had that been a portent? Had she been trying to warn me of some terrible fate, either hers or mine? Little Eyolf followed the Rat Woman into the lake to his death. The pull back to the van was growing stronger, almost umbilical. I worried about Richard worrying, and of the reindeer and juniper-berry stew he had been marinating, and his disappointment that I couldn't share it. Then I thought: why am I doing this? I've had my own special view of the canyon already. My feet are sodden. I am cold. I am alone in the Arctic vastness. I want to go home. So, defiant in the face of failure, I turned back.

The drizzle was melancholy grey. The emptiness was no longer majestic, but menacing. The perpetual daylight seemed weird, unearthly, the landscape bleak in its looming blankness. I was alone in a great incomprehensible emptiness. The wilderness hid – what? Nothing specific. Wolves perhaps, even bear, but it was not them I feared. It was something more obscure, some misty, prehistoric sense of fear itself.

I broke into a trot, close to tears. Then I heard clicking, and turned, but saw nothing but bogs, streams, woolly tops of clouds hovering in the canyon. Click, click, click. Deer? Click, click. Some nocturnal bird? Absurdly, I was being frightened by my jacket toggle clicking against my zip.

As I began the last stretch, the mist thickened. The red splashes on rocks, intermittent before, vanished. The cairns, distinguishable by Sami herders or *noaidi*, all looked alike. It was past midnight.

Then I passed the orange peel and white tissue paper. People! Towns! Lights!

And through the cloud loomed a cliff of white. I ran the last stretch. Richard was smiling out of the window. Our bed was made, lights soft. Xanthe snored gently in her cot, but Tallulah was waiting up. She poked her head between her curtains.

'I want to come in *your* bed.'

Richard lifted her down and she snuggled between us.

Richard said, 'I want Mummy beside me.' So she moved over, and we all hugged each other for a while.

My great-great-grandfather was a celebrated Calvinist Methodist preacher, the Rev. John Lewis. He was saturated with the spirit of the Welsh Nonconformist Revival, with its fire and fervency. The fire in his spirit was said to warm the congregations and his eloquence flowed like a stream of lava. At a Revival in Cardiganshire in 1859 he preached with such freshness and power that the congregation broke into spontaneous praise, *gorfoledd*, and remained in the chapel regardless of time, all day then all night. By morning the service still had not ended.

Like a Welsh bard John Lewis wandered the land, heralded by his reputation. He was the chief attraction at the *gymanfa*, the great preaching festivals held not only throughout Wales but in Manchester and Liverpool too. Thousands would gather on hillsides, as if at some ancient bardic fest, to hear him preach. The audience would discuss the relative merits of the preachers billed for the day; John Lewis was a favourite.

He was not a handsome man. His hair grew in a circlet around his bald pate then down beneath his chin like the ribbons of a bonnet. But his eyes burned.

For eleven years he was minister of fourteen churches in Llanrhaeadre-ym-Mochnant in the lovely Tanat valley in Montgomeryshire. He preached ceaselessly, walking the twenty-mile length of his parish between chapels and meetings of the *seiat* and the Band of Hope, tending the sick, taking funerals and weddings. By coincidence it was in Llanrhaeadre-ym-Mochnant that the most crucial event in the history of Welsh took place. Here, in 1588, William Morgan, vicar of Llanrhaeadre, published his translation of the Bible into Welsh. This was only sixty-two years after Tyndale's translation of the Bible into English (and for his trouble Tyndale was burned at the stake), and years before the publication of Bible translations in any other non-state language in Europe. It partly explains why Welsh has survived with such vigour.

John Lewis was born and bred amongst Nonconformists, and Nonconformists spoke Welsh. Welsh-speakers were chapelgoers, English-speakers church. When chapel and church met on the street, one would cross to the other side. The Calvinist-Methodists saw themselves as a lost tribe, bearers of the torch of Welshness, righteousness and education. Through the efforts of men like John Lewis, a powerful Welsh sermonizing tradition grew up, along with hymns, Sunday schools, cultural societies, *eisteddfodau*, and publishing.

But in 1852, at the height of the Welsh Revival, Matthew Arnold, Inspector of Schools, wrote: 'It must always be the desire of a government to render its dominions, as far as possible, homogenous.' Democracy works through majority rule, and a majority can only be created by a society which is homogenous. 'Sooner or later,' he predicted, 'the difference of language between Wales and England will probably be effaced . . . an event which is socially and politically desirable.' Surprising words from a poet entranced by Celtic literature and magic, from the inventor of the Celtic twilight.

Arnold's reports led to the Education Act of 1872, which imposed compulsory education in English. This caused the deep undermining of Welsh and the near extinction of Irish and Scots Gaelic.

Similar acts were passed all over Europe.

In the early 1990s I was writing about Romania, and toing and froing to the Balkans. On the fringes of Bucovina I met Hutsuls (outlaw descendants of exiled Polish aristocrats) and Ruthenian Lemkos and Boikos. With Richard and Tallulah I chugged down the

Danube Delta in search of the fishing Lipovenians, the bearded Old Believers exiled from Moldavia.

I mined the stacks of the London Library for histories of these peoples. Crepuscular days were whiled away between dusty Topography and musty Philology. The secrecy of these book-lined tunnels had an oddly sexual allure, like the recesses of a church. They also enabled me to postpone having to write anything. I began to dig out studies not only of obscure East European tribes, but also of the ancient communities of continental western Europe: The Frisians, inhabitants of ambiguous North Sea mudflats. The Basques, fighting for independence across the Franco-Spanish border. The battling Corsicans in their mountain fastness. The Walloons and Macedonians, the Ålanders, and the Ladin in their secret Dolomitic valleys. My imagination was caught. These were not exotic tribes from distant lands; like the Welsh, they were fellow citizens of a united Europe, yet many I had never heard of.

They were peripheral people, Europe's marginalia, pushed out to the edges of the continent and its islands. They inhabited wild coasts, and borderlands where cultures cross, and land so inhospitable that no one else wants it. But now they were being pushed even further, off the Beachy Head of existence into oblivion. Mass tourism and global communications, quite apart from Matthew Arnold's politically desirable homogenization, have brought up to half of the world's 6500 languages to the brink of extinction. Linguists estimate that a language dies, somewhere in the world, every two weeks.

Within the European Union people in forty different communities speak a 'minority' language which is not that of the state – and that does not include the more recent immigrants. All of them are endangered, if not already moribund. The prospects for the smaller languages of the world are even worse than for the threatened plant and animal species that we hear so much more about. But they are part of the same loss, the loss of diversity in all things.

Yet I also read of a 'resurgence of historic identities', of ancient tribes making their presence felt more strongly than at any time since the end of the Roman Empire. Far from arriving at the long-predicted end of nationalism, the UN is forever admitting new members, while old nation states keep finding sub-nations emerging in their midst. The break-up of Yugoslavia and the USSR, I read, revealed a 'devolutionary virus' that was attacking big political units all over the continent. I was intrigued by the idea of the EU being subjected in its infancy to this two-way pull – centrifugal and centripetal – towards homogenization, and away, back towards something more deep-rooted.

I was compelled by the image of ancient faultlines – Sautso Canyons – opening or reopening across the more recent map lines of the nation state. I thought about people across Europe bonded by their sense of being victimized, their burning resentments fuelled by often distorted histories, their spurned languages, their disparate and desperate attempts to keep their cultures alive. I wanted to know not just who they were, but who they thought they were.

And I wondered if it was right to talk of a resurgence of historic identities, or if we are witnessing a last gasp, a sort of ethnic death rattle.

When Richard was six, his mother asked him what he planned to do when he grew up. He said he was going to live in a bus and travel around with his family. Now was the time. After nine years, the excitement of South London's dog-shit parks and car crime had faded. The novelty had worn off conversations about childcare. Richard was tired of his job in a contemporary art gallery; he wanted to be free to pursue his two great loves, photography and painting. We would wait for our second baby to be born, then before Tallulah started school and we became mired in middle age, we would go.

We took to weekending at Turner's of Dulwich, Britain's longest-established dealers in motor caravans. Tallulah would bounce on beds, sit on loos, peer in cupboards and fiddle with switches, all with an enthusiasm that boded well for our future. The salesmen were a friendly bunch, devotees of the open road, but they had trouble hiding their contempt for our lack of experience. We disguised it by parleying in the jargon – wrap-around, zig unit, three-way fridge, Omnistor. This we picked up from what became our bedtime reading, the catchily titled *Motorcaravan and Motorhome Monthly*, with its section on 'How to Build Your Own Camper', and its invaluable feature, 'Tenner for a Tip'.

So it was that we rented out our house and bought a home with a difference, a home not boringly fixed in one place but with places to go, a home we could drive to a location of our choice, and park. Our home on wheels, self-sufficient, free.

It was converted from a Mercedes 308D van, a cross between a lorry and a caravan, built like an ox and able to heave its diesel engine over any mountain pass. Unlike boats, these humble roadsters are not given names, but their model types are enticingly adventurous. They are 'Cherokee' or 'Voyager', 'Kontiki' or 'Chinook'. Appealing to our outlaw fantasy, ours was a 'Corsair'. But it was known as the Mob. This was short for mobile home, although we discovered that a mobile home was not mobile, at least after its initial journey to its site when it became an immobile home. Nevertheless, the name stuck.

Until we filled it, the Mob's interior seemed spacious. Its decor was delightfully kitsch. If it were a Barratt show home, its style would be described as 'Streatham'. Co-ordinating dusky pink velour furnishings – pink carpet, pink cushions, pink curtains, pink carpeted walls – shimmered under four brass spotlights and a ticking brass clock: very Cynthia Paine. A red light indicated that the water pump was on, and so if money got short I could don black suspenders, get out my knitting, and sit in the window like ladies in the back streets of Liège.

The pièce de résistance was a cocktail cabinet with a plastic 'leaded' window and a light that illumined automatically when you opened it. There was a mini shower, and a mini loo called a 'porta potti', which flushed its contents into a 'cassette'. Everything ended in 'ette'. We would dine in our 'dinette', shower in our 'showerette', and each night we would sleep in our 'bedette'. Yet it was well built, solid.

Richard customized the Mob. He built a toy box in the luton above the driver's cab. This would be the girls' bedroom and playroom, a space six foot by four foot across and two foot six inches high – more a cupboard on its back than a room. As it was six foot off the ground, a safety net was added. Our 'double' bed was punitively narrow, so he made boards to attach it to the single bed on the other side of the 'corridor' (one foot wide), giving us a bed the width of the entire Mob. A strong box for my computer and his camera was built under a seat.

Tallulah was eager to take up residence in her mobile Wendy house. She was physically delicate, prone to chesty colds, but she displayed a promisingly adventurous spirit. I too couldn't wait to escape. As I paced the bedroom in the early hours, trying to soothe a colicky baby, I envisaged myself supine by a sunlit river, my daughters romping over me, with Richard doing something manly (and probably bearded) nearby.

But it took time to draw a line under our lives and for winter to pass and for Xanthe to reach the age of seven months when she stopped waking us four times a night.

At last we packed one wall of cupboards with nappies, the other with children's books, lifted our sleeping babies into the Mob, and left for France. It was April 1996.

ONE

Prouvènço, ma Patrio

First off the ship at Cherbourg but now where? We'd done it! No plans, no place to stay. Goodbye Stockwell, Hello Freedom! Pull into a layby, pull out the map.

We rocked down the Contentin Peninsular, enjoying our regal height and our ability to peer down into people's private back gardens. Richard said: It's good to arrive before the trees are out because it means we haven't missed anything, it's all fresh and new.

Xanthe slept, as she would (magically) every time we turned on the ignition. Tallulah climbed up to her luton and fell asleep. I prised a crayon from under her cheek. When she woke she cried, inconsolably. I think there was an element, even on our first day, of anticlimax.

We made a false start up a track to find it fenced off. Two farmers looked up from beneath a tractor bonnet in astonishment. I felt self-conscious because we were planning to do something illegal, and because I was peering down at them from our white expensive height. They suggested we spent the night beside the *mairie* in Veranguebec, but that wasn't what we had in mind. We boldly turned down another track into the Bois de Limors.

Stunted ancient oaks, mossy stumps, last year's bracken ginger and crunchy underfoot, not a sound but wind in the trees: this was more like it. Mysterious rootlings at the base of trunks suggested wild boar, even truffles. Richard sat on a stump to smoke his first pipe of the trip. He winced at the taste but liked the Hobbit-esque idea of it. Tallulah held the bowl to warm her hands.

As darkness fell in our deep dark wood, we prepared for our first night in our new home. In our frenzy of departure, we had never tested the Mob's gadgets, let alone used them. Gas cooker, water heater, porta potti, fridge, blinds, mosquito screens: everything worked. I lifted a lid beside the porta potti and lo! We even had a loo-roll holder.

For the first time, we made up our bed. The technique was as follows:

1. Prop underboard and mattress on forehead while pulling base out from underneath.

2. Drop board and mattress down without catching fingers.

3. Unscrew table and rest it on mattress.

4. Unscrew table leg.

5. Collapse Xanthe's car seat and squeeze it between front seats.

6. Haul bedding out of cupboards beneath seats.

7. With three boards, connect double bed with single bed to make one bed that fills entire Mob.

8. Stand reel of Sellotape on fridge to see which way it rolls, to ascertain which would be the head of the bed that night, and which the foot.

9. Spread out bedding accordingly.

In the morning, reverse the procedure, but with Tallulah bouncing on the bed, climbing on your back, and crawling into the bedding cupboard. Once you have asked 'Where's Tallulah?' at least ten times and she has been dragged out, hiccuping with laughter, you can re-erect the table and serve breakfast.

All this seemed fun at first, but there would come a day when we would dream of the time when 'making the bed' meant a quick flick of the duvet, not actually constructing the damn thing.

We walked in the Marais, bleached grasses waving into the distance. It was bitterly chill, the kind of April that kicks in with a winter that never was, worse for being unexpected. Xanthe was in the sling, wriggling when spoken to, and Tallulah was in the backpack, keeping up her usual lively chatter. When Richard insisted she walked, she refused to move. We tried to tempt her with open arms and running races, but she stood in the middle of the marsh and yelled, an enraged speck. Richard looked despairing. 'Is our whole trip going to be accompanied by Tallulah's screams?'

We were stopped by an angry man in a beret, Gauloise embedded in bottom lip. He berated us for trespassing.

'*Vous n'avez pas le droit!*' he kept shouting.

I envisaged phrases like '*Excusez-nous,*' and '*Nous ne faisons pas de mal,*' becoming staple over the next few months. We assured him that we would not stay the night (a lie) and parted, but we felt shaken by the reprimand.

By the time we got back we were sodden. There was nowhere to dry anything. A tiny glimmer of warmth escaped from the back of the fridge so we draped our clothes there, but there was no space for jackets.

That night Tallulah woke with a cry. In the morning she drew her nightmare: a frightened face peering through a mesh of what looked like barbed wire. I stuck it on a cupboard door, mainly because it was an expressive drawing, but I also wanted it as a reminder of her sensitivity and fragility. She was a highly intelligent and humorous child, but she had a morbid fear of noise, soldiers, policemen, dogs, monsters, other people's sadness, her own blood. What she liked was to stay in and draw and be read to, a house mouse.

The drawing stayed up for eighteen months. It rebuked us for plucking her from her cosy life and subjecting her to this scary peripatetic existence.

Xanthe was too young to share Tallulah's anxieties. She had spent her waking life roosting like a bird against my shoulder. Over the next few weeks she learnt to sit, so I was occasionally permitted to put her down with her toys, and so long as I was in view, she was content. And I nearly always was in view: for her our confined pink-lined space was like a glorious extended womb.

After three days we felt confident enough to move on. Richard put on the dashboard a list of instructions for himself:

Never forget how tall and wide you are (10′ 9″ high, 20′ long).
Always admit that you are the slowest vehicle on the road.
No road rage.
Keep calm and go slow if in doubt.
Look out for holes and bumps, overhanging branches, low
bridges, etc.

He had noted how to change gas bottles and fill the water tank.
Also how to empty the porta potti. 'Don't let it get too full. If it does
get to overflowing there are instructions in booklet for emergency
procedure (I think it involves drinking straight from the spout).'

We shopped in the nearest village. There was something so enjoy-
ably cheeky about taking our home to the shop and filling our fridge
right in the supermarket car park. Tallulah complained about French
food but as long as she had Special K all was well. Special K
disguised the taste of UHT milk, but it was more than that. For
Tallulah Special K became the equivalent of those sodden rags that
some children suck. It was her comforter, her nye-nye, her noo-noo.
Fortunately – and depressingly – Special K was available (along with
fish fingers, pasta, and Pampers nappies) in every supermarket in
every country in Europe.

When denied an ice cream, Tallulah had a tantrum. That night
she refused to go to bed in her luton, despite the inducements of her
toy box, and her screams woke Xanthe. We managed to get her up
her ladder, and she yelled for a pear, then she sicked it up all over
her sleeping bag.

Tallulah was getting a cold. She drank more Calpol in those early
days than in her whole life hitherto, which worried me as Calpol
was one of the few things that we could not buy anywhere on the
continent. She swallowed so much snot that she was sick in front of
the Bayeaux Tapestry. (Most viewers were plugged into explanatory
headphones, so missed this additional sound effect.) While Richard
cleaned her up, I breastfed Xanthe, gazing across the dimly lit
museum at scenes of extreme violence at the Battle of Hastings.

From April to May we ambled south. Tallulah was angry much
of the time. There were moments when I thought wearily, I know I

love her, but I can't remember why. We had never raised our voices to her before, yet now we did it constantly. Living in such cramped quarters was turning me and Richard into control freaks. I hated myself for it. Tallulah's life had been turned upside down, she was ill, exhausted and overstimulated. Perhaps we all were, but Richard and I were sustained by the adrenalin of the journey, in which Tallulah was only a passenger. She needed more emotional and physical space, but we didn't have that space. Before we left, friends had assured us that children are fine wherever they are so long as they are with their parents. But it wasn't true. Tallulah was not fine. I found it hard to accept that a three-year-old could suffer from what I considered to be the *adult* emotions of claustrophobia, boredom, and irritation, but she did.

Most of all she was lonely. She talked incessantly about her two best friends, Jazzy-and-Georgia, Jazzy-and-Georgia, wondering when they would join her. I couldn't tell her that the answer was probably never. She drew pictures for them and wrote cards that we didn't get around to posting.

Richard had worked since the girls were born, and now he was aghast at how little time they left him to get on with his own thing. He railed against their relentless demands. Before having children, he and I had travelled the world together, and he found it hard to adjust from our usual travel-as-time-out-of-life to a journey which brought our life with it – a routine life of daytime sleeps and 'I DON'T WANT SAUCE WITH MY PASTA'.

Richard intended to paint, but whenever he opened his paintbox Tallulah would insist on painting too. He enjoyed this for a while, but soon found that he never got time to himself. His precious gouaches were squeezed, fine brushes ruined, concentration gone. When Tallulah tired of painting on paper, she painted herself, from head to toe. So Richard decided to abandon painting. He would concentrate solely on photography, something he could do with a child on his back. Once he had accepted this, he felt better.

He and I took out our frustrations on each other. Our family became nuclear in every sense. In our tiny Mob, cast adrift in a foreign country, twelve combinations of relationships rebounded off each other twenty-four hours a day: parent with parent, each parent with each child, each child with parent, child with child. We were often on the brink of meltdown.

Nevertheless, I *liked* the lack of space. It made bringing up children so much easier. No possessions got lost, we never had to trudge from room to room in search of them. If either child woke at night I simply had to reach out. Nappies and wipes were always to hand. I loved the novelty of cooking, tidying, grinding Xanthe's food through the baby mouli, washing up, all in the space of a garden shed. I also liked spending each evening with a different view, a different front garden. I liked the way we lived right in the weather, yet without depending on it; just a thin metal skin divided us from rain or sun. I liked the way I could get out of bed in the morning and step straight outside to sniff the air. I liked the way Richard was always around, sharing every detail of our lives. I liked the way we lived completely inside our own adventure. Best of all I liked the proximity of my daughters' smooth little bodies. They were always within stroking distance.

I found that Tallulah's mood was paramount. If she was happy, we were happy. I was amazed by how much power a three-year-old can have over her parents. And once she was well again she often *was* happy. But one evening, when I was putting her to bed, I asked Tallulah which she preferred of the glories we had seen – the chateaux of the Loire? The Gorge du Tarn? The cathedral at Tours? The prehistoric caves of Périgord? She muttered, 'Stockwell.'

Richard dreamed of olive groves and vineyards and honey-walled farmhouses. The image pulled us south-east.

But as we crossed the Vaucluse, Richard said, now we know why the rest of France is so empty. Everybody's here. Everyone wants a piece of the loveliness, and now there's none left. Olive groves were uprooted and abandoned in garden centres, waiting to adorn some suburban garden. Promising-looking tracks into woods were blocked with chains and a stern *Privé*, and beyond the chains rose brand-new villas. We were forced to park by the road or in designated picnic sites which were fouled with litter. Beside the deserted Lac de

Sainte Croix, an unbelievable turquoise, someone broke into our Mob.

We sought my cousin Mathieu as though seeking sanctuary. He offered us a haven amongst the few hectares of vines he had bought on a hillside near Le Luc in Central Var.

Richard checked the dirt track and after sawing back overhanging trees deemed it accessible. We skewed from hummock to hummock, revving over mini crevasses that severed the red earth, the Mob lurching from side to side. Saucepans crashed out of cupboards. Tallulah clung on, eyes wide with fear, while Xanthe's car seat slid the length of its seat belt, then back again. At the top we skidded. We slid down, tyres burning and stinking, to within a foot of Mathieu's weekend cottage. Thankfully he wasn't here to witness this. We shovelled pebbles and dead grass under the wheels and Richard managed to accelerate out of danger. It was one of our worst moments.

We established ourselves between two terraces buttressed by a dry-stone wall. Lizards flicked between crevices. Awning out, washing up, bikes propped against the wall: this was us at full stretch. Central to the scenario was the well. We hauled up buckets of water, some for drinking, the rest for Richard to boil up on fires of vine prunings. After a month on the road, we could wash our clothes, and for the first time we had sun to dry them. We warmed up, and settled down.

I put the girls to bed. Tallulah thrust her head between curtains once pink, now striped with felt pen and dangling with dags of dried playdough.

'Mummy.'

'Yes, darling?'

'What are you doing?'

'Clearing up. Then I'm going outside.'

'I don't want you to go outside!'

'I'll be just there. You can see me from your window.'

'But I want you to stay in here.'

'Ssh. Don't wake Xanthe.'

'There are wolves and monsters.'

'Darling, there aren't. Wolves don't live in France, and monsters don't exist.'

'I still don't want you to go.'

I longed to be outside in the evening, drinking wine with Richard. 'I'll be just here, so close I can even hear you. You go to sleep now. It's getting late.'

'Mummy?'

'Yes?'

'Where does water come from?'

'Rain.'

'Yes, but what is it?'

'It's a combination of hydrogen and oxygen . . . Oh listen, it's time for sleep now. You know what Daddy says. This is Grown-Ups' Time.'

'I need a drink of water.'

The pump growled. She tucked her cup into a corner of her bed. I heard her burrowing in her toy box, then whispering to some beloved teddy.

Mathieu lived nearby in Cabasse, a medieval warren of tunnels and ancient gateways opening on to a *pétanque* pitch beside the river Issole. Under pollarded plane trees, around a moss-clad fountain, old folk sat side by side, some leaning on sticks. They wore sunglasses, which made them look blind. One was Mathieu's neighbour, Madame Herault, a square-shaped woman with a freckly face.

I noticed that Madame Herault's car had a yellow and red sticker on the rear window saying '*Dóu Païs Prouvençau!*' Yellow and red were the colours of the Provençal flag. I asked Mathieu if this was some sort of separatist subversion. Mathieu laughed. This wasn't Corsica! Madame Herault was passionately Provençal, but it was culture, not politics. She was a member of some Provençal club. Every week she would drive the ten kilometres from Cabasse to Le Luc to meet the friends who shared her passion. Every week they spoke Provençal, read Provençal literature, sang Provençal songs, and generally enjoyed being Provençal together.

So Provençal wasn't dead after all. Weeks earlier, somewhere in

Périgord, we had crossed the border into Occitania, the southern third of France, the land of the langue d'oc, as opposed to the northern langue d'oil, but there had been no sign of this either on the Michelin map or on the ground. In fact there was no outward sign of the language whatsoever – no shop names, no signposts. This seemed to me extraordinary. Until the nineteenth century Provençal was the standard and literary language of almost everyone in the Midi. Now this great medieval language, the language of courtly love and chivalry, at one time a respected language of law and administration, was on the brink of extinction. French had taken over completely. Provençal appeared to have retreated so far, and its prestige sunk so low, that it had become a purely private thing, spoken – if at all – at home.

Cabasse/Cabasso was one of the only villages to have its name signposted in both French and Provençal. It was the only reminder to outsiders that French hadn't always dominated here.

I was excited by the idea of meeting people who still communicated in Provençal, as if they were members of a secret sect. Mathieu said that Madame Herault's meeting would be at 8 p.m. on Tuesday, in Le Luc's Town Hall Annexe. I had hoped for somewhere less institutional – a café or bar – but undeterred, on Tuesday evening I cycled back down the cratered track between the vineyards. It was slightly intimidating and exciting to be out on my own. Without Xanthe strapped to me in her sling, I felt bare-chested. This was the second evening I had left her since she was born.

Le Luc was quiet. A few children, some Algerian, kicked a ball against the walls of the medieval church. A bedraggled woman with dyed-blonde hair sat alone outside a bar in the main square, drinking pastis. The Town Hall Annexe was empty.

The next afternoon we cycled into Cabasse to track down Madame Herault herself. It was a long ride between tiny poppy-flecked fields and vineyards, with Xanthe on my front and a rucksack of nappies and baby food and drinks on my back. Tallulah fell asleep, slumped against Richard's back, mouth open, while Xanthe kicked at her reflection in the bicycle bell.

Madame Herault was out. Two other village women left their

perches under the trees and flocked around like blackbirds. Madame Herault was at her daughter's, near the bridge, they said. I wheeled my bike, towering over them. One had dyed-orange hair and false teeth that she clacked together. Her name was Murielle. The other had a face as white and wrinkled as a peeled chestnut. Her name was Marie. When I asked them about the Provençal language they chuckled, as if this was faintly risqué.

'Do you speak Provençal?'

'Of course. *En famille.* My grandmother didn't speak anything else. No French,' said Marie. I studied her. This grandmother's grandmother: she could have been born in the mid-nineteenth century. Before cars and tourists, before not only geographical but also social mobility, before radio and TV, before compulsory primary education, which was introduced – in French of course – in 1882.

'But you learnt French.' This was obvious: we were speaking it.

'Not until we went to school. It was very difficult at first. We didn't know what the teacher was on about. But we weren't allowed to speak Provençal. Not even in the playground.'

'What happened if you did?'

'We were punished.'

They giggled. Their mixture of embarrassment and hilarity confused me; I had expected them to be proud of their language.

'When you're sitting round the fountain, are you speaking Provençal then?'

'Yes, most of the time. We're all Provençal here.'

Except, I thought, for your new neighbour Mathieu. Though brought up nearby, he was half-English, and his wife Quebecoise. These days their mixed blood is typical of Provence, invaded as it is by Peter Mayles and other itinerant Europeans, along with 200,000 North Africans. Thirty-five per cent of the population of Provence has been born outside the area.

'We speak French if someone doesn't understand Provençal,' explained Murielle.

'Not always,' Marie corrected her. 'Sometimes in the shops we tell strangers to get a move on. *Qué siès loungango!* She's taking a long time! They haven't a clue what we're talking about.'

So they used it like a secret language, the badge of exclusive members of a club.

'Chk, chk.' Marie tickled Xanthe under the chin. '*Boun Dieu! Qué siès poulido!*'

'There!' exclaimed Murielle. 'That was more Provençal for you.' The words sounded Spanish (*pulido* meaning 'polished' in Spanish) but the pronunciation was like Italian. 'She said, "My God! She's pretty!" '

'Thank you. But pouli*do*? You'd think that would be masculine.'

'Not pouli*do*, poul*ee*do.'

Marie and Murielle used the term Provençal in its widest sense, as another name for Occitan, or for what was sometimes known (principally by the northern French) as the langue d'oc. It meant the language spoken in various dialects throughout the first Roman *provincia* beyond the Alps, Gallia Transalpina, which was occupied for five centuries after the second century BC. Linguists use the term Occitan, confining Provençal to its narrower modern sense as the dialect of Occitan spoken in the historic province of Provence, where we now were. Occitan includes the multitude of other dialects spoken throughout the Midi such as Languedocien, Gascon, Limousin, Auvergnat, and Alpine Provençal. I learnt that one of the distinctive qualities of Provençal was that the final feminine 'a' of other Occitan dialects was here 'o' or 'ou'.

Madame Herault was walking home over the bridge. The meeting in Le Luc? She'd had to miss it. Yes, it was always in the Town Hall Annexe, she didn't know why I'd failed to find it. She had a hairy wart on her chin. She offered to show me her Provençal costumes sometime, but not now. Now was dinnertime.

I felt tantalized. There was so much more I wanted to know. I would have to cycle all the way back here tomorrow – we could never get the Mob over that track again until we left Mathieu's vineyard for good.

The next morning we cycled through Cabasse to the cliff-top chapel of Notre Dame de Greuve. We picnicked below a crucifix. From our vertiginous height we could admire the hermetic perfection of Cabasse, unlike Le Luc which was now fringed with a hideous *zone industrielle* and the usual plethora of out-of-town superstores. I focused binoculars on tangled streets, and vegetable gardens dropping like a skirt with a bias binding of river. Immediately below us I could distinguish seven of the twelve stations of the cross that straggled up to our eyrie, and the rocky façade to our right was dappled with trogloditic caves; at the base lay the Cistercian abbey of Le Thoronet, which Tallulah had described as 'all stone and glass, stone and glass'. This was Provence at its best, the Provence of Daudet and Pagnol that had elsewhere been discarded, without anyone seeming to mind.

Madame Herault was not at home. Someone thought she was working on her *terrain*. But there was no sign of her there either.

I persevered the next day, and the next. The mistral began to blow. Our awning bucked about, but we couldn't take it down for lack of shade. We were restless and irritable. Xanthe was teething. It was time to move on.

Tuesday came round again, so I returned to Le Luc. This time there was a class at the Town Hall Annexe, but two puzzled students explained it was about AIDS. I walked on to the main street and asked passers-by. One man gaped at me as if I was mad. 'Provençal? You mean the *patois*?' I was depressed by the shrugging lack of interest. Provençal? Nobody cared. Someone directed me to the defunct offices of the local newspaper, but they were deserted. Litter drifted in the doorway. I wondered if Madame Herault had invented the whole Provençal thing.

Then on our farewell visit to Cabasse we caught Madame Herault setting off in her car. She agreed to show me her costumes, but quickly mind you. We stood in her living room. Like Mathieu's next door, her house was tall and dark, one room per floor. From behind her front door she unhooked a bulky peasant skirt with a red sprigged pattern worn by her great-grandmother. Now, like all Provençal costume, it was reserved for festivals. Out came a wine-red shirt with a lace collar that Madame Herault had made herself, and a chemise that she had bought at the *brocante*. She had put together her outfits from whatever source she could find. Everyone did that, she said, a bit of this and a bit of that. Not many people were lucky enough to have inherited an entire outfit. She was warming up a bit now, enjoying showing me her treasures.

She had saved the best until last. It was her bonnet, and she put it on specially. It framed her face in crisp white lace, and with her wiry hair poking through she looked like an overgrown Mrs Tiggywinkle.

She recommended the Pentecost festival at Apt the following weekend. She couldn't go because her husband was ill, but normally she'd be there in full regalia.

Mathieu said there was another neighbour whose husband was a Provençal poet, a contemporary troubadour. Her name was Annie L'Antoine. She lived on a hillside, buried in greenery.

Annie was beautiful, with a square balanced face and high forehead. We sat in the shade of a scrubby cork oak in a typical Provençal garden: few flowers, prickly grass, quite rough.

Although her husband was a native speaker, Annie had learnt Provençal as an adult in Toulon. All sorts of people came, not just French, but incomers, even North Africans. Without learning Provençal, you would never fit in here, she said. You'd always be an outsider. She had a deep warm voice.

'Isn't it hard enough for foreigners to learn French, let alone Provençal as well, a language that isn't necessary any more?'

'Provençal *is* necessary. Without understanding the language, you can't understand the literature, or the people. You will always, ultimately, be excluded.'

Annie explained that the languages of France had nothing in common with each other. Celtic Breton is totally different from Romance Occitan, German Alsatian, or Basque Basque. And they are all different from French. They are not *patois*, whatever the French say – she was adamant about this. They are not bastard dialects of French. They lack the status of being recognized as national languages, but they are recognized linguistically as separate languages in their own right, with their own grammar, syntax and vocabulary, and their own *patois*.

There is no scientific definition for when a language is a language and not a dialect. It is a question of degree. A dialect becomes a language when it is sufficiently different from another dialect as to be mutually unintelligible, and to need its own grammar and dictionary. 'Sufficiently different' is a subjective response, and linguists can be no more precise than that.

In fact, both French and Occitan are Romance languages. They share a lexicon. Both derive from Latin. Not from classical Latin, the language of scholars and sophisticates, but from the popular proto-Romance language that coexisted with it. As the great nineteenth-century German philologist Friedrich Diez wrote so disapprovingly:

> We must only be cautious not to take this form of speech for anything else than it is usually conceived to have been, that is to say, for a vulgar usage of the common language, recognizable by a comparatively slovenly pronunciation of words, by a tendency to the elimination of grammatical forms, by the use of numerous expressions which are avoided in literature, and by sundry peculiar idioms and constructions.

The irony is that while pure Latin went into a lingering but terminal decline after the Germanic invasions, many of the slovenly and peculiar Romance languages flourish to this day.

Until the fourteenth century there was no concept of separate Romance languages: they were all different versions of the same language. Romance speakers throughout the Middle Ages distinguished themselves from Germans and Slavs by calling themselves Romans; their language was Roman. What became Occitan was known as '*romans*'; what became *català* was known as '*romanç*'; what became *castellano* (belonging to the 'castle area') and later, from the end of the fifteenth century, *español*, was known as '*romance*'; what became *franceis* and later *français*, was '*romanz*'.

However, since the collapse of the Roman Empire distinctions had evolved between the regions. French came under the influence of the Germanic Franks, while Occitan remained closer to Catalan and Italian. It was Dante who noted this distinction first: it is he who is credited with beginning the philology of Romance. In his unfinished treatise '*De Vulgari Eloquentia*', written after 1304, he divided the Romance languages into three groups, according to their words for 'yes': *si*, *oc*, and *oil* (later *oui*), the latter two deriving from the Latin *hoc* and *hoc illud*. Hence the langue d'oc and the langue d'oil. France was thought of by the Provençal troubadours as being divided into Catalans and Frenchmen, the Catalans including the peoples of Gascony, Provence, Limousin, Auvergne, and Viennois, with Dante placing the principal seat of the language of Oc in Spain.

These days, Catalan is considered so different from Provençal as to be a different language.

Each of these languages continued to evolve, like rolling snowballs gathering to themselves a word from here, an accent from there, shedding syntax along the way, breaking apart, dwindling, drifting for a while, stagnating, then getting on the move and growing again. Since the early nineteenth century, linguists have used the metaphor of the family for languages, with parent languages giving birth to daughters and sons and distant cousins: their books are filled with obscure family trees. But this suggests that there is some abrupt and painful moment of linguistic birth. Languages don't work like that: their evolution is haphazard and mysterious.

In AD 536 Occitania came under the control of the Franks – nominally at least – but it was not until 1481 that the region was transferred to the king of France, and not until the French Revolution was the area finally deprived of its political institutions. It maintained its jongleurs and troubadours, its literary language going back to the eleventh century. Even after the violent crushing of Languedoc's cultural individuality by the northern forces of the thirteenth-century Albigensian crusade, the language in Provence – then part of Catalonia – continued to thrive, and was even codified at this time. The mid-sixteenth century saw Provençal's first literary renaissance.

Nevertheless, the south of France never had the ethnic integrity of, say, Brittany, and this was one reason, along with the region's turbulent political history, why the French managed to extend control so effectively. By the seventeenth century the languages of Provence had been downgraded to a mere set of low-status *patois*.

The French language stems from Paris, or rather from the Île-de-

France region. In effect it was a regional dialect deliberately imposed on other dialects. Its adoption as a state language was a purely political move in the sixteenth and seventeenth centuries: the strengthening of state functions required the use of a common tongue. Until then the common tongue was Latin, understood by scholars and priests throughout Christendom. Latin was the only language taught in schools, and Latin, the esoteric language of the Church, was considered the path to sacred truth and thus was an inseparable part of that truth. The Reformation challenged this notion, and knocked Latin off its pedestal. It sought to spread the Word in a vernacular, accessible to all. Luther is sometimes said to have virtually invented German; Calvin was an almost equally important figure in the development of French.

Fundamental changes were taking place in the way people understood the world. The break-up of Christendom, economic change, scientific discoveries, but above all the printed word, the spread of newspapers, and empowering political tracts and speeches in the vernacular: these made it possible for nation states to emerge. In France that vernacular was French. The newly published books needed a market, which made it necessary to standardize the grammars and syntaxes. Turning it into a print language fixed it, and helped it to spread. It also created a sense of community with other readers. Most importantly, it boosted it as a language of power, with other dialects or languages relegated to second place. A huge proportion of the population – among them Corsicans, Bretons, Alsatians, Basques, and Provençaux – had seen the foundation of a national language which was not its own. So although Occitan persisted as strongly as before throughout the south, it was now vehemently condemned by French-speaking intellectuals as a barbarous *patois*.

Then came the French Revolution of 1789, and with it the Jacobin doctrine of nationhood, which was to shape the modern world, particularly the USA. The year 1789 was a key historical pivot and, as Annie pointed out, made France an appropriate starting point for our journey. The Jacobins stressed the ideological link between language and state, arguing that a common language was essential if not just the nobility and landed gentry but *all* citizens of one nation were to take part in the democratic process. A common language would mean commonality of purpose, ideas, and sentiment, an ideal fostered not only by the French and Americans but later by German Romanticism – and of course by the likes of Matthew Arnold. The Jacobins declared French '*La langue de la liberté*', and thus politicized it. Ever since, French has been invoked as the face of France and Frenchness. This is still the case.

The eventual abandonment of Latin as a state language in Europe led to a nineteenth-century golden age of folklorists, lexicographers, and philologists who toiled away to collect ancient tales and to create grammars and dictionaries of their vernaculars. It was a lexicographical revolution that created the conviction that languages were 'owned' by specific groups, which gave them a place in a fraternity of equals; they backed up the ideal of the nation as a unified body of people, a tribe.

'Vernacularizing' did not mean equality for all languages. In order to create political unity, one language had to lord it over others spoken within that state. Thus France, and later the French Empire, became *francisé*, Germany Germanified, the British Empire Anglicized. This created an awareness of the threat to vernaculars that were now being marginalized. While championing the French state, the French have paradoxically always maintained a fondness for their own folkloric and regional traditions.

It was even a Francophone philologist who, at the turn of the twentieth century, invented the now widespread science of linguistic geography, the cartographic study of living vernaculars. Jules Gilliéron, a pupil of a pupil of Diez, spent years steeping himself in 639 Romance-speaking localities in France, Belgium, and Switzerland. He sent out voluminous questionnaires, followed by his friend and collaborator Edmond Edmont, a shopkeeper with an exceptional ear for the nuances of phonetics and morphology. Edmont closed his shop and left home to spend four and a half years – without interruption – in the field. He was a zealous dialectologist. He filled quantities of notebooks that he sent back to Gilliéron in Paris. There was a sense of urgency to their work: they were aware even then that education, and centralizing French institutions, were threatening to destroy the very languages they were studying. They wanted to collect them before it was too late, and save them from oblivion, as if in a linguistic zoo.

Gilliéron presented his results in a collection of maps called a 'linguistic atlas'. The first *Atlas linguistique de la France* was published in 1902–10. It consisted of nearly two thousand maps, one for each notion or word that was studied, pinpointing exactly the different dialect forms of the word and where they were spoken. It was a laboratory of living speech. It revealed that words, like people, migrate; they sometimes leave their native land and travel, and along the way they encounter difficulties, or rivals from Paris; sometimes they are defeated, other times they triumph. Sometimes new words simply erupt, like a volcano, as if from nowhere, although in fact they are usually connected subterraneously with somewhere else. The remoteness of a valley has a big part to play, as does a means of communication like a river or railway line or road network, or today a global network of air travel and media.

Although some scholars regarded this gigantic work as a scientific event of national importance, a revolution in the study of linguistics, others received it with incredulity, even hostility. Some resented the notion that there could be languages and dialects that did not obey the rules of the French Academy, and were beyond its grammatical control.

'It's impossible to overemphasize the linguistic sensitivity of the French,' Annie said. 'If you put all the minority regions together, you would completely isolate Paris. People are afraid of that. Paris has never become sufficiently confident of the integrity of France to allow other identities to exist within it. And now there's the threat from English.'

It transpires that Gilliéron himself was not French but Swiss: that makes more sense of his obsession with the multiplicity of languages.

The reaction to the *Atlas linguistique* highlights the irony of all modern Europe: the more a country becomes centralized and homogenized, the stronger the reaction of many of its people against that homogenization, and the more heightened the awareness of ancient differences.

The French Revolution doomed the dialects of France, but it took education to all but finish them off. Annie blamed the Third Republic Minister of Education Jules Ferry, who in 1882 imposed compulsory (free) primary education in French – and French only. He was her personal villain. Like Matthew Arnold, one of his principal aims was to suppress other languages, to reduce them to subservient status, and eventually to eliminate them. Thus national unity and loyalty to the French state would be assured. As recently as 1925 Minister of Education Anatole de Monzie declared belligerently, 'The only one who is truly French in heart and soul, and from head to toe, is he who knows and can speak and read the French language.' Today, local speech habits are scorned.

Annie confirmed Marie and Murielle's descriptions of being punished for speaking their mother tongue. Perhaps because she herself had not experienced it, Annie was more forthcoming than they were.

'*Le symbole*,' she explained.

It could be a stick, or a pebble, and would be held or worn around the neck of a child caught speaking Provençal. The child continued to wear it until someone else made the same mistake, whereupon it was passed on to the new offender. Whoever was wearing it at the end of the day could be fined or sometimes beaten. Wearing *le symbole* was considered deeply shaming. Sometimes it could be a clog or a pottery cow, representing the bovine peasant, the country bumpkin, someone to be despised. This was why the old ladies had giggled about it: they were still ashamed. It was like the 'Welsh Not', a punishment introduced into Welsh classrooms after the 1870 Education Act. A placard saying 'Welsh Not' would be hung around the neck of a child caught speaking Welsh and this would be passed from culprit to culprit, with the child found wearing it at the end of the day being beaten or fined. But this happened on a much lesser scale than in France, and certainly not within living memory.

Annie's mother-in-law was punished so often that she stopped speaking her mother tongue; her parents would address her in Provençal, but she replied in French.

I wondered what it could do to your mind, to insert fear as a barrier between thought and sound. It would have almost the same effect as living under a totalitarian dictatorship. It would send you slightly mad.

Of course, there was another sort of fear, Annie added. Many parents discouraged their children from speaking Occitan because they feared it would hinder their social and economic advancement. Ever since the sixteenth century, the bourgeoisie had cultivated French at the expense of their own local tongues in order to get on in the world.

But why, I asked her, did people not rebel against this? Why were there no language activists? The public pressure, she said, is too weak and fragmented to achieve anything. Many people are still hostile to their own language for fear it will hold them back. It is seen to be of no use. It is ridiculous. Most people in Provence, even the Provençaux themselves, don't want to be taught in Provençal because it is inappropriate for a language hitherto only used at home.

Here lay the crux of the matter. We were to discover this all over Europe: that language death was always as much an act of suicide as murder.

There *was* a Provençal revival during the nineteenth century, she added, when the Nobel Prize-winning Provençal poet Frédéric Mistral and his disciples, the Félibrige, wrote in Provençal, and sought to standardize the different dialects. It was a renaissance that rediscovered the lyric poetry of the troubadours, and was partly responsible for the growth of interest in the Romance languages; it was Goethe who first recommended troubadour poetry to the young Friedrich Diez, and steered him towards the study of Romance. This was a strictly literary revival, however, not a political one, and was confined only to the dialects of Provence itself.

During the mid-twentieth century some militants, inspired by Catalans across the border, managed to agree to a standardized version of Occitan which would be admitted in school examinations. Meanwhile the 1951 Deixonne Act permitted a minimal presence of regional languages in public education, and left the door open for the development of grant-aided private primary schools known as *calendretas*, in which some instruction was in Provençal. But it was small fry. By 1994 there were seventeen preschool and primary *calendretas* in which Occitan was taught to 665 pupils, a tiny minority of the total school population. Those who have been taught in Occitan are never sure of being able to continue with it at secondary school, where it is an optional subject in only a very few. There are no efforts by the state to train teachers in Occitan. Most other measures to promote Occitan today are systematically curbed by public authorities.

'There's no question of wanting to break away from France, absolutely not.' Annie was vehement. 'Not like the Corsicans. I am Provençal, *and* French.' Besides, she added, the language was not dying, it was reviving. The situation had improved over the last forty years. As a child she rarely heard it; now it was being spoken more and more. I must have looked doubtful, because she insisted it was true. It is possible to take your baccalaureate in Occitan, and there are degree courses in it. There are forty minutes of Occitan broadcast on the public radio FR3 at the weekends. Forty minutes! I burst out laughing.

'Well,' she said sheepishly, 'it's better than nothing.'

'But languages come and go, perhaps Occitan has had its day?'

'No, no, no! There is a vast body of modern Occitan literature, and new Occitan songs. It's a living thing not something fossilized. There's a mass of new children's books in Occitan. Kipling, Saint-Exupéry, and soon Seamus Heaney will be translated into Occitan. Dictionaries and grammars are proliferating.'

'It seems that it has cultural value, but is it any use?'

'It may become of use. There's a new confidence blooming.'

'So how many Occitan speakers are there?'

'Oh, about ten million.'

I must have looked disbelieving. She added: 'Or so some people say.'

In fact there is no official data. The most accurate figures dating from 1992 suggest that of some twelve to thirteen million inhabitants, three million are theoretically capable of holding a brief conversation in Occitan, around two million use it from time to time, and one to two million use it with family and friends.

'Why have you learnt Provençal?'

'Maybe I'm growing older. I don't know. I felt a desire to rediscover my roots, to find out who I was.'

'And who are you? What makes you Provençal?'

'Hmm. Our history. But first and foremost, the language.'

'So Provence is a historical fact, and a linguistic community.'

'Yes. But above all, my Provençal identity is defined by my love of the place, with its vineyards and scents of pine and broom.' She leant forward, spreading strong hands on the table. 'When I go elsewhere, I see lovely places much greener than here, with big trees, and I think, how wonderful. No fires, no rampant house-building, no corruption.' She sat back and looked around her. 'But when I get back I smell the broom and pine –' she waved at the garden – 'and it wakens something in me, and I realize that despite everything, this is where I belong. I can't put it any other way.'

'Is it to do with the land?'

'Yes. I think so. My identity comes from my closeness to this place, to my *terrain*. Everyone is attached to their land. There is something symbolic about it. And it also comes from the products of this place. A cuisine attaches people to their region. My roots lie in what I grow – garlic, olive oil, olives, red peppers, wine . . . When people emigrate, they should take care not to become deracinated. That's how they lose their self-esteem. You must be confident of your identity. Wherever I live, I will always be Provençal at heart.'

And yet, I said, I had heard much criticism of North African immigrants to France who 'refused to integrate'. 'Integrate' was a big word here. It featured in much of the racist graffiti daubed on flyovers. How can incomers integrate, while also maintaining their identity?

'People are resented,' Annie replied, 'because they are seen to sponge off the state, pay no taxes, live separate lives. They are resented for taking, not giving. But there are many who make the effort. And we must respect their culture too. It's a difficult balance.'

The person I should meet, she said, was her husband Ferdinand

L'Antoine. He was a troubadour. He still followed instructions that were laid down in the mid-thirteenth century for the correct way to write lyric poetry, as inspired by the ancient Greek conception of the lyric poem as a vocal composition.

Of the 400 troubadours known to have been writing during the Middle Ages, most were kings or nobles, and composing and performing their songs was considered one of the highest manifestations of chivalry. Essential to the Provençal form was the use of the vernacular; after Welsh, Provençal is among the oldest of Europe's literary languages still being used today. As Johann Herder wrote in his 'Essay on the Origin of Language' in 1772, whose ideas helped to form the political programme of European nationalism: 'A poet is the creator of the nation around him; he gives them a world to see and has their souls in his hand to lead them to that world.'

Ferdinand L'Antoine was the troubadours' heir. Annie loved and admired her husband. I followed her into her kitchen where she dug through some papers.

'Here it is!'

It was a scroll wrapped in a ribbon. It unfurled as a L'Antoine paean to Provence, a love poem to his country. Annie gave it to me. Monsieur L'Antoine would be reciting more of his verse at the Pentecost *fête* at Apt.

'Apt, ah! Ça ç'est autre chose! Il faut que vous y allez!'

A straight road striped by wind-breaking cypresses, light and shade, light and shade, the trees black and sharp. The Mob purrs along, cushions on the floor, books strewn about, kids asleep, Xanthe with head lolling, legs splayed, fists clenched, Tallulah sweaty and uncomfortable, Richard in shades at the wheel, shoes off, poplars shimmering, up, up and, whoa, Mont Sainte-Victoire on our right, bulbous up its flank like a Michelin mountain, pumped up to its jagged crust. Would Cézanne recognize it? No. All the trees had been burnt.

Apt was ominously quiet. In chill alleys that enmeshed the cathedral, shops sold Catholic paraphernalia. Child-sized dummies modelled First Communion clothes. They looked like Cistercian nuns. There was no sign of any festival.

Then we saw the flags of Provence hanging like aired sheets from the windows of the *mairie* in the *grand place*. Two ladies in lacy bonnets and sprigged calf-length skirts and aprons tripped by, posies in hands. They seemed prissy. They looked as if they had stepped out of a National Trust tearoom. A table displayed Provençal publications, and drab-looking men selling the publications wore lapel badges with their names on.

But in the morning, Apt came alive. We were woken by music. The alleyways filled up with the old, the young, and the very young parading in nineteenth-century costumes, all crisp and clean and proud, pipes piping, drums drumming, accordions accordioning. The off-key toot of the *hautbois* hit the walls and bounced back. Some groups were got up like wenches in clogs, others like ladies of the manor, sporting parasols. They did it so well, so professionally. Everyone was immaculate, the women with their hair tidied away under bonnets. Unadorned by hair, their faces were plain.

Sometimes the procession stopped, and polite farandoles took place.

This was the coming together of everything I had been looking for, the ultimate expression of *la vie provençale*. But I felt unmoved. It seemed regimented and dull. I couldn't help thinking: this is fancy dress. This isn't what I meant.

The procession reached St Anne's cathedral. It filled until children had to be hoisted on shoulders. When there was no room for us all, the service was relayed into the little square outside. Every word was Occitan, and everyone seemed to understand it. The congregation sang hymns with vigour, seemingly exhilarated by the use of their own language, and I found this very moving.

We wandered into a bar and drank *café au lait* with a few other stragglers. Who, I asked them, was the event for? There appeared to be no other tourists – it was May, still just before the season. Why, they said, it's for us. It's a celebration of our culture, by us and for us.

Then I noticed a Vietnamese *épicerie*, and two Vietnamese children in the doorway. They ignored the festival. They were playing with a ball and didn't look up as the costumes and musicians paraded by. An Algerian woman in a veil, head bowed, scurried with her basket into the shop. They were the only people on the streets who were not participating. Was the festival indirectly for them? Was it a territorial statement? Was it a manifestation of reactionary chauvinism, a statement of 'us' and 'them'? After all, being Provençal meant speaking your grandmother's tongue, wearing your grandmother's lace. It meant having lived here, like Madame Herault's family, for generations.

The procession moved on. Each group sported a heraldic banner bearing the name of their town, twenty-one of them from across Occitania, from as far afield as Bordeaux and Toulouse. There was even a troupe from Vitrolles, a Gehenna of cut-price superstores and *zones industrielles* off the autoroute to Marseilles where we had gone to replace a window broken by the thief at the Lac de Sainte Croix. It was a place where the Front National supplies the mayor, where shaven-headed police in combat gear patrol the streets, and Front National posters promise a reward of 5000 francs for each pure-bred French baby.

I remembered that Provence was the heartland of support for Jean-Marie Le Pen and his racist Front National. Perhaps this festival marked a reaction not just against homeogeneity, but against another perceived threat, the newest epoch of migration into Europe. Settled people have always feared, and been undermined by, rootless people. It makes them return to their own roots in search of reassurance about the validity of their own community.

But the festival was not in any way overtly racist; I even noticed one or two black faces in the parade.

Amongst the banners was Cabasso, and behind it, mincing balletically alongside other ladies in bonnets, was the square, gingery form of Madame Herault. She had got here after all. We waved like mad and she permitted herself, in her dignity, a tight smile.

And there, up on a podium in black felt hat and jacket, stood the declaiming troubadour, Ferdinand L'Antoine.

'Pèr tout acò qué siès, Prouvènço, ma patrio,
Pour tout ce qu'a douna, tout au long de la vido!
Ti devèn tout l'amour e la recouneissènço.
Nosti Reire an paga soun degut à la Franço;
Estiman si valour e nosti liberta,
Acetarèn jamai qué siégon infama!
Pantaiaire madu, varlet de l'estamen,
Vosti plan desgradan, nani! Li rejiten!
Faguès li pourcarié s'agrado ei Parisen...
Nautre, n'en voulèn gès de badafro en Prouvènço.
Pas mai de TGV, qué de grand Tai nouvèu,
Enco ès en flânant que trouvan qu'ès mai bèu.
A nostri Fraire Corso, si deven acampa,
L'óunour e de saupre si faire respeta!'

'For all that you are, Provence, my country,
For all that you give, throughout our lives,
We give you love and recognition.
Our forefathers paid tribute to France!
Conscious of their valour and our freedom,
We will not allow them to be mocked.
Busy utopians, civil servants,
No to your degrading projects! We don't want them!
We don't need Provence to be scarred
By more TGVs, or new motorways!
To all our Corsican brothers, let us unite with one voice.
Honour is found by fighting for our identity!'

TWO

War-torn Borderlands

We drove north through the Alps. East of Vosges, suddenly the place names were German. We stopped for tea in a village called Westhalten, all window boxes and squat, sturdy German houses with steep roofs and walls painted with images of grape picking or heraldry. It was immaculate.

There was a feeling of being in the heart of Europe, but it was still France. This was Alsace.

We reached Strasbourg late. Bars were open, people strolling in warm air. We eventually found a space outside the hospital, on a slope so steep that Xanthe slithered down to the end of her cot, and it was difficult to stand upright in the bathroom. The next day we moved to a flatter quieter place on a *quai* near the old city, overlooking a rainbow-filled fountain, weeping willows, and Germanic buildings with pitched roofs, windows poking out of an expanse of tile. Flat-bottomed boats slid past full of tourists.

I'd been excited as we approached Strasbourg to see cars with a red 'A' stuck to the rear bumper. I wondered if this signified some kind of Alsatian separatist movement. Soon I discovered there was no such thing. 'A' meant '*Apprentie*'.

We collected mail from the central post office and sat in the van in a chaos of discarded envelopes, crying children, remains of lunch, while outside slender women in small black T-shirts tripped by.

There was a last-minute feed and nappy change, then we loaded Xanthe into the sling and set forth into the city. We had no money, and had overspent our budget, but when Richard managed to change some we were so relieved that we immediately bought ice creams, then the same again. Tallulah walked the streets with her face smeared in chocolate.

We drank beer in the pretty Place Kléber, full of the hum of voices and no cars. The clientele was young, mostly students. They were civilized and relaxed; they lolled on chairs. A bookshop was closing, and someone flung open the window of the floor above and Brahms floated out. For the next week Richard spent his evenings here alone, a tramp-like figure in dirty shorts with a grey string leading to the penknife in his pocket, hair all over the place, unkempt beard. No one would suspect that he had a valuable Leica at his side.

The Museum of Alsatian Art was in a handsome sixteenth-century building full of alcoves, tiled stoves, interior balconies, with displays of cake tins and jelly moulds, all very food-orientated. The displays were in French and Alsatian, my first sighting of the language. It looked like German. But when I asked the guard for some sort of pro-Alsatian organization, she didn't know what I was on about.

I was confused by the lack of public use of Alsatian, almost as if it didn't exist. Although there were Alsatian eateries and bars – *bierstubs* and *winstubs* – most shop names were in French. All street names were in French. A few years ago the authorities had tried to introduce French/Alsatian/German street signs, but the locals objected that it was too reminiscent of German wartime occupation. After that the revised French/Alsatian proposals failed to gain momentum.

I should not have been shocked. I should have remembered that French insecurities would not permit their minorities more than the faintest glimmer of folkloric frippery, and nowhere more so than here, where the Frenchness of Alsace had so frequently been challenged, not so much by the Alsatians themselves, but by the Germans.

Because of its agricultural and industrial wealth, but more because it lay across the paths of the great routes of commerce and communication – the Rhine, the Saverne Pass, and the Burgundian Gate – Alsace-Lorraine had always been a prize for both France and Germany. In his autobiography, *Tomi*, the Alsatian illustrator Tomi Ungerer describes how his grandmother had had to change nationalities four times: during the Franco-Prussian war in 1871, then in 1919, 1940, and 1945.

Before that Alsace had been invaded by the Romans, then the Alemanni – the first German tribe to arrive in western Europe, hence Alemagne. Then at the end of the fifth century along came Clovis and his army of Franks. It was incorporated into the Holy Roman Empire, devastated by the Swedes during the Thirty Years War, and made a protectorate of France at the Peace of Westphalia in 1648, ending centuries of German domination. During the French Revolution it was formally annexed by France.

The Alsatians were always torn between loyalty to France and to themselves. In early years people continued to speak Alsatian while the small circle of bourgeois aristocrats spoke French, but later there grew a division between French nationalists and autonomists. Nationalists maintained that France was 'one and indivisible', and that separatism amounted to treason; autonomists insisted that the 'one and indivisible' theory denied respect for the liberties, traditions, and customs which had been guaranteed by Napoleon.

However, the rise of the Third Reich gave both groups something more important to think about. As usual, the little people were squeezed out.

We decided to try the European Parliament. Surely someone there would be willing to discuss Europe's regions in general, and Alsace in particular. We found the complex of Euro-buildings on the edge of town, sheets of glass and steel, Euro flags, swooshing doors, security cameras, X-ray machines. It was like the check-in at an airport, appropriate for an organization with the slogan 'Europe on the Move', and appropriate for the delegates who spent their lives shunting from one Euro-city to another. I felt disorientated by my abrupt propulsion into this sleek world.

Leaving Richard with the girls illegally parked outside, under the hostile eye of an armed guard, I tried to get in. I was regarded with suspicion. Too dirty? Too scruffy? I talked my way into the reception, but was sent back for ID.

Even from the swooshing doors I could hear Xanthe screaming, with 'Robin Hood, Robin Hood riding through the glen' at full volume. The Mob was a furnace. Tallulah was drawing felt-pen hieroglyphics on her cheeks. My return to the air-conditioned world, now clutching my passport, was accompanied by the fading strains of 'Robin Hood, Rahbin Hood, Rahbin Hoooood'. The security guard shifted uneasily.

After explaining that I was researching Europe's regions, I managed to arrange a meeting with an Alsatian Euro-MP. While my accreditation was checked and I was photographed from every angle, I watched a file of enthusiastic Irish people being greeted by their Euro-MP from Cork. He was young and good-looking, with shoulder-length blond hair, and he sat in a wheelchair. He pressed the flesh dutifully, a bit of a ladies' man, and when they left I half expected him to get out of the wheelchair and walk away. Oh, he's a lovely fella, one of his lady constituents confided.

The Alsatian MP was self-importantly preoccupied. I made the mistake of apologizing – 'you must be very busy' – and he agreed that he was. I assumed that as an Alsatian he would be concerned with the status of lesser-used languages within Europe. However, the words 'federal Europe' and 'regions' had him shuffling papers and looking shifty, as if it was something shameful. He had nothing to say on the matter.

I talked my way into a debate in the European Parliament. In the last two decades the European Parliament has adopted a series of resolutions to promote regional languages and cultures, while in 1992 the Council of Europe adopted the European Charter for Regional or Minority Languages in the form of a convention. This was important because a convention is a treaty which is legally binding upon the states which ratify it. Its aim was to prevent the decline of Europe's languages – not migrants' languages, but non-official languages traditionally used in a country by nationals of that country. It aimed for recognition and respect, promotion, elimination of discrimination and assimilation, and 'trans-frontier exchanges'. France had refused to ratify this charter, arguing that it would be unconstitutional to do so since it was enshrined in the French constitution that French was the single national language.

I had failed with the Euro-MP; I looked forward to hearing something interesting in the European parliament, to discovering more about the airy stratosphere of European policy-making, before continuing our journey to discover if any of it had the slightest effect on the ground.

I was seated on a leatherette seat in a circular chamber, over-looking a handful of slumbering members, twenty-eight in all, heavily outnumbered by spectators, functionaries, and translators. The functionaries wore tailcoats and chains of office to distribute paperwork to each seat. I tuned in to the English simultaneous translation. The translators sat behind a screen, like Mafiosi on trial in Sicilian courts, leaning on their elbows and speaking into microphones, each with their bottle of mineral water. Seven serious-looking committee members sat on a dais. The level of debate was abysmal. The subject was Europe's economy, but I learnt nothing except that the delegate from Finland was against unemployment, the delegate from Germany thought jobs were necessary, the delegate from France wondered if there was to be investment in training. The high point was when a good British socialist stood up to reprimand the chairman, the President of the European Monetary Institute, for allowing speakers to bore on too long.

Bells woke me on Sunday morning, not pealing like English bells but a cacophony that summoned me to Mass. The air and buildings in the Place de la Cathédrale were saturated with bells, they res-onated off the walls.

I sat behind a nun and watched the theatrical arrival of white-robed and cowled sacristans with wooden crucifixes on their chests. They were led by an absurd little man hung with a mayoral chain like the EU functionaries, his blue uniform and tiny moustache pure Inspector Clouseau. Ten priests would be ordained that afternoon, and some were here now, preparing for a major event: they would be celibate for the rest of their lives. Two sat beside the priest in virginal white while he was resplendent in red and gold. One priest-to-be cocked his head in benign piety, hands folded as if in humble supplication to the Lord; the other had cropped black hair and sharp features, his arms thrust up his sleeves and held defensively against his body; he whispered to the pious one now and then.

When the priest broke the bread, we heard the amplified crack of the wafer. A woman with her hair scraped puritanically off her face swung a censer and the choir filled with smoke; it billowed into the dome and obscured the twelve mosaic apostles in the apse. She swung it each side of the altar (clunk, clunk as it hit its own chain), bowing all the time, then she swung it towards the congregation. The priest opened a silver box to spoon more incense into the censer, as if brewing some magic potion.

We would discover nothing about Alsace here. At the tourist office we learnt of a festival in Jetterswiller, twenty-five kilometres west of Strasbourg. Maybe here, far from the cathedral and Euro-functionaries and Inspector Clouseaus, we would find something genuinely Alsatian.

The village lay in rolling hedgeless fields, striped with maize, wheat, and hops. We followed people into a marquee where trestles had been covered with oilcloths. Merry folk were tucking into lunch. A man serving food made eyes at Xanthe, but she squirmed away in my arms; he addressed me in Alsatian, and it sounded, as it looked, like German. Around me I heard no French.

There was no messing with delicate portions or choice: my plate was filled by a slab of pink ham with a wedge of fat, a splatter of potato salad, followed by four different tarts, and washed down with quantities of chilled Alsatian white wine, deliciously *pétillante*. Everyone had rolled up their sleeves. No one was in traditional dress; they looked like farmers at an English village show – rosy-cheeked men with bright eyes and black hair, or big blond ones; grannies with swollen country legs. Everyone was in a good mood.

The rain began lightly at first: we trailed through it around the village lanes to inspect local crafts, which were unremittingly tasteless. Then drums sounded, and the procession began. Tallulah noticed drum majorettes in pink minidresses and insisted we followed them; she longed to be one herself. But the rain got heavier, the majorettes colder. Soon it flew off our waterproofs, filled Xanthe's eyes, and the procession was abandoned.

We rushed convivially back into the marquee and crowded round a stage to watch traditional dancing. There were the usual girls on squeezeboxes and drums, the usual nineteenth-century costumes. The children were pretty, the old women absurd in girly frills. A woman with buck-teeth was in charge; I had to hide a smile when she slipped in a puddle, but she stuck her nose in the air and marched off to fetch a mop. The other dancers sycophantically applauded. When two men had to lift her during a dance they faltered and nearly dropped her, and I secretly applauded too, the great big cross-looking dollop.

One blond well-built man danced with real verve. He had more presence than the rest. He knelt chivalrously to the ladies and twirled them on light toes. When I congratulated him afterwards, he beamed with pleasure. He was Michel Matz, the genial village postman. He danced all summer long, travelling from *fête* to barn dance; he had four more bookings today. He was Catholic and this was a Catholic village; Protestants inhabited the neighbouring village and wore a slightly different costume. One particularity of Alsace is that Protestants have historically been given more freedom than in the rest of France.

Another dancer joined us. She said they all spoke Alsatian – *Elsässerditsch* – at home, and that they and their parents taught the children. They studied in nothing but French at school, although there was talk of starting *maternelle* classes in Alsatian for fear of it dying out.

'But what's the point of speaking Alsatian now?' I asked.

The woman worked in a hospital where she came across older patients who did not speak French, so she found her Alsatian essential.

'But when they die will it disappear? Will the language die with them?'

'Possibly. There's always more and more *Parisianisme*,' Michel complained. The woman nodded. The language was dwindling. Recent surveys showed that of Alsace's population of 1,625,000, about 60 per cent spoke the language, but only 36 per cent of those entering primary school still spoke it. Most people under twenty-five spoke French amongst themselves.

'Does anyone want independence?'

'There's talk of more autonomy, but like in Brittany, not like Corsica.'

'*Non, non!*' the woman agreed vehemently, waving her hands in front of her face. '*Pas comme ça! Hou la la.*'

Although most Alsatians are pro-France, it is probable that the Alsatian dialect would be stronger if Alsace was still part of Germany; after all, most people argue that Alsatian is no more than a German dialect. Paradoxically, however, it was the loss of Alsace to Germany the first time, in 1871, that proved one of the most important stimuli in the creation of modern France, and therefore led ultimately to the present sorry state of Alsatian. The anti-German feeling that the Franco-Prussian war generated led to a stronger sense of Frenchness. It also led to the push towards nationwide education in French. This was because the disastrous annexation of Alsace was partly attributed by the French to German education, which was considered better than in France, and able to create a stronger sense of Germanness. At that time schooling was seen as the most important means by which a nation was created, so the French obviously needed better (Francophone) schools.

Michel knew from his postal deliveries that older people in remoter parts did not speak French, especially if they were at school under German occupation when all lessons were in German. Indeed, speaking French at all had been banned. It was forbidden to own a French book, and radios were installed in schoolrooms so that pupils could improve their German in order to understand Hitler's speeches. Because of Alsace's Germanic history and language, the Vichy government was quick to recognize it as part of Germany. Some autonomists had hoped the Germans would help free Alsace from the French, but they quickly found that life under the Germans was far worse. French-speaking inhabitants were deported, Jews slaughtered, and while the rest of the French put down their arms (apart from those in the Resistance) 130,000 Alsatians were conscripted into the German army and packed off to the Russian front. A quarter never came back.

Then in 1945 everything reverted to French. The French were welcomed back, and most people wanted to be as French – in other words as non-German – as possible. Not only German was banned, but Alsatian too. It was despised for being written as German, for being a German *patois*.

Michel hastened to point out that Alsatian was no such thing but a separate dialect, even a language in its own right, similar to the Swiss spoken in Basle, with its own literature and dictionaries.

In some ways things were improving. There were now more exchanges with towns over the German border, across the Rhine, where the dialect was the same. There was more cross-border co-operation, new cross-border businesses. There were interactions across the margins of their countries, as there had not been for many years. There were also attempts to give Alsatian more prestige.

But amongst the older generation the war was still very present: our road out of Jetterswiller grazed a vast wartime cemetery, acres of identical white crosses, and in Strasbourg cathedral at midday every Monday to Friday a prayer was still said for peace. Following the Second World War there was a consensus that nations should no longer be threatened by other nations – and nowhere more so than here in the trampled heart of western Europe. It was agreed that all West European nations should be equal in a liberal melting pot of modernization. All efforts went into healing wounds. The same applied to internal differences within a country. It was better that they should be effaced than lead to rivalries and more war.

In Alsace that still takes precedence over the feeble bleating of a lesser-used language.

THREE

The Åland Islands

The ferry from Lübeck landed at Trelleborg on the southern tip of Sweden on midsummer's eve. Richard turned down a grassy track to a meadow beside the sea.

I sat there, stunned by weeks of travelling. We'd made it. And on the perfect day. But now that we'd got here, I couldn't move. It took a while to rid my ears of the lonesome tinnitus of the autobahn.

Richard flung open the doors to fill the Mob with Scandinavian breeze. Its pristine freshness lifted the curtains and scoured every corner. It tugged our hair and pulled us outside to explore tonight's front garden. It was lovely. To one side sheep and sheep-bitten grass; to the other an overblown hedge of pink rugosa roses smelling of Ponds Cold Cream. Below the hedge was a narrow strip of pale sand, then half in half out of the sea a glut of rotting seaweed. This stank, but it was a good clean stink, not like the diesel stink of the road trains moaning across Europe day and night.

Midsummer's eve was a Swedish national holiday, and there was a gently festive mood. Strollers with dogs chatted quietly, and a hardy old woman in a bathing suit tottered down a jetty and climbed unflinchingly into the Baltic. Groups of younger people came by swigging from beer cans, but they were not yobs. Later, they'd be dancing round maypoles.

There was a feeling of innocence and youth. I felt invigorated, as if I too could take a plunge. I got as far as striding down the jetty and taking deep breaths, with the liberating confidence that I could fill my lungs without lining them with filth. It was the sort of air that makes you wake up early, go for a run, write a chapter, scrunch on a nutritious Scandabrod.

Nearby stood a group of wooden cabins – toytown holiday homes.

Each was painted ice-cream colours or rust red, each hung with tasteful lace, all ludicrously petite for such a tall race. Each patriotically flew the Swedish national flag, and inside families and friends gathered around tables in candlelight.

For the first time on our travels, I felt a rush of loneliness. We were just us four and our Mob, a solitary unit exiled in this strange new place.

A handsome man in round glasses peered at our number plate, and the peculiar position of our steering wheel. I feared he was going to reprimand us for being parked here, but instead he was charming, urbane. He was down from Stockholm for the summer. I fancied he was a writer, well-travelled, here to finish a book. I envisaged conversations about the poetry of Pär Lagerkvist around a wooden table with a vase of wild flowers.

'Welcome to Sweden,' he said.

So much for the taciturnity of the Swedes, I thought.

But he walked on. We never met again.

Then we witnessed something odd. A car drew up. Two men got out. They erected two identical tents, side by side. They sat in their separate doorways facing the sea, and cooked their separate dinners on two separate stoves. Then, side by side in their separate doorways, they ate their separate dinners. They stayed up until the longest day of the year ended, then slept in their separate tents. They never exchanged a word. In the morning they got back into their car together and left.

It reminded me of a Scandinavian joke. Two Norwegians, two Danes, and two Swedes are stranded on a desert island. When a rescue party arrives a year later, they find that the Norwegians have started a branch of the Sons of Norway patriotic society, the Danes have started a co-op, while the Swedes are still waiting to be introduced.

We drove north, away from big open farmland and red-oxide timber farmhouses towards a more secretive land of lakes and forests. I draped the long Swedish map over my knees. Two things interested me. No, three. The first was the way Sweden was pocked with bumps and troughs like acne skin. The second was the place names: Asby, Husby, Askeby, Enneby, Oppeby, Alby. It was disconcerting. I could have been looking at a map of the English Midlands, with Derby, Osbournby, Corby, Navenby, Appleby, Rugby, Naseby. This was the Viking connection. Linguists believe that Scandinavian settlement was probably more extensive in England than anywhere else in Europe. It reinforced a northern connection I had been feeling very strongly. Muesli, yoghurt, fresh milk, brown bread, comfortable clothes: I felt more at home here than in France.

The second object of interest was a necklace of islands linking Sweden and Finland: this was where we were heading.

The third was the empty vastness of the far north. But that was for later.

We reached Stockholm late one afternoon and marvelled at grandiose boulevards, the cupuloid cathedrals and exotic spires. I was amazed by the city's Russianness. But I should not have been amazed, for until 1920 – just within living memory – where the land juts into the Baltic north of Stockholm at Grisslehamn, the most westerly outpost of the Tsarist Empire would have been within sight.

One evening we joined the commuters and inched out to Saltsjöbaden to visit Swedish friends. We ate gravadlax with black bread and ice cream made from lingonberries and we talked about Scandinavia, about great spaces and forests, about extremes of light and dark, about churches we had to visit, and we pored over maps.

'Have you ever been to the Åland Islands?' I asked.

Ann-Sofie recalled an Ålander boyfriend taking her there to meet his family. His grandmother had been making bread. Ann-Sofie had noticed that she swept flour on to the board with a hare's paw. Ann-Sofie imitated the grandmother's sweeping motion; this image had stuck in her mind.

'I think they are very remote. Very traditional.'

The next evening we caught a ferry from Grisslehamn to the Ålands.

It was as if the Baltic – a sheet of satin – had been endlessly perforated. The map showed constellations of islands, six and a half thousand of them, some fine as nebulae, others merging into multiple stars, one or two of first magnitude. Then they drifted serenely past our portholes. There were red pimply ones and hairy ones sprouting lichen and bonsai pines, and now some with clusters of ochre-painted wooden boathouses with white flagpoles waving blue flags with a red and yellow cross.

The ferry docked at Eckerö on the main island, near an outsized yellow stucco mansion that dwarfed neighbouring houses to cabin-size. I wondered what it was doing there, so big and grand.

We drove where the road took us, over bridges, past inlets and pastel clapboard, until we found a meadow by a reedy shore. To one side stood an ochre windmill, to the other a maypole still decorated with leaves and ribbons and miniature ships from last week's midsummer frolics. And in front, the Sea of Bothnia, calm as a lake.

I carried Xanthe along a muddy path between reeds, Tallulah dancing at the end of my index finger. Near the maypole was an earth loo, clean and smell-free; and the small mud beach had been equipped with a wooden jetty and slide: it was so thoughtful, so wholesome. So still.

We snoozed on the beach. We sat out in the stretched Nordic evenings to watch Arctic terns diving for the fish that Richard kept failing to catch. When the mosquitoes became intolerable we retreated to our picture window and watched from there. This was the furthest north we had ever been. The midsummer light on the granite slabs that wallowed in the shallows was the colour of Tokay.

A lemon-coloured house overlooked its lawn that sloped to the sea. A man carried a bundle of logs into a hut. Smoke wavered from its chimney. Much later he and a plump boy, his son I guessed, emerged from the sauna and waded silently out to sea, flopping on their bellies when it reached knee-height.

One morning a party of schoolchildren came to swim, diving off the jetty with whoops of joy. They were tall and fair like Swedes. They spoke Swedish. 'Maypole' stems from the Swedish *maj* meaning 'decorated with leaves and flowers'. Their houses looked like Swedish houses. They could pay in Swedish kronor. All this was odd because this was not Sweden. Almost without knowing it, we had crossed the border into Finland.

But that is the thing about the Ålands. They are part of Finland yet not part of it.

We cycled over a forest floor cushioned with pine needles to a Russian battery left from the First World War. Nothing remained but half-submerged trenches and walls. Someone had made a photo display of frozen-looking Russians in big hats and boots, black against the snow. Half a century earlier, during the 1850s, a battle had been fought nearby between British and Russian troops; it was an offshoot of the Crimean War that was being fought at the other extreme of Europe, by the Black Sea.

Richard was excited by the bonsai pines sprouting from rock crevices, and he photographed Tallulah towering over them. I fed Xanthe, sitting on granite beside a nest of deer droppings, and thought about those Russians.

What were they doing in this remote outpost, so far from home? Who are the Ålanders?

If they are Finnish, why do they appear to be Swedish?

I rang the Åland *Lagting*, the legislative assembly, and arranged to meet its General Secretary, Lars Ingmar Johansson. He turned out to be an expert on the history of Åland and its autonomy.

The *Lagting* appoints the *Landskapsstyrelse*, the Åland government, and both are housed in a horizontal 1970s building fronted by a grandiose parade ground in the capital, Mariehamn. Lars Ingmar Johansson shook hands in his office upstairs. He was thin and grey in a grey suit; when he removed his glasses I saw that his greyness was fatigue. His secretary was away, he said, so he was fending for himself. We sat in his grey office, which was decorated with nothing but leather-bound copies of the Act on the Autonomy of Åland.

He outlined the Act. In many ways it allows the Ålands to function as an independent state. The government in Helsinki is responsible for foreign affairs, the judiciary, civil law, and customs, but everything else is left to Åland. It has its own postal service with its own stamps (bearing no mention of Finland), and it flies its own flag.

'We are taxed by Helsinki,' Mr Johansson explained, 'then a small proportion of the Finnish State budget is repaid to us, to spend as we choose. This is a big political subject here.'

'Why?'

'Because some people strongly object to paying taxes to Helsinki. They say you can't have real autonomy until you are in complete control of your own finances. Others like it because it makes us feel safe. They think we will always be taken care of, no matter what.'

For an ethnic Swede, cradle-to-grave security would be paramount.

Crucially, the Autonomy Act was Finland's undertaking to guarantee the Ålands' Swedish language. Because of its Swedish-speaking minority, Finland is officially bilingual; the Ålands, however, are unilingually Swedish. The teaching language in Åland schools is Swedish. It is considered no use to *teach* Swedish; the children must be taught *in* Swedish. Finnish is taught as a second language but isn't popular. University is more likely to be in Stockholm than Helsinki, and students don't want to waste time, as they see it, studying an obscure language like Finnish even if it is their national language: they prefer English or German.

He said that in the way it safeguards the culture of a small population living under the sovereignty of a larger nation, the Autonomy Act is now considered a model of its kind. He believed it could be a prototype for solving ethnic conflicts all around the world. During the Falklands crisis the Åland Autonomy Act was rumoured to be much in demand in diplomatic circles as a solution for the islands – under the sovereignty of Argentina.

Lars Ingmar Johansson stressed how equable relations with Helsinki now are; he implied that the Ålanders have everything a minority could want. But I sensed that relations with Finland were far more ambiguous than they appeared. I picked up that beleaguered small-island fear of being swamped, the prickly sensitivities of a culture that sees itself as under threat.

He was explaining the language situation. Because Finland is officially bilingual, the Helsinki authorities must be able to speak Swedish. But the Åland authorities do not have to speak Finnish. When Mr Johansson goes with a delegation to Helsinki, he can insist that the common language is Swedish, even though they are in the capital of Finland. From the gleam behind his spectacles I guessed he had done that, just for the hell of it.

I found the image compelling. It was as if an official writing from Cardiff to London could expect a reply in Welsh. As if a delegation from Cardiff could insist during any meeting in London that the language used was Welsh.

'Why?' I asked Mr Johansson. 'Why do you care so much?'

'Finnish,' he said, smiling slightly, 'is a very *difficult* language.'

For a non Finno-Ugrian, this is true. Finnish has a few loan words from the Germanic languages along with Iranian, Lithuanian, and Russian; it is similar to Estonian and Sami, and is thought to stem from the same Finno-Ugrian group as Hungarian. But it has no links whatever with any West European language. Even something as basic as the key to the Åland map: 'Bicycle ferry' is *Cykelfärja* in Swedish but *Pyörälautta* in Finnish. 'Bathing beach' is *Badstrand* in Swedish (*Schwimmstrand* in German) but *Uimaranta* in Finnish. 'Tourist Information' is *Turistinformation* in Swedish but *Matkailu- neuvonta* in Finnish.

Take these two verses, the first from *aftonland* (*Evening Land*), by the Swedish poet Pär Lagerkvist, translated by W. H. Auden.

> Det tänds ej någon lampa där för natten,
> för ingen lampas olja skulle räcka,
> och inget stamp av hästar skall dig väcka
> för att en gäst skall vidare i natten.

> No lamp is lit for the night,
> For no oil would suffice,
> And no stamping of horses will wake you up
> For a guest who departs in the night.

The second is from Finland's heroic epic the *Kalevala*, book VIII, lines 1–6.

> Tuo oli kaunis Pohjan neiti,
> Maan kuulu, ve'en valio,
> Istui ilman wempelellä
> Taivon kaarella kajotti

Pukehissa puhtaissa,
Walkeissa vaattehissa;

Lovely was the maid of Pohja,
Famed on land, on water peerless,
On the arch of air high-seated,
Brightly shining on the rainbow,
Clad in robes of dazzling lustre,
Clad in raiment white and shining.

Whereas the Swedish verse contains several words an English speaker would recognize, the *Kalevala* is completely unfamiliar. It looks more like Fijian.

A reason for the huge disparity between these cohabiting languages was first proposed in 1786 by Sir William Jones, a British judge stationed in India. He made one of the world's most exciting discoveries. He noticed astonishing similarities in grammar and vocabulary between Sanskrit and Germanic, Celtic, Romance, Greek, Slavic, and Iranian languages. 'Brother', for example, is *phrater* in Greek, *frater* in Latin, *bratre* in Old Slavic, *brathir* in Old Irish, and *bhrater* in Sanskrit. This suggested to Jones that the Indic civilization was far older than that of Greece or Judea. It was then thought that rather than being the parent of most European languages, Sanskrit possibly shared with them roots in one language, which came to be known as Indo-European. It was the study of it and its so-called offspring that established the principles basic to modern philology, with its studies of comparative grammar, classification of languages into families, and reconstructions of 'proto-languages' from thin air.

Modern scientists tend to agree that there must have been one dominant Proto-Indo-European language, albeit divided up into numerous dialects, and place its homeland in the Near East or in eastern Europe, possibly around the Black Sea. A few hypothetical Proto-Indo-European words, derivatives of which occur in most Indo-European languages, suggest that it was spoken by a Neolithic or early metal-using people in around 5000–3000 BC. Recently the British archaeologist Colin Renfrew identified the 'homeland' as Anatolia on the flanks of the Fertile Crescent region and reversed the spread of Proto-Indo-European by two thousand years to about 7000 BC, just as Europe's ice caps were retreating northwards. Renfrew argued that the language was spread not by conquest or migration, as was commonly thought, but by the cradle. The Fertile Crescent was inhabited by people who were among the world's first farmers, and as they bred, their Indo-European children needed more land, and so they fanned out, taking their techniques with them. They interbred with indigenous hunter-gatherers they met along their way, reaching Ireland and Scandinavia by 2500 BC. With them went their language, gradually changing as it intermingled with those they encountered. This theory is appealing because every time we say the word 'brother' we could be connecting with those who brought about the most important event in human history, the spread of farming.

Renfrew's theory confirms the studies of Europe's human genetic landscape by Luigi Cavalli-Sforza. The gene shift that he traced from east to west coincides with the spread of farming. However, Cavalli-Sforza noted another east–west gene shift that occurred a few thousand years later, and proposed that this signalled a flow of nomads who invaded western Europe from the Ukrainian steppes, beginning around 4000 BC. It is possible that *they* bore the Indo-European tongue.

However or whenever it spread, Indo-European remains a useful tool for classification. Swedish is classified as a northern branch of the Indo-European Germanic languages. The western branch includes English, which makes Swedish a distant cousin of English, along with every other West European language except Basque.

Finnish, however, is no relation. It is neither Scandinavian nor Slavic. It does not stem from Indo-European. It has a number of other morphological distinctions, one of which is that it is strongly agglutinating. This means that a single root word can be given numerous subtle changes of meaning by glueing other words to it.

Genetic distinction supports the linguistic evidence, and there is historical evidence too. Southern Finland was first populated in about 7000 BC when the Baltic was still a lake and the Ålands more extensive. They were hunters and fishermen who decorated their pots with comb-like marks, and they moved north across the Gulf of Finland. But it was not for thousands of years that any permanent settlements were made in Finnish swamps, when Finno-Ugrians moved west and north. Who were these people? Herodotus described the Indo-European-speaking Scythians transacting business with a bald-headed people who lived on the European side of the Urals. They found it impossible to communicate and could manage it only 'through seven interpreters and in seven languages'. It is possible that among these languages was an ancient form of Finnish.

However, I realized that when Mr Johansson described Finnish as a 'difficult language', he meant more than morphology and vocabulary. His difficulty was with what Finnish represented.

Although the Finns came from the south-east, trade and cultural ties were increasingly with the Swedes to the west. Swedes settled along the western and southern shores and on the Åland Islands, particularly after Sweden conquered Finland in the twelfth century. The Swedes became the urban elite, the bourgeois traders, industrialists, and shippers, as well as the colonial aristocracy, while Finnish became a low-status language of the backward masses. Until the mid-1800s it did not even have a full-fledged literary standard. So a division developed between town and country, bourgeois and peasant, Swedish-speaker and Finnish-speaker, us and them.

I sensed pride and defensiveness in the way Mr Johansson spoke. The Ålands may be small but they are rich; the language may be a minority tongue in Finland, but it is the language of the former rulers of Finland, of the upper classes, and now of a powerful neighbour. The former rulers were frightened of becoming the underdogs.

I began to feel sorry for 'them'. It was the Finns who struggled under first Sweden then Russia to preserve their extraordinary language. It is Finland that came into existence only eighty-odd years ago – within living memory – and has a population smaller than that of Greater London. The marvel is that Finnish has survived. Perhaps even more extraordinary than the way a language travels is the way it sometimes doesn't travel. Despite centuries of conquest, Finnish triumphed. When the Russian Governor General of Finland,

General Bobrikov, asked a Finn how long he thought it would be before all Finns were speaking Russian, the Finn replied, 'For six hundred and fifty-five years we were dominated by Sweden, and only ten per cent of us now speak Swedish.' This was shortly before Bobrikov was assassinated, in 1904.

So why were the Ålands not part of Sweden? Since the thirteenth century the Ålands had been subject to the Swedish crown, but being strategically crucial in the Baltic they had for centuries been fought over by Sweden and Russia. The Russians wanted the Åland harbours because they remain unfrozen for longer than any in Russia. The Swedes wanted the Ålands because they plug the Gulf of Bothnia, protecting northern Scandinavia, and because they lie close to the entrance to Stockholm. Both wanted them because they cross the Baltic like stepping stones. They provide a toehold in the other's camp.

Russian soldiers twice burned and pillaged the Ålands so savagely during the eighteenth century that these events became known as the Greater and Lesser Wraths. But life continued. Hunting expeditions by boat lasted several days in open fishing boats, the sails doubling as awnings over the bows when the hunters slept. Sheepskins served as mattresses, with seal-skin boots for walking on ice, the seal hairs lying against the ice to prevent slipping. Their houses were wooden cabins with beds stacked one above the other like berths around the chimney. The women worked lace to trim their sheets and pillows, and wove striped dresses and draped themselves in tasselled shawls decorated with flowers.

Hard winters see the Baltic freeze over. Once people drove sleighs from one country to another; now they drive in land cruisers.

The Ålands and Finland were finally wrested from Sweden by Russia in 1809. Administered as part of the Grand Duchy of Finland, Åland became an outpost in the defence of the Tsarist Empire. That explained the stucco mansion on the shore at Eckerö. We went back there one rainy day. A notice in three languages said that it was the former post office, built in 1828 by Carl-Ludwig Engel, the German architect who built the by-the-yard neoclassical centre of Helsinki, the Duchy of Finland's new capital. This handsome edifice – so expensive that it bankrupted its builder – became the Tsar's window on the West. For two hundred years a mail route had been established here, linking the Ålands and Sweden by the shortest route, and was maintained by a rota of farmers who doubled as fishermen; now it became not a link between two parts of Sweden, but Russia's eye on its long-time enemy.

In 1917 Finland took advantage of the chaos of the First World War and the Russian Revolution to declare independence. Helped by the Germans, the Finns conquered the Reds and drove out the Russians. This was followed by a White counter-terror in which thousands died.

This upheaval caused consternation in the Ålands. What was to become of these undefended little rocks? Neutral Sweden seemed stable and homelike in comparison. At a secret meeting the Ålanders agreed to cut their ties with Finland and reunite with Sweden. A petition was sent to King Gustav V of Sweden. It stated that, 'Affinity in origin, language, culture, way of thinking and customs as well as an assurance of future security under the sceptre of Sweden have urged the Ålanders to this action.' This was brave: three years later the leaders of the secession movement, Julius Sunblom and Carl Bjorkman, would be arrested, taken to Åbo/Turku on the Finnish mainland, and prosecuted for high treason.

By 1919 Finland had managed to establish a republic, which was legalized by Soviet Russia in 1920. Finland refused to contemplate the Ålands' secession, and in the same year passed the Autonomy Act for Åland, which the Ålanders, having not been consulted, refused to accept. Finnish troops invaded.

This situation created growing tension between Finland and Sweden, so Britain drew it to the attention of the newly formed League of Nations. The League of Nations concluded that the islands should not be allowed to secede from Finland, but instead become autonomous. Finland would retain sovereignty, and in return would guarantee the Swedish language, culture, and customs. The League of Nations also insisted on the Ålands' neutrality, thus giving Sweden guarantees that Åland would not constitute a military threat. Everybody ought to have been happy.

But they were not.

The Ålanders were bitterly disappointed that what they felt to be their historic destiny had not come about. In their deputation to the Swedish king, the Åland secessionists recalled their annexation by Russia in 1809 thus:

> With bleeding hearts the population of Åland, Swedish from ancient times, received the news that their islands could no longer belong to Sweden. Deeply distressed in their innermost being by this separation, which in the Åland view was contrary to human and divine law, the Åland people nevertheless did not abandon the hope which they nourished in their national soul of a future reunion of their islands with the kingdom of Sweden.

The secessionists, steeped in nineteenth-century German romantic nationalism, considered a nation to be a tribe which was the bearer of a national soul, and all those belonging to that tribe had the same origin, spoke the same language, and maintained the same customs and habits. They stressed the power of historical tradition and the historical differences between nations. When it came to political allegiances, Jacobin free will was less important than what had been historically determined; in fact a tribe or people was represented as the only legitimate foundation of a body politic. Helsinki – and the League of Nations – disagreed.

Disappointment at the League of Nations' decision turned into antipathy against Finland. Mr Johansson referred to the 'language war'. Between the 1950s and 1970s political speeches frequently referred to the threat of imminent Finnification. Finnish speakers became the enemy, given historical blame for Åland failing to reunite with Sweden. Antagonism was strengthened by reports of infringements of the Autonomy Act. Negotiations often broke down.

'Did you ever resort to arms?' I asked.

'No. We Ålanders are pragmatists. We are sceptical about extremists.' This was a very Swedish remark. At the heart of Swedish thinking lies the concept of *lagom*, meaning 'the right amount', whether of freedom, wealth, success, happiness. It's good to be average. It's nice to be normal. It's better to have just the right amount of social equality than to strike out on your own.

'Do you still want reunion with Sweden?' I asked.

'No. Some people do, but most are happier this way. Why should we want to be swamped by another country? This way we do better, since we pretty well run Åland ourselves.'

'What about independence?'

'No, the Ålands are just too small. Our population is only twenty-five thousand! Most of us you see here, living in Mariehamn.'

'So the situation is this: you didn't want autonomy, you had it thrust upon you. But now you like it. It's as if the idea has caught up with the reality, rather than the other way round.'

'Yes. You could put it like that. So,' he concluded, 'we have Swedish language, culture, and the philosophy of pacifism – that's what unites us. It is our autonomy that has given us our identity.'

We toured the self-government building, peering into the darkened parliament with its pompous tiers of plush red seats and waiting microphones. Mr Johansson was proud of it: this was the visual manifestation of the Ålands' coming of age.

We lingered in the lobby. I asked him about old Åland.

'We're completely modernized now,' he assured me. 'All the outer islands have telephones and electricity. All have roads.'

It was as if he wanted to make the islands normal, middle class, dull, that Swedish *lagom* again.

'No old ways?'

'Later this month there is an annual re-enactment of a traditional wedding. In costume.'

'That's all? A wedding faked for tourists?'

'Tourists love it!'

'Have you ever heard of a custom of sweeping flour on to a bread board with a hare's paw?' I imitated Ann-Sofie's sweeping gesture.

'No. This is modern Europe.'

I rushed to rejoin Richard and the girls in the park. Xanthe was yelling with hunger, so I fed her on a bench while Tallulah bounced on a bouncy castle. She bounced for an hour, her cheeks going pink. Every time another child entered through the inflated portcullis she cringed; she craved their company but was stifled by shyness. Richard shopped furtively for beer at the sole outlet for alcohol, the state-owned and ignominiously named 'Alko'.

We went to the *postipankki* for yet more money, and to KKK supermarket to spend it all. We needed nappies, but didn't know which size because at least four months had passed since Xanthe was weighed. The solution: place her on the fruit and vegetable scales. She sat there grinning and going 'Dadadada', and prodding a picture of a red pepper. Nobody here spoke above a whisper, so the hushed calm of Åland shoppers was ruffled by Tallulah gurgling with laughter.

'Which sort of fruit is she?'

We agreed she was a banana. Tallulah then demanded to get in too.

Mariehamn was boaty, clean, and dull, despite the strenuous efforts of the tourist office with its nature trails, re-creations of Stone Age villages and Viking feasts (horned helmets will be worn). Youths cruised in Oldsmobiles down broad American-style avenues. Of course, the American style was really Scandinavian style; land short-ages in the nineteenth century had forced 1.3 million Swedish speakers to emigrate to the USA between 1851 and 1923. They imprinted America with barely a trace of their language, but they left behind their architecture and urban design.

We bought sausages and baked potatoes and thin Finnish beer from stalls below an outdoor stage. An elderly trio played country and western music on accordions, but nobody listened. The wooden tables were full, and conversation was animated, but nobody spoke to anyone else; the conversations were into mobile phones. Hands glued to ears: we diagnosed Nokia elbow, the national disease. Our fellow lunchers were here, and yet not here; they looked towards us, but their eyes were glazed. It made us feel oddly abandoned and invisible. It reinforced our sense of being outsiders.

Richard studied the map and drove down a forest track to a rocky outcrop spread with violas and thrift. Tallulah jumped from rock to rock, talking to herself. The roar of distant breakers made white noise; close by, the sea was still, ruffled only by the plop of Richard's float.

Tallulah and I read *Jeremy Fisher*. The frog had just been caught in the jaws of a trout when Richard's astonished face appeared at the window. He clutched a twitching fish, eighteen inches long. We tumbled over ourselves to congratulate him. I expected Tallulah to beg him to spare the fish's life, but far from it. She urged Richard to bash it on the head with a plank, then spent a happy half-hour spooning the guts into a bush.

It was a scaly carp, which was surprising since carp is a freshwater fish. The Baltic is so low in salt that we even saw cows drinking from it. This was because the Baltic was once a lake. In fact it was twice a lake. Until the end of the last ice age it was ice-dammed. Then the ice melted and saltwater penetrated the basin, turning it into a sea. But the land, released from the pressure of ice, rose faster. The sea was dammed again and became what geologists call Ancylus Lake, and Åland surfaced. Then the sea rose again and breached the land barrier to the south-east, and all but the highest tips of Åland were submerged.

To Tallulah's delight, we grilled the carp and ate it for supper with waxy Åland new potatoes.

'Is it delicious?' she enquired from her top bunk.

'Yes. Would you like some?'

'No! Yuks! But you know the best thing?'

'What's that?'

'You got it for free.'

We woke jaded. I had fed Xanthe until dawn, propped against the window, half-asleep, listening to lapping waves.

I strapped Xanthe into the sling and took her and Tallulah for a walk through the woods. Moss was spongy underfoot, and lichen sprouted like silver coral, some with lacquered scarlet tips. I deposited the girls back at the Mob and continued alone, down a path lined with lilies of the valley. By a pile of dead twigs I noticed a pair of ears. A deer and I watched each other for a while. On my return we watched each other again until it suddenly fled its nest to bound away along the shore. The stillness settled back again.

In the Mob, Richard was building a Lego house while Tallulah was talking to herself on the loo.

'Here's a happy scene.'

'Yes,' said Richard. 'She demanded the Lego. Then as soon as I'd got it down she lost interest. Now I'm having a lovely time doing it on my own.'

Xanthe cried at the sight of me, little arms reaching up; my very presence reminded her of food.

Rolf Witting was the rotund editor of the leading Åland newspaper, *Nya Åland*. He put me on to a man called William Nordlund.

'You must meet him,' Witting said. 'He has a big heart for Åland. Maybe a little naïve, but a very big man.'

He rang Nordlund's wife and arranged for us to meet.

William Nordlund had been managing director of a firm of Lloyd's shipping brokers and an MP for the dominant Farmer's Party. In 1981 he had helped to set up *Nya Åland*. This was important in the history of the islands because it had marked the birth of a new independent voice in the Ålands, able to criticize the prevailing pro-Swedish view. It was a sign of the Ålands' growing self-confidence.

I looked for him down corridors of shining vinyl and pictures of anodyne seascapes. He held out his hand, and I felt a mixture of revulsion and pity for his semi-paralysed body, and the nursing home smells of disinfectant and stale air. He had had a stroke.

'Take a seat,' he said airily. 'Ah, you've chosen well. That chair once belonged to Admiral Nelson. It was his library chair. I've got the authentication papers to prove it. Want to know how I got it?'

'Tell me.'

'It was given to me by Peter Miller. He was Chairman of Lloyd's in those days. He brought it here in his private plane. I flew in that plane once. Peter Miller took me to the Channel Islands.'

I said my grandfather had been a Chairman of Lloyd's too.

'Peter Miller. Is he still alive?' he asked, taking no notice.

'I don't know. I know his name. I could find out if you like.'

'That's Peter Miller with me, at the wheel of the Nautical Club here in Mariehamn.' He indicated with his head a framed photograph. 'My wife was allowed to bring a few things for me from home. So she brought that. And that desk. It's an eighteenth-century English desk. And that barometer, that was bought in England too. Sometime in the 1920s. Then there's that fossil. It's five hundred and seventy million years old. I bought it in Selfridges.'

His Anglophilia was forged through shipping. Since Tsar Alexander II founded it in 1861, Mariehamn had been a ship owner's town. Åland farmers had always been powerful, but a boom after the Crimean War persuaded them to sell their own goods and to transport others by taking to the high seas. They built schooners, brigs, and barques, and sailed across the Atlantic and down to Australia, and it was Lloyd's who insured them.

Now twelve shipping companies are based here, of which the ferry companies are the biggest. The Baltic shipping lines, which are controlled by the Åland government, are the mainstay of the economy and are subsidized by the huge proceeds from duty-free sales. This makes Åland the richest part of Finland.

I sat there in Nelson's library chair in a nursing home in a remote little island in the Baltic while he told me about himself. He had been born in 1917 in New York, where his father, a carpenter, had gone to make his fortune. When Mr Norlund senior succeeded, he returned to Åland with William, aged nine.

William grew up during the 'era of disappointment'. Although he was in New York when the appeal for reunion with Sweden was made to the king, he shared the feeling of the day that this was their historic destiny.

'Reunion with Sweden will happen one day,' he assured me. 'The Ålanders wanted it, the Finns opposed it, and the League of Nations compromised.'

'Why do you want this so badly?'

'Because we are Swedes. It's obvious. We are Ålanders first, of course, and then Swedish. I don't feel Finnish at all. You'll see the difference when you get to the mainland. The towns are uglier, the people paler, their cheekbones higher. They are a different tribe.'

'What's the difference between an Ålander and a Swede?'

'Nothing.'

'What about your accent?'

'No. No difference. There's more difference between the accents on the Swedish mainland than between us and Stockholm. We have been given autonomy and the official policy is now to develop that, to strengthen our Åland identity, but we have none. We are Swedish. Everything here is just like Sweden. We are creating a new ethnic identity for ourselves now, but it's bogus.'

'Why aren't you happy being part of Finland?'

'Because Finland will have trouble with Russia again one day, and I don't want any part of it. It will happen! Greater Russia! Just you wait.'

'Do you speak Finnish?' I asked him.

'No. Why should I need to?'

'Well, to communicate with your fellow countrymen.'

'If I wanted to communicate with someone from the mainland I would do so in English.'

I took his hand. As I reached the door he called out, 'Yes . . . Peter Miller. Please give him my regards.'

We caught the last ferry to the outlying island of Kökar. We cruised in a rain-swept evening through a sea flecked with skerries that from time to time coagulated into larger masses with quaint troll-like names such as Lemland, Föglö, or Lumparland. Then they broke up and dispersed into the drizzle. Richard and I took turns to go up on deck and lean on the rail. Around us lay a hazardous maze for our captain to negotiate in the dark.

I had expected a landscape like the Outer Hebrides, dotted with poor fishing communities or ruined houses abandoned by emigrants. But there was nothing like that. Most of the islands were rocky sanctuaries only for seals and birds.

It was midnight when we landed. Richard drove into the darkness, peering right and left in search of a place to park. But there was just a lane lined with farms and water, with no access to unused land. I had hoped the girls would sleep on the ferry, but they had been wildly excited, Tallulah chatting nonstop, eating special treats, needing to be read to, and Xanthe shredding bunches of fabric freesias that filled the vases on each table. Now we were all beginning to despair.

Then we were crossing a bridge on to another tiny island called Hamnö. We stopped where the track ended, on a meadow between a mass of wild flowers and an eighteenth-century church, not a house in sight.

We built the beds and tucked up the girls, then went out. I stood beside Richard, buffeted by the wind on a promontory so narrow that we could hear the sea crashing against three sides of it. The white-painted church glimmered, and beside it a bell tower acted as a lighthouse. It flashed its lonely light. It had just guided in the ferry on which we had arrived.

After the rain, blustery sunshine, bright waves, a picnic on rocks beside clusters of orchids and thrift, scrubby elders coming into flower, terns shrieking Kee-arr, and Tallulah trying to feed me gull shit for my lunch.

There was bustle around the church. People arrived early, rattling on black bicycles. They wore wellies and flapping plastic macs; I could tell they were locals by the surly looks directed at us. We felt unwelcome here, perhaps because of our van, perhaps because of a mistrust of outsiders.

A ruddy-cheeked man in fishing boots helped his bobble-hatted wife to tend a grave. She emptied dead flowers on to a compost heap and refilled a vase with fresh ones. Not that the graveyard needed tending; the grass was perfectly shaved, and the lettering on the gravestones regilded, so that even those from the 1890s looked shining new.

Tallulah danced from grave to grave, covering her nose with pollen, peering at dates and asking, 'Was this a young-un?' She was always distressed when I said yes, that's Olaf Sundberg, he was a young-un; that's Julanda Soderlund, and Bertil Westerberg, they were young-uns.

'Why did they die?'

'I don't know. Maybe they were very ill. Children don't die like that any more because we have better medicines.'

'Will you die?'

'Not for a while, I hope.'

'When you die, I want to die at the same time. Then we can be in heaven together. But, Helena?'

'Yes?'

'What if there's no room on your cloud?'

An archaeological dig was marked out with taut string. I explained about 'archaeology', 'monastery', 'the past'. Tallulah immediately set to with a stick, and to her delight unearthed a jawbone that she thought belonged to a monk (it was a sheep's). She washed it and treasured it for the rest of our journey; she loved its teeth. Eventually it was incorporated into a bones mobile that dangled over her bed; when we went over bumps the bones would clack together.

We returned for tea to find Richard listening to Bob Dylan at full volume, while sweeping out the van. I fed Xanthe. A face appeared at our window. The face was young, and groovily sported a baseball cap the wrong way round over long floppy hair. He peered up from under the window and announced that 'a decision had been made not to allow camping'. We looked at him insolently, without turning down the music, wondering what right this man – this youth – had to move us on. This was the first time we had suffered such an indignity, and here of all places, the land of wide open spaces where the entire population is less than that of London, where there is even a law entitling us to camp and walk where we liked.

'I'm sorry,' he added.

We decamped to the south of the island, beside another rocky promontory.

In the 'town', Karlby, there was a petrol station and a couple of shops, nothing more. We had a drink in the island's only hotel, a long building ranged beside a creek with a few boats moored alongside. We were the only customers. We ordered a single frugal beer between us. We got talking to the barman, who doubled as the tourist officer. The preparations at the church were for St Francis's day, he explained, to be celebrated on the first Sunday in July. The church stood on the site of a medieval Franciscan monastery, one of only three in Finland. He urged us to stay on, and offered to change our ferry booking.

Did he know anyone who could tell us more about Kökar? He knew just the person. His uncle, Kenneth Gustavsson, was the archaeologist in charge of the monastery. He worked at the museum at Mariehamn, but he was from Kökar and still had an old family house here. He phoned his uncle but there was no reply.

'Don't look so disappointed,' the barman said kindly. 'Do you see that big white house over there?'

'Yes.'

'And do you see all that grass?'

'Yes.'

'And do you see the man mowing the grass?'

'Yes.'

'That's my uncle.'

We trooped up the long drive. The landscape was open, without fences or trees, so Kenneth Gustavsson must have seen us coming and wondered who we were. He took off his earphones and switched off the mower. He was surprisingly young to be the barman's uncle, in his mid-forties. He was narrow, moustached, and fair, but he was enveloped in a blanket of melancholy. Perhaps it was the acres of grass that made him feel this way.

The house was lovely but decaying. Paint flaked off the windows, the frames beneath the paint were black with rot. The clapboard was bulging and unkempt. It was not old – 1936 Kenneth thought – but in the damp nothing lasted. That was one reason why there were no remains of deserted villages: everything disintegrated.

'Shall we take off our shoes?'

'No, it's all right,' he murmured.

He led us into his drawing room. Frayed Empire-style furniture was arranged against the walls. We clomped over the parquet, our footsteps unnaturally loud in a house that seemed to know only silence. Melancholy hung there like dust motes. On the other side of the hall I glimpsed a child's toy, a framed photograph; their presence drew attention to a bigger absence. Perhaps his wife and children had stayed behind in Mariehamn, but I sensed their absence was more long term.

We perched on brocade at a walnut table. In the centre of the table lay a blue and white eighteenth-century German dish. I held Xanthe on my lap, and attempted simultaneously to take notes. Kenneth explained in his polite, gentle voice that he had begun his excavations at the monastery in 1982. There were few written sources, he said, but had been thousands of archaeological finds – pottery from south-west Germany, a beautiful medieval silver and copper chalice, fish hooks, rings, a belt buckle, a knife. There were medieval graves and a huge rubbish pit, he said, full of coins, ceramics, and bones. (I kept quiet about Tallulah's jawbone.) The monastery was sacked during the Reformation and abandoned for years, then in the eighteenth century a Lutheran church was built on the old foundations.

'Why are Åland churches always on their own on the edge of the sea?' Richard asked.

Kenneth explained that until fairly recently there were no roads; until fifty years ago there was not even a bridge to Hamnö; there had been a village around the church, but that had moved inland, and people went to church by boat. Hamnö means harbour, he explained, an ancient harbour that was on the Itineris sailing route. This was a pre-Hanseatic Viking trading route linking Denmark, Sweden, and Estonia; the Franciscans had followed the Vikings.

'In 1549 there were three hundred fishing boats in Kökar, employing about a thousand people.'

'Where are all the fishing fleets now?' I asked.

'I think people are bored with fishing. They are fed up with it. They want to do something different.'

'What do they do?'

'They work on the ferries. They farm. Tourism. People are coming back to the island. At the end of the First World War this island was overpopulated – there was no work. My father went to New York and Washington to make a living, then came back and built this house. At that time about a thousand people lived on Kökar. Then by the 1960s it had gone down to six hundred people. In the

1970s it went down again. There were fears that by the year 2000 the island would be depopulated. But it hasn't happened. In fact the population is going up. There are three hundred people here now. It's the tourism that's bringing them back. Most of them are people whose parents moved to Sweden in search of work between the 1940s and '60s. Most of them kept their Finnish citizenship and often their old houses on the island too.'

'Do they hate tourists? That's the impression we get.'

'When they first started coming it was exciting for us. Most were Stockholmers. It seemed as if at last there would be some fun here. But now it's irritating when you can't get a place on the ferry.'

'You have very strict landowning laws.'

'Yes. You can buy property in Åland only if you are a Finnish citizen, have lived here for at least five years, and can demonstrate that you have a good command of Swedish.'

Initially, this law was to keep the Finns out, but now it's to keep the Stockholmers out too. It is a piece of legislation envied by the minorities of the world. Imagine, I told myself, if a similar law was passed in Provence or in Wales. If you could buy property in Wales only if you could prove that you had lived there continuously for five years, not just for holidays, and spoke Welsh. Imagine if you could buy a house in Skye only if you first proved your fluency in Gaelic. Why not? The schools would fill up with Gaelic-speaking children, there would be demand for Gaelic teacher training, the Gaelic college at Sabhal Mòr Ostaig would burst with applicants.

Kenneth addressed himself mainly to Richard. I sensed that he felt uneasy with me. He seemed shy, but it may have been because my conversation was fraught with sotto voce reprimands. There had been no time to explain to Tallulah who this man was, or why we were here, or why I should be writing in my notebook. She interrupted, then tore around the room. When we left, Kenneth seemed more despondent than ever.

Grey sky, grey sea. We got up late, lulled by the rain drumming on our roof. I liked these days off, when we could catch up with reading to Tallulah, doing puzzles, and making masks from Rice Krispy packets.

But then we got on each other's nerves. Xanthe had been going to sleep when Tallulah activated her Talker Dolly. *'Maammaaaa! Ha ha ha ha ha ha!'* This woke Xanthe, who cried, so I was cross, so Tallulah cried. Then Tallulah climbed on to the heater to reach for some of Xanthe's clothes to put on Talker Dolly, fell off and cried noisily again, making me cross again. No, not cross, almost beside myself with rage.

'Why are you always so cross?' Tallulah asked.

'Why are *you* always so cross?'

'I only get cross when you get cross.'

'And I only get cross when *you* get cross.'

'The thing is,' she said, 'I do love you, Mummy, but I'm bored of you.'

I looked at her. A three-year-old doesn't say that sort of thing. But I couldn't blame her. I felt the same.

We were getting cabin fever. It seemed important to get out, despite the rain. We donned waterproofs to cycle into Karlby for supplies. The fields were saturated green, the rocks silver. The supermarket was shut – no milk! – but we found a shop selling local eggs and lax. It was more a shed than a shop, with a candle in one corner and in the other a man and a woman hunched over drinks behind a sign saying *reservat*. No hare's paw, but not far off. The woman behind the counter explained that the ugly hunks of bronze-coloured fish were hot roast salmon, while gravadlax is cold cured salmon. It was pale orangey-pink, not the bright orange stuff which is often farmed, she said.

On a nail hung a black and white photograph of a fishing boat. That's what we used to have, she said. Her husband, him over there having the drink, he was the fisherman. Fishing's finished now, he interjected. We just do the smoking and buy salmon from friends.

'Why is the fishing finished?'

'Because of the Norwegians.'

'What do you mean?'

'The Norwegian fjords are full of fish farms. They wait for prices to get high, then they sail in and undercut everyone else. And they aren't subject to fishing quotas and restrictions because Norway isn't part of the EU.'

'Do you regret joining the EU?'

'I don't know. We don't get much from it. And we feel very bitter about the Norwegians. Not the people, but the situation.'

We bought gravadlax and dill, and a loaf of local black bread, flat as a frisbee and so dark and rich it tasted of tar. The woman recommended it thinly sliced with lots of butter. She said it was cooked the 'real' way, not the 'easy' way. This took two or three days, using rye flour, with lots of kneading, then you bake it twice, once in an aluminium container. No malt! Malt's the *easy* way. It stops you needing to bake twice.

So the islanders still liked a little bit of hardship.

We gossiped about the Franciskus Fest. It was a new thing, she said, mainly to provide a focus for Körker emigrants returning home, as well as for Franciscans. The vicar was new, very young, and (whisper it) handsome.

'Does he have long dark hair?' I asked.

'Yes!'

'Might he wear a baseball cap?'

'I expect so. Everyone loves him. Oh, he's marvellous. He's just come from a parish in Sweden.'

'Is he Swedish?'

'No, Finnish of course, but a Finland Swede. From the mainland. He's just had a new baby, last week! But he's very nervous about the Franciskus Fest, oh dear me! I asked him, which do you feel more nervous about, the baby or the Franciskus Fest, and he said he didn't know!'

'We met him a few days ago.' I now felt embarrassed by the memory of his face peering awkwardly up, and our insolence.

'Are you from England?'

'Yes.'

'I thought I didn't hear any Yankee accents.'

'Do you get many English people here?'

'No, I would say, no. There is one man who comes from some-where near Oxford, I think. He has a Finnish wife. But that's all.'

'Well, we look forward to seeing you tomorrow.'

'Yes, let's hope the weather improves. The forecast is bad, a low, coming from the east, from Russia.'

We biked home against driving rain. Xanthe was in the sling, and the rain whipped her face; she became distressed, and so did I when we lost our way. At last we found our van and piled inside, stripping off clothes and hanging them in the shower where they streamed. Richard made tea.

'Do you want a cup?'

'*Do I want a cup?*'

'In other words, do you want me to cram chocolate into your mouth and give you a million pounds?'

I never drank my tea. I was too busy cooking risotto for Tallulah, heating up puréed liver casserole for Xanthe, feeding Xanthe, hanging up wet clothes, changing Xanthe's nappy, playing with Tallulah, breastfeeding Xanthe again, then putting her to bed. Meanwhile Richard read to Tallulah, repaired her safety net, tried to warm his feet in three pairs of socks under a blanket, wrote his diary. Meanwhile Tallulah ate Special K on the floor and reminisced about her nursery school.

'I loved all the teachers,' she said, 'but I didn't like the food.'

Then I got Tallulah undressed, helped her to clean her teeth, sat her on the loo, read her a story, sang her songs, cuddled up with her for a while. Richard warmed the risotto for us, poured drinks, we ate supper, read, made up the bed, then lay down.

Gusts of wind rocked the van. We were woken by a heavy-footed gull on our roof. The weather had cleared.

The church shone against the blue sky and sea, the air washed clean. People arrived throughout the morning, including two coaches that disgorged priests and nuns and attendant pilgrims who had come from all over Finland and Sweden. With a Franciscan foun-dation beneath a Lutheran church, it was an ecumenical festival, with Catholics and Lutherans together. Startling here, two of the Franciscan nuns were black.

We milled around the graveyard. Friends greeted each other and admired the fresh flowers. Some stood silently, looking down at loved ones.

'There's Kenneth Gustavsson.'

He looked cool in a brown leather jacket. He waved and came over. I said how lucky it was to have this sunny day after the gale, and he looked at Richard and smiled and said, yes, it's usually like this for the Franciskus Fest.

A service began, outside in the sun. Our vicar prayed at a microphone, dramatic in red robes, his long dark hair flapping over his face. He was assisted by two priests in white who (rumour had it) came all the way from Assisi. Kenneth explained to Richard that the vicar was dedicating a new bell in the wooden bell-tower-cum-lighthouse. Then shutters in the tower flew apart and two men appeared at the opening. One was young, the other old and frail. They were father and son, local farmers with ruddy cheeks and sideburns, awkward in unfamiliar suits.

A female priest said prayers, and the young man reached for a bell pull and began to toll the new bell. His father on the older, smaller bell joined him, and together they rang and rang against the blue sky on a lonely crag in the Baltic. It was so simple and so pure and joyful, I found myself suddenly choking back tears.

Inside, the church was decorated as if for a wedding. The aisle was lined with fresh branches of birch, light green and feathery. Two model ships were suspended overhead. Kenneth said that one had been given during the eighteenth century as a votive offering by a man who grew up in Karlby and as a boy worked on a Norwegian ship in the Mediterranean. There he was captured by Turkish pirates and taken to North Africa to be sold as a slave. He had vowed then that if he ever returned to Körker he would build a model of his ship and give it to the church. But this was not only a votive offering, it was a celebration of the seafaring lives of the people. It was also a reminder of life as a voyage, the ship of life. I liked that.

We lasted only a few minutes of the service before the children got restless. We wandered through the graveyard listening to the hymns. Later we watched 'medieval' theatricals. They were dull but it was lovely just to lie on the rocks, looking at the sky. We joined a queue at trestle tables for a smorgasbord of smoked salmon and poppy-seed rolls.

Kenneth leaned against a stone wall chatting to Richard, but he still avoided my eye. He appeared suave, urbane, more sophisticated than the other locals; he clearly enjoyed the Franciskus Fest, and loved the church, but he was an onlooker, not a participant.

With great excitement a woman introduced herself. She was the local girl who had married the Englishman. They came home every summer to see her family. She had kept a house on Kökar, and her brothers worked here as pilots for ships. She invited us to join her for tea in a café on a cliff. We sat at the windows admiring the view.

Lisa was an old friend of Kenneth's sister, and had often stayed in the big white house as a child. She remembered how lovely it was.

We asked her about the sea freezing over – we couldn't get over the idea of skating from one country to another – and she said, yes, she remembered it happening from time to time. A few times she had been going to Mariehamn to buy her spring clothes and the sea had been frozen. I had a vision of a tall young girl in the 1950s, with short styled hair and a brown coat and shoes, going off to Mariehamn to buy her spring cottons and being stopped by an expanse of lumpy ice. Even now, to the people of Kökar, Mariehamn must seem like a metropolis, and going there is still a big expedition, five hours in the ferry, there and back.

She said that Kökar was traditionally a smuggling and pirate island. Old habits die hard. Only recently, she said, there was a wreck near the island and everyone got in their boats and rushed over to it and came back with vast timbers. Before she knew it, lots of new houses had sprung up.

Lisa said that her family was unusual in that they had felt Finnish rather than Swedish. Her father had been a civil servant for the Finnish government, so in her early teens she had left Kökar to attend school on the Finnish mainland, then university in Helsinki. Several times a year she had to take the train through Porkkala, a part of Finland that was leased to the Soviet Union as a naval base from 1944 until 1955. As the train entered the Russian zone, the windows were blacked out. When they returned to the Finnish zone, the passengers were allowed to look out again.

(The following day we would be staying on the mainland with friends who lived beside that very railway line, in a yellow clapboard house that had been requisitioned by Soviet officers. Lisa would have passed this house on her way to school, but never seen it.)

We were joined by our handsome vicar and his ecclesiastical guests, the Franciscan monks, the priests from Assisi, and the two black nuns. The vicar recognized us and looked surprised.

'Were you at the Franciskus Fest?'

'Yes. It was lovely.'

'So you found a place to stay?' He was smiling, but the memory of Bob Dylan playing too loudly and my bare breast prevented me from saying more than 'Yes.'

Then everyone had ice creams. Tallulah spilled hers down Richard's trousers. He went outside to scrape them clean; he was very cross.

We boarded the last ferry to the Finnish mainland, joining pilgrims and nuns. Late into the night we cruised past dark islands, silent silhouetted pines, a mysterious velvet darkness and just the rumble of our engine. We landed at the end of the necklace slung between Sweden and Finland, on which the Ålands hang like beads. Long after midnight, this was Finland proper at last: grand, remote, untrampled. I thought of Sibelius, but it wasn't *Finlandia* – that was too swaggering, too martial – it was more like *Tapiola*, with its minor key suggestions of sadness, the ominous looming of forests, sudden shafts of light, fluty sprites. But even that wasn't right. Instead I kept hearing the single note – passionate, mournful, exquisite – of a Japanese flute. In the wooden architecture, in the modern architecture, in a Finnish neatness and attention to detail, in that eastern slant of the eyes, beside still lakes, beneath twisted pines, I thought of Japan.

FOUR

Samiland

Tallulah had noticed them first. They were on Stockholm's Ström-bron, leaning over the parapet to haul up lines of fish like whitebait. Holding Richard's hand, Tallulah had stopped to watch the youngest, a thickset girl, unhook the fish with expert fingers and drop them into a bucket.

She and her companions, a youth and an older man, had black hair and slant eyes and brown skin, a remarkable sight in Stockholm. They looked like Inuit. I caught Richard's eye.

'Lapps?'

He nodded. We were excited because this was the first time we had encountered the people of the Arctic. I was surprised to see them so far south; from Lapland to Stockholm is about as far as from Stockholm to London.

I imagined how these people felt, hooked like their fish out of the lakes of their homeland. I imagined them trapped in the urban jungle, nomadic instincts stifled. Perhaps they escaped to this bridge to breathe sea air and dream of home. In winter (I supposed) they clambered on to the ice-bound Strömmen, cars rattling overhead, to chisel out holes for their hooks, and sit in furry-hooded jackets waiting for a bite.

When we visited Alf and Ann-Sofie in Saltsjöbaden, we talked about the Lapps. Have you been to Lapland? I asked Alf. No, he said, we tend to go south for the summer, to Europe. But he did have a friend involved with setting up a Lapp museum, who had been struck by the resentment felt by the Lapps towards the Swedes and Finns and Norwegians, who they felt had oppressed them. I related our encounter with the narrow-eyed fishermen. Alf suppressed a smile.

'I think you'll find they were Japanese tourists.'

It was one of the tourist attractions of Stockholm, he said, the fact that you could catch fish in the centre of a capital city. Oh, I said.

The Lapps, Alf explained, do not resemble other indigenous peoples of the Arctic. They look like Scandinavians or Finns. They are blond or dark, tall or short, fat or thin. It is one reason why they have been so readily assimilated into Fenno-Scandian culture. Which, in turn, is one reason why their own culture is on the verge of being wiped out.

And by the way, they are no longer called Lapps. According to Johannes Schefferus, the seventeenth-century Swedish professor of Law and Rhetorrick who was the first to write about the Lapps:

> After the Swedes had learnt from the Finlanders that they were called Lappi, or banished persons, they also gave them the same name; then the Danes took it up, then Saxo, and so at last all the country was called Lapland from the Bay of Bothnia northwards, except only that part of it which lies on the coast of Norway, which retained its ancient name of Finland, as also that part towards the White Sea called by the Muscovites Cajanica.

Schefferus's book *Lapponia* was published in 1673, and was immediately translated into English, German, and French. For two centuries it was the major source. But the Lapps no longer wish to be known as Banished Persons. They call themselves Sami, and the place they inhabit – the northernmost tips of Finland, Sweden, Norway, and the Kola Peninsular of Russia – they call Sápmi, Samiland.

I was excited by the idea of endless days, endless nights, the sky shimmering with aurora borealis. I'd read a wonderful Sami poem that had been noted down in 1885:

> *Guovsahas viekka, viekka*
> *Lippaha, lippaha;*
> *Vaetsjer – oaiwe,*

Nava–gaddsa–juoelgek,
Ruona haelmek,
Lippaha, lippaha;
Buoide bitasj njalmest,
Gakkobitasj giedhast,
Viekka lippaha!

Northern lights – running, running
Fleet-footed, fleet-footed,
Hammer-head
Fists-helix-feet,
Green fringe
Fleet-footed, fleet-footed;
Tasty bit in mouth,
Bit of cake in hand,
Running fleet-footed!

It was the sense of perpetual motion that excited me most.

For a week we drove north. Finland's roads were straight and deserted and walled with black-green forest, which parted on to peaty lakes that stretched taut and shiny as black plastic. Driving, driving, Finland slipping by. The denseness of the forests had a pleasantly soporific effect and diverting to look at towns or Aalto churches became an unwelcome interruption of the rhythm. While Xanthe slept, Tallulah would curl up at my feet with her ear to the speaker listening to *Charlie and the Chocolate Factory*, dreaming of sweets.

I wanted our restless life to last for ever. I would lean back and envisage a future in which everyone lived on the road – the ultimate in the free movement of peoples. Cities would be deserted; our descendants would hardly believe that there was once an era of static living, in which people were shackled to one place, often for their entire lives.

In the market at Joensuu in Karelia, near the Russian border, there was nothing on sale but strawberries and peas. It was mid-July, and the wind bitter. Summer was late, the stallholders apologized.

I'd always been excited by the romance of the North. We drove through a region that was even called the Far North, then north again.

Reindeer began to appear at the roadside, both hinds and stags sporting antlers like absurd mossy headdresses. Some could barely see for the antlers that branched down over their faces. We were on the edge of somewhere grand, marvellous, empty. Lapland, the northernmost province of Finland, is the size of Ireland.

At last we entered Lapland. In its capital Rovaniemi, built on the confluence of the Kemijoki and the Ounasjoki, two great Arctic rivers, the Finns were hosting a tango-dancing contest. They strutted to and fro, necks stiff, over the stylish new bridge beneath fluttering Euro flags. The exaggerated drama of tango seemed bizarre but appropriate: for the extremes of light and dark; the extremes of joy and depression; the extremes of Lutheran asceticism and raging alcoholism; the extremes of a law-abiding people with the highest manslaughter rate in Europe.

Alvar Aalto devised Rovaniemi's town plan in the form of a pair of reindeer antlers. We parked on the brow tine to stock up with food and nappies before heading into the tundra.

Rovaniemi was also the last place in which to repair an oil leak and wobbly steering. Finns are famous mechanics, famous for their *sisu*, their self-reliance. We spent the night in a garage forecourt in the hope that the mechanics could squeeze us in first thing. The scheme worked well. At 8 a.m., while we were still having breakfast, Richard drove us into the workshop. Something wrong with your house? Take it to be mended. The mechanic lifted out a front seat and put it on the garage floor, and Tallulah, still in her nightie, sat on the seat amongst the grease and tools and engine parts and ate her honey toast.

A mile north, we crossed the Arctic Circle. From here on we would see the midnight sun – when not hidden behind clouds. A dotted line on the map marked 66° 30′ N latitude, a line linking Fenno-Scandia and Siberia with the northern tip of Iceland, the lower half of Greenland, and the frozen wastes of Canada and Alaska. In Finland, thanks to the Gulf Stream, the climate is warmer than in the west. A bollard marked the Arctic Circle, but in fact it is not fixed. The Arctic Circle is a line around the North Pole whose angular distance from the pole is the same as the ecliptic inclination, and its location is constantly shifting north and south. The total shift is between Kemi, on the coast, and Ivalo, a distance of 380 kilometres, a shift that takes 25,000 years.

Supposedly marking the Arctic Circle is Father Christmas Village. We had to take Tallulah here. What fun, we thought, to see Santy in situ! Tallulah didn't think much of it. No doubt it was picturesque when swathed in snow, but in summer it was cynical and tawdry, tinkling with unseasonal musak. A moth-eaten reindeer grazed in a pen. There was nothing decent on sale, but there were buckets of bright blue and red hats with pointy corners, like jester's hats. They were sold as Sami hats. I had no idea that anything so fanciful was still worn in northern Europe. But when I looked at the label I saw they were made of nylon, in Taiwan. Father Christmas himself, however, was very convincing. Tallulah overcame her shyness to sit on his lap, and when he chatted to me I found my heart pounding. It was like chatting to the king.

Lapland was officially declared Santa Claus Land in 1984, and the 'village' (really a shopping mall) was built soon after, as close as possible to an airport. The Sami, in their sweet pointy hats, were supposedly connected with Father Christmas, perhaps as elves in his workshop. Ironically, however, the Sami do not live here, and have not done so for centuries; they live hundreds of miles north. This error arose out of confusion over the name Lapland. 'Lapland' was supposed to mean the transnational region inhabited by the Lapps, i.e. Lappland, not the Finnish province of almost the same name. Father Christmas Village could just as legitimately have been sited in Sweden, Norway, or Russia. The Finns have profited hugely from this mistake. In winter people fly in, just for the day.

Another irony is that far from being a funny little stunted tribe, whistling while they worked in Santa's workshop, despised by Finns and Scandinavians, it is now thought that the Sami and Finns were once the same people. Over a third of Finnish and Sami vocabularies are similar. 'Bread' is *leipa* in Finnish, *laibi* in Sami; mother is *aidi* in Finnish, *eadni* in Sami. Like Finnish, Sami has a tendency to agglutinate. Tacitus, who in AD 100 was the first to mention them in writing, referred to them *all* as Fenni, people of the marsh (hence both Finland and what Schefferus called Finland – now Finnmark – in north Norway).

But a thousand years before Tacitus was born the cultures had probably already diverged. The southern Finns had adopted agriculture and cattle herding, and encountered other Baltic and Germanic peoples, while the Sami hunter-gatherers remained utterly dependent on the resources of their isolated northern wastes, and gradually domesticated the wild reindeer they found here. From around 1900–1000 BC they moved north through Finland and Karelia, possibly in pursuit of those reindeer, and mingled with any existing inhabitants they met along the way.

Gradually the Sami themselves divided up, each taking their characteristics from their occupations – Coast Sami, Forest Sami, Mountain (reindeer herding) Sami. As they dispersed, their languages evolved into nine or ten different languages, each with their own dialects.

Then over the last millennium, Finns, Scandinavians, Russians, and Karelians pushed north into Sami territory, where they colonized the Sami, married them, assimilated them, dominated them. Now the Sami number perhaps seventy thousand out of a total population of nineteen million. The coast and forest Sami have mostly disappeared. The reindeer-herding Sami are under threat.

They remain the majority in two Norwegian municipalities (in Finnmark) and only one Finnish municipality, in Inari, known in Sami as Anar. This is the home of the new Finnish Sami Parliament. This was where we were heading.

North again, the wall of coniferous forest thinning and shrinking, the days expanding. The light turned white as chalk, then silver by night. The shadows seemed perpetually long, as if sunset and sunrise each lasted twelve hours. We camped in forests. Thanks to our nomadic existence, Richard's hunter-gathering instincts were on full alert. He led us between trunks, eyes down. He knew exactly where to look: around stumps of spruce and pine, among pine needles, beneath birch trees, beneath bracken. Ha! He would brush pine needles off a tawny orange cap: a perfect specimen, no sign of maggots. He would pick it. The stem would be thick and white with woolly scales; it had no ring at the top, and instead of gills the area underneath the cap was spongy and pale; these were signs of a boletus, which was good since most boletuses are edible – except for Satan's boletus with its blood-red pores, which is deadly poisonous. Richard would sniff it. It smelled as a mushroom should. He slit the stem and pressed it with his knife and watched it turn a milky grey, faintly bruised-looking. This was promising too, an Orange Birch boletus which tasted good. Where there was one mushroom, there would be others, and soon he would fill a basket, along with a few brittle red-and-white russola.

We sautéed the boletuses and russola in butter and garlic. The Sami dismiss fungi as reindeer fodder, but we found them delicious, if a bit slimy. I preferred the russola, which had a firmer texture and a nutty taste. We'd been eating them for weeks now, with no ill effect. Of course, the diarrhoea that follows ingestion of a sweet-smelling mushroom like *Amanita phalloides* is usually followed by a brief recovery. You think you've made it. Then two weeks later comes death from renal and liver failure.

It was dark and solemn beneath the trees. Many had had their crowns snapped off by the weight of snow. The branches dangled lichen like a witch's wispy hairs. Tallulah and I would find pudding, in the form of bilberries, dangling from tiny stalks near the ground. She stuffed herself with them. But we couldn't go on; mosquitoes were bobbing through the undergrowth, our hands red with bites. With my jacket almost completely smothering Xanthe, we would flee to the Mob.

We had arrived at the height of the short but frantic mosquito breeding season. As Schefferus wrote in the seventeenth century:

> The gnats infest man and beast, the Raindears especially, which on that account are driven to the mountains; The men arm themselves by keeping a Continual smoak in the house, and in sleeping by putting a blanket over head and body. Abroad they

As for Linnaeus's absence of 'the iron din of arms', lo and behold, here in the forest, deep in the soil, wound a massive German defence network. Trenches interlocked with dugouts and gun emplacements. Near Tankavaara we peered beneath sod roofs into cave-like interiors, almost able to hear the clash of German steel, the tramp of boots, the bark of orders, all now swallowed up in black peaty water and green tufts of bilberry bushes and a stuffy silence. The reason for it is one of the more extraordinary twists of the Second World War.

In 1941 200,000 German troops arrived in Finland to help the Finns repulse the territorial claims of the Soviet Union, and to extend the eastern front up towards Petsamo (then in Finland) and the nickel mines and harbours of the Arctic Ocean. Many German soldiers were stationed in Rovaniemi, where they struck up friendly relations with the locals. The Finns made handicrafts that they bartered with the Germans for tobacco and food, and the Germans found the Finnish girls pretty. There were parties and love affairs, even the odd marriage. Together, for three years, Finns and Germans fought the Russians. But in September 1944 the Finns were defeated and forced to sign a ceasefire with the Soviet Union. The USSR imposed severe terms of armistice. Apart from the hefty reparations that would overshadow Finland for the next fifteen years, the Finns were to turn on their former friends and expel every German soldier from Finnish soil, or intern them, within fourteen days. When the Germans failed to leave, Finland declared war on Germany. Thus began the War of Lapland.

As the Germans were pushed up through Lapland towards German-occupied Norway, they left devastation in their wake. Seventy-five per cent of the total population of Lapland – 103,000 people – had to be evacuated, some to Sweden, some to other parts of Finland; those who returned in 1945 found their country obliterated. Houses, schools, churches, shops: all had been razed. The old market town of Rovaniemi, where they had lived and loved together, was reduced to a pattern of smoking piles of ash. Twenty-five thousand head of livestock were slaughtered, 20,000 reindeer. To slow their Finnish pursuers, the Germans blew up almost every bridge in Lapland along with 170 kilometres of railway track. They also planted 55,000 mines.

Incredibly, by 1949 Rovaniemi was almost completely rebuilt.

This wasn't the Samis' war, they were victims of it. They didn't avoid it; indeed, during operations in northern Norway it was rumoured that of all the soldiers the Germans most feared it was 'those with hair on their feet'. These were the Sami in the Alta battalion who took along their own sedge-grass and fur shoes, and who knew intimately the lie of the land and the great voids.

Have 'mankind found their way into the bowels of the earth' as Linnaeus wrote? Of course they have. Iron ore, gold, and limestone were discovered in Swedish Samiland in the mid-seventeenth century, even before Linnaeus's journey. This led to more loss of grazing land, more colonization and, worse still for the Sami, compulsory service that ordered everyone to give up one tenth of their reindeer to transport the incoming men and their goods. This impoverished many, who emigrated in such numbers to Norway and the coast that soon emigration itself was forbidden. Roads were built for transporting logs and minerals. The neighbouring Kola Peninsular is a lethal wasteland of nuclear reactors, rotting Soviet nuclear submarines, spent fuel rods, solid and liquid radioactive waste, and the Northern Fleet's arsenal of 12,000 strategic nuclear warheads. Add to that the industrial pollution produced by the nickel-processing plants and you get the Kola Peninsula, once home only to Sami reindeer herders, now the most dangerous place on the planet.

As for not engaging 'in wars to define its boundaries'? In early years there may not have been such wars, but there were other ways of defining boundaries. The governments' representatives in the form of the hated *birkarls*, tax collectors, exploited the lack of any clear international borders dividing up Sami territory. The Sami paid tax in the form of furs, which accumulated in stockpiles in warehouses in Stockholm and Russia. Since the power able to collect most goods had the strongest claim to Samiland, some Sami were charged huge taxes several times over by different *birkarls* representing different countries. And what did the Sami get in return? Nothing.

Then, when national borders hardened during the nineteenth century, the Sami suddenly found that traditional reindeer migratory routes were truncated: they were no longer allowed to cross in search of the natural resources they needed.

Both world wars resulted in the shifting of national boundaries that left many Sami displaced. During the Winter War of the Second World War, the Orthodox Skolt Sami found their territory invaded, villages burnt, and their forests and lovely still waters in the front line. They were evacuated to Finland, but when the war ended their land was on the wrong side of the new Russo-Finnish border. When the Iron Curtain came down, all contact with the remaining Russian Sami was lost.

Here and there a lake, a sheet of tinfoil, patched the forests. One was Orajärvi, the subject of one of the most beautiful Sami poems. It was known by Olaus Matinpoika Sirma, the first Sami from the Kemi region to be educated. During the seventeenth century he went to Uppsala University where he studied to become a priest, and where he helped Johannes Schefferus with *Lapponia*, and gave him two love poems which came from his home district. From *Lapponia* 'Orajärvi' was taken and published all over Europe, including in *The Spectator* during the eighteenth century. The poem was important not just because of its beauty, but because it was the only large sample of Kemi Sami. This language is now lost.

'Orajärvi' was said to have been admired by Goethe, Longfellow and von Kleist, and to have influenced their work. Perhaps from there it made its way across the Atlantic and into the pen of Robert Frost. A nomadic poem. It went like this:

> *Pastos paivva kiufvvresist javvra Orre Iavvra*
> *Ios kaofa kirrakeid korngatzim*
> *Ia tiedadzim man oinamam jaufre Orre Iavvra*
> *Ma tangast lomest lie sun lie*
> *Kaika taidæ mooraid dzim soopadzim*
> *Mak taben sadde sist oddasist*
> *La poaka taidæ ousid dzim karsadzim*

Makqvvodde roamaid poorid ronaid
Kuliked palvvaid tim suttatim
Mak kulki vvoasta laufræ Orre Iaufra
Ios mun tæckas dzim kirdadzim sææst vvorodzæsæaest
æ muste læ sææ dziodgæ sæsæ maina taockao kirdadzim
Aeka læ Iulgæ songiaga lulgæ, akælæ siædza
Fauron sietza, maan koima lusad
Dzim norbadzim.
Kalle ju leck kucka madzie vvordamadzie
Morredabboit dadd paivvidad, linna sabboid
Dadd salmidadd liegne sabboid vvaimodadd
Ius kuckas sick patæridzick
Tannagtied sarga dzien iusadzim
Mios matta lædæ sabbo korrassabbo
Nu ly paddæ soonapaddæ, ia salvvam route salvvam
Kaek dziabræ siste karrasistæ.
Ia kæsæmyna, taem aivvitæm puniepoaka
Tæmæ jardækitæmæ parne miela
Piægga miela hoara iorda kockes jorda
Lostaidæ poakaid læm kuldælæm
Luidæm radda vværaradda
Ouita lie miela oudas vvaldæman
Nute tiedam poerponne oudastan man kauneman.

Let the sun shine bright on the lake –
Orajärvi,
If I climbed a spruce tree tall
And knew I'd see the lake – Orajärvi,
On whose heather banks she stands,
Then I'd cut down all these trees.
Speeding clouds I watched
That moved towards Orajärvi.
If only I could fly like a bird.
Long have you waited there,
Your sweetest days, your fondest eyes,
Your warmest heart.

Even if you fled afar
I would still soon come to you.
What can be stronger
Than thread of vein, iron chains,
That press so hard
And swathe our heads, change all
Our thoughts? Youth's desire
Wind's desire, young thought long thought.
If I listen to them all
I'll walk the wrong road.
One desire I must take,
Then I'll better find the road before me.

The road before me displayed, for the first time, bilingual road signs. They pointed back to Rovaniemi/Roavenjarga, on to Ivalo/Avvil and Inari/Anar. Samiland proper at last, and my first view of the North Sami tongue. I was very excited.

A few scruffy stalls selling Sami handicrafts appeared at the roadside. They were hung with white reindeer skins and leather purses and moccasins. Huddled inside the stalls under plastic canopies sat Sami traders in puffa jackets. To one side stood Sami *kotas* with wisps of smoke escaping from the hole in the roof. At first they seemed sad, the Sami reduced to marketing themselves to tourists, an extension of Santa's village, but on closer inspection we saw that these handicrafts were of high quality. During the long dark winters the Sami had always concentrated on their *duodji* to sell in the summer, it was nothing new. Now they would come from their towns and over the summer sell goods they had made themselves, sometimes sleeping in the *kota*, but mostly using it by day as a cook tent and a place to keep warm.

We bought a reindeer skin for Tallulah to sleep on. The Sami trader handed over the heavy bundle of fur and (to her delight) gave Tallulah a carved antler knife too.

A Sami woman emerged from a *postipankki* and wobbled off on her bicycle. She was wearing a *girjjatgakti*, a floral dress with a swirly skirt, and on her head sat a curiously unbecoming Sami bonnet with red flaps that hung down below her ears.

Our first view of Anar was from above. In crepuscular light we looked down on a vast lake, a mesh of islands and bays and secret waterways. But we drove through town before we realized. Anar had been razed by the Germans. Now it was a one-horse shanty, a frontier town on the edge of nothingness. Not much of a site for the new Finnish Sami parliament.

I was looking for a Sami who could talk to us about Samiland, and the plight of the Sami. In Rovaniemi I had heard about a writer, Nils-Aslak Valkeapää, whose book *Beaivi Ahcazan* (*The Sun, My Father*), written in Sami, was awarded the Nordic prize for literature in 1991. I began to see Valkeapää's name often. I noticed *Beaivi Ahcazan* on sale in bookshops, along with other books by him, including one with his marvellous photographs of weather-beaten Sami with snow ageing their rough beards and another with his naïve paintings of reindeer herders travelling across frozen wastes in their sledges. I had found a photocopy of his *Greetings from Lappland, The Sami – Europe's Forgotten People*, the second book by a Sami to be published in English. It was a passionate angry book about the plight of the Sami, written back in 1971, but addressing issues that were today more pressing than ever: loss of language, loss of land, loss of culture. The Nordic countries, he wrote, were beating their breasts about Chile and Vietnam, but were unable to put their own house in order. 'Ja, ja, these advanced Nordic countries, the conscience of the world, the conscience of the world. Really highly advanced states carry out genocide without blood, without physical violence. That's how it is.'

He clearly smarted from the stigma once attached to being Sami. He angrily dismissed all condescending charges of 'primitive' and 'backward'. Instead, he said, he was well educated, and what's more, sexy. Women throughout the world had always been keen to know him better. Studying the photograph on the back of his books, I could see why.

Valkeapää was also a founder member of the World Council of Indigenous Peoples. It was clear that this was a highly talented man with a passion for his people and their place. I was determined to find him, though I had no idea how. It was thought he lived in the deep north, up near the Norwegian border, and I hoped I might find him in Anar. But I'd heard that he'd had some problem, that maybe his mother had died.

No one seemed to know of the Sami parliament, not in the supermarket, or the *postipankki*, or the handicraft store. Then we tracked it down to a school. It was closed for the night. We would return tomorrow.

The wide Lemmenjoki hurtled over its stony bed, lined with majestic pines and flowering rowans. Richard eased up on to chocks to give us that perfect flatness, Tallulah built a sandcastle, and I fed Xanthe. Richard was so happy: the river for tea and washing, wood for the fire, forest for fungus, Anar within cycling distance for supplies, and no undergrowth immediately around us to harbour mosquitoes. We hoped to settle here a while.

Richard piled high the fire, got the smoke good and thick, then fortified our home. He taped over every point of entry, every vent, every window. We risked suffocation or carbon-monoxide poisoning from our gas fridge, but at least we might be free from the *whiiiine*, the interminable nocturnal complaint.

Richard stoked up the fire. It was wonderful to have such abundance, since gas was impossible to find. It meant that I could give the girls a bath, even wash their hair, with Richard supplying us with blackened saucepans of steaming river water. Then Richard grilled a chicken on the fire, and tucked potatoes and carrots into the embers. I watched him wrapped in his jacket taking in the view. This was what he loved to do more than anything, sitting in silence, just watching, but usually he was prevented by the mosquitoes. Tonight there was nothing but river and trees and the birds asleep inside them.

We dabbled our feet in the cold fresh water. It was nearly midnight, but the pale cloudy light had not changed.

I was woken by Richard clambering over the bed with a torch. He was squashing mosquitoes. Our fortifications had failed. The walls were flecked with blood – our own.

*

At the Sami parliament I found a young Sami called Oula working in one of a row of offices furnished with Ikea-ish desks. In another, a young woman translated Finnish textbooks into Sami. She said they were at the earliest stages of providing Sami children with an education they deserved, and that the major problem was still a lack of resources, both of books and teachers, although there was now a Sami teacher training college in Guovdageaidnu, in Norway.

Oula waved me grandly to a seat. He was pale and serious, almost colourless. He was a student off to study law at the University of Lapland in Rovaniemi, but filling in here for the summer as an administrator. Everything he said was carefully considered, his narrow features concentrating on getting it right. Disappointingly, he was not wearing one of the blue and red pointy hats, but was in jeans and trainers, determinedly Western. He was defensive, and I wondered if he too was still shaking off the primitive image of the Sami.

The parliament, he explained, was dedicated to furthering the interests of the Sami in Finland, and to participating in the Samiradii, the Nordic Sami Council. It had just been able to flex its new young muscles. The Finnish government had recently given an international mining company permission to begin extraction, but the Sami had not been consulted. The Sami parliament protested, and the Supreme Court withdrew the permission. In future, it would be more difficult to open mines in Samiland.

The point, Oula stressed, is that the Sami are the indigenous people here. It's even mentioned in the Finnish constitution. No one really knows where they came from, but they see themselves as indigenous, and that's what matters. According to the International Labour Organization convention no. 169, the term 'indigenous' means that the people in question has inhabited its domestic area since before the establishment of the present-day states which govern them, or before colonization from outside. This is crucial for the Sami sense of identity and in disputes over land rights.

'Do you seek a separate Sami state?'

'No. We are one people, despite living in different countries. We are like the Kurds spread across the Middle East, if more peaceful.

But there is no desire to set up an independent Sami state. We are also Finns, Swedes, Norwegians, and Russians.' However, he did acknowledge a growing sense of Sami cohesion, particularly now that internal frontiers within the EU were going. Even the Russian Sami have begun to forge cross-border links.

I asked him about his own family, but he resented my intrusion into his personal life. He appeared shocked by my directness and was happier with the abstract. His personality was dry, perfect for a lawyer, and his paleness gave him a bleached-out look. I found him hard to warm to. I did discover that his family were well-to-do reindeer herders, traditionally nomadic but since the 1950s settled in Enontekiö, to the west. With the arrival of snow scooters in the 1960s it became possible to live away from the reindeer and simply visit them each day. Nowadays, he said, people have four-wheel drives for reindeer herding, even helicopters, and planes for transporting the tents. What about your family, I persisted, do they use helicopters?

'Yes, they have done.'

'So why are you becoming a lawyer?' I asked. This was a difficult subject. The herd had been in his family for generations, and when his father retired there would be no one to look after it. In the past it would have been impossible for Oula to leave. He would have had to work the reindeer all his life and his children after him. But it was a hard life, and he had other interests.

'What will happen to the herd?'

'I don't know.' He shrugged and looked away. 'Maybe my father will sell it.'

Then Oula confessed something curious and sad about himself. This young Sami, of classic reindeer-breeding stock, living and working in the heart of Finnish Samiland, had been brought up speaking no Sami. He had taught himself Sami in adulthood, but at home he spoke Finnish. So his father may have regretted that his son would not inherit the herd, but it was largely his own fault. Oula was highly educated; maybe his father had never wanted him to tend deer anyway. Maybe he had wanted something he considered 'better' for his son.

Oula explained that when his father was a child, he had been punished at school for speaking Sami, and he was afraid that his son would suffer the same fate. Maybe that was why Oula was so reluctant to talk about himself; maybe he shared some of the furtive shame about Sami culture. I'd read stories going back to the eighteenth century of priests accusing Sami speakers of speaking 'the devil's language'. The parish priest of Kemi, Pastor H. Zimmerman, once overheard a man in Sompio speaking to his children in Sami. Zimmerman got angry, grabbed a stick, and threatened to strike the man if he used 'the devil's language'. The man grew afraid and flew around the room shouting, 'Good friends, come and hear, the pastor is preaching.'

But things are changing, Oula added. Young Sami now are proud to be Sami, and proud to speak the language.

'So you are optimistic about the future of the language?'

Well, not exactly. The problem is that there are so many Sami languages. In Anar alone there were three Sami languages existing side by side, each mutually incomprehensible. Oula spoke the most widespread North Sami, which is spoken in Norway, Sweden, and Finland by about 30,000 people; since 1978 it has even had a common Nordic spelling, which will help its survival. Anar and Skolt Sami, on the other hand, can boast very few speakers now, only 400 of Anar Sami, and 500 of Skolt Sami. Skolt is not helped by using a Cyrillic alphabet. Yet these seem positively flourishing compared with Ume Sami, which at the last count was spoken in Sweden by ten people, and Akkala Sami, which is spoken in Russia by eight. Only seven other people in the world can understand what they are saying. How lonely they must feel, condemned forever to be foreigners in their own land, and knowing that with their death will die a way of communicating, a repository of collective memory.

Oula and I had been talking for three and a half hours. We were both exhausted. Then I asked him his full name. He wrote down Oula Valkeapää.

'Valkeapää? But that's the name of someone I very much want to meet, the writer!'

'Yes, my uncle,' he replied. 'My father's brother.'

In *Greetings from Lappland* Nils-Aslak Valkeapää despairs of parents who have failed to teach their children Sami; I now realized that he was talking about his own brother.

'I'd love to meet him.'

'Mmm.' Oula permitted himself a thin smile. 'You could, but he lives in Norway. I don't know exactly where.'

I felt bitterly disappointed. For me, Nils-Aslak Valkeapää had assumed almost mythical status, the essence of Samiland, handsome, impassioned, vibrant, talented. I now felt as if we had come all this way especially to find him, only to have him snatched from us.

I found the Mob in uproar. While Xanthe was asleep and Richard hunting for parasol mushrooms, Tallulah had been playing in a sandpit. When she complained of being bothered by flies, Richard lifted her shirt to find she was belted with blood. She was completely traumatized by this sight and had to be calmed with sweets. Above our two ceiling vents mosquitoes bobbed in a suffocating cloud.

'It's appalling,' Richard announced. 'I can't stand these insects any more. Let's be like the reindeer. Let's go to the coast.'

Within two days we had reached Porsangen Fjord, where Norway breaks up into the Barents Sea. I kept being reminded of the Scottish Highlands, the same worn-down mountains, the saturated golden light and barren islands. Ochre-painted cabins clung to a shore flecked with buttercups. Huge nets hung out to dry. There was the occasional boat, the occasional jetty, but everything was dwarfed by the scale of the space and the mountains.

Then we came across the nomads. Nothing but a church of the Finnish Mission was marked on the map. We were crossing a bleak snow-patched plateau between Porsangen and Alta fjords when we began to see scattered wooden houses, some with turf roofs and *kota* alongside, the occasional one with a car parked outside or a caravan. Some were ramshackle cabins with dogs rummaging through rubbish. It resembled a gypsy camp I had once visited in Romania, where people had built themselves houses but still lived in tents outside them, as if uncertain whether to join the majority or cling to the old ways. The place seemed deserted.

One slope was patterned with the elaborate fences of a reindeer corral.

An old woman flagged us down. She was dressed in frilled and floral *geassegakti*, but with a cardy on top and instead of boots filled with beaten rush grass, she wore shiny après-ski boots. Her lips collapsed on toothless gums. She held a plastic bag and seemed to want to sell us something. It was a tiny purse made of white reindeer fur, decorated with red and orange wool. She had made it herself, she indicated. We didn't want it, we had no room for souvenirs, and we had few Norwegian kroner. But she was desperate, so we bought it.

A wisp of smoke leaked from a stovepipe sticking out of the roof of her tin hut.

Her bent-backed husband emerged from the hut. He wore a beautiful hat of red, white, and yellow bands of braid, and from the top flopped the fanciful blue four-cornered cap typical of the Guovdageaidnu district, some 200 kilometres south. It resembled the hats I'd seen at Father Christmas Village, but this one was hand-embroidered, perhaps by him. Like his wife, he had no teeth.

He wanted us to buy a pair of miniature reindeer skin shoes. By now we had no kroner left. He begged us to take them for 50 kroner, then 30, but we had nothing to give. He stood there for a long time after we left, with a bewildered expression, clutching his plastic bag.

It was late, the children needed tea and bed, we needed somewhere to stop. We spent the night nearby, tucked out of the wind in a roll of the fells. Yet that was an excuse: I had wanted to escape from the old couple. I was overwhelmed by a sense of loss – actual and impending – that was too painful to witness. Gone was the reindeer *pulkka*, gone the hay-filled boots. As a Sami writer explained to us later, that couple was in culture shock; they had gone from nomadism to barcodes in less than twenty years.

I was ashamed and confused. I saw myself through their eyes, as the inadvertent symbol of all that had destroyed their way of life. I could see it in the way they looked at us, despairing, bemused.

I was also shaken by the sight of such destitution here in Norway, one of the wealthiest countries in the world. Why were they still travelling from base to base, struggling to survive off so little?

But perhaps I shouldn't have pitied them: perhaps they wanted to keep on the move. Perhaps they didn't mind camping in their squalid hut, begging from passers-by. Perhaps it was even something in their blood, an instinct developed over the millennia that they had been following their herds. I read a poem by the Norwegian Carl Schøyen, and I thought of that old couple.

My sleep I must sleep where the herds run in our own valley,
Only there where I know the language of the living
Can I understand the words of the dead.
I cannot rest amongst these settled peoples.
John, you must come quickly,
I heard the dogs all howling –
I know my time will soon be up.

Those people did not live here all year round. In spring they had left their winter quarters in Guovdageaidnu to follow the deer nearly 200 kilometres to this, their summer quarters. In that sense, the lives of these nomads had not changed. They were still adjusted to the Arctic climate and to the feeding, mating, and migratory rhythm of the reindeer. The animals do not need to be driven; in fact it is all the herders can do to keep up when in spring the does at the head of the herd take off along the old routes. No one knows exactly why the reindeer migrate: possibly hormone secretions, possibly the urge to seek out familiar mating and calving grounds, possibly the need for fresh moist lichen and grass, possibly the urge to escape mosquitoes. Generation after generation, the same routes have been followed, crossing the same mountain passes, the same valleys, the same rivers and lakes, up to this same seeping marshy fell, Aisaroaivi.

Come autumn, as the trees are turning, the herd will assemble on their own along the great fences, and then the sorting takes place in the corral before each herd heads south again, back over those same mountain passes, those same valleys, those same rivers and lakes, to the winter pasture, home in Guovdageaidnu.

Although the nomads appeared to roam freely across the fells and forests, in fact their winter and summer territories – and the routes between – have always been firmly demarcated. This is their *siida*. The concept of land ownership was always alien to the Sami; instead they relied on a complex system of rights. A *siida* would include not only grazing rights, but also fishing rights on sections of river, and hunting rights, all 'owned' by an extended family or families. There were no 'Private' signs or other barriers. Some *siidas* crossed others or overlapped. But everyone knew which was their *siida*. It was their homeland.

Their nomadic lifestyle prevented the Sami from forming any sort of government, even if they had wanted such a thing. Their loyalties were not to any Greater Samiland, but to their *siida*. Tragically, it was the lack of formal ownership or organization that made land appropriation by outsiders so easy.

The nomads would soon be rounding up the herds for calf-marking. Oula had said that his father was doing it now, before the calf left its mother and joined the rest of the herd, ownership unknown.

Tallulah stuck pictures from a Sami magazine over the walls of her top bunk. When she went to bed she wanted to hear how a child like her would have travelled across Samiland on a *pulkka*, dressed in furs, Xanthe trussed up beside her in a wooden *komsa*. Their cheeks and noses would be smeared with lanolin to prevent frostbite; if her nose turned white we would rub it with snow to revive the circulation. If there was a thaw, she would travel by night over the crusty *cuonu*. There would be no sounds in the Arctic nights but the tinkle of reindeer bells. The only lights would be the occasional distant oil lamp shining from a cabin window. By early morning we would reach the grazing grounds where we would rest, brew up coffee – there was always coffee – and she would get cosy round the campfire. A *kota* would be pitched, cooking utensils and food and clothes unpacked from the draught reindeer *pulkka*. Then when the icy night came, off we would set again, through the forests, over the fells, across frozen lakes. It made her cry because she wanted to be Sami, but never could. She cried herself to sleep, snuggling on her reindeer skin, clutching her bone knife.

The next morning we returned to the timber church. By 'Finnish Mission' it meant not Finland, but Finnmark. It stood bleak and lonely in the moor, beside the rushing Repparfjordelva, propped up on bricks to keep it off the mire. A crow perched on the spire. We peered through locked windows at sparse rows of wooden pews and a kitchen with an oil lamp and a candlestick and some neatly washed up cups. One room was clearly a schoolroom. It had a puritan look. But in fact these churches are scenes of almost sexual abandon. The congregation wail and cry, speak in tongues, the atmosphere thick with emotion, charged with an almost shamanistic ecstasy.

There was no effective conversion from shamanistic/animistic beliefs until the eighteenth century, when the *noaidi* were banned, some executed, their painted drums burned. Linnaeus described the lengths to which missionaries went to seek and destroy the hidden drums.

Having procured information of any Laplander who kept such things concealed, he [the missionary] first requested to have them brought forth. This their owner refused. After having long entreaties, to no purpose, he laid hold of one of the Laplanders' arms, slipped up the sleeve of his jacket, and so contrived at length as to open a vein. The Laplander was near fainting, and, entreating him to spare his life, promised to bring the drum required; upon which the arm was bound up immediately. This plan has been frequently pursued with success.

The translator in the 1811 edition adds: 'A notable method of converting these poor people from pagan superstitions, and of exemplifying the mild and just spirit of the Christian religion!'

For all the success of the drum-destruction, it was a century after Linnaeus's visit before the Sami would be converted. But when that conversion came, it came with a storm. It began around the nineteenth-century pulpit of the part-Sami revivalist preacher Lars Levi Laestadius. Following a dramatic conversion of his own, he began preaching in the 1840s, advocating strict temperance, honesty, and peacefulness. His sermons were fired by a consuming fervour. In a movement that paralleled the Calvinist Methodist revival in

Wales, Laestadianism spread like fire throughout Scandinavia. Large farmhouses came into demand for meetings, and services were provided by itinerant preachers who, like my Welsh great-great-grandfather, covered huge distances by sleigh, horse, or boat.

Laestadianism is still a powerful force in Sami life. Nomadic Sami attend church when they can, about twice a year, at Lady Day and Easter, when they listen to sermons, have their children baptized, get confirmed, get married, get spiritually high. Laestadians have a sceptical view of modern culture, which may explain why Sami customs have survived as long as they have.

The sun came out and we left the plateau for the waterfalls and meadows and birch woods of the lower slopes. It was fresh and so beautiful. And there, trotting through the trees, came the herd itself, each gentle-eyed doe trailed by its calf, pausing to nibble a leaf here, a bud there, grunting and snuffling, one step ahead of the gadflies.

The lushness grew lusher as we descended to Alta. After weeks in the outback, it looked like a metropolis. In the supermarket a middle-aged woman in complete Sami *kofta*, her floral *geassegakti* with its frilled hem draped with a shawl, her grey hair tucked under a bonnet, waited at the checkout, basket on arm. No one stared, it was quite normal. We were in one of the most northerly towns in the world.

We were here to see Stone Age rock carvings made over a period of four thousand years, between 6200 and 2500 years ago. They are shallow incisions chiselled into several hundred slabs of granite, not in caves but outside, exposed to the elements. They depict bears, reindeer, elk, boats, stick-like men with priapic erections, lively men and women holding hands and dancing in a ring, and fishermen holding up their catches of dish-sized flatfish. These were halibuts, and the halibut is the only fish motif that recurs throughout the four thousand years of carving, suggesting that since cod was the main diet of these coastal peoples, the halibut had special ritual or religious significance.

The images disappeared beneath lichen and moss and were rediscovered by chance only in 1973. They have recently been coloured red, partly to make them more visible, but also because it is thought that this was how they might have looked, the same dried-blood red of the images painted on *noaidi* drums, made by chewing alder bark.

Much of the imagery is familiar from modern Sami life. There is even a reindeer corral identical to the one at Aisaroaivi, with its clearly marked fence – the oldest known picture of a reindeer fence. There are figures holding drums, and the ritual bear hunt that was until recently central to Sami culture. This adds fuel to the Norwegian/Sami 'indigenous' debate. Are these rock carvings Sami or Norwegian? No one knows, but a surprising number of people care. It matters to the Sami in the fight over land rights. So what if we're talking six thousand years ago?

The site overlooked the flat-topped fells that encircle the fjord, their golden flanks plunging to ice-blue water, all – even at the end of July – snow-capped. No one knows why the carvers chose this site, but it's possible that Stone Age man was simply moved by the drama of the landscape. Why not? Such sensibility brought the humanity of the rock carvers closer; I liked the idea that they had time left over from hunter-gathering, chipping tools out of quartzite, defending themselves from predators, and worshipping their unknown gods to sit back and admire the view.

In the museum shop we found tapes of music composed by Nils-Aslak Valkeapää. Not content with being merely a writer, photographer, and illustrator, he was also a singer and composer. He was celebrated for his *joiking*, the often wordless improvisational singing, but he had taken *joik* into new realms by adding not only the traditional *noaidi* drum, but also synthesizers, birdsong, splashing water, the sound of oars grinding on rowlocks. As we drove around Alta fjord, we listened to the music. At once it evoked the looming and splendid grandeur of the very mountains we were driving through, the loneliness, the rhythm of the reindeer moving over the fell, the mournful emptiness, the cry of a gull, the awareness of perpetual darkness even during the days of perpetual light. I had never before heard music that so perfectly expressed a place. *Joik* has never been about a person or place, it sang the place, almost like an incantation. Valkeapää's music was Samiland, Samiland was the music. I didn't want it to stop.

We reached the fjord edge: we could go no further. We were on a promontory of a glacial moraine that almost embraced this inlet and turned it into a lake. Above the opposite arm, a rubbly cliff tumbled to the water, with the odd birch and juniper clinging on; behind us, the land rose in a bank covered in harebells, white and pink clover, crowberries, bilberries, and sorrel, and bouncing with moths. Along the shore at Kafjord stood a simple Lutheran church, its wooden tower reflected in the sea – one of the very few churches in Finnmark to survive the Germans' scorched-earth retreat.

As the tide turned, water whooshed through the strait.

People stood on the beach fishing, and Richard joined them. As evening fell they left, and we had the entire world to ourselves. Richard kept on fishing. I looked through the window and saw him catch a small coalfish. I was rushing out to congratulate him, when he ran to the sea and hit something with a rock. By the time I had joined him, he was hauling a slippery flat fish – more than a metre long and still fighting – up on to the shingle. It had been swept by the tide into the weedy shallows and stranded there; Richard had heard it thudding its tail to flap itself back into the sea, and without thinking – instinct took over – he waded in. Like a Stone Age Sami hunter-gatherer he wrestled it to land. It was a magnificent halibut.

It weighed so much that Richard could barely lift it. Without wasting time, he gutted it. There were almost no innards, just a small pouch: the rest was firm white flesh nearly six inches deep. He cut it into steaks which we packed into our fridge and icebox. Some he cut into chunks which, after lighting a fire, he grilled on the beach. You couldn't get much fresher than that, he exulted. We lived on it for weeks. I picked sorrel and chives and bilberries from our wildflower bank, and over the next few days baked the fish with each of these: the sharp acidity of the sorrel was best. Two weeks later there was still enough fish to make a fish pie for seventeen.

Now there was no night. Richard would come in from fishing at around midnight, when the light was white. Blinds and blackout material kept the children asleep, but everyone else seemed energized by the endless days. At four o'clock in the morning we would hear fishermen climbing out of their cars to spend a couple of hours casting.

As they helped each other disentangle their lines from the seaweed, Richard chatted to his fellow fishermen. A rotund woman said she was Sami, although she did not speak the language. She knew someone we should meet called Odd-Mathis Haetta. I recognized the name – we had two books by him about the Sami. He was a flamboyant figure, fascinated by Sami traditions and beliefs. He had been head of Sami Radio during the battle over the Alta Dam in the early 1980s.

Now we found him teaching at the Institute of Adult Education in Alta. I liked his face. It was impish – pointed, with slanting eyes, and thick black eyebrows like trains that shunted up and down independently. They gave him a cheeky, humorous look.

We left Xanthe asleep in the Mob, and Tallulah danced along, pausing to gaze at fish in a tank, then having to be dragged away as we crossed the stylish new building to his office. He pointed out remains of the old pre-war school building, and this prompted memories of the German retreat. He immediately lost his shyness as he recalled his mother telling him that they had been ordered by the Germans to leave their home and all possessions. He still remembered it vividly, he said. He was four and a half, a little older than Tallulah.

He was born in Guovdageaidnu, which the Nazis had selected as a military base. During the retreat of 1944, almost every house, barn, byre, church, school, and shed was torched. Special commando troops were brought in to do it; the buildings that survived did so because they housed German troops.

'Is there still much bitterness about what happened? Even amongst our generation?'

'Oh yes, I should say so.'

They were given two weeks' notice, but were forbidden to take anything but a few clothes. Everything else was to be left in the house, and was burned with it. Reindeer herders were forced to take their deer to the slaughterhouse; cows and horses too, with some horses requisitioned as pack animals. Some people hid their animals in remote places unknown to the Germans, others did the same with treasured possessions – photo albums, family mementoes, fishing tackle, and, rather than be evacuated to a strange land, thousands of people – old, young, newborn – spent the gruelling winter of 1944–5 hidden in caves. Many died; others were caught and shot, some forcibly evacuated.

The town of Alta suffered even worse. By the time the Germans left, not one single dwelling in Alta was left standing.

Mr Haetta's family had Sami relatives in Finland, so they fled there; they felt more at home with the Finns than with their fellow countrymen, whose language was completely alien. They returned after the war, and Finnish labourers helped to rebuild Guovdageaidnu. So although he was Norwegian, Sami was his first language, Finnish his second. When he was twenty, he went to Tromsø in Norway to train as a teacher. Norwegian became his third language, English his fourth.

We sat in his office, Tallulah sprawled on the floor drawing on paper he provided. He had children too, he said, he knew how boring it was when grown-ups talked.

He was intrigued by shamanism. He had managed to get himself into a trance-like state. He had two ways. One was hyperventilation: even if you do it for only two minutes, he said, you begin to lose your balance. The other was drumming. This produced hallucinations and a shamanistic state. If you combine these, you can see strange things, he said, and you stop knowing if they're inside your head or out. Ritual helps too. *Noaidi* were rare today, but he knew one in Guovdageaidnu, and a group in Oslo.

'Do you use mushrooms?' Richard asked.

'I never have, but people do.'

They use the toxic scarlet and white fly agaric. I had read descriptions of *noaidi* in action and independent descriptions of the effects of eating fly agaric: they were identical. The *noaidi* dry the cap and swallow it without chewing, allowing symptoms to begin up to two hours later. Their muscles twitch convulsively and dizziness is followed by a death-like sleep, and in this state the *noaidi* experiences intense visions. On waking he is filled with elation and energy, bounding about. It is thought that Sami *noaidi* got the idea of eating fly agaric from the reindeer, which go wild – literally – for this mushroom.

Observers have described *noaidi* waking from the dead to leap about with extraordinary energy, as if wearing seven-league boots. Alexandra David-Neel described Tibetans leaping about in a similar state when she crossed the Chang Thang in Northern Tibet in the 1920s. But those Tibetan *lung-gom-pa*, although in a sort of trance, had achieved this state through meditation and gymnastics not hallucinogenic mushrooms, and rather than shamanism had a personal spiritual and physical aim.

'If I was a *noaidi*,' Mr Haetta observed wistfully, 'I could predict what was going to happen to us. Whether any Sami are going to be around in a hundred years' time. But I'm not. All I can do is study our past. I like to use the image of rowing: it's best for the Sami if we look backwards, and understand who we were, where we're coming from, whilst moving forwards.'

This had created in him passion for genealogy. This was typically Sami. Where so many Sami had been assimilated into the majority culture, their language lost, to be Sami it was vital to know who you were. He was the seventh-generation Mathis in his family – he produced a sheaf of documents listing every family member. This genealogical obsession stemmed from the days before the Scandinavian missionaries introduced surnames. Where there were so many Mikkels and Mathises, you had to be able to establish which Mikkel – son of Mikkel, or son of Mathis? Maybe it also helped to situate yourself in a land of such emptiness. Perhaps it was reassuring when you were alone on the fell to know that somewhere out there you had a tight web of relatives to hold you in place.

There was an equally precise vocabulary for different family members, as if it were necessary to situate yourself and your relatives exactly in society, and therefore in the world. Mr Haetta had made a list of them. His mother's elder sisters were his *goaski*, their husbands his *máhka*, but his own older sister's husband was his *sivjjot*. His mother's younger sisters were his *muotta*, while his father's younger sisters were his *siessa*. His mother's brothers were his *eanu*, her brothers' wives *ipmi*, but his own brother's wife was his *mangi*. With just one word, he knew who was who.

I asked him to write down these words, and he took my notebook. I cringed. Now he would see that I had been taking notes around the edges of Tallulah's mad drawings. Every page was colonized by dancing women and hairy monsters. There was a sad boy picking wild strawberries (sad because he couldn't find any), a boy who got frightened because he went too close to a yak; and – my favourite – a boy in a pram whose mummy stopped to take a photograph while he was blown away by a tornado. Some days the drawings poured forth in an unstoppable stream, especially when she was sitting on my lap as we drove along. She drew freely, without inhibition, her imagination tuned to perfection. Mr Haetta returned my notebook without remark, but now I had blown any professional credibility I might have had.

Then suddenly his own credibility was thrown into doubt. For all his passion for his tribe, in a sense he had betrayed it. His wife was Norwegian (she played trombone in the Nordic Women's Big Band) and they had not taught their children Sami. In theory they were therefore not Sami, since the only definition the Sami had agreed upon was knowledge of the language.

As we left, Mr Haetta advised us to visit Guovdageaidnu. That was the Sami stronghold. We should meet his cousin, Madam Bongo. Bongo, he added, was a common local name. Then there was Alf-Isak Keskitalo, a man passionate about Sami culture and politics. He was *the* expert not just on Sami language, but on linguistics per se.

The map marked a road that briefly hemmed the Alta river then diverted into the mountains. It dwindled to a dirt track. A sign announced that this was a winter path for snowmobiles until it rejoined the main road in twenty-seven kilometres. We debated turning back, then decided to risk going on, and rocked through forests of spruce and mountain birch, up and up until we emerged on to open fell. The track was lined with poles that would project above the snow to mark the route through what in winter would be a perpetual nightscape.

We climbed higher, clinging to our seats as we lurched over potholes. Our van was designed for gliding between campsites, not this. A cupboard swung open and books crashed to the floor. Xanthe cried out. I stumbled over the books to comfort her and to slam the cupboard shut before we all – including Richard, our intrepid driver – were maimed by Lewis Carroll and friends. Tallulah slept through this.

Out on to a pass. The world fell away. We tried to press on, so as to be in time for a meeting with Alf-Isak Keskitalo, but now the ruts were impassable. Richard reversed to a sheet of mossy granite. It was late afternoon. Clouds sagged, losing us in drizzle. It would take hours to struggle back down and then find somewhere to stay, so we decided to park up for the night.

Tallulah lay stretched along the bench seat, books strewn around her, still asleep. Xanthe stared out of the window, apparently stunned. We sat for a while, settling into the silence. Then over the crest of a hill came a herd of reindeer, their white tails stuck up like the white marker poles. They were looking for lichen.

Jeagil is crucial to the Sami way of life. Lichen is very slow growing, partly because the growing season here is so fleeting – just a few summer months. This means that if lichen is trampled by feet or tyres, or is grazed, it can take up to thirty-eight years to recover. Thirty-eight years was longer than I had been alive. It also means that reindeer need vast areas for grazing, which is the main reason why the Sami are nomadic. This was what the Norwegian government, when they proposed to dam the Alta, failed to understand.

Until recently the Sami were basically self-sufficient. The herds formed the basis of their entire existence. The deer provided almost every article of clothing and almost every morsel of food. The reindeer supplied skins for boots and belts and tents; their bones were beautifully carved into knives; and then there was the meat. Sinews were sold to itinerant merchants for thread in surgery, while reindeer hair was used for stuffing lifebelts. Even skulls were used as shoes on cold winter days. These were traded with non-nomadic Sami for wool, milk, vegetables, and fish. But now the market economy has taken over. Cash is needed. So the small family-sized subsistence herds have grown into vast super-herds (subsidized by the EU) leading to overgrazing, erosion, then desertification.

Lichen is also vulnerable because it takes its nourishment directly from the air, so if the air is polluted – as it is by factories in central and eastern Europe – then the lichen and therefore the reindeer are polluted. Even now, reindeer herders feel the effects of Chernobyl.

There is another interesting fact about lichen. The unique nature of this plant was discovered only after the invention of the microscope. Unique because although it looks like a single plant, it is in fact two in one: an alga and a fungus. The alga host, the green part, creates food through photosynthesis, while the fungus parasite, which often grows as a sheath around the algal cells, absorbs water from the atmosphere; the complex organic compounds are then exchanged. This helps it to survive the savage Arctic climate.

Just how fundamental lichen is to Sami life is indicated by the language. Odd-Mathis Haetta had compiled a list of Sami words in everyday use precisely describing the different growths – hairy or bearded, curling or dangling. *Beassejeagil, bohccejeagil, fiskesjeagil, láigejeagil, nállojeagil, oaivejeagil, ránesjeagil, roncejeagil, smar-vejeagil.*

If the Sami words sound good, the biological words sound even better. The different types of growth habit of the lichen? Crustose, squamulose, foliose, and fruticose.

The Sautso Canyon, northern Europe's deepest fissure, split the earth somewhere over the mist-swathed fells. I wanted to find it. I had an overwhelming urge to be out there on my own, with the elements. Richard generously offered to stay behind with the girls. They clung to me as hard as they could: Xanthe insisted on a feed, and Tallulah *needed* me to read the whole of *The Tale of Johnny Townmouse*. It was almost as if they sensed that something terrible was going to happen if I left. But I tore myself away.

At the garage outside Guovdageaidnu a woman ate cake beside the magazine stand in full Sami regalia. A red braided belt buttressed her capacious bosom. Then the little town itself unfolded under multicoloured Sami flags. The main shop stocked rolls of blue cloth and red braid for edging. Most of the women were wearing *kofta*, but no men.

Madam Bongo lived outside town beside a lake. Threatening clouds swung low over the vastness, the rain hanging on the horizon, Tallulah said, like hair. It drew apart from time to time to provide a tantalizing glimmer of a lit-up world beyond.

We found Madam Bongo going into her *kota*. She was dressed in full midnight-blue *kofta*, with its braided red and white swirly hem, and her chest was draped in the fringes of her shawl and an elaborate silver necklace. Her colours shone against the monochrome grey-green tundra. A leather handbag hung regally from one wrist.

Tallulah followed her in; Richard found them sitting together beside the fire, chatting. I put Xanthe to bed then tiptoed in under a flap of canvas. Inside, the *kota* seemed huge, the staves soaring to a hole in the centre; it was, Madam Bongo said, large enough to sleep twenty. Birch twigs had been laid as a ground sheet, with reindeer skins on top. We sprawled on them, around Madam Bongo who sat at the circular stone-edged hearth in the middle of the *kota* and tended her fire. Smoke gathered at the roof hole, turning blue before it was sucked into the night.

It was a scene we could have witnessed over thousands of years. The Alta stone carvers lived in tents like this.

She stirred a cauldron of reindeer stew that hung from a chain off a cross-pole. She had puffy red-rimmed eyes and swollen wrists, and seemed tired, but when she smiled her smile worked its way into every crinkle of her expressive old face, and her narrow eyes disappeared. She found it hard to move about, so kept her utensils within reach. She ladled the stew into enamel bowls. It was delicious, not chewy.

'I cook it twice.'

She'd been born in a tent and grew up in it, with seven siblings. Her father was a reindeer herder. In winter they would line the *kota* with wool, and they could close the top when it snowed or rained.

They slept on skins and under skins and woollen blankets, and kept very warm, she said.

'What did you eat?'

'Reindeer.'

'What else?'

'Reindeer.'

'No vegetables?'

'No vegetables, not even potatoes. Sometimes salt fish,' she conceded, 'but mostly reindeer, hung up in strips outside to dry. We had salt, tea, and coffee, but no milk.'

'No reindeer milk?'

'No, too much work.'

'It was a hard life,' I observed.

'No,' she retorted. 'Not hard. A good life.'

Tallulah was loving this. When she pulled a hair from her mouth Madam Bongo laughed. 'I too have eaten much reindeer hair!' Tallulah rolled about on the skins and kept us from feeling too sad.

After coffee and cake, we helped Madam Bongo to pile the skins in a heap on one side of the *kota*, and – for fear of rain – to cover them in plastic. The magic was over. We carried the pots and pans inside her wooden house. It was built after the war, she said, after the Germans burnt the old one. They'd always had a house for winter. It was full of engine parts and stank of cats. She seemed tired, and keen for us to leave, but she didn't mind us spending the night outside.

At the Guovdageaidnu museum the young woman at reception was informing visitors that the collection's origins were the few houses and barns left standing in 1945. Everything else was burnt, she said in a singsong voice, by the Germans. How did you know they weren't Germans, I asked when they left. I could tell by their accent, she said. They were Dutch. And I always keep an eye on the number plates.

'What do you tell the Germans?'

'I say everything was "destroyed in the war". I only say more if they ask.'

'What's their reaction?'

'They mostly don't believe it.'

Alf-Isak Keskitalo was the curator. He resembled a troll, his face completely round and fringed by a red beard. When he smiled, his mouth split into a semicircle, like an Edam cheese. Xanthe was learning to crawl in a three-legged way across the museum floor, to the delight of Tallulah, who got down with her beside a stuffed reindeer and made a lot of excited noise. I left them to it, with Richard distractedly in charge, and went off to the back regions with Alf-Isak.

Three hours later I emerged exhilarated and exhausted, yet deeply sad. Our conversation had ranged around the circumpolar region, then on to Friesland, the Basque Country, the Ålands, Ulster, Greece, Wales, the Caucasus, the Romanies, the Kurds, the Sioux. Tucked away in his Arctic outpost, his mind ranged freely across the languages and cultures of the smaller peoples of the world.

He had found that culturally the Samis' closest relatives were not other inhabitants of the Arctic, but Native Americans. He had been astonished by the similarities of dress, the *kota*-like teepee, and above all the *joiking*. Later I would listen to a group of Navajo singing in London, and if I closed my eyes I could have been listening to grumbly Sami *joik*. This suggests that the first journeys to the Americas were made not from Asia across the Bering Strait into Alaska, but somehow across the Arctic, or by boat via Greenland.

Again and again we returned to the difficulties the Sami faced in keeping their language alive. Since the Alta Dam battle and the subsequent legislation in 1992 there was schooling in Sami in Guovdageaidnu from infancy right up to teacher training or journalism college. There was also a school of reindeer herding. In many ways things appeared to be improving. Sami speakers no longer felt stigmatized. But he feared that the survival of the language depended on the isolation created by nomadism; once people settled, watched TV, drove to the supermarket, they would quickly be assimilated. It was, he said, incredibly demanding to maintain a Sami career, learning in Sami and continuing to study on the outskirts of society. Not many people were prepared to pay that price. It was easier to join the herd. Guovdageaidnu was a Sami enclave, but these days it was too narrow for most people.

It was not just the isolation of nomadism, it was the language itself. So much of the everyday vocabulary concerned reindeer herding. There were over 160 words for snow, each one precisely describing conditions for sleigh driving or for deer to nuzzle through. There were numerous words precisely defining different ages of reindeer calf. Without nomadism, the language had little purpose beyond itself.

Alf-Isak estimated that 5000 people now spoke North Sami in a 'society context', when they went shopping or met friends in the street. Since 1992 administrative and legal documents could be in Sami. But he complained that the political will was not there to put legislation into practice. Even officials at the municipal office couldn't speak Sami, and they ought to be the role models. The mayor of Guovdageaidnu himself did not speak Sami.

'He must have a hole in the head!' Alf-Isak exclaimed.

The tragedy, he said, was that it didn't have to be like this. If there was the will to change, things would change. The trouble was that local politicians weren't angry enough. But if the language dies, they will be to blame for its murder.

'Will the language die?'

'Well, what do you think about a language spoken by 5000 people? Just how viable do you think it is?'

I shrugged, weighed down by the tragedy of witnessing a society in its death throes.

He foresaw a time when he, and the singsong girl at reception, would be the last remaining speakers of North Sami. Its existence was so precarious that he feared it would die in his own lifetime. Each week he wrote a column in the Sami press about some learned aspect of philosophy; when nobody wants or is able to read it, I will go, he said. I think he felt that Sami – at least North Sami – was his personal patient. He had shouldered responsibility for its survival. He was here because of the language; it was his raison d'être. If the language died, he would have no reason to stay.

'Where would you go?'

'New York. I am a member of the American Academy of Science. Or maybe Cambridge.'

'In the steps of Wittgenstein.' Throughout his life Wittgenstein was in thrall to the relationship between language and the world.

Alf-Isak's face split into his troll-like grin. 'Exactly.'

'What does it mean to be Sami? Who are you? Is there a Sami character?'

He said that there were two different Sami temperaments – the nomadic temperament and the settled temperament. Take Nils-Aslak Valkeapää, for example.

'Oh, Valkeapää! Yes! He has been on my mind all the time.'

Well, his art stemmed from a nomadic mentality. Alf-Isak Keski-talo didn't like it. It was not for him. He couldn't relate to it. His own family were sedentary Sami, and this gave him a very different outlook; he knew this well because he had been married to a reindeer nomad's daughter, and after fifteen years he couldn't take it any more. He couldn't stand her restlessness.

In general, he could say that the Sami temperament was unlike that of the Canadian Inuit, who was morose, but had an expression: 'Never in anger'. The Sami were more frivolous, angry, undisciplined, volatile, childish. They felt more like central Europeans, like Hungarians. They were intensely religious to the point of madness – teetotal, excessively moral, hysterical. They were not dangerous like the IRA, they were humorous. They were also prone to depression – he himself had been clinically depressed. Then he looked at me.

'But what we really like is fun. So much fun! Oh yes!' and he threw his head back and opened his great half-moon, and laughed.

Through directory enquiries I tracked down Nils-Aslak Valkeapää to Skibotn, on the Norway coast. We slowly made our way towards him. I was so looking forward to meeting him. But there was no answer. I phoned again and again. At last a frail voice answered. I explained that we had come all this way, how much I wanted to talk to him. He apologized. He had suffered a very bad car accident and only that morning returned from hospital. Maybe some other time.

FIVE

The First Word

When we were searching for the Sami parliament in Inari, Xanthe did something intriguing. While in her sling she made a clucking sound, as if smacking her lips. I looked at my watch. Yes, it was four hours since she'd been fed. She'd always been a punctual baby. By imitating the sound of suckling, she signalled that she was hungry, but without having to cry.

From then on she did this daily, every four hours, until she learnt to speak. Cluck, cluck, cluck.

Perhaps she found it more pleasurable to cluck than to cry. Perhaps it was also her first attempt at language. Wittgenstein defined language as being a way of representing the world by *depicting* it; for him language was essentially pictorial. In his *Tractatus* he gives no examples of pictorial propositions, but now Xanthe had provided one. She had an image in her ten-month mind of herself suckling, and the sound of suckling stemmed from that image of the fulfilment of her needs. It was what linguists call an 'iconic sign'.

As a newborn baby she cried without awareness that crying had meaning. She had no idea that she was communicating. She cried because she was hungry or tired or in pain, and I just happened to be on hand to meet her needs. Gradually she learnt to cry and communicate at the same time. She would hurt herself and cry with her arms out, waiting to be picked up – waiting for a response. She began to communicate joy and amusement. But by Inari she needed to be more specific. She was learning to articulate her needs with more precision.

I interpreted this (erroneously, of course) as an example of her thoughtfulness. As if she knew that I disliked the sound of her wails. This was absurd as babies have no thought for anyone but themselves. Even Wittgenstein himself, when he wrote the *Tractatus*, was living an exceptionally isolated life, talking to no one except his teacher, Bertrand Russell, and partly because of this he looked at language not as a communicative instrument but as an instrument for reporting to oneself, for describing.

Xanthe was surrounded by a babble of sounds. She had begun to babble herself, imitating our conversation. Now, at the age of ten months, she had understood that she could make sounds with meaning. It is assumed that a child learns by imitating its mother, but I had never clucked myself. I had never taught her to cluck. This was something Xanthe had invented for herself. I had an idea that Xanthe, by beginning to use the fundamentals of language, in some way mirrored the process of language development itself, all those millennia ago. Xanthe's clucking suggested that language evolved when some proto-human learned to express the image of his needs being fulfilled, then developed further when other people understood what he meant and responded.

According to Wittgenstein, it is the use of language that distinguishes us as human beings. Later, when he became more extrovert himself, Wittgenstein viewed language less as a descriptive process for interpreting the world to oneself than as a social tool. Language, he said, was a social phenomenon, governed by rules that are only to be found within a social group. This was confusing: the opposite of what he said before. Before, he implied that Xanthe would have clucked whether I was there or not. Now he seemed to be saying that without us, her social group, she would never have clucked.

Wittgenstein was absolutely opposed to the anthropological outlook of the Enlightenment, which judged peoples of utterly different circumstances in the light of its own principles. He proposed instead a sort of cultural relativism. For Wittgenstein, all forms of life were equal, and just as language could not be judged from afar but had to be examined and understood from the inside, so with society. Thus Sami society – permeated as it is by its language – is as 'valid' as any other.

A few weeks later, in Denmark, Xanthe's hitherto impressive vocabulary of 'Dadada', expanded to include 'bllll', with her tongue wobbling about between her lips. Then one miraculous day it was 'banana'. Not a special word, and the event was banal enough, but to us it was thrilling, like opening a window on to Xanthe's personality. Suddenly she was human, not a pet. Tallulah was touchingly excited. And of course it was thrilling in its very banality. Noam Chomsky, the American philosopher-linguist-biologist, puts forward an explanation for this miracle. He argues that every baby's ability to make sense after only a few months of the wall of sounds surrounding it is so extraordinary that there must be some innate and distinctively human predisposition towards language. It cannot only be a social or behavioural phenomenon, or the mysterious essence of the uniqueness of humanity. Chomsky believes that human beings have a natural propensity towards language, even that Xanthe could not resist the urge to make intelligible sounds. Chomsky talks about language in an infant's mind 'growing' rather than being learned, as if it were almost a physical thing, like her teeth emerging, its pattern of growth not created but *shaped* by its environment.

Chomsky argues that babies must be genetically programmed to perform this super-difficult feat, and that therefore all languages must share some basic structure that corresponds to this programming. Every baby can do it, whether it is born to parents who speak English, Provençal, Sami, or Pidgin. Therefore there must be universal properties to language: they must share fundamental structural similarities. Although Chomsky has never claimed to know all the world's languages, he argues that they are all subject to the same constraints, structured by the same (deep) principles, using grammar to create sentences made up of a finite vocabulary. Their differences, he argues, are superficial.

Chomsky's ideas about the universality of language came to be linked with politics. In leading the American resistance to the Vietnam war, and more recently voicing criticisms of the war in Kosovo, he has put into practice his belief in the fundamental superficiality of our differences, the fundamental sameness of humankind. It is a sort of holistic approach to languages that makes their squabbles seem trivial. If all our differences are superficial, he seems to say, let's abandon those superficialities, and reduce ourselves to a linguistic common denominator, whatever that might be. Should the administrative documents of the Guovdageaidnu municipal government be published in Norwegian, Sami, or both? If they are basically the same, what does it matter?

The problem is that Chomsky and other twentieth-century linguists have concentrated not on the multitude and variety of languages, but on the universal set of principles and constraints that make up their grammar. Chomsky is interested in the light shed on the workings of our minds by the child – Xanthe – who (he argues) uses those universal constraints to identify and use the grammar of her mother tongue. Chomsky views different languages as a sort of social epiphenomenon; he is not interested in the culture that may go with the grammar. Therefore the endangerment of individual languages is also not of interest.

Anyone can learn a language; but the tragedy is that none of us will ever live long enough to learn them all. Languages can therefore never be tools of communication per se, but tools of communication within certain groups. The language helps to define the group, to give it its identity. If by speaking a language we intended to communicate with the largest number of people, Church Latin would have survived as the European lingua franca and spread throughout the world. But it did not. Particular vernaculars took over. If we wanted to communicate with the world, Volapük, Esperanto, Ido, Interlingua, or any other universal language would have succeeded, but they did not. People felt no connection with these artificial hybrids; they meant nothing to their community, to their immediate relationships.

The creators of Esperanto and the rest understood the huge potential in a universal language, and perhaps with the Internet English will become that universal language. God understood that linguistic homogeneity led directly to heaven. He knew that with only one language mankind was invincible. Feeling threatened, he was forced to divide and rule. And down on the ground, scattered abroad upon the face of all the earth, those divisions are clung to, passionately. Whether or not the Guovdageaidnu documents are published in Sami matters to those whose language is under threat, and with it their own historical and cultural sense of themselves as a people.

SIX

Friesland

By the end of August we were on Rømø, an island rising – just – out of the windswept dunes and mudflats of the North Sea. We had meandered south through Sweden and Denmark. Now Ulla and Eigil Hoydal, friends of friends, had lent us their weekend house in which to celebrate the great event, Tallulah's fourth birthday. We had met them to talk about Friesland, but gone away with their keys.

You won't find any hills, Ulla warned, but we get a lot of sky. She had decorated the long thatched brick house with prints of Nolde's sea and sky scapes, all luminous, brooding intensity.

Today's build-up was huge. For over a month we had been crossing dates off a chart, and I had sung 'Happy Birthday' every night for seventy-two nights. Tallulah had announced that the only thing she desired (thank you, Roald Dahl) was chocolate bars. Anxious to compensate for her being stuck in a van in the wind off Jutland, we obliged with a lunch box of Mars Bars accompanied (boringly, she thought) by a toothbrush. Tallulah cried when the unwrapping was over.

Party preparations occupied most of the day. Expectations were not high, they were stratospheric: last year she'd had thirty friends, a bouncy castle, and a magnificent home-made cake in the shape of an angelfish. So we hung streamers, inflated balloons, decorated the cake, dug paper plates and party hats out of the top box, cut up sandwiches, stuck grapes and cubes of cheese on to cocktail sticks, grilled sausages, and poured Ribena.

'Tallulah! You can come in now!'

Her eyes were wide with excitement. We sat round the Hoydals' table, candles glimmering, and crunched Hula-Hoops. We partied as hard as we could. But after blowing out her candles Tallulah sighed wistfully, 'I wanted a noisy party.' Richard and I looked at each other. Then we did our best to make noise. We shouted and sang, we played Hunt the Thimble. But the cracker of false jollity had been pulled, and inside it was empty. There we were in a stranger's house, hundreds of miles from family and friends, just the four of us.

The Frisian islands fall like droplets off the coasts of Denmark, Germany, and the Netherlands. They act as breakwaters for the mainland, bearing the brunt of North Sea storms, lying in a fugitive domain of shifting sandbanks intersected by winding channels and the cavities of vast estuaries.

'They look rather desolate,' observes Carruthers in Erskine Childers' marvellous thriller *The Riddle of the Sands*. And his co-conspirator Davies replies: 'Desolate's no word for it; they're really only gigantic sandbanks themselves.' Norderoog, Wangerooge, Langeoog, Borkum, Rottum, Griend: even their names are outlandish.

Rømø was almost the most northerly. We were looking for vestiges of Frisian culture, mainly in the form of the Frisian language, but there were none. There were dunes studded with clumps of marram grass, woods of shrivelled pines, German and Danish cars whizzing along the central road, and there were vast white churches gleaming against darkening skies and flecked below by the white headstones of allied graves. But there was no one speaking Frisian. The only reference to Friesland was a fishing boat tied up in the harbour named *Frisia*.

Ulla Hoydal, who was born in this part of North Slesvig, remembered encountering Frisian speakers years ago, and Eigil Hoydal had had the occasional Frisian speaker attend the village primary school of which he was headmaster, but basically it had died out.

Why?

There were other competing dialects like Sønderjydsk, Plat Deutsch, High Danish and High German; Frisian had been squeezed out. Danish itself felt squeezed, having lost Norway then Iceland, South Slesvig, the Faroes, and Greenland. Now it was threatened by

German and English. Danish was becoming defensively assertive in response, at the expense of Frisian.

For two centuries the death of North Frisian has been predicted. If we were to find anything still living, we would have to go south, to Germany. Not that the Germans are exactly renowned for tolerance of minorities.

We drove down a country lane and knew we'd crossed the border because of the remains of a wire fence and a peeling wooden sign saying 'Achtung!' The goose-stepping Nazis were still there in that alarming exclamation mark, a piece of punctuation that makes you jump to click your heels and obey.

But there was no one to obey. A wooden hut stood empty. I felt a twinge of nostalgia for the frisson of old border crossings. This was the modern EU, with signatories of the Schengen Agreement losing border controls. Yet this border had been battled over by Danes and Germans so many times: 1864, 1866, 1920, 1940. Lord Palmerston remarked in 1864, 'Schleswig-Holstein's history is so complicated that only three people have ever understood it. One, Prince Albert, is already dead. Another is myself, but I have already forgotten it all again. And the third is a Danish statesman, and it drove him mad.'

Briefly, all of what the Danes call North and South Slesvig was for centuries under Danish sovereignty. Then in 1866 it was conquered by the Prussians and became part of the German Empire after its foundation in 1871. The region south of the Ribe became German. This lasted fifty years until, after the First World War, a referendum decided that the northern half be returned to Denmark, while the southern half remained German. A small German minority remains in the north, and a large Danish minority remains in the south. North Frisia is now a district in the predominantly Danish area of German Schleswig-Holstein.

Today, the line on the map dividing Germany from Denmark looks arbitrary. Physically, both sides are the same; the same massive dykes fortifying land against sea, the same expanse of marsh and mud teeming with birds, the same sands and streams, the same piebald cows, the same avenues of white wind turbines turning and turning – the only verticals in this horizontal world.

Then there are the same great Nolde skies.

We picked our barefoot way across tidal flats. Weed had dried to crusty plates, and we stepped gingerly from plate to plate, trying to stay clear of the slime. The undersides of these plates were still moist, and where their surfaces were not crusty enough, the mud oozed between our toes. Rivulets ran past, but I wasn't sure if they were running out to sea or were tidal driblets running in. There was no clear-cut coast; sea and land melded, each trespassing on the other. That evening the sea was nowhere to be seen, but surreptitiously the tide came in, sending whorls of milk chocolate with a scummy froth eddying round our feet.

In fissures samphire sprouted, and we gathered enough for supper. We ate it like asparagus, dripping with butter, and it tasted of a vegetable sea. We followed it with field mushrooms and russola that Richard had found that morning on Rømø. He was nervous about the russola, not certain he had identified them correctly as the edible paludosa, but we took a chance, and they were nutty and delicious.

We slept twenty yards south of the border, sheltered beneath a dyke. On the marshes birds moved in sudden inexplicable unity from patch to patch.

A man in khaki climbed out of a Land-Rover. You can't camp here, he said. The whole area is a bird sanctuary, all 285,000 hectares. But Richard explained about the children, how small they were and already tucked up. The man nodded curtly, then relented and drove away.

The cold was sharp when the sun went. We sat beneath the Milky Way listening to the wind whistling in our beer bottles and watching a tangerine segment of moon rising. From time to time it was obliterated by dense flocks of birds, off on some unknown night-time mission.

A hare hopped by, grazing in the dark, unaware of us.

We were at the end of the earth, elemental and lovely. But we knew come winter, when sea and land battled for supremacy, how bleak it could be. Within the beauty lay its opposite, which made the beauty greater, more tragic and more fragile.

Nolde surrendered himself to this landscape. 'I did not paint what I wanted to paint, but what I had to,' he wrote. 'Everything ancient and timeless fascinated me. The great swelling sea is still in its original state, the wind, the sun, the starry sky are still the same as they were fifty thousand years ago.'

This is the most sparsely populated corner of Germany. There are nearly twice as many cows as people.

In the eighth century the first wave of Frisians came from their original settlements between the Weser and what is now the west coast of the Netherlands to this, the most remote coastland of the North Sea. At the turn of the millennium a second wave arrived. No one knows why. Possibly escaping the Vikings' threat, possibly pushed out by the belligerent Franks and their expanding empire. What is certain is that they already knew the region well; they had been trading here for so long and so effectively that in those days the North Sea was known as the Mare Frisicum. They reached the Faroes, Shetland, and the Orkneys. Amsterdam was a Frisian town. They even reached the Baltic.

They occupied coastal parts of what were to become Denmark, Germany, the Netherlands, and Belgium. Today there are some 411,000 Frisian speakers – 400,000 speakers of West Frisian in the province of Friesland in the Netherlands, 9000 speakers of North Frisian in Schleswig-Holstein, and a mere 2000 speakers (at most) of East Frisian in an obscure part of north Germany called the Saterland.

The Frisians settled into their watery abode, on storm-swept islands and a mainland that was barely land at all but an amphibious country. They made the monumental effort to build dykes, and having protected and drained the fertile marshland behind the dykes they proceeded to farm it. Agriculture flourished. Some dykes are over a thousand years old. The dyke beside us towered nearly eight metres high and stretched 132 kilometres; beyond it waves broke; behind it, we were safe. Behind us rolled waves of older dykes, 'sleeping dykes' that had now retreated into the second, third, or fourth row as more and more land was reclaimed.

Night after night we sheltered in the lee of these dykes, marvelling at the number of them, and the phenomenal effort behind them.

Dyke builders had sometimes been summoned from the Netherlands, but mostly it was local farmers who shouldered the responsibility for protecting – and extending – the land. They paid for the dykes, built them, and maintained them. They struggled out here in storms and fought to plug the breaches. There were famous tempests in the Middle Ages when entire islands disappeared for ever and whole towns were obliterated. One seventeenth-century storm killed 8000 people in North Frisia and washed away 50,000 farm animals. In 1976 there was a terrible – fatal – storm, so terrible that these days land reclamation has become less of a priority than protecting what already exists.

When not battling against the sea, the Frisians braved it. They launched into the breakers to fish, and joined the crews of German, Danish, and Dutch ships that ventured as far as Greenland in search of whale and seal, declaring '*Rüm hart, klaar kiming!*', 'Wide heart, clear horizon!' The eighteenth century was their heyday, the height of Frisian expansion and wealth. Sailors returned with Dutch blue-and-white tiles for their houses, and when they retired they sat in rocking chairs sucking carved meerschaums, looking out over the polders. They kept their beds in cupboards, cosy behind doors.

There was never a Frisian state, nor any concerted attempt to create one. There was not even a great city, which might have acted as a focus for unity. Loyalty was to one's own *harde* – court or administrative district – or to one's own island, but never even to North Frisia, let alone to the rest of Friesland. There was not even a common language. To complicate matters, each Frisian language subdivides into numerous dialects, most of which have evolved in such isolation as to be mutually unintelligible, even from one adjacent island to the next, or village to village. North Frisians who need to communicate across dialects have always done so in High or Low German or Danish.

There were no Frisian political movements, no battles for independence. The North Frisians find it hard enough to agree amongst themselves, let alone with East or West Frisians. Besides, independence wasn't needed; isolation on the periphery of Europe already allowed each of the Frieslands enough self-government. They had long had their own Frisian law, the *Lex Frisionum*, which was orally handed down through the centuries and eventually written down in 1426. Fundamentally this concerned relief from paying taxes to the sovereign – this was the essence of Frisian freedom. There was also the freedom from military service, which was granted in exchange for manning the barricades in the front line against the sea.

The Frisians looked after themselves. To them, winning or losing land was more important than winning or losing battles.

Nevertheless, there is a shared sense of identity, and that identity has been shaped by the sea, by their shared struggles to contain it. These experiences have taught the Frisians self-reliance, and paradoxically it is that very self-reliance that they share; independence is what binds them.

During the nineteenth century there was a tentative National Awakening in North Frisia, inspired by ideas of Romanticism, with works of North Frisian history being published for the first time, and North Frisian linguists suddenly excited about studying their own language. *Liiwer düüdj as slaaw*, 'better dead than a slave' – the battle cry of a fourteenth-century leader of the West Frisians – became the favourite slogan. But when Prussia annexed North Frisia in 1867 and attempted to Germanize the region, any nascent nationalism was quashed. Within two years Bismarck was able to report the satisfactory progress of Germanization, and North Frisian language classes were banned.

Political strife – and poverty – conspired to send thousands of North Frisians overseas, mainly to America, and the subsequent depopulation further dented Frisian life; their places were filled by Germans.

North Frisia recovered and during the 1920s and '30s reached a literary and political high. The literature was dominated by the idea of a homeland. At that time the Schleswig government appeared keen to assist the North Frisians, and agreed to introduce Frisian in schools, but in fact internal documents reveal the true long-term objective to have been an extension of Prussian *Eindeutschung* – a word which, in the light of what happened later in Poland and other Second World War conquests, has deeply sinister overtones.

Innocent of what was to come, 70 per cent of North Frisians eagerly voted the Nazis into power in 1933. Nolde himself was a member of the Nazi party. But within five years it had become illegal to speak in public of a Frisian minority. The North Frisian farmer–poet Jens E. Mungard, committed to the idea of a separate Frisian culture, died in a concentration camp at Sachsenhausen.

We ambled south, past a village called Nolde. Emil Hansen was born here and loved this backwater so much that not only did he build a house and garden nearby, he even took it for a name. Despite voyaging as far as the South Seas, it was to this simple rural world of space and seclusion that he always returned. We spent one morning in the boxy red-brick house he built on a mound in Seebüll in the 1920s. Here, after the Nazis branded his often savage Expressionism 'Degenerate', Nolde retreated to live out his wilderness years, secretly painting his 'unpainted paintings'. Now his widow ran it as a retreat for other artists. I had thought that the dissonant clash of colours in his flower paintings was the work of an ecstatic imagination, a sort of orgiastic expression of the dissonance of the age, but in his Seebüll garden he had brought those paintings to life. Yellow dahlias burned beside orange freesias and purple roses in a lurid floral conflagration. In the middle of them, unperturbed, sat a hare.

Richard wandered across the surrounding monochrome flatness and returned with a basket of wild plums and field mushrooms. It was early September, with mists and mellow fruitfulness on their way. We parked in a field and lunched on found food.

> *Frii es di Feskfang,*
> *Frii es di Jacht,*
> *Frii es di Ströngang,*
> *Frii es di Nacht,*

Frii es di See,
Di wilji See,
En di Hörnemer Ree.

Free is the fishing,
Free is the fight,
Free is the beachcoming,
Free is the night,
Free is the sea,
The wild sea,
And the Hörnum harbour.

We could have added, 'Free are the fungus and the fruit.'

I wondered if not only the physical distance from Berlin drew Nolde back here, but also that sense of wild freedom. Despite a brief flirtation with *Die Brücke* in Dresden, he was always the lone wolf.

The Second World War brought an influx of refugees. In a Frisian museum of vernacular architecture we were shown round by a woman with broad hips and arthritic legs so wide apart you could have fitted a horse between them. She wore her iron-grey hair in earphones. She was, Tallulah pointed out, a cross old biddy – at least until it came to the tip. Her name was Frau Schuck. She turned out not to be Frisian at all; she was Prussian. She had been sent here after the war when her home became part of Poland. The Russians had chased her out in 1944. Her husband was killed, and she was resettled here in underpopulated North Frisia. She missed her own *heimat*.

But the greatest blow against North Frisian culture and language was struck by refugees of another sort – tourists. For some reason post-war Germans came in thousands, the rich transforming the shivering island of Sylt into an unlikely St Tropez of the north. I watched them on a stretch of seaside mud that masqueraded as a beach. Each goose-pimpled family had hired a sort of enclosed settle, like an open-fronted beach hut, and in this they huddled.

Today only one third of the inhabitants of North Frisia consider themselves Frisian, and only one fifth of those can speak the language.

It felt like a treasure hunt. A pamphlet we found at the Nolde museum had told us about the Frisian museum, and a note we found there alerted us to the North Frisian Institute at Bräist/Bredstedt. This institute described itself pompously as 'the central scientific institution for the preservation and promotion of and research into the Frisian language, culture, and history in North Frisia'. It was housed in a former school.

A librarian sat behind her desk facing the stacks – modern, grey, cool, calm. It wasn't often that English people and their children turned up in Bredstedt, but she seemed unsurprised and guided us to the relevant shelves.

'Of course you'd be interested in Frisian,' she said matter-of-factly. We looked at her expectantly.

'Because some of the dialects are so like English. They are closer to English than any other language in the world. Look at this.' She produced an English–Frisian dictionary. It listed English words beside a number of different Frisian dialects, and we noted the following:

English	Bökingharde (Mooring) Frisian
sheep	*skiep*
rain	*rein*
smoke	*smoke*
help	*helpe*
cork	*koarke*
open	*iepen*
afternoon	*middei*
nose	*noas*
name	*namme*
Wednesday	*Woansdei*
man	*man*
tooth	*tosk*

Bökingharde is increasingly becoming a standard. But it resembles English more closely than it does its immediate Frisian neighbours.

Given Frisian dominance of the North Sea, it is hardly surprising that there are some connections, but to be so very similar suggests that while the invaders of Britain may have come from Saxony, they were mainly Frisians. Later a Frisian professor of linguistics in the Netherlands would dismiss the connection with English as a kind of myth. Danish and Norman French, he pointed out, would have heavily influenced Old English, while Frisian was influenced by Dutch and German. Nevertheless, I found the similarities with Bökingharde Frisian astonishing. Perhaps Frisian was the 'missing link' between English and Germanic lexicons.

Xanthe crawled between the stacks. For weeks she had been doing this in churches – down aisles, round pulpits, up chancel steps, between pews. Tallulah found it deliciously funny and, bubbling with naughty giggles, would get down with her and crawl along too. Their hands and knees were filthy, but it gave Richard and me a few moments to ourselves. Today noise levels swelled and the librarian showed signs of restlessness, so we had to leave.

She gave us a phone number, and one call led to another, which eventually took us to the head teacher of the Danish-Frisian school in Risum, the stronghold of mainland North Frisia. He invited us to meet him that evening.

We drove through a dismal landscape of rain and farmhouses stranded in polders.

It was a primary school, one wall daubed in graffiti masquerading as a mural. The children had gone home; Jörgen Hahn stood alone at the entrance with his golden retriever. He was an unlikely head teacher, with a straggly blond ponytail. He was forty-four.

Xanthe needed a feed, so I stayed behind in the van. She seemed to go on interminably. Eventually she was satisfied, so I locked the van and carried her through deserted classrooms in search of the others. The walls were hung with childish paintings and laminated illustrations of farm animals with their names in Frisian. Since Tallulah was born I had visited a few London primary schools, and they always made me want to cry. The sense of effort and kindness was so overwhelming, the paintings so touching. This, in the wilds of North Friesland, was the same.

I found them in a small, comfortable staffroom (with a fish tank to amuse Tallulah). Hahn sprawled in an armchair, his huge retriever at his feet. He had a battered presence, handsome in a rangy, rugged, hook-nosed, leathery-skinned way. He looked like a teacher who wanted to get out on the pitch with the lads, and was adored by them.

'Look,' Richard suggested, 'why don't I get a couple of beers from the van?' I could see that he was fired up by his conversation with Hahn. Afterwards Richard would talk of meeting Hahn as a sort of turning point for him, the moment he understood what I had been on about – not folklore, not fancy dress, not petty nationalism, but ordinary people struggling to retrieve their pride in themselves in a homogenized Europe.

Hahn was passionate about Friesland. He had been born nearby and had grown up determined to work at a grass-roots level to keep North Frisian alive.

'This is the only North Frisian school in the world,' he boasted. It had been founded in the 1950s by a group of soldiers returning from prison on the Eastern Front. They had been recruited by the SS. Frisian males, tall, blond, and free, were considered the epitome of the Aryan race – the irony being that they were not German at all. They were to be the elite, and they signed up in droves. They returned in 1946 disgusted by war, and sickened by having been exploited by the Nazis. Together in prison, hundreds of miles from home, they had dreamed of their watery land. They would try to rescue what remained of their non-German world. This little school, set up under the auspices of the much more powerful and well-funded Danish minority, was the result.

I was moved by the image of battle-scarred, hardened SS officers, who had committed God knows what brutal and brutalizing crimes, returning here to retrieve some non-German innocence in this little place of childish paintings and struggles with sums.

Hahn was their heir. I wondered if he too was escaping from something. His face had a battle-scarred look.

Hahn had five teachers, who taught in Frisian, Danish, and German. Each child could choose their language of instruction, but leavers were expected to speak all three. All the teachers were multilingual enough to be able to understand each other. He said the success of the school was such that although most of the parents were at school during the 1950s and '60s, when Frisian was dismissed as a liability, a hindrance to progress, many had now chosen to send their children here. They even had a half-Lebanese, half-Austrian child who had chosen to be taught in Frisian.

Hahn himself taught in Frisian, but was fluent in four languages – Frisian, Low German, High German and Danish – and slipped easily between them in a way that, he said, might seem confusing to the monolingual observer. It was a common prejudice that the multilingual spoke many languages less well than a monolingual spoke one language. In Hahn's experience, his languages had broadened his horizons immeasurably.

'Wide heart, clear horizon!'

He smiled, a rough, broken-tooth smile. 'Precisely.'

'Is there racism against the Frisians?'

'No,' Hahn said, 'none these days. After all, we aren't recent immigrants. We've been here forever, or as good as. Before the Germans anyway.'

Moreover, the North Frisians had the protection of the wealthy and successful Danish minority, who in turn had the protection of the whole of Denmark. No, there was no racism. They all got along pretty well. If anything, the quarrels had always been between the different groups of North Frisians themselves.

The problem was that this little school – all fifty pupils – was unique. Most North Frisians are illiterate in *Friisk*. This hardly encourages copious North Frisian literature or other media. There are a couple of North Frisian publications, but most of the articles are in High German; each week North German Radio broadcasts a handsome two minutes in Frisian; as for television, there is none at all. Even now, North Frisian is in hiding. It has almost no public life. Although some of the gospels were translated in 1955, there is still no North Frisian Bible, so it is still not possible to get married, to declare your love and commitment to each other, in church in your own mother tongue. Some register offices have recently introduced North Frisian, and a few people – but a very few – are able to live in streets that have revived their original North Frisian names.

But under German Federal law it is still forbidden to announce the name of a North Frisian town in North Frisian.

Nevertheless, to his own and everybody else's surprise, the number of *Friisk* speakers was said to be growing. As chairman of the National Frisian Association, Hahn made annual EU-funded pilgrimages with groups of fellow North Frisians to other European minorities – they'd met the Welsh, Scots, and Irish – and wherever he went people complained of dwindling numbers, except here. He felt it was because fellow North Frisians were searching for their roots in a homogenous world.

I began to see Friesland, with its shifting coasts, its treacherous sands, its invasive estuaries, as a metaphor for the unsettling amorphousness of modern European culture.

Soon, he predicted, the Danish–German border would disappear, the nation state would shrivel and die, and then they would come into their own. In fact, he felt that the North Frisians' success was such that although they were one of the smallest minorities in Europe, the way they peacefully coexisted with the majority could be a model for the rest of Europe.

Tallulah had found a box of books to occupy her, but Xanthe was tired and needed to be held. She sat on my lap throughout this meeting, which didn't make for easy note-taking. Inexorably, it became obvious that she needed a nappy change. No one mentioned it, but before we were asphyxiated we drew the meeting to a close.

Richard photographed Jörgen up against the mural with his dog, in the last of the light. He looked rough and solitary. There'd been no mention of a family, of his own children.

We parked on a hummock beside the road, opposite a sleet-blown farmhouse. I rushed the children to bed. As Tallulah snuggled into her sleeping bag we tried to remember where we'd been that morning, but failed. I loved those full-up days, but sometimes they wore us out.

Richard and I sat at our window drinking beer, voices low, lights a warm glow. We looked over a sullen view of fences and ditches and cows munching and pissing in the mist.

Richard felt inspired by Hahn. He admired his vigour and

enthusiasm. He was of the same courageous stock as Tacitus's Malorix and Verritus, the Frisian commanders who astonished the people of Rome by sitting down uninvited in seats of honour beside the emperor Nero, believing themselves entitled to this as nobles of a renowned nation, brave and free. And then there was Gemme van Burmania, the Frisian who refused to kneel at the coronation of the Hapsburg Charles V, insisting that 'We Frisians only kneel before God'.

But I felt a seeping melancholy. Frisian pride and struggle seemed pitiful somehow, a huge expenditure of energy in an indifferent world. The insolence of Malorix and Verritus looked childish. Nero may have awarded them Roman citizenship for their bravado, but he still sent them packing from their squatted territory on the Rhine, back to Frisia.

I wondered if melancholy was a condition of the place, a characteristic induced by mudflats and mist. Of course it was! The Frisians had shaped this landscape, and in turn the landscape had shaped the character of the people. It was this melancholy that Theodore Storm evoked in his nineteenth-century *novellen,* most of which are set along this coast. Loneliness, longing, homesickness, the transitory nature of man before the infinite: they recur again and again in his work. They reflected the Frisian loneliness and struggle, and also our own. I felt a growing sense of exile, something constantly underlined by Tallulah's homesickness, and by the bleakness of the view.

A farmer emerged from his thatched farm to sort through piles of wood in the morning drizzle. He stood to watch us leave, hands on hips, scowling. Perhaps we were parked on his land; perhaps we should have asked his permission.

'Give him a wave,' I suggested, and Richard waved, and the farmer's face lit up and he waved and waved back. We drove past a grove of poplars, and when we looked back there he stood, a solitary speck against an emptiness of damp grey, still waving.

We swung round the North Sea, crossing the vast embanked Nord-Ostsee Canal, a motorway of water, the world's busiest canal. It was built just before Childers wrote *The Riddle of the Sands*, when it was still called the Kaiser Wilhelm Ship Canal. Carruthers and Davies are towed along it in their little yacht the Dulcibella, dwarfed by great locks and the soaring hulls of commercial barges. The Kaiser ordered it built to move ships from the Baltic to the North Sea without them having to round the northern tip of Danish Jutland, where they would be vulnerable to enemy guns. It is when the Kaiser himself makes an appearance on board the grim Grimm's tug that Carruthers, lurking unseen on deck, suddenly gets the point.

Yes, I understood at last. I was assisting at an experimental rehearsal of a great scene ... when multitudes of sea-going lighters, carrying full loads of soldiers, not half-loads of coal, should issue simultaneously, in seven ordered fleets, from seven shallow outlets, and, under escort of the Imperial Navy, traverse the North Sea and throw themselves bodily upon English shores.

After the First World War its name changed to the Kiel Canal; Kiel lies at its Baltic end, and was the setting for the sailors' mutiny in 1918, one of the first sparks of post-war rebellion which forced the Kaiser to abdicate and sent him packing to an obscure Dutch suburb.

We circled Hamburg, crossed the desolate Lüneburg Heath, lunched by the Weser, then rode north again, to East Friesland. All this was Childers' territory: the chocolate-watered estuaries of the Weser and Jade, then the obscure crescent of coastal towns fringing their marshy peninsular. Here Carruthers and Davies measured channel depths, tiptoed in fog over sandbanks, measured tides. Childers intended his book to alert the somnolent British public to the danger posed by Germany; it was published with great prescience in 1903, eleven years before the outbreak of war. But later he was accused of inflaming British hostility to Germany and actually helping to ignite the war.

I noticed that after almost annual reprintings until the war, *The Riddle of the Sands* did not reappear again until 1927. It transpired that after Childers was demobbed from the RAF in 1918, he promptly went to war against a different imperial power, fighting for home rule for Ireland. In 1922 he was caught in possession of revolver without licence, found guilty of treason by the Irish Free State, and executed.

I suppose his publishers had waited a decent interval before reprinting a novel by a condemned traitor. I found it unnerving to hold a book written by a hanged man. No mention of his untimely death is made in the preface of the 1931 edition, which was written by his son, who in a final twist became President of Ireland.

By evening we reached a patch of farmland beside a moor, somewhere west of Oldenburg. East Friesland had shrunk until it was a Frisian island in a German sea. We met a farmer on his tractor. Could we spend the night in his field? By all means! He manoeuvred the tractor into a vast silage field, as flat as a football pitch and ten times the size. He drove around it as though selecting a site, and we processed behind him. Park where you like, he said, waving his arm grandly.

East Frisians like him may have lost their language, but they retain a sense of being Frisian, of not being German. The Germans have them as the butt of their jokes. Frisians play little part in *The Riddle of the Sands*, except as 'stolid' onlookers, but I felt sure that as a member of the IRA Childers would have sympathized with any Frisian desires for home rule. However, there were none.

The farmer drove away, leaving us alone in an emptiness of green.

We played football. I had Xanthe as a third leg; I swung her feet towards the ball, and thus she kicked it. She got hiccups with laughter. From afar came the oom-pah-pah of a brass band. I envisaged jolly burghers in breeches quaffing beer and sausages. I longed to join them. But Xanthe's cot was already prepared, Tallulah's toys and books flung back in her toy box, her reindeer skin unrolled, her sleeping bag spread on top. It was time for stories, songs, and kisses. Then Richard and I sat outside, warding off a new, damper sort of cold with whisky and extra squares of chocolate from our secret stash. Richard swore by these morale-boosting palliatives.

The reclaimed land was so flat it looked concave, *below* sea level. It was a sea of its own, a green sea, with farms and villages stranded in it. The horizon was so wide it bent, as if following the curvature of the earth. The vast fields were divided not even by the verticals of hedges, but by ditches; the only verticals were church spires, rising like beacons. Then there was the odd windmill, one or two still working, with sacks of grain piled outside waiting to be milled, like in Tallulah's books of nursery rhymes. This was West Friesland. Almost without noticing, we had entered the Netherlands.

There was nowhere to park. Every green space was occupied either by an immaculate garden or by an intensely cultivated farm enclosed in ditches and wire. There were no woods to hide in. And as we kept being reminded by passers-by, free camping was illegal in the Netherlands, and subject to on-the-spot fines. Outside Leeuwarden (known in Frisian as Ljouwert) we reached such a state of desperation that we were forced to ask a farmer if we could stay in his yard. We spent the night beside a black hill of plastic and tyres holding down steaming silage.

Ljouwert, capital of West Friesland, was presided over by a Frisian cow, a bovine vision in bronze. It was modelled on a real cow, a pedigree from the Adema herd, bred in the famous stock farm of Knol Bros at Hartwerd. It had the ideal vital statistics. Its udders were veined and swollen, its gleaming flanks tactile, and it gazed over the city, proud and comforting. It was known as *Us Mem*, 'Our Mother'.

There is something almost religious about the place of the cow in the Frisian psyche. The great lactater, the great breeder, the great fount of Frisian wealth, she is far more convincing a mother figure than the Virgin Mary. Gazing up at *Us Mem* I felt shrunken and unproductive.

The Frisian Studbook is the Frisian bible.

But Frisianness lay in the farms, not the city. Although still widely spoken, by the eighteenth century West Frisian had been ousted by Dutch in government, judiciary, schools, and church. West Frisian – *Frysk* – became a home language, but also a rural one. We studied the map. The islands were hopeless; they'd lost it completely to Dutch settlers and tourists. But just inland, north of Ljouwert, was the West Frisian heartland. A few hundred metres from the dyke that shielded the mainland from the Waddenzee lay a region of polders and isolated farms and poor coastal villages: this was the Terpelân, the most anciently populated Frisian area, pimpled with prehistoric mounds.

I wanted to be out there in the *âldlân*, patting cows, chatting to farmers. I wanted to make friends. Our previous night's host had been kind to give us shelter, but there had been no friendly exchanges. When he emerged in the morning to milk the cows, he'd been unable even to raise a smile.

We needed time to penetrate the taciturnity. The tourist office produced a list of farms that admitted a few campers. One farm gave its address in Frisian, and had a West Frisian name, Grut Kûhoal. We drove there.

We had chosen well. There was an eighteenth-century barn, thatched and massive, with a red-brick house tacked to one end. It crouched among trees out of the wind, shoulders hunched over an ancient *terp* that raised it out of the floodwaters, and was surrounded on three sides by a ditch, like a moat. It was on *terp*s like these that Frisian civilization began. A thousand years before they built dykes, the Frisians were great *terp*-builders. They used mounds of manure and refuse to keep their feet dry. From here the Frisians could have surveyed the sea – which would have been much closer then – on watch for long dark shapes in the water, moving ominously closer. Many *terp*s were built at the height of Viking power.

Now most *terp*s have been levelled off to fertilize poor surrounding soil. Thanks to ditches and pumping stations Grut Kûhoal no longer risked submersion. The drained fields swelled away from the ditches, like the camber of a road. They were soft looking, cushioned in grass.

Grut Kûhoal specialized in breeding sheep and glossy black Frisian horses. The stable hands clomped around in wooden clogs that lay scattered around the entrance to the barn. We shared a field with three Dutch couples in caravans, but they were so reserved they could barely meet my eye, let alone return my cheery greetings.

Morning sun shafted through elders when the Frisian horses were led out for exercise. Tractors thundered by, the drivers remote and lonely up in their cabs, off to harvest. This was agro-industry on a vast scale.

Tallulah loved Grut Kûhoal. It had a romantic, melancholy air of abandon. There was a rundown rabbit hutch, and a dovecote with a dead pigeon on the ground that Tallulah liked to prod with a stick. In a field screened behind ash and sycamore we found a rusted swing, and in the centre a tree laden with apples that Mrs Dankert, the proprietor, didn't have time to pick. Both seemed magic to Tallulah, especially the apples. She didn't eat them, she just loved the fact that a tree could produce such abundance. Help yourself, said Mrs Dankert, shrugging.

Best of all was a solid Dutch girl called Kim, who Tallulah fell for. They couldn't speak to each other but they swung on the old swing. Tallulah would slip her hand into Kim's, gazing up at her silently, adoringly. Kim was more interested in baby Xanthe, but Tallulah didn't notice this.

Grut Kûhoal looked like a classic West Frisian house, perfectly proportioned with tall windows reaching almost to the ground. We longed to talk more to Mrs Dankert. Richard managed to engage her in conversation, and asked if he could photograph her house, but Mrs Dankert brusquely declined. She was busy with the horses and the harvest, and besides her husband was very ill. Richard was bitterly disappointed. This was why we were here. Was there anyone else she knew who might be willing to talk to us? No, they're all just farmers, she said. But that's what we want, Richard explained. She shrugged.

We celebrated Xanthe's first birthday. We decorated the tent and Xanthe sat at the head of the table in her stripy rompers and party hat and laughed at balloons, and when we overcame our inhibitions regarding our fellow campers and sang 'Happy Birthday', she hummed along. We had a traditional Frisian Orange cake, a cake that celebrates the Frisian descent of the House of Orange. It was a success, the sun shone, and even Tallulah said she had enjoyed it, though it was a bit short and there were no party games or friends.

'Is Kim coming?' she kept asking.

'I don't know, darling. Maybe later.'

'But I want her to come now!'

'Why don't we save her some cake?'

'Yes! And biscuits. And sandwiches. And Cheesy Wotsits.'

When Kim turned up she accepted Tallulah's gift with her Dutch matter-of-factness, then disappeared. We never saw her again.

Days went by. Tallulah tired of prodding the dead pigeon. She was wan and coming down with a cold. Xanthe was teething and exceptionally clingy, and breastfed all day, just when I was trying to wean her. Richard vanished on errands of his own. There were always urgent reasons why he should get on his bike and cycle as far from us as he could.

Loneliness and claustrophobia: we were pulled between extremes. Richard coped by immersing himself in fungus. All day long he scrambled over fences, slid through ditches, braved bulls and dogs, in pursuit of his quarry. I was used to his recondite enthusiasms – eighteenth-century cookery, bonsai trees, the music of Philip Glass – and this was one of the things I loved about him, but now fungi superseded them all. He drew up charts of the most common species, listing likely sites and seasons ('The Miller, white funnel, pink gills, decurrent wavy cap, grass in open woods, early to mid-autumn; Jew's Ear, brown leathery semicircle, elder, spring to late autumn; agaricus bitorquis, stout & slightly funnelled with age, hedges & gardens, through tarmac, spring to mid-autumn'). Like Theodore Storm, I think he found contentment in the physical solitude.

I was struck by our resemblance to Storm's 1874 *novelle*, *Wald-winkel*. A botanist, coincidentally named Richard, shuns the outside world and lives in a forest retreat in Friesland. He spends his days foraging for botanical specimens, leaving his ward Franziska, his housekeeper, and his dog incarcerated in his mansion for hours on end. In the end Franziska gets fed up and elopes with someone else, leaving Richard to find solace in his dog.

But I wasn't complaining. Every evening we lit the candle and dined in our tent on the day's pickings. Best were the squat little puffballs with white crinkled domes like scurfy scalps that tasted of tofu. They thrived on these sandy pastures of the north. We followed them with yoghurt in tall litre bottles, and Gouda – not the waxy stuff of British supermarkets, but strong hard *oude* Gouda, a cheese almost as tasty as Cheddar.

I envied Richard's sense of purpose; I was in limbo, waiting for Mrs Dankert to change her mind.

One afternoon Xanthe and I cycled along the Wadden dyke. Combine harvesters roared on every side, and would continue to do so late into the night, headlights shafting across the flatness. Beyond the dyke lay not the sea, as I expected, but polders grazed by horses and cows, then mudflats, and only then, in the far distance, an oil rig and the outline of Ameland Island. I couldn't tell the land from the sea: they melded into each other. The grass was green, green without a weed, not a dandelion, not a buttercup, a lurid unhealthy green coloured by chemicals. We cycled home through villages of unbearable neatness and quietness. In Ferwerd a villager polished his flagpole.

We were outsiders, surrounded by an infinite desolation of pasture. I wanted to be inside a real Frisian house, living and breathing, with a real Frisian person. Richard would find the opportunity to have little chats with Mrs Dankert. She was mellowing, he reported, but the answer was still no.

The evenings were growing damp, and the wind got up. The tent walls sucked in and out like a diaphragm, and bruise-coloured clouds hurtled across the sky. The candle guttered.

As summer departed, so did most of the other campers, and with their departure Mrs Dankert began to waver. As the temperature dropped, Mrs Dankert warmed up. One afternoon she invited Richard as far as the kitchen. She had something for him, she said. The walls were tiled blue and white, but otherwise looked disappointingly like any other kitchen done up in the seventies – the usual units. In one corner under a blanket hunched a frail old man. He shook Richard's hand, then handed him a pamphlet. It was the latest publication from the Fryske Akademy in Ljouwert, of which old Mr Dankert was a member. So the Dankerts were, after all, enthusiastic Frisians. Richard thanked Mr Dankert but he held up a thank-you-halting hand.

The remaining camper heard us bemoaning our lack of progress with the Frisians, and at last overcame his reserve. His name was Hans Romp. He was not Frisian but a 'Tukker' from Twente, a region near the German border where he spoke a Dutch dialect called *Twents*. He was amazed that we had found it difficult to approach people here; in his experience it was all they wanted to talk about, they were so proud of being Frisian. Frisian this, Frisian that. There were Frisian flags, Frisian T-shirts.

'You could just get someone off their bicycle and ask them,' Hans suggested. 'Listen, maybe I can help.' He had a Dutch friend who worked with a Frisian who lived nearby in Blija.

It was raining when Anke Vellema and his wife Julie answered the door and found us unravelling Xanthe's sling and struggling out of unimpressive waterproofs. We left our paraphernalia and bikes streaming in their hall.

'Sit down,' they said, indicating a large leather sofa. It was a detached brick house in a row in Blija's main street, built eight years earlier on the site of Anke's grandfather's house which they had demolished. A Frisian house at last, but disappointingly one that could have been anywhere in the world: venetian blinds, a rubber plant, nothing of interest on the walls. It was bland. The floor was tiled. Every time Xanthe pulled herself up on the sofa, I waited for the crack of her skull as she hit the tiles, and this made it hard to concentrate. The Vellemas had no children and seemed nonplussed by ours. In fact they were bemused by our presence altogether, but they were a nice couple, happy to oblige. They sat side by side on another black leather sofa, Anke bulky and blond, Julie small and dark, positive and negative. When anyone shifted, the leather creaked.

Anke was Frisian born and bred and proud of it. I'd noticed the name Vellema in a graveyard, and he said '-ma' was a typical Frisian suffix meaning 'son of'. Miedema, Vellema, Binema, Anema, Boesma, Jansma, Sipma: I'd seen them all.

He spoke Frisian, though he didn't write it well, and only didn't speak Frisian when someone couldn't understand. Julie was not Frisian. She had moved here from elsewhere in the Netherlands when she was eight and had been forced to learn Frisian because it was all the other children spoke.

'Is the language under threat?'

'Oh yes,' they chorused. The threat starts in school. For the first couple of years Frisian can be the language of instruction, but from the age of seven or eight, everything is taught in Dutch. Frisian is taught for a few hours a week in some schools, but not many. There's no state curriculum, so it's up to the schools themselves to decide how much Frisian they teach. Then there's the media. All foreign programmes are subtitled in Dutch, not Frisian, and although there is a short Frisian programme five evenings a week, it tends to be watched only by the older people.

'Twenty-five years ago everyone here spoke Frisian. People say that in a hundred years there'll be no more Frisian.'

'Does it worry you?'

'A little,' Anke admitted, and Julie nodded. 'I wouldn't want Frisian to die out. It's part of my identity. I like to read Frisian writers.' Until the nineteenth century there was very little written Frisian, but the philologist Joost Hiddes Halbertsma, a friend of the Brothers Grimm, brought home from Heidelberg notions of Romanticism that led to a spread of popular Frisian literature. Today about ninety books are published annually in Frisian.

Anke's grandfather had spoken only Frisian. He had worked the land. I could see him in Anke, a solid labourer of few words, evenings in the brown-painted bar up the road, a game of pool, a glass of *beerenburg*. But there wasn't much work any more. There used to be big rich farms – cattle breeders, seed potato growers, sheep breeders – but there were too many younger sons needing farms, so the bigger properties got broken up. Now there was not enough land to go round. And what there was had become far less labour intensive. The gigantic machines had caused unemployment. Besides, agriculture wasn't as profitable as it used to be. And the fishing's all but disappeared. So people have moved away, to America, Canada, South Africa.

The following week Blija would be hosting a welcome-home party for the village diaspora. It had become an annual event. Flags of the world fluttered over the village.

An influx of middle-class Hollanders, commuters, had replaced them. Anke was lucky. He hadn't needed to emigrate, he had found a job in Ljouwert as a planner in a car factory, while Julie worked as a nurse in the hospital's surgical ward. He said he rarely spoke Frisian at work, but she found it useful with older patients.

'Are there problems between you and the incomers?'

'No, no. We all get along pretty well. No problems. No antagonism at all. We are Frisian first, but Dutch too. We feel comfortable with our situation.'

'Any links with the North Frisians?'

'None. Never have been. We have enough trouble trying to understand the different dialects here, let alone in the North,' Anke said.

'So there's no desire to reunite, to form a transnational Frisian state?'

'None at all.'

'Do you want to break away from Holland?'

Anke laughed. 'Certainly not! We're far too small. There's no independence movement whatsoever. People even say, what's all this fuss about bilingual place names? That's a new thing, started last year. They say, don't let's overdo it with the signs on the road. Don't exaggerate with the Frisian. Frisian is nice *but* . . . it's not such a big deal. It's not the be-all and end-all of our lives.'

I felt impatient with their acceptance of the status quo. What was Childers' word? Stolid. They'd been Frisian and free, never bowed under the feudal yoke, with their *Lex Frisionum* handed down by Charlemagne himself, and now they were content to sit back. The Vellemas expressed concern about the disappearance of their culture, but were impotent to arrest its decline. After the Second World War, when Europe was in a state of change, the West Frisians could have made a bid for independence, but there was no such desire. They wanted no more enmities; they sought freedom beneath the benevolent blanket of protection. I understood this, but found the lack of fire dispiriting. It was all consensus culture, like the pragmatic

Hollanders – no hot blood, no demonstrations, just send a letter and hold a meeting.

An anti-German feeling – albeit thoroughly suppressed by 'good' Europeans – further isolated the West Frisians from their East and North Frisian cousins. Maybe some of those crack Frisian SS units had been stationed here. Memories of the war, and a newer fear of economic domination by their overbearing neighbour, drew the West Frisians and Hollanders together.

Tallulah and Xanthe had been model children, crawling after two toy cars they had found on a shelf. I was constantly amazed by how much fun they could squeeze out of so little, and how much they enjoyed each other – probably because they had no one else. But the floor tiles made the noise deafening. It was getting late, and I could smell the Vellemas' supper cooking. We thanked them, then made an undignified exit as we struggled back into our waterproofs, Richard heaved Tallulah into her seat and I strapped Xanthe to my chest.

The next day we had to tie the tent down. Richard, in anticipation of a hard winter, thought we would benefit from a 'get tough' stance, and insisted we continued to breakfast under canvas. We huddled in jackets around a table sticky with dew. Xanthe was still in her woolly all-in-one night suit, and Tallulah in her pyjamas with a rug over her knees in a bad mood. Richard persisted with shorts and sandals and dismissed us as wimps.

Now when we cycled along the dyke we had to battle against the wind in one direction, and cycle with our brakes on in the other. On the dyke crest Xanthe cried as the wind tore against her face, forcing a retreat. We saw that it wasn't the sea alone that was the danger, it was the wind-blown sea. White wind turbines rotated like mad.

That evening Richard struggled with flapping canvas that tore his hands, and dismantled the tent.

Then at last his charm prevailed. Mrs Dankert's invitation excluded the children, we could tell, so we left them in the Mob and followed her through the barn. She lumbered along, broad hips swaying from side to side. She reminded me of *Us Mem*. Heavy, bovine, ungainly gait.

She led us down a tiled corridor then through a brilliantly convincing wood-grained door into a panelled sitting room.

'There!' she huffed. 'Here it is!'

The Dankerts had bought the farm in 1972, and with a government grant had restored it to the original 1783 colour. Unfortunately, this was the colour of sludge. It was over-furnished with uncomfortable-looking armchairs draped in antimacassars, and hideous swirly carpets: 1783 meets the 1970s, the decade taste forgot. A door opened into the hall which was lit by windows over the front door, then we entered the room Mrs Dankert called the parlour. This was more formal, painted a more faecal shade of brown. It was dingy, unused as a museum. A carpet covered the table. A life-sized photograph of her mother in Frisian dress hung over the mantelpiece; beside it a traditional Frisian clock, its face painted with a bucolic Frisian scene, had stopped several years earlier.

Both she and her husband were Frisian to the core; they'd been born a few miles away.

The best thing was the windows, which stretched over ten feet high on two walls. The Dankerts had removed ugly modern windows, and this made their house no longer typical of the area, she said. Most had been modernized.

She rested on a chair arm, silhouetted against her fields and horses. My husband used to be a big farmer, she said. Big time. She stated it unsentimentally, but sadness pervaded the room. And now I'm too old to drive the horses, she muttered. There was no sign of children, no family snaps, no toys for visiting grandchildren: I supposed she'd have to sell the farm when Mr Dankert died.

Then she stood, and with a theatrical flourish opened an unnoticed door in the panelling. Hidden between two gilded Corinthian pilasters topped with a motif of nuts and corn, an image of abundance, was a red-painted apse. She said it never had a religious purpose – it wasn't a secret chapel – but would have been to display the family's collection of porcelain – Chinese, Japanese, Delft – brought back by Frisian merchants. The collection would have stood on its shelves, shiny and fragile, a display of wealth. Now there were just a few stranded bits and pieces. When she closed the secret room it was as if she closed the door on Friesland's glory days.

Now the parlour was funereal, as if Johannes Dankert was already dead.

'Contrary to common misconception, and in defiance of probability, Frisian is flourishing.' Durk Gorter ran his hand over his hair. He was all movement, bright and quick, a changeling in Friesland. I liked him at once. He was a relief. Dr Gorter was a professor of linguistics at the university of Amsterdam and a sociolinguistic researcher at the Fryske Akademy in Ljouwert, where we now were. He was also at the heart of the EU's Mercator project that was documenting, researching, and advising on all lesser-used languages of the European Union. There could be few people in the world better placed than Dr Gorter to know what was going on.

'At any rate,' he added, 'the latest surveys show there's been no *decrease* in the number of Frisian speakers in the last twenty-five years. It's very surprising.'

'How would you explain it?'

'Education, an awareness of being Frisian, a fear of its loss. It's incredibly interesting. But let's get something straight. What do you mean by a "speaker"? Someone who speaks Frisian at home? Or only in public? Someone who can read it? Write it? The latest data shows that we have 400,000 social users, and of them 350,000 use it at home while the rest use it occasionally. And that figure has been pretty stable for twenty-five years.'

'Who passes it on?'

'That's another surprise. It's not the mother tongue as such. The latest evidence shows that it is the grandfathers who keep it alive. But I'm pretty sceptical about that. It's something I want to follow up.'

And contrary to what the Vellamas had said, there *were* links with the other Frisias. There had always been times of Frisian unity, with medieval gatherings at Aurich in East Frisia, in the days when West and East Friesland were both ruled by Saxony. Today contacts are encouraged through the Fryske Rie, which has representatives from North, East, and West Friesland, and tries to maintain an awareness of being Frisian, of having that in common. But it's also a rural thing, Durk Gorter added. We share a way of life.

'What makes you Frisian?'

'For me, I suppose the language is the most important thing. But it's a combination of things. The landscape ... I don't know ... there's also an intangible feeling of having a common past, *and* a future. I co-authored a research project about ten years ago and we discovered that at least three-quarters of the inhabitants of West Friesland consider themselves Frisian. It's not just a reactionary thing. We want to be Frisian in the future too. There's no independence movement, but we do want a greater say in Frisian language and culture.'

'But how can Frisian cope with modern language developments, technological data, and so on? How can it be part of the modern world?'

'Yes ... Our language is not something fossilized. It's still living and changing. Of course, to a certain extent Dutch is still assimilating us. We use all their technological words. We have to. And English is spreading at a phenomenal rate. EU policy has been supportive to an extent, with the European Bureau for Lesser-Used Languages. This is important. But we must observe the other tendencies, for example the millions given to translating state languages. Minority languages like ours get support for specific projects, but we're small fry.'

What was so interesting, he said, was the way in which globalization was running parallel to regionalization. Why? Why were people developing an interest in their roots?

'I think many people fear a global culture will destroy their identity, and this gives them a feeling of goodwill towards Frisian culture and language. They fear the negative effects of a McDonald's culture. You might call it McDonaldization. For a local example, take *beerenburg*. It was a typical Frisian drink. Almost every village had its distillery, its different local brand. Now they've introduced *beercola*, and you can get it all over the Netherlands. It's mass produced, very popular. All the young people are drinking *beercola*. So you see, the product has been expanded but diluted. It's the essence of what's happening here, a cola culture mixing with a *beerenburg* culture, and diluting it.'

'So what's the prognosis? Will Frisian still be around in a hundred years?'

'A hundred years ago people were predicting the end of Frisian. And look at it now! So I think the outlook is optimistic. I think it will be here on the mainland a hundred years from now, if in a different, diluted form.'

As we left we asked if there was anywhere in Ljouwert where we could find traditional Frisian cooking. Dr Gorter thought for a while, and then said, no, he didn't know of anything.

SEVEN

Flemish v Walloons

The Leuven Stadhuis glowed in autumn sun, a fantastic flamboyant Gothic confection, iced with pinnacles and spires of stone. We passed it several times on our way to the university arts faculty, because we were lost. A law student offered to show us the way, if we didn't mind dropping off his laundry en route.

He sat beside Richard, directing him through tangled medieval streets, over canals, through the Grand Place, past the lumpen cathedral, past the icing-sugar Stadhuis again, past enticing-looking collegiate courtyards, past the gabled façades and stalls of the Groot Markt where we could eat *moules et frites* with Trappist beer. It was teeming; the student boasted that Leuven had the highest concentration of bars in all Europe. It looked like a Belgian Cambridge.

The student had beautiful golden hair that curled over the shoulders of a dark gold corduroy jacket. He seemed nice, civilized.

'Is Belgium going to separate?' I asked him from the back of the Mob.

He half turned in his seat and replied, 'Yes, I think it will.'

'Why?'

'Because we Flemish are fed up with having to subsidize Wallonia. It's OK for, say, thirty years,' the golden-locked student observed, 'but there comes a time when we don't feel like paying any more. There comes a time when the Walloons have to start doing something for themselves.'

A short dapper Flemish man with dark hair was waiting at the arts faculty. He opened the back door of the Mob and climbed in, and bent gravely to Tallulah.

'Good morning. My name is Guido Latre.' Tallulah's face was

streaked with felt pen. She turned shyly to me, not sure what to make of this approach. He took her hand and tried to shake it, but she giggled and hid her hand behind her back. As always, she tried to deflect attention on to Xanthe, *sweeeet little baybee*, waggling Xanthe's bare arm, and glancing back under her lashes at Dr Latre. He had the common touch, rare in an academic. He was Senior Lecturer in English at the Catholic University of Leuven, the largest university in Belgium.

He perched on the edge of our sofa as we drove along. Tallulah was excited to have a stranger in her home, and bounced around on my lap. Dr Latre looked more like someone in advertising. His mac was from Aquascutum, and he carried a little handbag which he held primly in his lap. I became conscious of our scruffiness. Tallulah's pen-streaked face, Xanthe's bare feet, my trainers with holes around the toes, Richard's beard, now reaching Edward Lear-like abundance: we all insulted the professor's sartorial perfection. Then there was the overwhelming odour of fungus. Richard had ranged his latest haul of Ardennes ceps along the dashboard to dry in the heat of the engine. They smelled like old socks.

The café Dr Latre chose was uninteresting enough to be child-friendly. He hung his coat and sat neatly, dapperly, at the head of the table in his beautifully pressed moss-green suit.

I slid on to a purple velour banquette with Xanthe on my lap while Tallulah, to her delight, was enthroned in a high chair. I knew it wouldn't be long before the children needed attention, so I quickly asked Dr Latre about himself and Belgium and Leuven, but he cut me short. 'Let's just order first.' He summoned a waitress and in Flemish ordered tomato soup for me, large steaks for him and Richard, and chips for Tallulah.

'There!' he declared. 'Now we can talk!'

But first there were complaints about mayonnaise on the chips, then visits to the loo. Eventually the girls went to play behind the net curtains, bursting out at each other with shrieks of excitement. An elderly woman with stiff hair ate on, regardless. Her fat feet, squeezed into high heels, poked out from under the tablecloth; I waited for the girls to trip over them.

'Now we can talk?' Guido enquired, politely. He was anxious not to seem critical, said he had three children of his own, but I knew that in Belgium children are well-mannered, obedient, and *bien propre*.

I asked him about himself, and he said that although he felt an untypical academic, he was a typical Belgian. Looking at him, I knew what he meant. Here was no tweedy intellectual, but an urbane man about town, immaculately oiled and pressed. He was a Belgian archetype. As he worked through his mountainous plate, dabbing pursed lips with his napkin, I was reminded of no one more than Hercule Poirot, minus the moustache. I pictured him in bed with his wife, his hair smoothed down under a hairnet. But that wasn't fair. I wasn't quite sure what to make of him. His Poirot qualities – an unctuous smugness – were combined with a genuinely charming simplicity, and I warmed to his honesty as he described his up-bringing in a poor peasant family in west Flanders, and his route up in the world.

There was one rich boy in the neighbourhood, he said, son of a lawyer, who was driven to school in a big important car. One day the important car drew up outside their house and the rich boy's mother stepped out. Guido's mother was in the garden hanging up the washing. She went to greet the elegant wife of the local notary, wiping her hands on her apron. The notary's wife announced that she had chosen Guido to be her son's friend, and that she wanted to send them both to England for a month. The notary would pay. Guido's mother was flattered that her son had been so royally chosen, and pleased that he would go abroad, but she refused to be patron-ized by the notary's wife, so she agreed that he should go, but insisted that he would pay for it himself. So Guido persuaded the local farmer to let him sit on a machine that collected potatoes from the fields of Flanders, and every time the machine picked up stones or copper fuses instead of potatoes, Guido would remove them. The copper fuses were remains of First World War shell cases. He was allowed to keep them. Some he sold for copper, others to tourists. And so it was that the First World War paid for his trip to England.

He never looked back. Now he was so multilingual that he taught not just English, but Middle English. His speciality was Chaucer.

Not surprisingly, his other great love was the poetry of Sassoon and Owen; he was organizing an exhibition about the war poets for the EU in Brussels.

But Guido stayed true to his roots, and lived in a working-class district of Leuven. This kept him in touch with what 'ordinary' people felt about Belgium.

'And what do they feel? Is the country on the point of breaking up?'

'I think not. The media talk about separatism, and so do intellectuals and politicians, but I think the man on the street wants to stay Belgian. You only have to look at what's happening now with this awful paedophile case. When the bodies of the murdered girls were unearthed, there was an outcry that united people in their grief. It didn't matter whether the victims were Flemish or Walloon, or whether Marc Dutroux, the paedophile, was Flemish or Walloon, all that mattered was that he had raped and murdered these children, and our police and judiciary had fouled up. Suddenly we were all just Belgians, and angry. Again, when King Baudouin died in 1993, everyone came together in their grief. He was a symbol of national unity, loved by both sides, and his death was mourned for what he stood for. I hope *I* am going to remain a Belgian at any rate.'

'What unites Flemish and Walloons?'

'I think we are united by the *absence* of any sense of nationalism. Ask anyone here, "What is your nationality?" and before you get an answer you get ten seconds of hesitation. Are you Flemish or Walloon or Belgian or simply European? I think it's that hesitation that unites us. Perhaps it's also a negative thing. We can define ourselves as *not* Dutch, *not* French, *not* German – there's a small German minority too, you know. That negativity, that ambivalence about Belgium, is something we share. We also share the way in which people – older people anyway – tend to owe their allegiance to their cities more than to their country. But I also think we are more Belgian than we believe. National pride only strikes us when we go abroad. When we're in the Netherlands, then we become more certain of our identity. There are things we Flemish share with the Walloons rather than with the Dutch.'

'What sort of things?'

'Let's see. We share a brief but very intense history – a colonial period, some might say not a very glorious chapter, then occupation by Germany during two world wars. We share the same inadequate, antiquated judicial system. What else? We both like steak and chips!'

'*Tintin*?'

'Yes! *Tintin*, *Asterix*, a love of all *bandes dessinées*. Beer. The Catholic Church, of course. And other things, such as a strong concern for minority groups like the handicapped. There is also a sense that we were once a tribe, the Belgae. We are all taught that in school, how Caesar reputedly said that of all the Gauls, the Belgae were the bravest. Although the territory they covered was seven times larger than our current state.'

'And what drives you apart?'

'Well . . . so many things. Unlike Northern Ireland, it's not a religious thing. What divides us above all is our languages. There *are* good Belgians who are perfectly bilingual, but not many. We are also incredibly different in other ways. Belgium is where North and South Europe meet.'

'Or collide?'

'Yes! That's right! Although ninety nine per cent of the collision is verbal, not physically violent as in Northern Ireland. In some ways we Flemish are like the Dutch: ours is a country of regulations. We are puritanical. Wallonia on the other hand is a country of fixers. More corrupt, less rigid. Our mentalities are different. Let me give you an example. I teach here, and also at the Francophone university of Louvain-la-Neuve. When I tell a joke at Louvain-la-Neuve, I get roars of laughter, then rapt attention again. Here, I make the same joke, and the immediate response is hesitation. You can see the Flemish students asking themselves: this is Shakespeare, but it's also a joke, is this allowed? Then they decide it is, and so they laugh, and they do so louder and for longer, and it takes them longer to settle down again. I have to plan for laughter time when I give lectures here.'

'It's a lack of confidence?'

'Yes. I see it in all sorts of little ways. Take the swing doors. Here, the Flemish students see me coming and want to be polite, but at the same time don't want to be seen to be deferential. So they become awkward. Either they go over the top, holding the door for me, flattening themselves against it, or they are rude and let it slam in my face. Now, my Walloon students at Louvain-la-Neuve see me coming, they fling open the door with a flourish and announce, "*Après vous, Monsieur le Professeur!*" They have more flair, more charm, more confidence.'

'And that's a historic thing?'

'Yes. The Flemish are the majority, but until recently they were the underdogs. They dug potatoes. The Walloons owned the mines, the Flemish worked them. In the army the Walloons were the officers, while the Flemish were the soldiers. During the First World War that made for some pretty interesting situations when the soldiers didn't understand their officers' orders. The Walloons had never felt the need to learn Dutch. There were no important jobs in Flanders, only big flat fields. A lot of people died on the front because they couldn't understand each other.'

'How absurd.'

'It is, or was. People remember such things, and it's caused a lot of bitterness. Another reason for our lack of confidence is that many of us never really feel at home in our own language. Flemish means a collection of Dutch-related dialects. My mother tongue was a broad West Flemish dialect. I didn't even learn pure Dutch at school; my teacher spoke a purer version of the local dialect. So we all had to learn pure Dutch before we even began on French or any other language. But now the Flemish are earning all the money, and the Walloons are having to learn Flemish after all. The mines are closing, heavy industry is disappearing, there's a lot of unemployment, and during the 1980s the Flemish took the initiative. Flanders is Belgium's Silicon Valley. It's where the jobs are. So the Flemish are getting more confident and are less bothered about learning French.'

'Why haven't the Walloons rebuilt their own economy?'

'It takes a long time. I don't know. Maybe after two world wars the Flemish are used to rebuilding.'

If Belgium stays together, he said, it would not be for economic reasons, it would be for emotional ones.

It was here in Leuven that the division of the country first became a possibility. After a misty and complex start, Belgium was part of France until Napoleon fell, whereupon the Congress of Vienna ceded it to the Dutch. William I imposed the Dutch language throughout Belgium, alienating not only the Walloons, but also the militantly Catholic Flemings, who feared that on the back of the Dutch language, Dutch Calvinism would also be imposed. Revolution broke out in August 1830, and the international community accepted Belgium's independence in 1831. But within a couple of years separatists were at work. The Francophone south grew rich while the Flemish north grew poor; there was simmering resentment and mutual incomprehension.

Seven years after Belgium's birth, Hendryk Conscience, the Walter Scott-inspired Flemish novelist, published *The Lion of Flanders*, which celebrated the Battle of the Golden Spurs, the victory of the Flemish over the invading French in 1302. Even allowing for a bad translation this is an unreadable book, but it was hugely popular in its day, translated throughout Europe. What was important was that it established a literature in Flemish, and helped to create the myth of the great historical Flanders. Soon Conscience would be setting up the proto-fascist Heilig Verbond (Holy Union), which used pageantry inspired by the Freemasons to promote the Flemish cause, and proclaimed 1302 as Year One in the Flemish calendar.

The principal complaint of the Heilig Verbond was the dominance of French. All major newspapers were in French, the Church leadership spoke French, the greatest Flemish writers wrote in French. Ruling families on both sides spoke French. There was no Flemish in the Lower Courts until 1873, no Flemish allowed in the lower stages of secondary school until 1883. Although Leuven is in the Flemish north, the teaching (as in all Belgian universities) was in French, the 'language of culture'. Agitation in the 1920s led to dual language teaching at Leuven, but by the 1960s the Flemish students felt increasingly resentful. They hated French, the language of the officer class. They had read Conscience. They demanded a Flemish-only university. The Walloons had to go.

It was a very difficult and emotional time, Guido recalled. There were riots. He arrived at Leuven just after they were over but the bitterness remained, and there were still banners all over the place, 'Walloons Out!' There was huge hostility between the two communities. The government fell. And it was decided: Flemish-speakers would keep the medieval institution, the oldest Catholic university in the world, founded in 1425 by Duke John IV of Brabant, but it would be divided in half. The Flemish would remain in the old buildings in the Flemish city, while the Walloons would move to a new green-field site in Wallonia.

It was like a divorce, Guido said. It was drastic. In Leuven there was a sudden loss of students, and the available funding was cut in half. What to do with the library? They divided it book by book, odd numbers out, even numbers to stay – though (he added hastily for us) the *Encyclopaedia Britannica* was left intact.

It was the beginning of Belgian federalism, which led, in 1993, to Belgium devolving into three regions, run effectively by three regional authorities – Flanders, Wallonia and Brussels – overseen by a national government. This, Guido said, was what Belgium's politicians had always wanted. They had for years used divide and rule as a way of furthering their own ends; politicians need scapegoats.

'So what will happen next?'

If the nation state dwindled, he said, Belgium might disappear. We would have a separate Flanders and Wallonia under the umbrella of the EU. One problem was that there were pockets of Flemish in Wallonia, and vice versa, not to mention the small minority of Germans; German was the country's third national language. And there were plenty of intermarriages. Workers of both ethnic groups had always moved around. On the other hand, the EU might have the opposite effect, and enable both regions to make the choice to stay together, and to view each other not as rivals, struggling to dominate, but as equals and compatriots.

What *he* wanted was a Europe of the Cultures. He was involved in advising the Minister President of Flanders on one such initiative whose aim was to promote a two-track Europe, one of nation states and another of cultures. By this he meant not geographical regions but peoples who shared a culture, whether or not they shared a state.

Tallulah had pushed some chairs together to build a house. She was coaxing Xanthe in. But Xanthe had another plan. She wanted to practise walking. Richard was forced to take her hands and stagger around behind her, negotiating the other diners.

'Look, darlings!' I called desperately. 'Come over here. It's pudding time. There's something called a "Child Ice".'

Guido summoned the waitress. Even in Flemish there was no mistaking the words 'parasol', 'chocolate sauce', 'cream'. I was touched that he should take so much trouble for Tallulah. She climbed back into her high chair and watched Guido eagerly, wriggling in anticipation, her intelligent face shining.

'It'll be the best thing you ever tasted,' I whispered. 'Just you wait!'

We did wait. At last it arrived: pinnacles of pistachio, chocolate, and coffee ice cream draped in a frill of whipped cream and scattered with chocolate powder, and peeking cheekily from the summit a striped cocktail umbrella. It was a Knickerbocker Glory of Stadhuis proportions. But it was not for Tallulah. It was for the professor. Tallulah's 'Child Ice' was a meagre blob of vanilla melting in the bottom of a metal bowl.

Tears splashed on to the vanilla blob, but there wasn't time now to order anything else. The professor tucked his napkin into his collar, plunged in his spoon, and devoured his confection with such concentration that he failed to notice Tallulah's disappointment. Or was this his revenge?

We insisted on paying the bill.

'Oh no!' The professor was aghast. 'But I've been eating like a Burgundian!'

As we put on our coats, he bustled around the banquette, flicking a napkin at the detritus.

*

It was complicated trying to cross back into Francophone territory. Road signs changed language every few miles. This was because the linguistic frontier, that divides Belgium horizontally, undulates. From previous visits I remembered bilingual road signs, but they seemed to have all but disappeared. Now French signs directed us to Bruges, Liège, or Ypres, while Flemish ones pointed to Brugge, Luik, or Ieper. One of the few signs we saw with a linguistic overlap had been painted out.

Walloon villages consisted of a grey church, a string of two-storey houses with window surrounds of red stone fronting directly on to the road, and a bank. They were somnolent, deserted, with blurred edges as if smothered in a coating of dust. They looked like black-and-white photographs from the post-war years. Yet amongst the dreariness would gleam a patisserie with its pyramids of petits fours and pralines, displayed on dishes as glittering and luxurious as in a Bond Street jewellers. The displays had an absurd valiance: however gloomy the economic forecasts, as long as one could preserve the bourgeois niceties of pralines, all would be well in Wallonia.

Sylviane Granger was Professor of Linguistics at Louvain-la-Neuve. We found her exiled to a fortress that rose from the centre of a moat of interconnected roundabouts. Twenty years earlier there'd been nothing but fields. Unscalable ramparts and walkways surmounted multi-storey car parks, and protruding from the top was a crane. The campus was still under construction. We found our way up subterranean steps, and emerged into what had, with a touch of irony, been named the Grand Place. Instead of the fairy-tale Stadhuis there was a concrete space with two litterbins, a bench, and one ill-looking sapling. A student sprawled on the bench nodding along to his Walkman. It reminded me of Basingstoke.

Sylviane was tall and in a hurry. She strode into a café and ordered *chocolat chaud* for us all. Her black hair was swept off a handsome face. I liked her energetic warmth. She wasn't a politician, she stressed, just an ordinary person, and could only tell us what she felt about Belgium from the Francophone point of view.

'But that's what we want.'

She had arrived in Leuven (or Louvain as she called it) in 1968, at the height of the uprising. Although she had good friendships with some Flemish students, as a Francophone she found the anti-Walloon graffiti and posters very upsetting. The divorce was acrimonious. For all her protestations of enthusiasm for the new campus – no cars, lots of facilities for kids, the marvellous achievement, etc. – she obviously missed the medieval town. They'd been moved out faculty by faculty, beginning with Applied Science. Few girls studied science then, so the students lived in Louvain-la-Neuve in monkish solitude.

The Walloons came off badly, she thought. They'd waited decades for funding; the new faculty of psychology had been inaugurated only last year.

The two universities were microcosms of what was happening in Belgium: polarization.

'The sad thing is that it boils down to a nasty little question of money. The latest bone of contention is the health service. According to the press, the Flemish want to split it because they say we cost too much. That more Walloons than Flemish get ill. The Walloons are presented as the poor relation. I really hate that. If they split the health service, what's left? That'll be the beginning of the end. We already have separate schooling. The army and the judiciary? Well, the judiciary's not up to much, and the army, well we don't have much of one, only professionals now, no military service. We'd only be left with an empty shell. And so they want to ditch us.'

'What would happen to Wallonia?'

'We could never survive alone. We would have to become part of France, and we would be their forgotten little province, stuck on the edge, treated even worse than Brittany.'

'Look at Luxembourg. They've managed it.'

'They have the banks.'

'True.'

'When I was young things were better, because we were forced to learn Dutch at school, and the Flemish were forced to learn French. OK, so the students got frustrated because after four years of the languages they still couldn't understand a word, but at least they had made the effort. Then it stopped in the seventies because it was considered that English would be more useful as a second language. This was a big mistake. OK, so Dutch isn't much use if you want to travel the world, but in fact the Belgians aren't great travellers. Most of them just stay here.'

The Walloons had the advantage of learning French as their mother tongue, not Walloon. This was because they had all but killed off their ancient tongue. Sylviane seemed to scorn the very notion of something so peasant-like. During visits to Belgium in the mid-1980s I only ever heard the odd *Nom di Dio* or *Bôdjou*. It was the language of farmers; my Liègeois friends laughed at them contemptuously, while harbouring a secret nostalgia. They were right to regret the demise of Walloon. Like Provençal with a smattering of low German, it is a separate Romance language, not a French *patois*, and supposedly descends from Roman legionaries who settled here, the word Walloon possibly stemming from the Germanic root *wal*, meaning 'foreigner', i.e. non-German. As in Wales, and Wallachia, and Gaul.

It was the familiar story of attempted obliteration by nineteenth-century schools, of divisions by dialect, of flurries of enthusiasm in the late nineteenth century, of that enthusiasm being killed off by the First World War and bourgeois ambitions.

The Francophones had enough to think about, keeping their end up linguistically, without having to bother with something so inelegant, so easily mocked. Walloon did you no favours when you were looking for a job in Paris.

What united the Belgians, Sylviane said, was enthusiasm for Europe. All the students were ardent Europhiles. Everyone here was. *Unlike* the English, she scoffed. She went on to be startlingly vitriolic about the English – our xenophobic tabloids, our incomprehensible lack of good European feelings. I was beginning to cringe, wondering why she had agreed to see us, and then it transpired that she was half-English herself. Granger – I should have guessed. Before rushing off to give a lecture she insisted on paying the bill.

'I want to because it's good to have Americans here.' She smiled. Richard and I looked at each other, puzzled, but kept silent. We felt like frauds.

EIGHT

Who is Bernardo Atxaga?

Along the promenade bins overflowed and litter tore past shuttered shops and caught in the dead leaves of stunted palms. On the tideline Tallulah scavenged panty liners, condoms, flakes of polystyrene. She preferred the plastic ear-wax removers. She built up a good collection of these. She pretended they were lollies.

This was where we had hoped to spend several weeks by the sea, settling in, recovering from the ferry journey across the Bay of Biscay.

To travel by ferry through night-day-night had been Tallulah's greatest ambition, the highlight of her short life. Our cabin on the *Pride of Bilbao* made the Mob seem palatial, but she loved the bunks. It was November. We tucked the girls up and couldn't resist the temptation of leaving them while we had dinner in the restaurant. When we returned we found both girls lying in puddles of their own sick. This, however, didn't lessen their enthusiasm.

Bilbao in its valley was invisible under a pall of pollution. I imagined the Mob vibrated as we drove down into the city, like a plane descending through turbulence.

We parked in the Casco Viejo, the old heart, on the right bank of the Nervion. The soupy water curved out of sight between old industrial buildings, and I kept thinking of Chicago. Around a bend in the Nervion, on the site of the old Euskalduna Shipyards, Frank Gehry's Guggenheim was rising like a titanium lotus from the mud flats, a symbol of Bilbao's post-industrial rebirth.

I was surprised how much I liked Bilbao, rough and workaday as it was. I liked its gritty heroism. Bilbao is the westerly limit of the Basque Country that spreads from here to Bayonne in south-west France. It is also the industrial heartland of Basque nationalism. In a park old men in *txapelak*, Basque berets, leaned on walking sticks, their shoes gleaming. Flowerbeds were dead, the bandstand boarded up and daubed in graffiti. ETA, ETA, ETA. A taxi rank said:

E

Taxi

A

Now we wanted to stop somewhere and steep ourselves in the Basque Country. The Bilbao tourist office had recommended this shit hole, Arrietarra. *Gracias por su visita*. Thank you for nothing.

Below the Spanish was written: *Eskerrik Asko Etortzeagatik*. It was the first time I had seen this arcane tongue, of European languages among the least known to linguists.

The neighbouring beach was worse. Skinny dark-eyed men sidled along the rocks, supposedly fishing. Taking Xanthe for a walk, I glanced up to see a man alone on the cliff. He stood, silhouetted against the shale, a malevolent presence. He stared down at me, then pointed his stick at a pigeon, and I saw it was a gun.

At night, by the deserted November surf, I heard feet crunching on sand; whispering; trigger catches being released. I lay taut, heart racing. If in doubt, someone had said, press the horn. But our horn didn't work with the ignition off. We couldn't reach the ignition because Xanthe's cot was in the way. We couldn't drive without collapsing the cot and swivelling the driver's seat to face forward, by which time any burglars/kidnappers/murderers would be inside the Mob. Even if we collapsed the cot and swivelled the seat we couldn't move because now the windscreen was enveloped in our latest purchase, a metallic quilt like the eyeshades worn by elderly Americans on planes. It was designed to keep in the warmth, but it was secured from the outside. We were mute, blind, and paralysed.

Tallulah caught my insecurity. She was jumpy, terrified of the candle – fire! – and had a sudden fear of the fierce expression on the face of her Lion King hot-water bottle. She had nightmares. Xanthe was restless too. They were so clingy that when I went to the loo they *both* had to come, sitting on my lap and making gargoyle faces in the mirror.

Six days later ETA would kidnap someone on his way home to

Getxo, a smart suburb of Bilbao, a few miles south. Cosme Delclaux, the 34-year-old son of a Bilbao industrialist of Belgian descent, would be ETA's forty-fifth kidnap victim in twenty-six years, of whom the police had succeeded in rescuing only five.

Richard studied the map. He noticed blue freckles that indicated a beach north of Gernika. If that proved another squalid disaster, we would abandon the Basque coast. But only on beaches could we stay without hassle for more than a few days. And besides, cut off from the rest of Spain by mountains and sierras, it was to the Bay of Biscay, the Bizkaiko Golkoa, that the Basques had always turned: fishing, exploring, being pirates and conquistadors. They even claim to have invented whaling, a practice they taught to the English, Dutch, and Danes, and in pursuit of their gigantic quarry may have reached the Americas before Columbus. First it was the steep valleys that shaped Basque identity, and then it was the sea. After the sea, the cities.

By evening we were cresting wooded hills above the milky Ría de Gernika-Mundaka. Way below twisted a bird haven of iridescent salt marshes and shifting sands. And at the Ría's mouth, tucked into its lonely bay, lay Laga, one of the most beautiful beaches I had ever seen.

At the far end blackened limestone stacked up to form a barricade that sheltered the beach from the north-east. Behind us, to the west, rose another rampart; between, they met in a green valley coursed by streams to splash in, pimpled with dunes to hide and seek in. There were pines for shade, a spring for water, a flat place to park, and a discreet whitewashed building tiled with terracotta: the Restaurante Toki-Alai. Then beyond, the surf-striped sea.

A sign said *Kanpaketa Debekatua*, 'No Camping', so the drawback could turn out to be the Guardia Civil. But until they arrived, we'd found a beach to call Home.

The sand was a golden crescent of crushed shells. We added our footprints to the gulls', and to the giant webbed prints of end-of-season surfers. They bobbed like seals on the massive Atlantic breakers.

Here I was less afraid: it was the beauty of the place, but also the reassuring presence of the bar. The girls were sleeping, the lights low; we sat at the window gazing at the stars and a gas rig twinkling on the horizon, and the coruscations of a lighthouse on the spur of Matxitxako. Richard planned a series of paintings with the exact dimensions of our window, 48cms x 134cms. The canvas size would seem familiar since these dimensions had so long framed his view.

We drank Rioja and loved the cosiness of our Mob. Onions, red peppers, garlic, and spicy chorizo sizzled on the stove. The waves were a constant background roar, like jets. White noise.

We spent three weeks splashing in the shallows and sand-castling. Xanthe practised walking in the firm wet places exposed by the spring tides. Richard dug pits and buried Tallulah vertically, up to her neck, like a Moldavian in her grave. 'Bury me! Bury me!' I heard her cry, halfway down the beach.

The sun veered out of autumn clouds. I carried Xanthe in the backpack up on to pointy hills that were astonishingly green and un-Spanish. Every wall, every signpost, every bridge, was daubed ETA, ETA, ETA. One more loquacious graffito demanded 'Freedom for the Basque Country' in English, French, German, Spanish, and Basque, to be sure of getting the message across. Membership of ETA was illegal, and you could get two years in jail for making graffiti; to manage such elaborate wall-painting, the artist must have been helped by the locals. The least they can have done was turn their backs.

We scrabbled up through flowering gorse and groves of young pines and eucalyptus, and I took deep breaths of happiness. It was just so beautiful. Xanthe demanded leaves and flowers – squeaked until she got them – then discarded them. This game was repeated until she fell asleep, snoring softly in my ear. Now I could see the orange segment of our *hondartza*, our beach, then the ironed expanse of sea, deserted but for a solitary fishing boat catching the afternoon sun.

I climbed through abandoned terraces, past what I mistook for a ruined barn until I noticed smoke leaking from its chimney. Tails of red peppers hung out to dry, apples were yellow on the tree and the maize beige and dying back. A rheumy old man in a *txapela* was scything hay and forking it up into the shape of a beehive; his greeting hung on the air, then scattered.

Portentously, red roof tiles were held down by rocks.

Half-built villas indicated the outskirts of Elantxobe. A steep lane descended to a miniature plaza with a vertiginous view of the sea. A bus arrived from above, and as I wondered where it would turn, it parked on a disk and with great aplomb was revolved.

Then we plunged down a cobbled gash, down, down. Xanthe's head flopped against the backpack frame and she woke – as always with a smile. We reached a cluster of fishing boats that bobbed behind a harbour wall. Warehouse doors opened on fluffy mounds of blue fishing nets, and old men leaned on railings, smoking. They returned my greetings without friendliness or unfriendliness: they weren't bothered either way.

The Cape of Ogoño encircled Elantxobe almost totally, leaving the narrowest possible mouth – the merest pout – opening on to the sea. It was a strange, hidden, mysterious harbour.

We climbed back up the canyon, so steep that my calves ached, so dank that moss cloaked the walls. Tiny houses formed tightly packed ziggurats against the cliff. A woman in slippers darted after her cat, '*Miz-miz, miz-miz*'. A baby cried. There was no room for cars, and no cars could cope with this gradient. An old man toiled painfully behind me. I asked him if there was a supermarket and he pointed his stick to the sky and gasped, '*Arriba!*' – 'Up.'

Oddly, there was no fishmonger, but there was a tiny butcher's shop. It opened on to a cave, its back wall formed by the rock face. In the gloom stood a knot of old women with string bags. They fell silent, then parted to let me in. Xanthe's presence made me feel less intimidated, and one of the women chuck-chucked at her, but she shrank into the backpack. Chorizo dangled phallically from the ceiling and red meat seeped in white trays. The women left, murmuring goodbyes to the butcher. One waggled her finger in Xanthe's face, and Xanthe gripped my ear in terror.

The fridge juddered. The butcher and I exchanged smiles. Slowly, a game evolved. I would ask for something in Spanish and he would repeat the words in Basque. His wife joined us, beaming. Hello, I would like some ham – *Egun on, xingarra nahi nuke,* they chorused. *Aygoon onn, chingarra nahee nookay,* I repeated. Polite laughter. They made me say it again. I loved the sound of it. The butcher got out a receipt book and wrote it down. Beef – *Idikia.* A slice of beef – *Idiki xerra bat* (*Eedeekee chayrra bat,* I repeated). I would like a chicken – *Oilasko bat nahi dut.* A hundred grams – *Ehun grama.* A litre of milk and half a dozen eggs – *Pinta bat esne eta dotzena erdi bat arraultze.* Yes! You're getting it! But it's very difficult! They seemed proud of that. (Later, Richard noticed that one of my purchases was horse. He said nothing and made a stew. The girls and I ate it without suspecting. So the last laugh was on me.)

The butcher wrote down some expressions. The word order, it seemed, was precisely the opposite of English. *Etxe zuri txiki polit bat* meant, literally, 'house white little pretty a'.

I was intrigued by the look of this Scrabble-winning language. No 'q's, 'w's, 'c's, 'v's, or 'y's, but a plethora of high-scoring 'x's, 'z's, and 'k's. I'd noticed that like Irish it had a particular script for public notices, with a curve over capital 'A' like a pair of bull horns.

Like Finnish and Sami, Basque is strongly agglutinating and suffixing. Instead of using prepositions ('to', 'of', 'for', 'by', 'with', or 'from') to indicate the role of a noun, it is the end of the word itself that changes. Xanthe being with me – *with* the mother – is *amarekin.* The bag of shopping for me – *for* the mother – is *amarentzat.*

We ranged further, and the butcher wrote words he loved, words that don't consist of combinations of words, but which were coined by Basques simply because they liked the sound of them. 'Crab' is *karramarro;* 'rubbish', *zarramarra;* 'spider', *armiarma;* 'whisper', *zurrumurru;* I'd never seen words like this before. Each one was greeted with increasing laughter. They were wonderfully onomatopoeic but they also looked so good. 'Scribbling', he wrote, was *zirri-zarra;* 'chatterbox' was *txantxan.*

Euskara remains basically the same language that was spoken here thousands of years ago. Basque theologians tried to prove it was spoken in the Garden of Eden, a pre-Babel babble. One Basque abbé even claimed it was the language spoken by God. Slightly less outlandish connections have been made with Caucasian languages, North African, Iberian, Etruscan, Finnish, and Pictish, but all have been discredited.

In fact, there is not one shred of evidence that Basque is related to any other living – or dead – language. Genetically, Basque is on its own. It is the last remnant of an almost lost cache of pre-Indo-European speech, spoken in this isolated mountainous pocket before Indo-European nomads and farmers and conquerors set out from the east. The ancestor of Basque – proto-Basque – existed in Europe before the ancestors of any other living language. It was spoken during the last ice age.

For Basque nationalists, the uniqueness of the language is a strong psychological barrier against assimilation. The language's difference from Spanish and French is so extreme that it is hard for them to swallow it.

Centuries of Roman imperial rule left a smattering of Latin loan words but, like Welsh, Basque not only refused to die, it flourished. Clearly the Romans were not interested in the area; occupation was limited to providing road access for their legions across the Pyrenees, and they did not establish more than a couple of towns in the region.

When the barbarian Visigoths and Franks established kingdoms in France and the Iberian peninsula, the Basques made a habit of raiding them from the hills. They were punished but, far from being conquered, by AD 700 had actually spread north to form Gascony (from the Latin *Vasconia*). The Moors never came here either.

The Basques were always belligerent, never trusted. The eleventh-century *Chanson de Roland* describes the massacre of Charlemagne's Frankish army on the Pass of Roncesvalles as a conflict between Christians and a vast Muslim army aided by demons from hell. It makes no mention of the Basques. But the *Chanson* was written nearly three centuries after the event. The fullest and most contemporary sources attribute the massacre not to Muslims but Basques. Einhard's *Vita Karoli Magni* written in the early 830s (about fifty years after the massacre) described Charlemagne withdrawing across the Pyrenees to Francia through the forested confines of the pass, whereupon the detached rearguard was ambushed by Basques.

Without alerting the front of the army, which marched on oblivi-ously, the Basques forced the rearguard back to open ground. Here they slaughtered every Frank to the last man, including Roland, Charlemagne's nephew and Lord of the Breton Marches. It was the only major military defeat in Charlemagne's long career. The Basques were lightly armed, and thanks to their pastoral ways knew every sheep track through the mountains: they melted away, and the outrage was never avenged. Einhard bemoans their treachery, 'per-fidia'. The perfidious Basques. They were never effectively subdued.

The mountains and forests they inhabited were criss-crossed by medieval pilgrims on the road to Compostella. This would have been a prospect both intriguing and worrying for those who read the popular pilgrim guidebook by a writer known as 'Aimery Picaud'. He described the Basque penchant for bestiality – a mule was as good as a woman for their perverted purposes, he wrote – and 'a Basque is even said to fit a chastity belt to his own mare or mule, to prevent anyone else getting at them'.

Confused and bloody years saw the Basque Country by the end of the Middle Ages without a state. Politically divided, subjects of different kingdoms, the Basques now lacked any sense of Basque identity. At that point the language could have disappeared. But prosperity returned with the growth of industry, fishing, and above all the voyages of discovery. Basques flocked to the New World, while the ports of Bilbao and San Sebastián (Donostia in Basque) became hugely powerful in servicing the new transatlantic shipping. Bizkaia and Gipuzkoa became the wealthiest provinces in Spain, and also the most egalitarian, free from the rapacious nobility who sucked up the wealth of much of the rest of Spain. In fact, during the sixteenth century the crown granted to both provinces the recog-nition that *all* native inhabitants were of noble status.

How did the language fare? From the sixteenth century a growing number of Basque texts were published in France, but after the French Revolution the linguistic centre of gravity moved to the now richer south. But the aristocracy despised the language and, although the Basque Country saw the founding of the first private secular school in Spain, all teaching was in Spanish. There was no Basque literature to speak of; until the nineteenth century, publishing in Basque was confined mostly to dull works of devotion.

The late nineteenth century saw a Basque *Berpizkundea*, literally 'rekindling', when stories, folktales, and songs were collected and published. But Basque still had a hard time. From the sixteenth to the nineteenth centuries, and at times throughout the twentieth century, publishing in Basque was often viewed as subversive. It was a possible indication of treachery in this sensitive frontier region, wedged as it was between the mutually hostile monarchies of France and Spain.

Then came linguistic suppression under Franco. No schooling was allowed in Basque, and the speaking of Basque was punished. The only Basque publications were those produced by exiles in the Americas. Today, Basque is losing ground in the south, and in the valley of Roncal it has disappeared altogether, just in the last few years.

Yet the miracle is that the language has survived. It has survived since history began, in linguistic isolation against the military, political, and cultural odds. Not only survived, but expanded. Since Franco's death, efforts have been made to increase the number of speakers, and so successful have they been that for the first time 80,000 on the French side have some knowledge of Basque and, according to the 1991 census, 660,000 on the Spanish side. Nevertheless, Basque speakers remain heavily outnumbered in their own country.

Richard took Tallulah to the Toki-Alai while I put Xanthe to bed. They returned to fetch me. Tallulah eagerly pronounced both bar and loos 'lovely'.

'Helena?' Tallulah whispered. It was more like 'Heddna?'

'Yes?'

'The bar smells of fag ends, Heddna, but don't worry about it.'

Old men played a card game called *mus*; one had the rasping voice of a rattlesnake, and skin as mottled. He was treated by all with particular respect. It was obviously the local bar, and he was the local paterfamilias. Beyond the bar a glazed veranda overlooked the sea, and here dozens more groups smacked cards on to green baize. They were a dour-looking lot. Tallulah watched them shyly, sucking the ice from her orange juice, then skipped off to join Richard in a game of pinball. I ordered a glass of *txakoli*, Basque white wine made along the coast at Zarautz. The barman looked startled by my choice, and a bit doubtful. It was young and sour.

This was to become our local. Richard loved its maleness. He'd write his diary, beer to hand, play pinball, watch sport on the TV over the bar. He became such a fixture that gifts began to arrive at his elbow: a bowl of salted nuts, a selection of tapas. Tallulah loved it too. There was a jar of lollipops and sometimes the *patrona* would haul one out. We ate Sunday lunch on the veranda. *Sopa de pescado*, *bacalao a la Vizcaína* with red peppers and kidney beans, and local yoghurt: Basque cooking at its finest.

I took Tallulah back to bed, and Richard joined us later, all fired up. The barman, it seemed, was a passionate Basque. His name was Unai. On a scrap of paper he'd illustrated the Basque dream. Across the top he'd scrawled '*BRUSELAS*', and orbiting in bubbles a spherical '*GALIZA*', a triangular '*BASQUE*', and a long thin '*CATA*'. A scribbled river linked '*VITORIA*' to '*BRUSELAS*'. Underneath was the word '*INDEPEN*', while '*ESPAÑA*' was violently scored out. The message was clear. The already autonomous regions of Spain – which included Galicia, the Basque Country, and Catalonia – would devolve, but under the umbrella of the EU. Vitoria, capital of the Basque Country, would deal not with Madrid, but directly with Brussels.

We watched a ragged gang – there must have been twenty of them – saunter along the tideline. They wore hooded sweatshirts and boots, and threw sticks for their mongrels to hurtle after. Later, when Tallulah took me to the stream to give Barbie a sail in a Tupperware box, we found ETA scrawled in gigantic letters in the sand.

Two land cruisers prowled the dunes. An officer from the Guardia Civil climbed out, guns dangling like supernumerary genitals. At first

I feared we would be moved on but he ignored us and scoured the cliffs with binoculars.

Perhaps the Guardia Civil were searching for the ETA supporters or perhaps for the kidnapped Delclaux. We didn't ask. We kept out of the way. With creepy symmetry, today *El Mundo* had published detailed revelations of a Spanish marine (known only as 1964-S) who, four days earlier, had been horrifically tortured by the Guardia Civil amongst dunes like these. His crime had been to give testimony against a Guardia Civil lieutenant about his role in a GAL death squad. GAL (Grupo Antiterroristas de Liberación) was a group of Guardia Civil who over the previous decade had used torture and assassinations to wage their own secret war against the Basques. The revelations fuelled a loathing of the Guardia Civil, already reviled as an instrument of centralization, as the occupying force.

We climbed steep steps. Tallulah was jealous of Xanthe being in the backpack, but she was too excited to whine. Evergreen oaks enclosed us; clouds cushioned the summit. We reached a locked gate. Behind it yawned a hole in the hillside. Three youths bounded after us. Two wore tartan bondage trousers; the third had a black goatee. The guide produced a rusted iron key and let us in.

Santimamiñe was someone's home, he announced, from about 15,000 BC until 2000 BC. In this limestone cave people would have sheltered from the *zirimiri* – and at the end of the last ice age the climate would have been even worse than now – living off deer and boar that roamed surrounding forests. The curious thing about the cave mouth, the guide explained, is that eight metres of mollusc shells have been excavated. Archaeologists believe that the shells were food gathered from the Gernika estuary, but that they were also for personal adornment. Who were these shell-decorated cave dwellers? Were they direct ancestors of our guide, and of the youths personally adorned in tartan trews and goatee?

Basque ancient history is riddled with lacunae. But such evidence as there is points to the uninterrupted presence of the same people here for thousands of years. It is possible that our companions were descendants of the aboriginal inhabitants who evolved out of the

Neanderthals in a pre-Indo-European Europe. It is possible that we were in a Stone Age cave with descendants of the original hunter-gatherers who inhabited it. Our journey into the ground was also a journey deep into European pre-history.

Geneticists like Luigi Cavalli-Sforza have found that the Basques are strikingly similar to each other, and strikingly different from their neighbours in the Iberian peninsula, and a bit different from their neighbours in south-west France. They have the highest proportion of the gene for the rhesus-negative blood group in the world, and among the highest percentages of type-O blood, as opposed to Indo-European speakers who are predominantly rhesus-positive. They may have clung not only to their ice-age language, but also to their ice-age genes. Both suggest that the inhabitants of Santimamiñe and other caves dotted around the western Pyrenees were not disparate tribes but a single Basque tribe. This historic connection is crucial to the Basques' ability to define themselves as a 'nation', enabling them to use their past to demarcate their territory, and to support demands for the reunification of all Basque provinces, French and Spanish.

We walked into the hollow mountain. It grew dark and slimy – it was only ever inhabited at the mouth – but deep inside, through a forest of stalagmites and tites, lay a natural chamber bearing drawings of bison, a horse, and a bear. Some ancient proto-Basque crawled down here, his flaming taper throwing shadows up on to glistening walls, to make these drawings: perhaps objects of worship, perhaps sexual totems if Aimery Picaud is to be believed, perhaps an early example of the Basque passion for graffiti. I was struck by their Picasso-esque fluency (and Picasso made much of the sexual side of his bestiary) but also by their resemblance to cave drawings we had seen seven months earlier at Rouffignac, just over the Pyrenees. Did these cave dwellers travel and view each other's art? Possibly. Genetic studies suggest that they were one and the same people, and although there are no written records of the Basques until the Romans brought literacy in the first century BC, it is probable that they spoke the same language.

*

Richard returned from the Toki-Alai with news from Unai. For the first time in sixteen years a Spanish president would be visiting Gernika, tomorrow. All today, Unai reported, the town had been closed. In fear of an ETA outrage, not a single shop was open, not a single bar.

Some places become so firmly associated with acts of atrocity that it is hard to think of them as normal places where people get on with their lives. Dunblane, Lockerbie, Verdun, Gernika – in Spanish, Guernica. The bombing of the small market town by German and Italian fascists in 1937 is recognized as the most notorious event in the Spanish civil war. But through Picasso, the word 'Guernica' has transcended place and time to become a very definition of the screaming terror of the innocent victims of modern warfare – women, children, and animals.

Gernika was not the first. A month earlier, Durango had met the same fate. In fact, Durango was bombed four times, killing over 250 people and wounding three times that number. But Picasso did not paint 'Durango'. Gernika, home of the famous Oak, around which representatives from across Vizcaya democratically debated the *Fueros*, the exemptions from royal law, was the spiritual heart of the Basque Country.

Over the next four weeks Gernika/Guernica became our local town, but I never got used to it. Its name never lost its emotive edge.

It wasn't a special town. It had no clear shape and few interesting buildings. We ambled under a pleasant, shady arcade. The old centre had been flattened.

On the afternoon of 26 April 1937, the bell at Santa María church suddenly began tolling as the fascist Condor Legion flew out over the sea then turned low up the Gernika estuary – our beautiful bird haven. The first wave brought 250-kilo blast bombs that shattered the buildings; the second wave brought incendiary bombs that ignited fires throughout the town, and delay-fuse bombs. The fire engines stood by, useless because the water pipes had been destroyed. In three hours 29,000 kilos of bombs were dropped on Gernika.

The third wave brought machine-guns to rake the people as they fled. No one has ever established how many were killed. Estimates range from 200 to 1654. Counting the dead was hindered by their bodies being bundled by Franco's troops into a common grave, without even an inscription, and by the lists of the deceased being torn out of the register office.

Only the year before we arrived, in 1995, were the Basque dead at last given their own memorial.

The Basques had found themselves supporting the radical leftist Republicans almost despite themselves. Their tendency was traditionally conservative and Catholic; but they were prepared to side with anyone willing to concede even a limited autonomy to the Basque Country, and this the Republicans did at the eleventh hour in October 1936, after civil war had already broken out.

Basque nationalism had got going in the mid-nineteenth century when a late but vigorous industrial revolution in Vizcaya attracted immigrants from the rest of Spain in such numbers that by the early twentieth century they and their descendants outnumbered the Basques. It created an explosive reactionary situation, exacerbated by the increasingly centralizing tendencies of Madrid. It provided fertile ground for the ideas of nationalism and self-determination which were spreading throughout Europe.

The result was the formation of the Basque nationalist party the PNV (Partido Nacionalista Vasco), today the Spanish Basque Country's most powerful party. It was overtly racist. Membership was open only to those who could prove Basque blood on both sides. 'Let your daughters marry none but Basques!' was the slogan of the day. It was seen as vital to preserve the purity of the language in order to create an 'ethnic' barrier against the Castilian immigrants. At the time the concept of race was fashionable, and seen as legitimate. One positive effect was to revitalize Basque language and literature. Neologisms poured forth, including the word *euskadi*, literally 'collection of Basques'. Having given their country a name, they pressed for its autonomy. Having achieved this in 1936, the Basques were forced to reciprocate by becoming a dubious ally for the Republican cause. Within months Gernika was destroyed.

Reprisals were ferocious. The Basques had aspirations towards autonomy, however limited, that could not be tolerated by the

Nationalist victors. Not content with winning, Franco indulged in a frenzy of vengeance. Soldiers, and anyone else caught up in the civil war, were packed off to prison and labour camps; many were tortured, others were shot. Franco ran the Basque Country as a police state and attempted to destroy the very identity of the Basques, whose distinctiveness was seen as a political threat. Into the shattered cities and ruined economy, thousands of Spaniards from Andalucia were transplanted to work in new state industries, which were deliberately sited in the Basque Country in order to submerge Basque culture. For the thirty-six long years of Franco's rule most Basque festivities and cultural events were banned. Basque books were burned, Basque universities closed, Basque was banned from church, and all Basque names had to be translated into Spanish in civil registries and official documents. Over a hundred thousand intellectuals and politicians were imprisoned, or fled to exile, taking with them twenty thousand children.

All contact with the French Basques was outlawed – the Pays Basque was in any case soon under occupation by the Nazis. It was the darkest time in Basque history. The prevailing mood was of utter despair.

During the late 1940s Franco began to relax slightly, and the Basques began a clandestine resistance. In 1952 a group of Bilbao students formed a pressure group called Ekin, from the Basque for 'get busy'. They learnt Basque and read the Existentialists. Ekin obviously fulfilled a need because it grew rapidly. In 1959 it renamed itself ETA, Euskadi Ta Askatasuna, 'Basque Homeland and Freedom'. Supported by Jean-Paul Sartre, financed by bank robberies, armed by Czechoslovakia, ETA was to provide Franco's Spain with the only active opposition to his dictatorship.

Initially protests were mild – nothing more than displaying the distinctive (but banned) red, white, and green Basque flag, and calling for action – but again Franco reacted with savagery. People were randomly arrested and beaten, and anyone who was arrested was systematically tortured.

By 1960 ETA concluded that nothing was to be achieved by passive resistance, so turned to violence. It began with known tor-

too proud to allow someone else to do their washing. So I left the clothes soaking overnight in French powder – *efficace sans frotter!* – and the next morning rinsed and squeezed until my knuckles were raw. I hung the washing line between the wing mirror and the roof ladder. Coat hangers dangled from the bikes and the windowsill.

Then it rained. Our dripping clothes had to be rushed inside. The warm space over the fridge was quickly occupied with pants and socks. I hung some sodden rags off each cupboard handle and every rung of Tallulah's ladder, but this meant that they all had to be removed when we opened the cupboards or used the ladder, and there was nowhere else to put them. Since it was raining, Richard and both children were also vying for space.

The solution was to give the clothes a blast from our newly installed Eberspäcker heater, the technology favoured by long-distance lorry drivers. But the washing remained damp. By morning the windows were running with condensation. We would give the clothes another blast. Silence. A flat battery.

It was a dank day. The beach was deserted. A flat battery meant not only no heat, but no flushing loo, no light, no water, no gas. It also meant no going. We needed milk again, and food. Two small children stranded without food, water, or heat on a wet winter's day on the Atlantic coast: Tallulah announced in the way she knew best that this situation was intolerable.

Eventually we were able to borrow some jump leads, and we were away, damp clothes swaying in our faces.

Now the sky turned black and the waves exploded. Even the surfers disappeared; our only companions were a colony of gulls. We would breakfast in pitch dark, the rig still glimmering on the horizon, the Matxitxaco lighthouse still pulsing.

Rain drilled the ground like metal rods. The stream that Tallulah and Richard had dammed swelled into a stinking torrent. Not surprisingly, Basque has a plethora of words for storms. *Ortzantz* means 'thunder', *hortzgorri* – 'red cloud', *ortzi* – 'sky' or 'rain cloud' (it seems these two are interchangeable), *ortzikara* – 'time when a storm is brewing', *orzoski* – 'calm air'. This was *ortzikara*. With plenty of *hortzgorri*. It rains as much in the Basque Country as in the west coast of Ireland.

The washing failed to dry and began to smell of rot. Days passed while we waited for meetings with assorted politicians. We tried to get on with each other despite almost suffocating in rotting clothes. I had to wash the entire load again and, like a Zanussi revolving, the story was repeated. We had to buy a new battery.

The problem wasn't just the laundry, it was the mess, stumbling over toys, the mountains of washing-up, winter coming on and rain and sand and sea water coming in. Black moods threatened to ooze out of me. But Richard kept us going, always cheery, always holding up the prospect of some pleasurable event, a drink at the bar, a trip to Gernika, some delicious cheese.

Tallulah would escape into her top bunk where she coloured herself in; she was like a Red Karen tribesman, tattooed from head to toe in blue. Richard spent the days squatting on rocks in the rain, gazing along the length of his rod, hoping for a bite. Xanthe put on and took off her plastic necklace. Despite having her bouncing on my leg, I managed to escape into Bernardo Atxaga's *The Lone Man*.

Atxaga is the first Basque novelist to be translated into English. In *The Lone Man* the accumulation of seemingly inconsequential detail created a tension so gripping that I read all day and all night, heart pounding. During the World Cup in 1982, a man known as 'Carlos' cannot resist being drawn back into the 'organization' – ETA – when he agrees to hide two terrorists in the hotel that he owns outside Barcelona. Also staying in the hotel are the winning Polish football team and their phalanx of police guards. When a more monkish style of policeman arrives, disguised as a TV producer, tension mounts as Carlos and the 'producer' try to outmanoeuvre each other.

Carlos is a seductive character. Tall, handsome, sexy, brave, in control, a loner with a touching need for human contact. His façade is cool, but underneath he is tormented not only by fear, but also by a conscience that refuses to forget some of the less glorious acts of his ETA terrorist past. It's a vista of loneliness, guilt, boredom, loss of identity, police-loathing, and a passionate, romantic love of the Basque Country. I suspected that it was the closest I was ever going to get inside the mind of an ETA terrorist.

Sunday in the Toki-Alai became the focus of our week. The *menu del día* was bean and sausage stew followed by pork chops in batter and chips, then ice cream and coffee. We washed down this gargantuan lunch with red wine from Gernika, served chilled. The stove blazed. Richard sat as close as he could, his jeans – drenched from a morning walk – steaming. The windows fugged up and obliterated the sea, but we could hear it raging, rain banging the roof and tumbling to the sand. It was like being behind a waterfall.

A party occupied three neighbouring tables. They were in their thirties and forties, men with ponytails and prayer shawls and black leather, women with pierced noses and dreadlocks plaited with blue wool. We couldn't place them. Too old to be students. Terrorists? Since reading *The Lone Man*, we suspected everyone of being a potential terrorist. As Carlos says, almost everyone of his generation has spent some time in prison. They turned out to be the 2CV owners club.

We were hardly able to prise the Mob door open against the wind. Xanthe went straight to bed for her afternoon sleep, Tallulah straight up her ladder and into her toy box, where she sat reading, coughing, interrupting herself only to ask me for a 'gunk tissue'. Mould was growing along the side of her bunk.

She stayed up late building nests for teddies. When she was asleep I peeped behind her curtains and found soft toys wrapped in blankets and squeezed together into a box, the whole space submerged beneath a silt of white hairs, as if her reindeer skin had begun an unseasonal moult.

That night the storm raged. Richard and I lay silent, but both aware of the other and our mounting anxiety. The wind came in gusts, like sobs, pausing for breath, then heaving and moaning again, sometimes howling. We were under siege.

The storm paused for breath. We drove up hill, took a sharp right at the multilingual Freedom for the Basque Country graffiti, to the village of Akorda. Unai was waiting in the shelter of his arched stone porch. He was shorter and plumper than he looked behind the Toki-Alai bar; it was the first time I'd seen his legs. He wore carpet slippers and a denim jacket slung over his shoulders like an old woman's cardy.

Behind him rose the half-timbered walls of his family house, a classic early eighteenth-century Basque chalet, with shoulder-thick walls built of rubble picked up from surrounding fields, mortared and whitewashed, pocked by tiny squinting windows with stone architraves; the long gables of the terracotta roof sloped steeply against the rain to give it a low-browed look. Within the porch lay the usual scruff of buckets, tools, a wheelbarrow, pepper garlands, stacks of wood. Unai seemed awkward, less confident without the protection of his bar.

'Come and see,' he said, and led us round the back. An old man in a *txapela* was wheeling a barrow laden with pumpkins big as Space Hoppers. Others were strewn across the fields. These were for the cows, six of which were tied up in a barn. They never went out, Unai said. It was too wet and steep.

While the girls clucked and mooed at the livestock, we stood on some dung and chatted. All Akorda people spoke Basque, Unai said. They were the clientele in the Toki-Alai.

'When strangers come into the bar, how do you know what language to use?'

'Mostly I listen to how they speak to each other. Otherwise, I use Spanish with the older people and Basque with the younger ones.' He called them *euskaldun berriak*, literally 'new Basques'.

'So the language is reviving?'

'Yes, I think it is.'

Unai had been educated mostly in Basque, at a state school in Gernika, and then at the state university in Bilbao, where he had studied what he called 'workers' law'.

'Is there much work for Basque lawyers?'

'A lot of jobs require you to speak Basque. But you need–' He held up two fingers as though to poke them up his nostrils. Unless you have fingers in pies? Yes, that sort of thing. Unless you have friends in high places. That's why he was working as a barman. He was soft-featured, with large gentle eyes like his cows.

'Do Basques and non-Basques get on?'

'We have nothing to do with each other. We don't like each other, but it's not like Belfast. We don't fight. We simply avoid each other.' There weren't many 'foreigners' in these parts. Elantxobe had few non-Basques. Outsiders weren't welcome; it was very tight and inward-looking. So much so, he said, that people from Elantxobe couldn't even speak to people from parts of Gipuzkoa because their Basque dialects were too different. Even to people from the next village, he added, laughing.

Other Basques deny that the dialects are so mutually unintelligible, and blame this misconception on anti-Basque propaganda, put about by people – Castilians – who didn't want the language to prosper.

The number of dialects is disputed. The founder of Basque linguistics, the first to classify the language into dialects (and sub-dialects) put the number at eight. I'd seen his famous dialect map, created in 1869, in the museum in Gernika. Its French author was working several decades before Gilliéron produced his linguistic atlas of France. His name was L. L. Bonaparte (1813–91). A few enquiries revealed this to be a nephew of Napoleon, and supposedly a dead ringer for his uncle, born in England, raised in the Papal States, married to a Basque speaker with the un-Basque-sounding name of Clemencia Richard. Thanks to her, Prince Louis Lucien devoted his life to studying Basque, and was among the first to inspire the Basques to take their language seriously and to write in it.

We stood there, Unai rhythmically kicking a pile of grass. 'Spain,' he muttered, as though it were a separate country. 'Bah! It's very ugly, all flat and brown. Very ugly. Not like this. There's none of this.' He sent up an arc of lush greenery.

'Are you Basque or Spanish?'

'My ID card says I'm Spanish. I know I'm Basque.'

Patches of black forest and verdant meadow chequered the hills down to Laga. Unai's love of this place reminded me of Carlos. I mentioned The Lone Man, and Unai nodded approvingly. Atxaga was a Basque superstar. What moved me most about Carlos was the loneliness of his exile. Beneath the crude Mediterranean sun, he yearns for the Atlantic, for the green and blue hills to heave into view. 'Was there anything worse than exile? No, apart from prison, apart, perhaps, from death, there could be nothing worse.' I sometimes felt the same.

An old woman in a wool skirt joined us in the barn: Unai's widowed mother. She greeted us warmly, then forked up some grass for the cows. Unai, in his carpet slippers and cardy, watched her work. This made me uncomfortable, but his mother didn't appear to mind. She didn't ask for help. I was struck by the respect she showed him.

Xanthe was frightened of the dark house. She buried her face in my shoulder. Then our eyes adjusted. There was a cavernous chimney breast, and overhead a beamed ceiling, a cosy place to hibernate during the long dark winters, a modern version of the mouth of Santimamiñe. The stone flagged floor sloped, to facilitate scrubbing. The hall led into a bright functional kitchen. The TV was on in one corner, and Unai's mother was brewing coffee. It came with glasses of potent *patxarán*, anisette; normally they had this for breakfast with fat cigars.

'*Every* day?'

'No, just at weekends.'

'*Every*body?'

'More the old men.'

I couldn't sit for my coffee; Xanthe was in a walking-practice mood, insisting on staggering round the room at the ends of my fingers, my back bent over her. Give her to me, cried Unai's mother, sweeping her up, but Xanthe was north European through and through: she never got accustomed to the southern cuddles. She was happy to smile but only from the safety of my arms.

Unai's mother perched with a bowl of black beans. They were smooth as Apaches' tears. She sorted the best for sale in Gernika market where she had a stall, the second best for themselves, and the rest were discarded.

Unai's mother was called Jone, which Unai said was a classic Basque name – so much so that the female terrorist who Carlos hides in the cellar underneath his hotel bakery is dubbed 'Jone' by the press; we never discover her real name. What Unai didn't know was that it wasn't a genuine Basque name at all, but a neologism coined by Sabino Arana, the nineteenth-century founder of the PNV, father of Basque nationalism. He was so determined to stamp out the Romance words that had infiltrated Basque – in T. S. Eliot's words to 'purify the dialect of the tribe' – that he devised Basque versions of Spanish names, and decided that male names should end in 'a', and female in 'e'. Jone was his version of Juana, Joan.

Unai said his name was Basque for cowboy. Oh yes! We laughed, but it didn't suit him. He was too gentle for that. When Unai's father had gone to Gernika to register his name, he was informed that Spanish names only were permitted, so he had had to think some up on the spot.

Jone spoke quickly to Unai in Basque, and he excused himself. He returned with an old book. He opened it reverently and handed it to us. Loopy sepia recorded every transaction that had taken place on this farm since 1718. The accounts book had become a family heirloom. I noted that the language was Castilian, not Basque. Unai said, we've always been oppressed.

It was interesting that the book had stayed with the house and not moved on with previous owners. This was because *etxe* means far more to a Basque than just 'house'. It is a symbol of continuity, and a focus for identity, even a political base. Ever since the Middle Ages each family had become closely associated with a particular house, so much so that the overwhelming majority of Basque surnames are geographical: they derive not from people's professions (Smith or Taylor), nor from an individual characteristic (Black or Brown), but from the place where some ancestor lived. Atxaga means 'crag', plus the common suffix '-aga', so presumably one of Bernardo's ancestors lived on a crag – if, that is, Atxaga was his real name, which for some reason I suspected it wasn't. (It turned out to be a nom de plume, his real name being José Irazu Garmendia.) Even today the house name is often better known than the family name, and is used for identification. A distinct Basque tradition is the non-particle inheritance: family properties are never broken up for division among the family as they are under the Napoleonic Code, but are passed on intact to (usually) the eldest son. The master of the house is the *etxeko jaun* (*etxe* – 'house' + *ko* – 'of the' + *jaun* – 'lord'). He became a powerful paterfamilias of the extended family, pre-eminent in local society. There was no feudal system: regular meetings between these heads of household in front of the village church, the *anteiglesias*, formed the basis of rural democracy. Thus the sense of place, and proud ownership of that place, is fundamental to Basque identity, and roots the Basques to their land. On the French side the Napoleonic Code was enforced, and some people believe it has destroyed the Pays Basque. One French Basque we would meet had seen his *maison natale* broken down to minute, unworkable plots, and the rest of his family forced to emigrate to California.

As we drove home we saw that the mountains were topped with snow. There was a new sort of cold, a throat-catching cold. We took the precaution of parking not by the shore, but tucked in behind, sheltered by pines. We played hide and seek behind the trunks, then as darkness fell the rain hammered down.

The Lone Man engrossed Richard now, and I suddenly thought: we must meet Atxaga. I identified Atxaga with Carlos – hard, tall, shaven-headed, confused, romantic, sexy. I would track him down. This plan excited me. Leaving Richard to give the girls their evening 'bowla' (Special K), I donned waterproofs and boots and set off through the dark, through the trees, to the bar telephone. I kept my eyes on the ground to protect them from wind-blown sand, but also to negotiate the puddles. One was so huge that we were now cut off from the road – not a puddle but a lake. I skirted it, and jumped the narrowest point. I vaguely noticed wires on the ground but was thinking of other things – how I would find the Harvill Press phone number, what I would say.

The bar seemed darker than usual. I headed for the phone. Everyone chorused: it doesn't work!

Cursing, I headed back. This time I paid more attention to the wires. A huge pine had been felled by the storm, bringing down a telegraph pole. Where we had been playing hide and seek was now a tangle of branches and splintered timber. A few metres east and the Mob would have been crushed. We had escaped from the waves, only to find ourselves at risk from the trees.

I climbed the bank to be smacked in the face by wind-blown rain. I could only just make out the sea but I could hear it roaring all around me. The lighthouse flickered, and as a cloud scudded off the moon the whole scene was briefly illuminated as a horrifying, exhilarating maelstrom. Metal oil drums used as bins had been swept from the car park down the beach; I tried lifting one to test the weight, and could barely move it. I turned my back to the wind and was almost lifted off my feet; at that moment the remaining lights in the Toki Alai were extinguished.

It was like the end of the world.

Today the nationalist Arrano Bar was open. It was a prominent building on the Juan Calzada Kalea, a busy Gernika thoroughfare; we treble parked outside. A banner draped across the façade read in metre-high red letters: '*PRESOAK*'. We had seen this word all over the Basque Country, as graffiti or on posters. We'd seen women at crossroads waving it on placards. '*PRESOAK!*', '*PRESOAK!*' I was haunted by it. It was as if the Basque Country was obsessed with disseminating washing instructions. Was there some message here for me?

Sandwich boards declared '*PRESOAK EUSKAL HERRIRA!*' Dotting the Basque text were mugshots of bearded men, like Muslim fundamentalists. '*EUSKAL PRESOAK MUGAGABEKO GOSE GREBAN!*'

The floor was strewn with discarded napkins and cigarette butts; heavy metal screamed from two huge speakers above the bar. Tallulah cowered from the noise. I was glad we'd left Xanthe asleep in the Mob outside. I felt intimidated, but also excited. It looked like a radical student bar, with a mass of ETA notices and more posters of bearded men.

Our requests for beers were ignored. Clearly Castilian was not welcome. Thudding music emphasized the sense of antagonism. We tried again, this time asking if anyone spoke English. The barmen suddenly heard us. They didn't speak English but one of the drinkers offered French. I explained why we were there.

'I understand. You mean not only Basques, but Corsicans, Bretons, Catalans?'

I nodded. 'You've got the point.'

'I would. It's central to the Basque idea.'

He asked how long we'd been in the Basque Country, how we got here, where we were staying. I told him everything. I was aware that he could suspect we were spies, especially following the kidnapping when police surveillance had been stepped up. He decided to trust us and bought Richard a beer and me some coffee. But Tallulah was upset.

'This isn't *our* bar,' she complained. There were no good things to eat, no pinball, no lollies, only fag ends. Richard took her aside, leaving us to talk.

The man said he was a primary school teacher, teaching solely in Basque in a state school in Gernika. Since Franco's death hundreds of such *ikastolak* had sprouted on both sides of the border, and were the basis for the Basque revival. Ticking off his fingers, he explained that in the Basque autonomous region a child could study:

A. All subjects in Spanish with a class of Basque.
B. Half and half.
D. All subjects in Basque with a class of Spanish. Most people here chose D.

'What about C?'

'In Basque there is no C.'

He taught in *euskara batua*, a unified Basque that had been forged during the 1960s. At home, he spoke his own dialect.

This building, he explained, was headquarters of the Gernika branch of HB, Herri Batasuna, 'Popular Unity', the left-wing nationalist party. This much I gleaned, but the man was drunk, and his French execrable. He must have sensed my impatience because when a plump woman with ragged dreadlocks and a nose ring appeared, he asked her if she knew an English speaker. There was someone. She made a call. This person's English was so good that when Gerry Adams last visited the Basque Country she had acted as his interpreter. The name 'Gerry Adams' was spoken in awed tones. Our contact would finish work at around 8 p.m.

The dreadlocked woman's name was Otsanda, Basque for 'Young She Wolf'. She produced a pamphlet in English entitled 'Peace Proposition for Basque Country; Democratic Alternative'. It was ETA's offer of a ceasefire if the Spanish government met certain demands. These demands were the right to the self-determination of the Basque Country as an independent nation, the release of all Basque prisoners and the return of Basque refugees, and the reuniting of all the Basque lands on both sides of the border. 'That and no other is ETA's daily commitment in prisons, in exile and in the Basque society.'

The struggle was romantic, heroic. There was the David-and-Goliath appeal, and the charm of a fight hinged on to something so ancient and extraordinary as the Basque language. It was easy to see its attraction as a cause. Besides, the Arrano was the hottest bar in town; this was where the fun was; it would be easy to be sucked in. But it was only a short step into the vortex of terrorism. I couldn't get rid of the sickening image of Cosme Delclaux, the industrialist's son, locked in some 'citizen's prison' in the back of a factory or some half-built apartment block. I thought of the anguish of his wife and children, his own terror. His kidnapping had prompted pro-peace demonstrations throughout the Basque Country: HB and its affiliated Basque Union of Nationalist Workers were the only political organizations not to condemn it. The schoolteacher said HB 'neither condone nor condemn' ETA's violence, but the number of pictures of ETA 'heroes' on the wall revealed where allegiances lay.

In a way I envied their sense of immortality and mission. ETA represented an irresistible challenge to authority, not just anti-Spain, but anti-bourgeois, anti-nuclear, feminist, environmentalist. More than that, joining ETA had become a moral imperative, a signal of your impeccable Basque credentials, the sense of loyalty and identity, the martyred elite.

The teacher offered to show us somewhere to park for the night. But Richard seemed reluctant to get in his car.

'What's the matter?' I asked.

'The matter is that the man's drunk. We don't know where he's taking us. And we've left Xanthe asleep in the Mob.'

What was I thinking of?

That evening the Arrano was packed. Music screamed. Again we left Xanthe asleep in the Mob, outside. Our contact was late. We ordered beers. Young She Wolf indicated with a flattening gesture that we were to wait, the contact would come.

Her name was Idurre Torrealdai. She apologized for keeping us waiting. Richard offered her a beer, but she declined and ordered orange juice. She was strikingly different from everyone else in the bar. She was young and pretty with her auburn hair neatly cut, and she wore brown jeans and a conventional beige jacket. She wore feminine make-up. She worked in a travel agency. She had long white medieval hands, hands that looked as if they had been encased all her life in the softest gloves, yet she said she came from a family of workers. Her grandfather had worked in the armaments factory.

What was most surprising – and perhaps shouldn't have been – was that when she spoke, out came a strong Belfast accent.

'*That's* it!' she shouted over the music, with breathy Irish emphasis. 'I love Ireland. I'm so in love with it, it's something so special.'

'I suppose there are a lot of similarities. The religion, the weather . . .'

'That's it. And the ancient culture. I feel very at home there. We know that Northern Ireland and the Basque Country are not the same, but there are many similarities. Maybe an outlook and focus.'

'What are the differences?'

'What's that?'

I shouted it louder.

'Oh, differences. Well, we don't have the same sectarian divide here, and it's not a religious thing. Most of us are Catholic, Basques and non-Basques. I don't go to church myself. I'm a Marxist. But I respect that some people feel the need for religion, like my parents. We know we can't do everything the Irish do, but we can learn from each other.'

'Do you have many contacts with Sinn Fein?'

'*Oh* yes.'

'Is HB the Basque Sinn Fein?'

'*That's* it.'

Idurre sucked down the last of her cigarette then took Tallulah's hand and led us outside. Tallulah turned to give me one of her anxious-but-trying-to-be-pleased smiles and reached for my hand. I needed reassurance too. I had no idea where we were going.

We blinked in a brightly lit room of tables spiked with upended chairs. It would be quieter and less smoky, Idurre explained. There were photographs of the bombed Gernika. It occurred to me that the memory of their collective suffering was crucial to Basque identity. And there were more photographs of bearded men. They were founders of HB, and heroes of the Basque movement. They looked like bearded Palestinian martyrs.

HB owned the building but this room was rented out to a gourmet society. I laughed at the incongruity of a bourgeois activity taking place in this hotbed of militant socialism, but Idurre frowned.

'Haven't you heard about our Basque cooking?'

She introduced us to John, a weak-looking older man who she said was her boyfriend. He didn't speak English, and I didn't dare use Castilian. He spent the evening sitting alone in one corner, eating crisps and watching us, like a minder. Tallulah settled in my lap and fell asleep.

I explained to Idurre why we were here, travelling round Europe, the Basque region–

'There I must stop you,' she interrupted, holding up a long madonna hand. 'Not Basque region. Basque nation. We are talking not only about the free province of the Spanish state, but also about Navarra which has been divided from us within Spain, and about the three provinces of the Basque Country that have been separated from us by a political border and are now part of the French state.'

'OK, Basque nation.'

Idurre described herself as a militant activist. Her soft conventional appearance masked a dynamic, energetic, passionate woman. I couldn't see her staying with John for long.

Why, I asked her, did HB – and ETA – continue to fight when they appeared to have everything they wanted – Basque schools, Basque media? They had more autonomy than any other part of Spain.

'Because the oppression hasn't really changed. Did you know that under Franco we weren't even allowed to speak our own language? My mother was punished for speaking Basque.'

'How was she punished?'

Idurre refused to elaborate. Later I discovered that one favoured punishment was to shave women's heads and exhibit them to ridicule in the main square.

'Today there are political and economic reasons why we are not allowed to be free,' Idurre continued. 'We are richer and more successful than other parts of the Spanish state, which is why they want to hold on to us. We could easily survive alone. And that is what we want. To be socialist, that is to say Marxist, and free.'

'But what more do you want? You even have your own police force now.'

'I would say they aren't "our" police. The Guardia Civil trained them. And we don't have any proof' – Idurre lowered her soft Irish voice – 'but we know that some members of Israel's army also trained the Basque police. Very right wing. It's very frightening for us. They are tools of oppression. I suppose you know we have many kinds of police?'

We nodded. 'If you were being burgled, who would you call?' I asked.

'If I was Irish, I would call the IRA.'

For some reason we all laughed at this, like an explosion of tension.

'Does ETA function as a punishment squad, like the IRA?'

'Not at all. They are only a liberation army.'

I asked her about Gerry Adams, and her eyes shone. She had been lucky enough to meet him, and Martin McGuinness, but she had been translator to a lesser Sinn Fein luminary. Gerry Adams had, however, been to Gernika: the Irish liked coming to the Basque Country because they were so popular and felt so at home.

I got the impression that the more sophisticated militants of Northern Ireland were looked up to almost as leaders. Most of her friends had links with Cuba, but she considered Ireland her second home.

'Do ETA and the IRA train together?'

'That's it.'

I was intrigued and unnerved by this European underworld. Later a French Basque militant would give me copies of *Enbata*, a political journal that he wrote for, which carried news of militant separatists in Ireland, Brittany, Corsica. They all knew each other. An IRA bomber who blew himself up in the Strand had a Basque girlfriend; she turned up at his funeral. Idurre knew her. She lived near Getxo.

'And *Presoak*? What does it mean?'

'It's about our Basque prisoners. That's it. There's a campaign to improve their conditions in prison. To move them closer to home. Every time their families go to visit them, they have to travel all across Spain. Each time the families go, there are demonstrations. *Euskal presoak mugagabeko gose greban* means 'Basque prisoners on unlimited hunger strike' – they take turns to go on hunger strike to protest against the conditions. They are much worse treated than any other prisoners, beaten more often, tortured. Ultimately we want them to be given an amnesty and set free. Ultimately we want freedom for all Basques.'

For all I knew, Idurre herself was a member of ETA – she said it had thousands of members. She expressed no sympathy for Delclaux. But she was quick to dwell on the atrocities of GAL.

'Do you condone ETA's violence?' Richard persisted.

'HB neither condones it nor condemns it.'

A year before, a faction questioning the armed struggle had been voted down, since when HB had become even more radical. I was beginning to understand that Idurre couldn't condemn violence, because violence had become an expression of Basque identity. It went beyond loyalty to HB. Where ethnic boundaries are weak or threatened, and where an identity is weak and divided, it can be rejuvenated through violence. Violence has a power of its own. It creates its own cycle of reaction and repression, followed by more violence, which thrust Basque activists more closely together.

Richard pointed out that HB's share of the popular vote was declining, and that 20,000 people had come to Getxo to demonstrate against the Delclaux kidnapping, and she replied with details of a demonstration *she* had attended last Saturday in Bilbao for the release of the ETA prisoners. She also argued that Gesto por la Paz, which had organized the Getxo demonstration, was not really interested in peace, just in doing whatever was opposite to HB. She called it 'auto-opposition'. I didn't believe this. It sounded like political point scoring, a skewed paranoia.

'Quite apart from the man's suffering, what about the threat to foreign investment in the Basque Country, the threat to tourism?' Richard sounded aggressive. 'You're trying to haul yourselves out of industrial decline – isn't the violence just going to hold it back?'

Idurre was tough. 'We don't necessarily want foreign investment and tourism. They could both destroy our culture. What we want is independence, the power to run our country as we like.'

A meeting ended upstairs and bearded men bunched up on the landing, watching us over clip files. They resembled the fundamentalists on the walls; they resembled Gerry Adams. Many had learnt Basque not at home but in prison, where Adams learnt Irish. Maybe we looked odd: an earnest little group, Idurre and two strangers and their sleeping daughter, surrounded by tables and upended chairs. I hoped they could accept us. Richard looked like them with his thick black beard.

One year later all twenty-three HB leaders would be arrested, accused of collaborating with ETA, and jailed for seven years.

We turned back to Idurre. Richard asked if, with the breakdown of political borders under the EU, would they not achieve a kind of reunion with the Pays Basque without having to continue the armed struggle? Idurre was ambivalent. She was so caught up in the 'movement', fixated almost, that she was barely aware of the rest of Europe except as a homogenizing threat to the uniqueness of Basque culture.

'The French Basques are misled if they think they'll get anything from the EU. That's what the French government tells them to keep them sweet.'

Only one thing was certain: until they achieved independence, on their own terms, with the whole of the Basque nation reunited as a socialist country, the armed struggle would continue.

Tucked away in Gernika, she seemed isolated, out of touch. I tried to change the subject. I wasn't keen to seem critical, not while we were in that room with John watching over us. I was craven, and wanted her to like and trust us, not to think we were hectoring her. This wasn't the sort of place where you would be wise to disagree. But Richard persisted bravely.

'If you did achieve independence, would you send back all the non-Basque immigrants?'

'If they want to be here, and have the same rights as us, I think that's OK, but only so long as they want to be Basque. They must be real Basques.'

'And what does it mean to be Basque?'

'It's hard to say. We're thought to be very hard-working, very driven. But above all, it's the language. The language is the basis of every single culture. They should learn the language, participate. But in my opinion, many don't want it.'

'So if they didn't want to be real Basques, they would have to leave?'

'I don't know . . . maybe . . .'

It was as if she and her colleagues had been so busy with their heads down, battling away for their nation, that they hadn't noticed that ethnic cleansing of the kind she appeared to espouse was costing thousands of lives in Yugoslavia.

'Will you achieve independence?'

'I *must* think that. But there's a lot of work to do. Maybe my grandchildren will have it. Who knows?'

'That was good, wasn't it?' Richard said, as we carried the sleeping Tallulah back to the Mob.

'Yes, but I couldn't stop thinking about Gerry Adams.' I don't know why this bothered me. Perhaps it was because it was all too easy to empathize with a cause in which I was uninvolved; but as regards Northern Ireland, I found myself – by default, being English, Scottish, and Protestant – on the side of the enemy. Richard more so: there's even a town in Northern Ireland called Pomeroy.

We stayed that night on the Pablo Picasso Kalea. The plaintive carillon sounded each half-hour, an endless reminder of the sadness of this town's past.

We drove east through fishing towns with their gritty mix of old port and tower blocks, and through the resort of Zarautz. Zarautz gave me an uncertain feeling. It is to here that Carlos's conscience keeps forcing him to return, to the back room of a cinema where he has imprisoned his kidnap victim, a businessman with an English wife, and where Carlos murders him.

By evening we had reached Donostia. We parked for the night on the seafront, sheltered from behind by the steep Monte Urgull. After the storms, the road was strewn with seaweed and sand, and chunks of broken paving, but the waves were a good forty feet below us, and tame now. A fishing boat heading out to sea implied a favourable forecast.

While Richard put Xanthe to bed I went out with Tallulah. Monte Urgull shielded the bar-infested streets of the old town. Tallulah skipped beside me, excited to be out in the dark warm night. We ate tapas and admired babies under pink blankets asleep in pushchairs.

In a bookshop Tallulah lingered over picture books; for me there were works by Atxaga, though nothing in Basque. I bought an essay Atxaga had written about the difficulty of being a writer in a language without a literary tradition, with no basis and nothing to work from. He argued that the first duty of a literary language is to be unobtrusive, but if you lack enough antecedents you cannot create the habit of reading in Basque, so a writer who writes in Basque inevitably uses a language that is obtrusive, because of its rarity and everything it stands for. As a young writer he launched himself into the deep end, without realizing quite how deep it was, but he persisted, and created a literary market. He gave credit to the Basque linguists who had created *euskara batua* and thereby given

Basques a common literary language. 'The journey continues,' he wrote, 'and I think most of us believe that things will turn out well.'

Donostia was far more Spanish than Bilbao. I was lulled into a warm, Mediterranean feeling.

Then at midnight the storm revived. The Mob swayed; hail drilled our metal box. Richard put on his waterproofs and climbed on to the roof. Waves clawed at him, greedy for a victim. The wind heaved but he clung to the roof rack, and managed to get a rope over the chairs and bike seats. When he returned the door whipped out of his hand and slammed back against the Mob and towels flew off their pegs.

A police car crawled past, shafting a spotlight on to the sea wall, looking for breaches. No other cars were left here now.

Richard struggled back outside. In the teeth of the storm he fought to prepare the Mob for departure to somewhere safer. He undid stablizers, came off chocks, removed the silver screen from the windscreen, dismantled Xanthe's cot. He drove carefully as the sink was piled high with dirty dishes. I lay in bed cradling a child in each arm, blinds closed, as we cruised through the buffeting night, turning invisible corners, braking at invisible lights. Ours was a secret world. Outside our cocoon the storm-torn streets were deserted.

In the morning Tallulah was red-eyed with fatigue. She sat in her pushchair like an invalid, staring at the November waves. They were exhausted too. A tractor drove up and down the Playa de La Concha, filling a trailer with storm detritus.

We pushed our invalid (and backpacked Xanthe) to the far end of the bay. Here was what we had come to see: Eduardo Chillida's masterpiece, *Pienes del viento* (*Combs of the Wind*). I'd known his work since 1980, when for some reason I had bought a catalogue for a show at the Carnegie Institute in Pittsburgh. Chillida was little known in Britain but the cover photograph struck me. It was of one of these steel combs thrusting towards the Atlantic breakers. Another, hazy in spume, cupped its claws as though in prayer. In 1977 Chillida dug them into these rocks.

We climbed over brick terraces built against the cliff, braving waves that shot up through a blowhole. The combs were smaller than I'd imagined, but had a presence that was both grand and elemental. I liked the idea that they caught the wind as it streamed towards the city, and untangled it. But there was more than that.

Only now could I appreciate the Basqueness of the Combs. The upright arm, proud and at the same time spiritually reverent in the way it raised its chalice-like hand, also suggested the discoidal shape of a pagan Basque tombstone. Another comb was muscular and defiant, clenching its barbaric fist at the elements, yet allowing those elements to pass through and leave it unscathed. The third was like an anchor or knotted roots. They were heroic, standing alone on the craggy Basque coast, protecting the city. They were rugged, yet full of feminine curves; they were macho, yet fluid and full of air and open-ended mystery. Even the materials – steel for this sculpture, iron and granite for previous versions – were products of the Basque Country, the foundations of Basque wealth, the ore dug from Basque soil. 'Nere herri zaharrari,' Chillida wrote, 'nere aberri gazteari, nere lan osoa bihotz bihotzez opa diot.' 'To my old country, to my young homeland, I offer with all my heart my entire work.'

Chillida has had one-man shows throughout Europe and the USA, hobnobbed with Miró, Calder, and Chagall at the Fondation Maeght, exchanged works with Braque, exhibited with Rothko, shared prizes with Willem de Kooning, but he has remained Basque through and through. He was born here (in 1924), married a French Basque, has played goalie for the local team, and now reportedly lived on Monte Igueldo, the cliff above his monument. I longed to meet him, but was too intimidated to try. He was too grand and also too handsome. No, we would do better to stick with Atxaga, who in my mind resembled Chillida – tall, dark, with high forehead and deep-set eyes – but was less famous.

I managed to contact Atxaga's British publishers. Bernardo! He was the *most* wonderful man, spoke *excellent* English. And where did he live? Donostia! I was to call back for his number in a few days.

Over the Ría Bidasoa into France there was no border checkpoint, but at once the Basque Country was less rough, the towns prettier, the architecture more feminine. In place of tower blocks flung up beside a port, there were pretty houses carefully conforming to the local style, with bull's blood shutters and verandas occasionally painted a daring green. Few shops bore Basque names, and I missed the cheery red, white, and green Ikurriña. There were still bilingual signposts and occasional ETA graffiti, but the Basqueness was weaker, more self-conscious, more touristy. Voltaire's patronizing dismissal of the Basques as 'the little folkloric people who sing and dance' must have annoyed them for centuries. The language was in a bad way, with no official status. It seemed unfair. French Basques have been allowed to give their children Basque names only since 1993.

The blinds lowered on a beautiful day, the first for weeks. I felt lighter myself, happy to leave a sombre, oppressive culture for something more frivolous, more chatty.

Autumn sun saturated the gold woods hemming La Rhune. This is the westernmost mountain of the Pyrenees, and to Neolithic Basques one of the holiest – judging from the number of dolmens, stone circles, and tumuli. We made a picnic, and set off up it. Tallulah equipped herself by wearing one of her doll's dresses as a smock and filling her pockets with teddies peeking out of socks (their sleeping bags).

The views were soon exhilarating. Green hills tufted with golden trees undulated away to the snow-white canines of the Pyrenees. Immediately to our west spread the Atlantic, edged by the sunny port of St Jean de Luz, Donibane-Lohitzune in Basque, then in the distance the conurbation of Bayonne, Baiona in Basque, the northerly limit of the Basque Country. Autumn crocuses bloomed at our feet. Everything was luminous after weeks of rain, washed like a water-colour, the colours Pre-Raphaelite golds and browns and muted greens melting into russets and Indian reds, a romantic landscape of farmhouses and barns and crags and clouds and sheep. Griffon vultures were strips of fringed black pasted against the blue.

The valley way below cradled the rooftops of Sara, a village notorious since the days when Basques used these tracks to smuggle sheep and cows over the border. There's always been north–south co-operation. There was often marriage across the divide, land-use agreements, freedom of movement, transhumance. Because of the way the valleys run north–south, the Pyrenees were a linguistic bridge between the two Basque regions, rather than a barrier. The dialects run in north–south stripes, across the Franco-Spanish frontier. Someone in Sara would be better able to understand a Spanish Basque over the pass than a French Basque to the east.

During the Franco-Spanish wars of the eighteenth and nineteenth centuries, the valley people regularly refused to serve in their national armies, and instead warned their neighbours over the border of the approach of hostile troops.

More recently, they helped to smuggle ETA activists on the run. During the ETA trial for the assassination of Méliton Manzanas, ETA kidnapped the West German consul in Donostia, Eugen Biehl. They offered to release him unharmed in return for lenient treatment of the ETA defendants. Biehl was held captive in the Pays Basque, but he escaped and sought refuge in a café. Local French Basques noticed he was in his socks, and realized who he was. Instead of offering him shelter or summoning the French police, they immediately returned him to his ETA captives, and not a word was said. Later a deal was reached and Biehl released.

Sara also featured in Atxaga's novel *Obabakoak*, the first Basque novel ever to be translated into English. *Obabakoak* includes a dream-like short story about his encounter with the seventeenth-century Basque writer Pierre Axular, who was buried in Sara church. They are together on an island, which symbolizes the Basque language. A boat approaches, but some of the passengers pretend interest in the island, some are jealous of it, some are determined to destroy it, and others bemoan its smallness and fragility but do nothing to help it. It expressed something of the loneliness of being stuck with a language that almost no one understands.

I thought of our own mobile island. Tallulah seemed frustrated and confused by the wall of foreign sounds that surrounded her. Her parents were not what she needed: she needed people of her own size who were on her level of incomprehension, not just of the Spanish world, but of the grown-up world in general. It made my heart bleed for her, but there was little we could do. For a while we tried an imaginary friend who lived in her pocket, but this wasn't enough.

Now the going was hard, the ground shaly underfoot. Tallulah called it 'the crumble stumble'. She was starting to whine, so Richard was forced to heave himself along with Xanthe on his back, Tallulah under one arm, and his camera bag under the other.

We lunched on a ridge. Richard parked the snoring Xanthe in the shelter of a ruined sheep byre. Now we looked down on the vultures; they prowled, croaking, in a rock-hugging flock, wings spanning up to eight feet. I quickly picked Xanthe up and held her safe in my arms. We were above the tree line, exposed and vulnerable. I dared not look down. Before having children this would not have bothered me in the least. Now I worried that Tallulah might topple over. Everything hid danger for my children. I watched over them constantly, and this watchfulness made me tense.

We headed east, into the remoter foothills of the Pyrenees beside the swollen River Nive. Torrential rain permitted the sun through for an occasional brilliant shaft, then closed in again. It got us all down.

In the *marie* at Esterençuby I enquired if there was anyone local who was expert in Basque matters. Two ladies exchanged glances over their desk.

'Monsieur Etchemendy?'

The other one laughed. '*Bien sur!* Monsieur Etchemendy!'

He was a teacher and novelist with a *maison natale* in Esterençuby. We arranged to meet at his home near Mauléon the next morning.

I also phoned Atxaga's publishers and got his agent's phone number in Barcelona. She was out. From then on, we would phone her repeatedly. She didn't know where he was.

Wrong turns through autumn foothills ever more remote took us to the end of a steep drive. No surprise that his name in Basque was Etxemendi, meaning Mountain House. A traditional Basque chalet was wrapped in a red-ochre veranda, with the entrance on the first floor, bedrooms below.

Madame Etchemendy retreated shyly after providing Xanthe and

Tallulah with her grandchildren's toys. Different toys! They got down on the floor for some serious play.

Jean Etchemendy was in his fifties. He taught agriculture and economics, but his interests were wide-ranging in all things Basque – linguistics, literature, history, singing, and politics. He was involved with the formation of *euskara batua*, and had published two novels in Basque, his latest selling 5000 copies, which I thought pretty impressive. He knew personally thirty-three people writing (and being published) in Basque, but he acknowledged that Atxaga was unique in managing to earn a living from it.

Monsieur Etchemendy was not physically prepossessing. He had reddish hair and narrow features, a down-turned mouth and teeth that sloped inwards, and a faint stoop. One thumb was a stump. But he had a fiery look in his eye. He launched into a passionate tirade against the French state, airing grievances going back to the eighth century. Most of his bitterness was directed towards the French secret service. He described it as Machiavellian. Young unemployed Basques who had compromised themselves in some way were used to infiltrate ETA and other Basque organizations both as spies, and also to carry out atrocities – bombings and shootings – in order to discredit the Basques. He could discuss it with us because we were outsiders, he said, but not with colleagues or friends. You didn't know who was who. It was too dangerous. One young man he knew had recently mysteriously disappeared, and Etchemendy was convinced he had been 'made' to disappear by the French police. He said it had taken him years to understand this, but now everyone knew it. The Spanish police were brutal but the French were cunning. ETA itself, he claimed, was now financed by Madrid and Paris, and manipulated by both.

'Sounds like Romania.'

'Yes, it sounds like paranoia, but it's true.'

His own writing was overtly anti-French. This was not a problem, he said, but if a writer had altercations with the police, his writing would be held against him.

We sat in his living room, typically Basque with white-tiled floor, white bobbly textured walls, hefty dark cupboards and chests, and the odd Catholic ornament. A coffee table was draped in Basque linen, old and delicate. I moved it out of Xanthe's reach and, when the table was bare, she laid her cheek on it and rested there awhile. She and Tallulah were tired and hungry. We had brought a box of *pains chocolats* and envisaged enjoying them over café au lait, but they vanished into the kitchen.

Most people here spoke Basque, he said, and considered themselves Basque first, French second. When he was at school he was beaten on the hand with a ruler when he spoke Basque. Catechism and confirmation classes were held in Basque, which provoked conflict between the teacher and the priest (he punched his fist into his palm, though he didn't mean exactly that). The church was always pro-Basque. Now, he said, there was more interest in *choses basques*, it was being taught in some schools, and you could take your baccalaureate in Basque, in certain subjects.

He glared around the sitting room at nothing in particular. There were growing desires not for independence, which was unsustainable, but for autonomy. There was not even a Basque *département*! During the French Revolution the Basque provinces of Lapurdi, Zuberoa, and Be Naparroa, which had always been deeply conservative and Catholic, were hostile to revolutionary innovations, and many Basques became victims of the Terror. The provinces were therefore abolished, and merged with the non-Basque region of Béarn in a *département* now called Pyrenées-Atlantique. They lost their identity. In official terms, the Pays Basque did not exist.

The Basque political press was full of the campaign to establish a Basque *département*, much of it with the support of the PNV over the border.

With twisted logic, he said that in the past he had espoused violence because the violence of ETA and its affiliates was as nothing compared with the violence of the French state that had destroyed an entire culture. However, he now despised violence. For him the way forward was democratic. He cupped his hands above his head and said that with the help of the EU what they wanted would fall to them, eventually. This was what Richard had suggested to Idurre in Gernika, but she had been too cut off, too blinkered to see it that way. With the breakdown of political borders, there were already cross-frontier businesses and political parties. Already there were signs that the two halves of the Basque Country were coming together. They had very different lifestyles, Monsieur Etchemendy acknowledged – the French Basque economy relied on tourism and agriculture, the Spanish Basques on industry – but nevertheless links both political and economic were growing apace. The French Basques saw their Spanish counterparts achieving autonomy, their own police force, their *ikastolak*, and they wanted these things too. *Euskadi* – the Basque state – was now closer to being a reality than at any time in history.

While he was talking, I noticed that for the first time Xanthe had taken five or six steps unaided, arms aloft. It was a great moment. Richard and I both cried out. But Monsieur Etchemendy was in full flow, and it required all my concentration to keep up with his thickly accented French.

We admired a new conservatory full of lobelias and geraniums. Here Monsieur Etchemendy worked overlooking the pregnant hill behind the house.

'I want to tell you something special. Something I have kept secret until now.' He looked around furtively. 'I can tell you because you are sympathetic to Basque, and because you are not a threat to my work. I don't want other people to steal my ideas.'

He opened a notebook.

'English and Basque!' he declared triumphantly. 'I've been working on this for some time. Connections between the languages. There are many linguistic links that I have discovered for the first time. No one else has done this before. Look! If I break down the agglutin-ated words, you can see how it makes sense.'

The fact that he didn't speak English had not deterred him. To prove his point, in his curly French script he transcribed the verb 'to be' into my notebook in Basque and English.

Basque	conglomerate	English
niz	ni-iz	I am (is)

hiz	hi, yi – iz	you are (is)
da(r)	d-are	he is (are)
girare	gu-are	we are
zirare	zu-are	you are
dirare	dir-are	they are

His etymological proposals looked far-fetched to me. No, no, he insisted, look at this: *aho*, meaning 'mouth', and *ots*, meaning 'noise', together made up the word *ahots*, meaning 'voice' – mouth noise. *Ahots* sounds like 'voice'. He looked up at me, eyes shining. I smiled enthusiastically, but I didn't get it. Did the Basques not like being on their own? Did they fear that their linguistic isolation meant that their language lacked legitimacy in the eyes of the world? I don't know. But finding such connections seemed to be a national pastime.

'You must have a drink!' Etchemendy exclaimed suddenly. We returned to the sitting room, and Madame produced a bowl of crisps, which the girls devoured, and a bottle of whisky. It transpired that she was not Basque, but had learned a little of the language, and always encouraged their children to speak it with their father. He was a man obsessed. We raised our glasses.

'We must drink,' Monsieur Etchemendy announced, 'because what you are doing is so important. You are going to disseminate the Basque story to the world.'

We followed the River Bidouze towards Mauléon. We needed somewhere to sleep. There was a track to the right. A sign forbade vehicles but Richard ignored this, shifted our workhorse into first gear and cruised up the mountainside. Squat Basque ponies called *pottocks* glanced up in surprise, and vultures croaked over a sheep's carcass. Close-up the vultures looked hideous, their oversized wings hanging like a voluminous cape, their necks puckered with genital-like skin thrust towards their prey.

As the drop into the valley grew sheer, I began to lose my nerve. It was not only the perilous gradient, but also the possibility of snow. We could be cut off up there, stranded for days. There was no shelter: what about the wind? But Richard kept on. He had to: there was nowhere to turn.

As we reached the top, at 705 metres, a flock of vultures flapped out of a wind-torn pine, sinister harbingers of death. On the sole flat space Richard managed to turn and face downhill: if we had a problem we could at least bump start back down the mountain. He tucked us in below the summit, in the lee of the wind, and switched off the engine.

Silence. Just our own breathing, the clock ticking, me scratching my scalp.

There was nothing here but a white barn-like structure, bare and forlorn. We had seen it from Monsieur Etchemendy's house, and marvelled that anything could be built so high. We went out in the dark, once the girls were asleep, and hoisted each other up to peer through the windows. It was a chapel to St Anthony, patron saint of lost things.

Way below towns glimmered. We surveyed them from our splendid isolation. To the west, facing into the wind over our crest, we could make out the lighthouses at St Jean de Luz and Biarritz. Looking the other way, south-east over the Haute-Soule and then along the Pyrenean ridge back, the mountains stood silhouetted against the moonlight. They were enveloped in a secret blackness. There were no streetlights, no headlights, not even a flickering candle. This was how these mountains have looked for thousands of years, since Palaeolithic Basques traversed them with their sheep, or since the perfidious Basques melted away after slaughtering Charlemagne's Franks. I felt like a cave dweller, alone in an empty world, and I felt a shiver of fear, an inexplicable Palaeolithic fear of blankness, the unknown. I hastened back to our Mob.

I said, 'I bet the highest mountain will be covered in snow in the morning.' And it was.

I fretted about the cold. The children were encased in woollen sleep suits, and Richard and I kept on our thermal underwear. We were permitted a few blasts from the heater – not many in case they flattened the battery. We lifted Xanthe's blanket screen to warm her compartment. When she woke the windows dripped with condensation and her hands were icy.

Dawn broke when fingers of light thrust through the clouds to prod the earth. Mist lurked in crevices. Tallulah stood by the window, entranced, Xanthe beside her, both patting the glass.

It was a relief to be back at our beloved Laga. We were welcomed into the Toki-Alai like long-lost friends, in time for another spoiling Sunday lunch. Now everyone had left. If we belonged anywhere now, we belonged here.

It would have made sense to continue our journey eastwards to Catalonia, but there was still Atxaga to track down. Atxaga, it transpired, no longer lived in Donostia, but in a village near Vitoria, far away to the south. Could we go there? His agent felt this was unnecessary since Atxaga was currently in Mexico. So that was that. We had returned for nothing. Even our sturdy ox couldn't make it that far.

But the agent kept us hanging on. Atxaga was due to speak at a Basque literary festival in Durango in mid-December. She gave us a Bilbao agent's fax number.

Rivers bulged and broke their banks. Foliage of shredded plastic caught on lower branches and trailed there when the swell subsided, only to be swept on when the rain next fell. Even Unai said he had never known it so wet. It had been raining solidly, remorselessly, for six weeks. We longed to leave the Basque Country, but were trapped here until the Durango festival. Even Xanthe was a bit less cheerful than usual; because she was never with other children, she was never ill, but now she had her first snotty nose. Tallulah, on the other hand, never seemed able to recover.

I was increasingly obsessed with my itchy scalp. I had lice. Soon we were all infested. In such close quarters, our whole beings felt infested. We filled up with water in a garage and doused ourselves in anti-lice shampoo. Only afterwards I read the warning: do not use if allergic to lindane. Lindane, I recalled, was an ingredient in wood treatment, but had been banned in Britain as a carcinogen. I wondered for a moment which I should be more anxious about, lice or lindane, then emptied the bottle over my head.

We followed signs to a car park, then made our way into Durango's rough town centre. Washing festooned the balconies of overhead flats. People coming towards us carried plastic bags of books and posters. We followed the empty-handed crowd in the opposite direction into a marquee full of stalls and people. They were mostly young with children on their shoulders, beards, and big boots. I felt at home here: they looked like us. This was the literary market Atxaga had been pivotal in creating. The mood was excited, and people clustered round the offerings of different publishers and record producers. There were new publications in Basque, and translations into Basque ranging from Josef Skvoreky to Shakespeare to children's books. The enthusiasm was palpable. Atxaga had a new book out, and people were snapping up copies; he would be here, somewhere, since he was coming to talk about it. I fought my way to his publishers' stall and caught someone's eye.

'What should I be looking for?'

'Someone short, fat, with curly hair, in his mid-forties.'

He didn't fit my image. He didn't sound like the sexy Carlos. He didn't sound like a latter-day Chillida. I battled across the marquee to a seminar room where he was due to speak, but there was no sign of a short fat middle-aged man. After waiting so long, coming all this way, I was determined not to miss him, and one of the technicians agreed to summon Atxaga over the megaphone. No response. Another technician confided that Atxaga would not show: he hated this sort of thing.

'Then,' I said, indicating the already filled rows of seats, 'there'll be lots of disappointed people.'

Now it was standing room only, and the clock ticked by. It was like awaiting a pop star. Then the technician waved from the door: 'He's here!' And he was: round face, curly mop of hair, nothing like Carlos. He was harassed – nervous and late. It wasn't a good time to approach him, just before he was due to speak.

'Go on,' Richard urged me. 'Follow him. You've got to do it. You'll never have another chance.'

Xanthe was on my hip. I approached. He was immediately charming, but his handshake was soft. He was soft all over. He apologized for not returning my faxes and calls, but after getting back from Mexico he was stuck in snow for five hours. He mimed the boring wait, drumming his fingers on an imaginary steering wheel.

'Can we meet after the talk? I've been trying to track you down for weeks.'

He looked hunted. 'No. No. Not tonight. But I'll tell you what I'll do. I'm going to give you my personal fax number.' He turned towards a sinister-looking youth with acne-scarred skin and dark glasses and a large gold watch. He resembled a Mafioso bodyguard. 'This is my Bilbao manager, Alejandro Zugaza. The fax number is his, but it will be passed straight on to me.'

I studied the 'manager's' card: I had already used this number several times to no avail.

'Call me. We can arrange another meeting.'

Why, I wondered, was he so secretive? What was he hiding from? Was it to do with ETA? Or was he simply fanatical about his privacy? Who exactly was this man? I wanted to ask him these questions, but now he was being swept on to the podium, launching into a speech in Basque.

I had a premonition that our meeting was never going to happen.

We struggled into the cold night air. It smelled of roasting chestnuts. Tallulah noticed a poster advertising philosophy classes with a picture of a naked man, head in hands, kneeling in the centre of a road that narrowed to the horizon.

'What's it about?'

'He's thinking about things, like "Why am I here?", "Where am I going?" '

'Why am I here?' she echoed. 'Where am I going?' A frown puckered the white space between her blue eyes. 'Why doesn't he just get in his car and find out?'

NINE

A Time of Inconvenience, at an Inconvenient Time

In the cloister of La Seu Vella we stood well back from the glass-less arches with their exquisite Gothic tracery. I held on to a stone column, and tried not to take flight over the dust-blown *huerta* that stretched from Lleida's hazy industrial fringe into a beige sky.

The honey-coloured sandstone, the decay, the eccentricity, the exoticism, the monumentality: it could have been India. From the base of the Moorish *zuda*'s perpendicular crag rose a cacophony of hooters, squealing brakes, metal shutters crashing for lunch, barking dogs, a crying child. Even a group of men loitering in the car park had dark-skinned Indian looks.

It was less like a cloister than a Mogul palace courtyard; I am a member of a harem; Akbar reclines on silk cushions sipping sherbet . . .

A crying child.

Richard was running back through the nave on to the paved *plaça* that descends in tiers to where we left the Mob. To where we left Tallulah in it, alone. To get here had meant a four-day haul across desolate sierras, hundreds of miles of fawn mud, the Mob only just holding its own against gusts of wind. And now that we'd arrived, she didn't want to see La Seu Vella. She was sick of views, sick of cathedrals, sick of us. So we went to see it on our own. Now she had unlocked the Mob and was lost and screaming in the acres of stone, dwarfed by the immense Gothic portal, terrified by a well-meaning nun.

Later I could hardly bear to think clearly about what happened, and the might-have-beens. I was racked with guilt. I felt it was a bad omen for our sojourn in Catalonia. After Richard rescued her distraught little figure, the police drew up. They advised us to move on; the place was full of thieves. Gypsies, they said.

I promised myself that when we reached Barcelona we would go to the park, go to the zoo, or swimming, give Tallulah a fix of child friendly activities. Christmas.

We were well into the Christmas spirit. The Mob was festooned in tinsel and streamers and dangling with Father Christmases and angels made of painted dough. In Durango we had found a paper Christmas tree that we decorated with red bows and bobbles. But how were we to drive across Spain with a fully decorated Christmas tree? As ever, the resourceful Richard found a solution: he sewed it on to the back of one of the seats.

The Mob climbed through pines until the globular rocks of Montserrat gleamed smooth and bald around us. We had to park beside a barrier above the serrated gorge that plunged to the River Llobregat and do the last stretch on foot. Then we were swept into the Montserrat machine. Car parks, cavernous restaurants, cafés, hotels, shops, a post office, funicular and cable car, a monastery, a baroque basilica, and all for the sake of a tiny black Madonna, not even the original, only a copy. At first I felt Protestant distaste for this conjunction of Catholicism and cash, but as we were funnelled with the hordes along the side aisles of the basilica, and propelled upstairs to the tiny chapel overlooking the altar and neared *La Moreneta* herself, I began to catch something of the near hysteria around me, the fervour and excitement.

A wedding was in full swing below. The congregation wore black furs, the bride white. Tallulah wanted to stay and watch through the grilles, we could see the bride's bowed glossy head, but the people behind pressed us forward. There was *La Moreneta* in her little octagonal inner sanctum just ahead. A young man bowed and kissed her, mumbled a prayer and was swept on. Now it was our turn. Her large solemn head, too big for her tiny body, gave her a touching childlike look; her hand, holding a ball – an orb, an apple, the earth – was presented through an opening in her glass cage for the faithful to kiss, and their lips had worn it down.

Then we were forced on, down past banks of candles shimmering in tubes of red, green, and yellow plastic, a magical coloured quiver, then back out into the cloister.

The cloister walls throbbed as the church bell tolled. Another wedding was nearly over; dark-suited guests congregated outside the west door, black hair elaborately embroidered with combs. As if given a signal, they semicircled the door and a couple ran out, clutching each other, shielding their heads from a hail of rice. Three different brides were awaited in a queue by three bridal cars, one a big tax-haven Mercedes from Andorra, a Catalan principality.

We followed tracks through evergreen oaks, the eastern end of the Pyrenees glinting on the horizon, past shrines built to remind us of the mysteries of the rosary. Between the shrines nestled little memorials to the Catalan great and good – composers, artists, writers. Because that is the thing about Montserrat: it is not only the most-visited Catholic shrine in Spain, it has also become the spiritual heart of Catalonia, the symbol of Catalan nationalism. Up here among the misshapen rocks, Catalanism hid out during the Franco era: Montserrat was the only church allowed to celebrate Mass in Catalan, the only place where couples could get married in their own language, the only place where they could dance their fawn-like *Sardana*. Gradually Catalans blurred the edges between a holy shrine and a Catalan one: the Catalan cause became a moral and spiritual crusade.

Initially the Catholic Church had supported Franco's National Catholicism, and collaborated in the post-civil war process of stripping Catalonia of its separate identity. But that support amongst Catalonia's clergy was not unanimous. The first sign of ambivalence took place here in 1947 during celebrations to mark the enthrone-ment of the Virgin, an event that was to become the first mass mobilization of Catalan nationalism after the civil war. Seventy thou-sand people congregated on the mountain in front of one of Franco's ministers and the Papal Legate, to be addressed in outlawed Catalan. There was nothing Franco's men could do. Their embarrassment increased when someone unfurled from an inaccessible peak the four red stripes of the banned Catalan flag.

Nevertheless, it was not until the 1960s, after the Second Vatican Council denied the legitimacy of National Catholicism, that the bishops began to dissociate themselves from Franco's dictatorship. In 1963 the Abbot of Montserrat, Aureli M. Escarré, opened fire against the Franco regime in *Le Monde* and was forced into exile. But by then Spain had started to secularize, so no one cared so much about the Church's position any more – it was too late.

Down into the raffish stink of Barcelona's rush hour. In view of what happened later, we should have paid more attention to *La Moroneta*. We should have kissed her hand, asked forgiveness.

We spent the night in the only free space we could find, on a bus stop on the dual carriageway Ronda Litoral that hurtled alongside the port of Barceloneta. The next day I kept my promise and took Tallulah to the zoo. She was in a sort of heaven. While we were away, someone removed the back window and stole everything of value. Everything except Richard's Leica, which he sensibly had with him, and my valuable but uninsured Apple PowerBook, which I kept locked in our under-seat strong box.

We were shattered. But it was important to hide the break-in from Tallulah. Xanthe was too young to understand, but Tallulah was easily frightened. Although she sometimes terrorized us, she was an exceptionally sensitive flower: lily-white skin, rosebud lips, slender form, easily wilted. It was vital that she should not become more afraid than she already was of tucking up in strange places every night. So while Richard spent the next few days dealing with police, passport replacements, credit card companies, repairs to the Mob, all delayed by the approach of Christmas, I kept the girls amused. We found a swimming pool and the Parc de la Ciutadella that Tallulah declared was nearly as lovely as Battersea Park, which was really saying something.

Richard and I lay in our metal box on the mean streets of Barcelona, our heads level with the legs of passers-by who, we now suspected, bore us malign intent. We listened to every conversation, every approaching footstep. Drunks bashed the walls, and each time Richard would start out of bed, reaching for our only weapon, a sacred stick from Madagascar that was designed to scare off evil spirits when brandished in their direction; it was also capped with a lump of horn so would be an effective cosh if we ever dared use it. Then the voice would recede, and he'd climb back into bed, both our hearts racing.

The burglary added to my feeling of being infested: I was still obsessed by lice, and now Xanthe had worms too. We were infested inside and out.

We had a week before joining friends here for Christmas so we fled south to Tarragona. Plan for the week: park up, hang out, sit around, do nothing, take in the view.

We found a patch of waste ground between the Roman blocks of the city wall and a row of windowless hovels with tin roofs. Others knew of this waste patch. Gypsy families came and went, and others; used condoms lay like squashed slugs in the dirt. It wasn't salubrious, but looking one way we could see the illuminated cathedral, and the other the Costa Daurada. We rode a rampart five hundred feet above the Mediterranean.

We hadn't intended to sightsee, but we couldn't resist the draw of the cathedral. It squatted, unfinished, like a tuskless elephant confined by little streets. Inside it soared with mysterious gloom. We had it to ourselves. Candles glimmered in chapels. Like La Seu Vella it was in the Transitional style, between Romanesque and Gothic; perhaps it was this unfinished, transitional feeling that made it seem so alive. Perhaps it was also the exquisite fifteenth-century altarpiece carved from alabaster and limestone, wonderful both in detail and as a soaring golden whole. The details ranged from perfect angels with meekly folded hands and feathered wings to minute bugs and animals entwined within the filigree.

The cathedral was built on a Moorish mosque that was built on a Roman temple. Medieval houses were built on Roman masonry that was built on unhewn cyclopean Iberian blocks: the strata of Catalan history were on view just beside our Mob. Inside the Archaeological Museum I studied models of Tarraco in its heyday, capital of Roman Spain, a mass of mosaic-floored villas, a vision of splendour and pleasure: most of the statues were of Bacchus or Eros. This was Catalonia's frolicsome heritage, not the dark, dank, obscure taciturnity of the Basques.

The Roman lettering on inscriptions was clear and unfussy, and the Catalan lettering was the same. No funny archaic script for Catalan: Catalan is not a marginalized folkloric language, but normal, confident, mainstream. Its only idiosyncrasy is the full stop between double 'l's – 'l.l' – to guide pronunciation ('l' as opposed to 'll' which sounds like 'y').

It is a Romance language like Castilian, but it is not a dialect of Castilian, as Francoists claimed. It is a splendid independent language, closer to Occitan, with its own dialects such as Valencian, Majorcan, and Rossellonès, and with a vast body of literature, both medieval and modern.

In the museum there were few concessions to Castilian – only once or twice did I notice a translation. Catalan has not just survived, but triumphed. Catalan is a major success story.

While organizing new passports in the British consulate in Barcelona, Richard had encountered a frustrated Italian who had been unable to find a Castilian school for his daughter. There were none. In the previous two years, Catalonia had gone from being bilingual to monolingual. There were no dual road signs: all were in Catalan. On a road sign for Lleida someone had scrawled the Castilian 'Lérida'. So it's come to that, I thought: the Castilians having to fight back. The Italian complained that whereas Castilian could be used not only all over the rest of Spain but also in most countries in South America, Catalan was of limited use, but the Catalans shrug and reply that Catalan is as useful as many state languages. After all, the population of Catalonia, a burgeoning, flourishing, dynamic region, is the same as that of Finland: seven million people. The Italian father was not convinced: he was looking for a British school instead – but there was none.

Catalan's success came despite the hiatus of the early Franco years, when Catalonia was subjected to a vicious form of cultural cleansing. As in the Basque Country, everything Catalan was prohibited –

books, press, theatre, radio, songs, flags, folklore, dance, history, but above all language. Speaking Catalan in public became an offence. A Catalan could legally be thrown off a tram in Barcelona by a Spanish-speaking tram guard for speaking his or her own language. The University of Barcelona lost its Catalan teaching staff, and many primary school teachers were transferred to the rest of Spain, while teachers from Castile or Extremadura were imported to replace them, as agents of de-Catalanization. Between 1938 and 1953, 3800 Catalans, mostly minor officials, were executed by Spanish military tribunals. Now it looked as if Catalan sought revenge.

How had the language managed such resilience? It had been an incredible struggle, political and cultural, and one that the Catalans were proud of. It was a struggle that was even bigger than it seemed, because Franco's repression was nothing new, it merely stepped up a campaign of repression and assimilation by both France and Spain that had been going on for centuries.

Unlike the Basque Country, Catalonia was never an isolated stronghold, but a thoroughfare between Moors and Christians, Iberia and the Mediterranean, north and south. Apart from the sea, it had no clear frontier. Nevertheless, by the eleventh century the region from Perpignyà (Perpignan in French) down to Valencia, was referred to in documents as Catalonia. During the Middle Ages it became the dominant Mediterranean power, and until the eighteenth century maintained its independent institutions, currency, customs, and tax systems, and, crucially for modern Catalonia, it maintained Catalan as the official language. Crucial because the Catalan sense of identity, like that of so many European tribes, depends not on race or on religion but on language. Basque nationalists have race as well as language as their defining collective identity; Catalan nationalists have only language. In his book *Construir Catalunya*, Jordi Pujol, the Catalan freedom fighter and now President of Catalonia, defined Catalanism as a 'fact of mentality, of language, of feelings. It is a historic fact, and it is a fact of spiritual ethnicity. Finally it is a fact of will. In our case, however, it is in an important sense an achievement of language.'

Castile always hated and resented Catalan separatism, and eventually, after a year-long siege by Franco-Spanish troops, managed to subjugate the region in 1714. Rosselló and Cerdenya, north of the Pyrenees, had already been annexed by a centralizing French government, and now Castilian laws and centralism were imposed on the south by the Spanish King Philip V. Reprisals against the Catalans were harsh. They were far more heavily taxed than Castilians, and decrees were passed against public use of the language.

Even so Catalan remained the dominant tongue. In the nineteenth century Castilian became the language of instruction in schools, but Catalan still managed a comeback.

The *Renaixença* was Catalonia's nineteenth-century literary movement, fostered (as always) by ideas of Romanticism. It was a movement fuelled by the burgeoning wealth of a newly industrialized Catalonia, by a powerful middle class who espoused the values of industriousness, thrift, and initiative – values that Catalans boast of today. This industrious class enjoyed a sense of superiority to the rest of still backward Spain, and this added to the sense of a separate identity, of Catalanism, which was given literary encouragement by the *Renaixença*.

The movement transformed written Catalan from an archaic language far from spoken Catalan, without standard rules for grammar and spelling, into a modern literary language.

In the early nineteenth century not only was written Catalan pretty anarchic, only the tiny proportion of Catalans who were literate also read it. Most of these had been educated in Castilian. But in 1814 a Catalan grammar was published, then in 1832 the New Testament, and a year later a poem by Aribau called '*Oda a la Pàtria*' which had perhaps the most profound impact of all by (unintentionally) identifying language and homeland.

The Catalan movement grew, and saw the revival of the medieval Jocs Florals, the poetry contests with their annual prizes, aimed at stimulating interest in the language, like a Welsh Eisteddfod. Literary quality was not great; what mattered more was quantity, and also the politically correct sentiment of the day, which was patriotism.

Catalan faced further setbacks under Primo de Rivera in the 1920s, when public use of the language and flag were again banned – even

Barcelona's Law Society was dissolved for not having published its list of members solely in Spanish. This only encouraged separatism, and Catalonia achieved its apogee with its short but intense period of self-government leading up to the Spanish civil war. Then Franco arrived.

After the civil war, 60,000 Catalans found themselves in exile in France or South America, or in concentration camps within Spain. Opposition to Franco withered away, partly because of his military power, partly because the Catalans fought amongst themselves. The pre- and post-civil war era witnessed strife between a tedious and bewildering plethora of acronyms – POUM, ACO, CCMA, FSFC, LOAPA, FNC, PCE, MSC, UDC. These divisions may have been a mark of laudable Catalan individuality, but they seriously hindered Catalonia's struggle to re-establish democracy.

Franco was confident that by cutting off the majority of the Catalan population from its language – in schools, media, politics – he would succeed in withering Catalan national awareness. And indeed, by the 1950s, the new generation was illiterate in its own mother tongue, and considered Spanish the sole language of culture. The spoken language was corrupted, and they were ignorant of Catalan cultural heritage and history.

Nevertheless, Catalan triumphed. To rediscover it was a huge effort, but it was one the Catalans were prepared to undertake.

Franco's dictatorship was increasingly seen as the negation of collective Catalan identity. Clandestine cultural, political, and militant movements got underway, and succeeded thanks, above all, to Catalan will. Despite fascist attacks on bookshops, publishers, and other cultural organizations in Barcelona and Valencia up until the mid-1970s, there were congresses, prizes, thousands of Catalan organizations in labour and student movements, a tireless programme of awareness-raising, strikes, and political chaos. One of the first popular impulses came in the late 1950s with a resurgence of Catalan folk songs and early rock music; this was young Catalonia, singing in its own tongue, defying the complacent middle-aged middle classes who were still content to kowtow to the Franco regime.

Franco died in November 1975 and, after emptying every cellar of every celebratory bottle of cava, Catalonia began its painful process of rebirth. In 1979 a referendum ratified the Catalan Statute of Self-Government.

There were economic crises, infighting, but with entry into the EU in 1986, and the public works project needed to provide the infrastructure for the Barcelona Olympics, Catalonia flourished. Catalanization flourished too. The number of Catalan speakers swelled sharply. Catalan media took hold and official use spread. Although Spanish still remains the dominant tongue, there has been a huge increase in the number of Catalan books published, and over a hundred public and private radio stations now broadcast in Catalan.

Although a separate language, Catalan's resemblance to Castilian is another reason for its success. Castilian immigrants have always learned Catalan with ease, and quickly become Catalan themselves, unlike the Castilian immigrants into the Basque Country who find themselves faced with a language unlike any they have ever encountered. And unlike the Basques, who traditionally feared that their language, their race – and their morals – would be corrupted by incomers, the Catalans have embraced immigrant workers and turned them into fellow Catalans.

And like the English, the Catalans themselves have always been in a state of perpetual evolution.

Catalonia has also been hugely successful economically. Unlike the Basques, the Catalans feel so self-confidant that they see no need for terrorism. The Catalans do not seek independence. They are too pragmatic to break away from Spain; instead they choose to protect their autonomy by running the country. Direct contact with Europe has helped Catalonia to begin to escape from gradual absorption by Spain; Catalan nationalists hope for a utopian future in the eventual dissolution of conventional nation states, and in the reconstruction of the historic territories of nations, based on their languages.

We were swept unwillingly along the main road to Valls. Richard noticed an unmarked gateway to the right. We turned up the dirt track, branches of umbrella pines slashing the Mob, unable to believe that this was the way to the magnificent Roman aqueduct of Les Ferreres. Then there it was, a golden dart flashing across the wooded valley.

As it left the valley its single tier deepened to two and then, where the valley was deepest, to three. Along a narrow trough at the top the Romans channelled water from the Gaya River to Tarraco. Tallulah and I walked to its middle, 124 feet high, where I suddenly lost my nerve. My legs loosened, I couldn't look down and I couldn't go on. Tallulah ran blithely ahead, and I had to cover my eyes; I couldn't watch, even though the parapets lining the trough were taller than her. I crawled back. Richard took Xanthe in the backpack but I couldn't stand the sight of that either: Xanthe had no harness. I had to summon him back and take Xanthe off him. It was absurd. Before having children I'd have run along it without a second thought.

It was a strangely deserted place. The previous April we had fled from tourist hordes at the Pont du Gard in France, but here, beside an aqueduct of similar date and only a few feet lower, there was nobody. Not a place to park, not a litterbin, just a stony track. Closer inspection around its base revealed the remains of a bench and spotlights, but all had been vandalized. There were remnants of campfires too and smashed bottles. The place was despoiled. The aqueduct itself was hung with ivy and brambles, and weeds sprouted from its masonry. Topping the hill beyond were the dwarfing towers of the new university. Later, the full moon turned the arches from gold to silver, but the ancient magic was desecrated by university spotlights, and by howling cars on the brand-new motorway.

It was happening throughout Tarragona: the skeletal arms of cranes constructing residential blocks, obliterating the view and belittling the Roman city. One day we saw a suited man with a clipboard inspecting our little spot, so by now even our condom-spattered waste ground will have gone.

It was happening throughout Catalonia. I was beginning to look at everything with a premature nostalgia. Catalonia was a victim of its success. I couldn't warm to it.

*

We celebrated Christmas with friends in Barcelona's Barri Gòtic. It was a fun-filled cava-fuelled interlude. We dined on goose and tobogganed in the Pyrenees. Tallulah had a week-long fix of English children and their toys. She was in heaven.

I shopped for presents in the market in front of the cathedral, and was surprised to find rows and rows of obscene terracotta men squatting with their pants down. Each was accompanied by its pyramidal turd. A straight-faced stallholder explained that he was *Caganer*, 'the Shitter', and a regular at Catalan Christmases. He was a reminder of the Catalan's relationship with the earth, rooted and peasant-like – easy to forget in the centre of Barcelona – and of the Catalan's traditionally scatological sense of humour. Or so the man said.

This would come to mind when we visited Dalí's museum in Figueras, and saw the outside walls covered with what were supposedly bread rolls, but which to us were clearly coils of shit.

We spent Christmas Eve in Santa Maria del Mar. Xavier Torra, a counter tenor, sang the sixteenth-century Catalan *Cant de la Sibil.la*, and his mysterious etiolated song made audible the bleached-out melancholy of the church itself, the purest and most stark expression of Catalan Gothic.

> *Un rei vindrà perpetual*
> *Vestit de nostra carn mortal:*
> *Cel cel vindrà tot certament*
> *Per fer de tot el jutjament.*

> A king will come who is eternal
> Clothed in our mortal flesh:
> He who will surely come
> To pass judgement on us all.

Torra's piercing Sibylline voice penetrated every lofty space. Like cold air it flowed down the central nave into the semicircular apse, then warmed on the white heat of white candles and rose up slender columns to the ribs of the roof to disperse around the Gothic vaults and float down again. The roof ribs stood out against the planes of stone, like the ribs of a Catalan galley – or, literally, like the body of the church, not a plump body but a skeletal, ascetic creature.

Catalonia was the Mediterranean's greatest medieval maritime power, with Barcelona ruling an empire that included not only Valencia but southern France, Sicily, Malta, and much of modern Greece. Maria del Mar, patroness of sailors, was so celebrated by the seafaring Catalans that when Jaume I conquered Mallorca in 1235 he promised to build a church in her honour. The promise was not fulfilled until the Catalans made their final conquest – Sardinia; Alfonso the Benign laid the first stone in 1329. It was worked on by almost the entire adult population of Barcelona; built by workers for workers.

At one time its empty interior was filled with Baroque furnishings: choir, pulpit, paintings, reliquaries, embroideries, and statues in each side chapel and niche, like Barcelona cathedral. But in 1936 – within memory of many of that Christmas Eve congregation, and despite the church's worker origins – Anarchists burnt the lot. Fire raged for ten days.

Where the Basques' civil war was principally a war of nationalities, Catalonia's was a war of class. Orwell makes this clear in *Homage to Catalonia*: the chaotic infighting, the internecine squabbling between Trotskyists, Leninists, Marxists, Anarchists, the loathing of the institutions of church and state and their representatives. He describes almost every church in Barcelona in 1936 as gutted, every wall scrawled with the hammer and sickle. He describes loudspeakers blaring revolutionary songs down the Ramblas, and the complete absence of 'the wealthy classes'. 'There was much in it that I did not understand, in some ways I did not even like it, but I recognized it immediately as a state of affairs worth fighting for.'

For the Catalans, the Spanish civil war was fought by an anti-Republican Spain against a self-governing Catalonia, but it was also a civil war between Catalans – however much the propaganda of resistance fighters might deny it.

I read somewhere that the puritan English prefer Santa Maria del Mar the way it is now, in its plain immensity, without its Baroque

paraphernalia, but not me. To me it seemed bereft, gutted, emascu-
lated like the counter tenor.

In a strange way it also reminded me of Tarragona cathedral. It
reminded me of Gaudí's Sagrada Família. It reminded me of Barcelona, of all of Catalonia. It was that restless sense of being in
transition, unfinished, incomplete. Not quite Spanish and not quite
French. Not quite one thing, not quite another.

On the mountain of Montjuïc rose another, parallel city: a city of
the dead. Avenues of cypresses stood sentinel along narrow streets.
Coffins were housed vertically in six-storey apartments with the best
views in town. Some sepulchres were capped with the family name:
Família Cervantes, Família Puig. Some front doors were clamped
shut behind a slab of stone, like the lid of a snail, but others had
glass doors that allowed glimpses of plastic flowers, vials of holy
water from Lourdes, a statue of Our Lady of Montserrat. There
were framed photographs of loved ones, mostly black and white and
formally posed, but some were holiday snaps of people cavorting on
beaches during happier times. They were vitrines, showcases of
people's lives. A man less loved had only a stamp in the cement
reading: 'Depositado El Cadaver J. Lopez Gris'.

The necropolis was windswept, unkempt. I wandered there, wal-
lowing in a New Year's Day melancholy. Fallen trees straddled the
avenues; plastic flowers were strewn about. Odd-looking men gathered in Andorran cars at the entrance, and looked as if they were
doing deals. They didn't look as if they were here to pay respects.
More cars arrived and some young people got out and danced. They
had their car stereos on and car doors open, and they jerked around
the cemetery gates, the tail end of a New Year's Eve party.

On the south flank of Montjuïc lay a quarry, plundered for the
stone to build Santa Maria del Mar. People said that after the civil
war, when thousands of Republicans were shot, uncounted bodies
were buried here. They had no catacombs, no pantheons or crypts,
no photos or vials of holy water. On wet days, it's said, you can
smell their decay.

We were living just above it, in a car park near the summit. It was also a prostitutes' hangout but that didn't bother us. We had a grandstand view of the red lights of a Ferris wheel, hypnotically flickering, ever turning.

We spent three weeks here, peering down from our pinnacle. From above, the city was a sequence of concentric semicircles, bound on the east by the Mediterranean where it lapped Barceloneta with its brand-new beach. In the centre was the higgledy-piggledy mess of the Barri Gòtic – we could pick out the slab of Santa Maria del Mar's west front. Around it wove the grid of the Eixample, by day blocks of brown criss-crossed by the black parallel lines of roads, by night speckled blue, orange, red, and white. Then – exactly a hundred years on – the most recent Olympics-propelled revamp that crawled up Montjuïc below us, and over the other side up the encircling Collserola to Norman Foster's twinkling Olympic communications tower that rose like a rocket in lift-off from the peak. It was a self-confident, burgeoning, fizzing view.

There are few cities whose planning is so clearly a product of nationalism. Though many of the new buildings were inspired by orientalism, or even by Flemish gables, it was Catalanism that fuelled the *Modernista* rebuilding from the 1860s, when the first stone of the Eixample was laid, and Catalanism that was behind the most recent revival. One of the chief *Modernista* architects was Josep Puig i Cadafalch, a contemporary of Charles Rennie Mackintosh, a reader of Ruskin; he studied at the University of Barcelona under Elias Rogent who (Puig recalled) in class would stress the importance of being a Catalanist in architecture, of using Catalan Gothic cathedrals as a starting point, as the equivalent of the pantheon for the Italian Renaissance.

And rising above the city were the absurd gloops and swirls, the parabolas and hyperbolas, the dribble castle pinnacles of Gaudí's vast and unfinished Sagrada Família. The dun colour of the stone and organic growths of its towers recalled the globular rocks of Montserrat. But close up, the more recent sculptures adorning its façade resembled on one side identical portraits of Richard Branson, and on the other models of Darth Vader. For all the effort, money, plans, and work, it is a ludicrous building. Nevertheless it was Gaudí above all, Catalanist extraordinaire, who turned Catalan nationalism into stone.

We'd plunge down into it all. Barcelona's streets were too narrow to park in, so I'd wait in with the children, hazard lights flashing, while Richard scurried about getting gas, milk, phone cards, going to the post office, making calls, filling the drums in the launderette. They were confining, claustrophobic moments.

Tallulah was a frenzy of post-Christmas excitement and anti-climax. I felt we were approaching some sort of crisis. But suddenly she was seen picking up Xanthe's toys and sweeping the floor, then scratching at the carpet with a nailbrush.

'From now on, this is what I'll do,' she announced. 'I will clear up, and clean up. After I've been naughty, I will do this, I won't say sorry.'

I praised her to the skies.

'When I grow up, I'm not going to be an artist after all. I'm going to be a servant.'

'Wonderful idea. Will you be our servant?'

'Yes. First I'm going to marry Daddy, then I'm going to be your servant.'

Single men loitered on the pavement, watching us. One moment of inattention, I felt, and they'd be on us. Richard parked his bicycle outside the launderette, and within four minutes it had gone; fortunately it was locked, and he found it abandoned up the road.

There were plenty of good days in town too. I spent one alone with Tallulah. We sat over coffee and croissants in the sun-filled Plaça del Pi (yes, Tallulah, very funny) and felt guilty about poor Richard who had vanished with Xanthe into the industrial hinterland in search of a new cooker switch. I cherished having Tallulah to myself. Around us other tourists wrote postcards and consulted guidebooks. We basked in the sun and in our self-indulgence; we didn't do enough of this sort of thing.

Then on to the Palau Güell, Gaudí's 1886 mansion built for his patron, the Catalanist and industrialist Eusebi Güell. Tallulah was absorbed by every detail, loving the different marbles and the black and gold. She was a wonderfully intelligent companion, but however hard we tried to like it, we failed. It was sombre – morbidly so, like a vast tomb – pompous and gloomy. It resembled Castle Drogo, though was more kitsch. But unexpectedly, up on the roof, amongst the chimneys and ventilator shafts, Palau Güell came to life. Playful forms – cones, obelisks, fungi, spirals, totem poles – were sheathed in fragments of smashed tiles, bottles, and porcelain, the polychrome *trencadis* that Gaudí made his own. It was like a sculptural roof garden where Gaudí had at last been allowed to go wild.

We hooted down ventilators, and stared over the rooftop into a bedsit with washing strung out of its grimy window. A North African man sat on an iron bedstead and changed his shoes on brown lino then went out.

We lunched in the Plaça Reial, the most graceful square in Barcelona yet so seedy, full of loitering junkies. A man in slippers fed pigeons from a plastic bag and stroked them when they hopped on to his hand. Buskers, cripples, Moroccans, youth hostels, boarded-up shops, Tallulah smiling over sausages and chips and saying, 'Lishous.' It was one of those perfect days.

Another day we strolled among Gaudí's snaking *trencadi*-clad seats in Parc Güell, part Disney, part Hansel and Gretel, part Ludwig of Bavaria, much of it decorated with obscure symbols of Catalan patriotism. It was Palau Güell's roof writ large. We played hide and seek in the 'forest of one hundred pillars', a building intended to be a market place when Parc Güell was first conceived as an exclusive housing development.

That night we shared the car park with lovers. One couple was shamelessly naked; another car was so steamed up you couldn't see in.

At the Parliament of Catalonia the security guards were intimidating in their black and red uniforms. When I passed through the metal detector, the alarm sounded. I handed the guard my bag and keys, and tried again. The alarm went off again. I removed my jacket, which had zips, and tried again. No good. I was wearing a T-shirt and tight trousers without pockets: I had nowhere to hide a weapon.

Then light dawned on the guard's face. 'Martens?' he asked. I looked blank.

'Martens?' he repeated, pointing to my boots.

'Yes,' I said.

He trod hard on my toe. I felt nothing. He managed a smile. 'Metal toe cap.'

He waved me through.

In the grandiose entrance hall, flanked by columns, I spoke on an internal phone to a woman in 'Protocol'. I clodded in my Dr Martens up the red-carpeted Staircase of Honour. A sepulchral light filtered through a stained-glass roof. The protocol woman was on the phone, and waved me to wait outside. I paced about, increasingly impatient. A guard invited me to look around. I wandered the gloomy *Modernista* halls, past hefty doors studded with bronze, past black and gilded marble pillars. The attention to detail and the eclectic use of materials was impressive, but the whole effect was hideous.

It was once the arsenal of the hated Ciutadella, the vast eighteenth-century citadel built by the Bourbons in a pentagon that spread over 150 acres. The Catalans were heavily taxed in order to finance the building of the symbol of their own repression – the Catalan Bastille. Demolished during the 1880s, during Barcelona's last urban revival, most of the area was turned into Tallulah's favourite park, but the arsenal remained and was redesigned as a royal palace by Pere Falqués, a contemporary of Gaudí. The Queen Regent refused to accept it in 1900 (perhaps she also found it hideous), so in 1932 it became the parliament building. This was short-lived: seven years later Franco's troops entered Barcelona and turned the Parliament Palace into a barracks. The Assembly Hall was closed, and Franco forbade anyone from entering it for thirty-seven years. Now it was open, as a symbol of the latest Catalan renaissance.

Their ancient democracy is something the Catalans are immensely proud of. Even in the Middle Ages the Count-King did not rule Catalonia and Aragon by divine right. The citizens insisted that he was only *primus inter pares*, first among equals, as shown in the famous Catalan oath of allegiance to the king. 'We, who are as good as you, swear to you, who are no better than us, to accept you as our king and sovereign lord, provided you observe all our liberties and laws – but if not, not.'

The woman was still busy. The guard invited me to sit down, then to warm my hands on the night-storage heater near his post. I pestered him to pester her, and she made out she was frightfully important and preoccupied. Eventually she thrust some pamphlets into my hand and I left.

Conversations with friends produced the following:

1. The Catalans are an unruly lot, more anarchic than anyone in Europe, and they need a strong government and a strong church. That's one reason why Franco survived so long.
2. Catalans are politically fickle.
3. They loathe the Guardia Civil, though not as fervently as the Basques.
4. Until recently Catalonia produced 79 per cent of Spain's GDP. Now that figure was diminishing slightly, but not much.
5. The Catalans know themselves to be the most well-educated, sophisticated, and successful people in Spain.

Robert Llimós added that all anyone cared about was soccer.

Robert Llimós was a Catalan painter, friend of friends. He lived in an apartment next door to the Palace of Music, a flamboyant *Modernista* building decorated with *trencadis* and florid figureheads.

We were buzzed in, up a marble staircase illuminated by a stained-glass window. He met us at the top, a dark-eyed man with grey curly hair. He was small, slightly plump and round-shouldered, in his fifties, a friendly crumpled figure in his paint-spattered shirt. He had a reputation as a womanizer and bon viveur. Yet there was sadness in his eyes which belied that.

Behind him a studio stretched the entire depth of the building with full-length windows at each end. We gasped at the space and light. He steered us in. It had been built as a studio, he said, indicating the skylights, but when he moved in it had been divided into five rooms. Now he had exposed the ceiling beams and built a chic little office like a capsule up against them; a secretary typed there invisibly.

He sat us on a sofa at one end, drawing up a chair for himself. There was colour everywhere – on a joyful poster he had designed for a festival at Cadaqués, on trolleys of oils and brushes and pots of varnish, and on canvases stacked against the walls. There were simply drawn linear outlines of figures in primary colours against a brushy ground – odalisques, mother and child, figures reclining on beaches. The figures were pared down to a curve for a head, a second for a bent back, a third for pulled-up knees, a line for feet flat on the ground. There were older works, and some he was still working on, and they showed how he was struggling to perfect this linear form. The contrast between the confident line and the more hesitant, breathy ground set up a dynamic of opposition and move-ment which I liked, and which prevented them from becoming formulaic.

When I asked Llimós if he felt himself to be a Catalan artist, he was wary of seeming provincial. He considered himself to be both international *and* Catalan. There was strong local support from Catalan collectors, but he had also lived in Miami and New York. However, Barcelona was where he felt at home. When I asked him what – if anything – made his work specifically Catalan, Llimós said it was the Mediterranean quality – not only the frolicsome beach scenes, but also the Matissian colour and sensuous curves, the light. There was a sense of the connection with France, not only with French Catalonia but with the whole western Mediterranean culture. It was a connection, he reminded us, that went back to Roman times. Contemporary art in Madrid was darker, more dramatic, more *sol y sombre*; here it was more poetic, more fun.

'What about Tàpies?' Richard asked. 'He's all browns and blacks.'

Llimós nodded. 'Tàpies is different, but he is an artist from the Franco times. Those dark colours were the fashion in the fifties. Barcelona *was* dark.'

Yet there was an element of that in Llimós' work too. It was not completely French in feel. There was a dark side as well: his work formed a bridge between Spanish and French culture. The use of black and other dark backgrounds behind the vibrant foreground set up a dissonance, a jarring sense of unfathomed depths and uncertainties. He had recently shown a series of work about Bosnia and Rwanda. Goats and piles of skulls stood out against a sombre ground.

Even during Franco times he had made political work. One moving painting from the 1960s was about a young Catalan who had 'jumped' from a window – shown in the painting being pushed by a Francoist disguised (thinly) as a fascist eagle. It was a brave painting to have made at that time.

His latest work was an Olympic Man, a piece of public art for Atlanta, Georgia. He was erecting another version in Barcelona. It was to be a three-metre-high bronze man, all sinuous lines, stepping through a threshold – into the twenty-first century. It would be coated in multicoloured polymer: Multi-Racial man. The use of colour outdoors was something a Catalan would be familiar with, what with Gaudí's *trencadis* decorating so many Barcelona buildings. Robert replied that he didn't normally like polychromatic sculpture but here it worked because he had applied the colour as if by brush marks. Richard said he liked the resolution of the formal problem of bringing together his painting and sculpture. I didn't say anything. I couldn't help thinking of the banal homogeneity of the 'United Colors of Benetton', and privately referred to the sculpture as Benetton Man.

Tallulah was spending the day with friends, but Xanthe was with us. She tottered off around the studio, left arm aloft as if still holding my hand. She enjoyed the expanse, but I had to keep an eye on her in case she crashed into Robert's maquettes or the paint trolleys. She was into kissing, big time. She kissed the walls, the door, the floor. Then she'd plump against my knees, kiss them, and wobble her head from side to side saying, 'Row, row.' She wanted me to sing 'Row, row, row your boat, gently down the stream'. She insisted, wobbling her head so eagerly (to indicate dancing) that I had to give in. I looked at Robert and Richard, sitting there discussing contemporary Catalan art, then I bent my head and sang it, all the way through, including the bit where the crocodile comes and everyone screams.

She was satisfied and tottered off again. She kissed a sculpture, then she came back for more. Robert was very tolerant and able to ignore her mostly, and when he couldn't ignore her any more he made fond and friendly faces.

He revealed that there was now a tragic personal element to his darker subtext. Six months earlier his only child had been killed in a car crash. He mentioned that this had become a problem for his work. His light-filled bathing scenes he now found inappropriate. He didn't know how to proceed.

He took us downstairs to his own apartment. It was clean, dark, and lifeless. His sadness pervaded it. He was separated from his wife. Racks were filled with unsold paintings.

We kept trying to leave Barcelona, but events conspired to keep us there. Richard was waiting for photographs to be developed, I was waiting for my Apple PowerBook to be repaired.

We were also waiting for Jaume Plensa to return from Paris. Plensa was Barcelona's artistic flavour of the month, a sculptor with a show at the Miró Foundation, just below our eyrie on Montjuïc. His London dealer had given us his number.

We met him in the Foundation café. I enjoyed the familiar art-world cool of these places. It was neutral, restful. I felt comfortable with the smell of filter coffee, the black and grey clothes of the international art scene, the smooth feel of the catalogues, the racks of postcards. We could have been in any contemporary gallery in the world. Catalonia was filtered out, we were in Art Ville, and Richard and I were at home with our tribe.

Plensa was small but broad-shouldered, Spanish-looking with dark rimmed slightly bulging eyes. It was his eyes that were so startling: they were khaki-coloured like his shirt. He was born in Barcelona in 1955.

His work was mostly containers inscribed with verse – Blake, Baudelaire, Dante – or with a single word. Hate. Cave. Nest. Mouth. There were transparent brick boxes and rooms like see-through cells. The top lighting gave them a sinister monumentality. The transparency was illusory. Rather, they were cloudy, unresolved, frozen, hinting at something other. They suggested fragility, ambiguity. The words had nothing behind them. There were words everywhere, but the sculptures were not about the words themselves, more about the spaces around them. Not silence, but the resonance of a thought, the reverberation of a word or a poem.

His work lacked the sense of fun of the *Modernistas*, or of Miró himself – that Catalan flamboyance – nevertheless I asked that same question: did he see himself as a Catalan artist? He was vehement that he did not, he didn't believe in such a thing. He was born and bred in Catalonia, but he didn't feel especially Catalan. Quite the opposite: he felt himself becoming increasingly international – he had worked in Berlin, Leeds, Paris – while Catalonia became increasingly introverted and provincial. He scorned the way every 'official' document now had to appear in Catalan, including his own weighty catalogue.

He was an individual, he stressed, not part of any group; he tried to see himself as an island in a sea of artists. Richard pointed out that rather than being an island, perhaps his concern with himself as an isolated individual was part of the Catalan attempt to preserve the uniqueness of the language and culture and its autonomy, in a sense the experience of being peripheral. He shrugged. He had no time for the Catalan cause.

'Don't you know that there are hospitals where, eventually, they have to switch off the life-support machine? It's the same with languages. There's a time when they have to be allowed to die.'

'But Franco tried to murder Catalan, and failed dismally. In effect he pruned it, and it's grown back stronger than ever.'

'True, but it doesn't concern me. If English ends up being the common language, so be it. It's more important that we can talk.'

This suggested another contradiction. His work was about words, but it was not about communication. It was more about silence, the spaces between words. Moreover, his work was avant-garde. It spoke only to a small group.

It was true that he used a range of literature much broader than Catalan, or even Spanish, and he made work far removed from the sunny Mediterranean scenes of Robert Llimós. They were darker, and tackled greater complexities of making concrete such abstract concepts as silence, absence, emptiness.

'What I love so much is that line from Blake, "One thought fills immensity". Do you know it?' His black-fringed khaki eyes lit up.

'*The Marriage of Heaven and Hell*?'

'Yes! I love that. "One thought fills immensity".'

I thought again of Santa Maria del Mar: one thought, one voice, rising up and filling the immensity of those Gothic vaults. His work had a similar puritan, lonely theatricality. And again, that sense of incompleteness, of transition. The ambiguous sense of perpetual motion that is Catalonia.

He was terrified of being labelled, and thus marginalized. He denied his Catalan base because he was frightened of seeming provincial. It was not just that he sought to broaden his appeal: he also sought the elevated status of the 'international' reputation. This is common enough. Most British artists are afraid of seeming homespun. But I found myself determined to bring Plensa's work back down to earth, to make connections between it and Catalonia. Much international contemporary art is rootless, its language intelligible only to itself. To me, the Catalan qualities of his work made it more interesting. It gave it a context and brought it alive.

And I suspect Plensa was being disingenuous, because he had agreed to show in the most Catalan of galleries: set up by Miró (Catalan to the core, though in fact a Jew), designed by Sert, funded by the Catalan government and city of Barcelona.

His attitude also showed how successful Catalonia had become: his Catalan identity had receded as an issue because it was now so self-confident. This made Catalonia less interesting for me too. I was more interested in the underdogs.

As the Foundation's press officer summoned Plensa away, the *Caganer*, the earthy shitter of Catalonia, intruded on Art Ville. Richard was called aside by an armed security guard. For a second I thought he'd been arrested. Then I knew. We had been robbed again. This time the police had caught the thief in the act. This gave us a momentary thrill, until we saw the damage. One picture window was smashed, a knifed blind hung limp. Nothing had been stolen.

This was because there was nothing left to steal. Richard had his Leica with him at all times, like a fifth limb, and my laptop was still being mended. But repairs would be expensive. We were ordered to accompany the police back to the *commisariat*.

This time there was no hiding it from Tallulah. She was unexpectedly brave. She clenched her little fists.

'I'm going to give that burglar a great big bruise.'

But he was kept from us. We sat on a bench beside a simple-looking man who was lost and then found. An armed guard in a bulletproof vest stood on the pavement behind a bulletproof screen. Nobody came near us. One hour passed, then another. Wires trailed from the ceiling down stained yellow walls. The rooms were as grim as Plensa's little cells.

Tallulah and Xanthe chased each other up and down corridors, in and out of grey offices, behind filing cabinets. Now that Xanthe was walking, Tallulah was thrilled to have a playmate at last, not just a doll.

We were summoned upstairs, but only to complete numerous forms in triplicate. Tallulah asked loudly, 'Why are the policemen all so big?'

'Perhaps they eat their greens.'

They were a dour, unsmiling lot. Drab walls were plastered with mugshots of 'Dangerous Delinquents'. They were members of ETA. They were ordinary-looking, in their thirties, the women with neatly styled hair. Several faces were stamped with an 'X: arrested in Santander'; 'X: arrested in San Sebastián'. Two were stamped 'RIP (BOOM)'.

It was late when we were allowed to leave. Richard had bought two crabs. He reckoned we deserved them. He cooked them up outside the police station where we spent the night, and we washed them down with white Rioja.

Broken window flapping, we trawled the industrial outskirts for replacement parts, then escaped to a beach at Gava to lick our wounds and repair the Mob. I spent an entire day stitching up the blind, but it never worked again. Richard fitted a new window, but it wasn't quite the right size – only millimetres out, but enough to stop that working too.

We lay on the beach and tried to enjoy it. I thought of Robert Llimós, and the delightful images his beach scenes conjured up of seafood, long lunches under trellises, sophisticated lazy days. The reality of the Costa Daurada, the Golden Coast, was a mess of half-built speculative *urbanizaciónes* daubed with graffiti, and a beach of unwashed sand spiked with shards of broken glass and concrete. One afternoon Tallulah gathered from the tideline so many used sanitary pads that she could wall her sandcastles with them.

We returned to town. I collected my repaired PowerBook. Richard rushed about getting last-minute supplies while I guarded Mob and girls. Xanthe was asleep and Tallulah sprawled in her bunk drawing monsters and picking her nose. I sat up front and tapped at my beloved laptop. A man's face was at the window.

'Quick! Problem! The back of your van! A cat!'

He smiled but also showed concern. I was confused by his Spanish and flattered by the unsolicited offer of friendship. He opened the door and helped me out. We bent down together to peer under the chassis in search of this cat. He turned to me and smiled a warm smile. Then he ran away. I stood up, puzzled, and watched him disappear into the labyrinthine Barri Gòtic. Then I saw the Mob's front door swing open. My laptop had gone.

I paced the pavement, pulling at my hair and sobbing. I hadn't lost my diaries, which were in tiny notebooks, but I had lost notes, lists, addresses. More than those, it was the machine itself that I cared about. It was uninsured, and I would never be able to afford another. But I was most distraught at my own stupidity, and the betrayal of what I, in my foolishness, had mistaken for friendliness. Barcelona was crawling with crime, poverty, drugs, destitution. I couldn't wait to escape. I foresaw a time when the thieves would steal the Mob itself with all its contents, and we would be stranded in Catalonia, cavorting on the beach among the sanitary pads with nothing to hide our nakedness but sheaves of police reports.

We'd been warned against lingering on Catalan beaches in winter.

The sun was warm, the sky blue, but there was an underlying dampness. We had ignored this warning. And now Tallulah was coughing and her temperature rising. In the Dalí museum in Figueras she enjoyed the jokes for only so long before she tried to collapse on Mae West's lips.

We crossed the Pyrenees. In Perpignyà, the capital of French Catalonia, I was on the lookout for evidence of Catalan on shop fronts or street names, but found none. As if stamping the place with French authority, with incredible insensitivity the main road through Perpignyà had been named rue Jules Ferry, commemorating the nineteenth-century Minister of Education who, by introducing compulsory education in French, held more responsibility than anyone for the decline of Catalan in France.

Later I would be thankful that the French had marginalized their minority languages. I would have been hard-pressed to explain Tallulah's symptoms in Catalan. As Jaume Plensa said, it was more important that we could talk.

We sought refuge from the rain and from the malevolence of Barcelona with friends on the edge of the mountains. To reach their farm we had to cross a ford, then drive a mile up a rutted track. We parked in a field below their house, and spent the day lolling in front of their log fire. Rain reached monsoon levels. A stream at the bottom of the field was swollen, engorged. Babette offered to summon her doctor, but Tallulah seemed to be recovering. She was happy to be in a house. Roland serenaded her on his guitar. She fell for him, but not with her usual wild joy.

Roland and Babette had some important guests for dinner, connected with Roland's work. We stayed in the Mob. The girls were asleep. Suddenly Tallulah began to thrash around and cry out, 'Carry me, carry me.' I found her sweating, delirious. I lifted her down and watched the mercury bounce up the thermometer until it stopped at 104. She moaned and complained of a headache. It was the moment I had been dreading.

Our first-aid manual had long been among Tallulah's favourite bedtime reading. We would pore over methods of preserving amputated digits in cling film, and rescuing an electrocuted woman by standing on a telephone directory and prodding her with a broom. We would laugh at the absurdly happy expressions on the faces of the victims and the lack of blood. But tonight the manual was no use. Richard pulled on his waterproofs and sloshed across the field, and forced himself to interrupt the dinner party to ask Babette to call her doctor.

I held Tallulah in my arms, wrapped in a rug. She was shivering. I sang to her, and she murmured that she wanted 'little songs', nursery rhymes, not grown-up songs. The lights were low; rain thrummed on the roof. Xanthe snored gently in her cot. It was 11 p.m., a dark and stormy night at the end of a flooded ford and a mile-long track, but within five minutes the doctor was knocking at the door.

He was young, thorough, impressive. He laid her out on the sofa and twisted her head from side to side, then moved her legs up and down. I knew what he was looking for, but neither of us uttered the M word. I was touched by how much trouble he took, how closely he enquired into her medical history. I found myself reluctant to let him go, this competent visitor from the real world. Only as he left did I remember that we would have to pay him.

He diagnosed an ear infection and severe bronchitis. It was serious, but not as serious as we had both feared, and not serious enough for hospital so long as we reacted quickly.

Typically French, the prescription was voluminous. There were seven different drugs, all of which came in sachets and had to be mixed with precise quantities of water. The list included a nasal spray of bottled seawater, and six sessions of 'clapping'. Richard and I looked at each other over Tallulah's prone body, and then looked at the doctor, blank. You must find a kinaestherapist, he explained. This turned out to be a type of physiotherapist who would bring up her catarrh by rhythmically patting her chest.

The drugs could not wait until morning. Roland offered to drive Richard down the track, over the flooded ford, then five miles to the nearest chemist. But it transpired that Roland's son had taken the car, so the important guest was prevailed upon. It wasn't much of a dinner party.

'*Suppo?*' the doctor asked, as he signed off.

'*Pardon?*'

'*Suppositoires?*'

'*Non.*' Here I drew the line. '*Pas pour les anglais.*'

TEN

Vendetta

In pink sleep suits they careered joyfully up and down carpeted corridors. Tallulah would charge ahead, then hurtle back into the tottering Xanthe, sending her flying. Richard sat at the bar sampling Pietra, a Corsican beer made with chestnut flour. The barman had florid sideburns and an earring. His manner was brusque; he lacked the courtesy of Catalans or Basques. He seemed to find it demeaning to serve a foreigner. He had the resentful look of an exploited islander.

Rap music thudded through the decks. It was the end of January. The *Danielle Casanova* was empty.

So we were surprised, as we cruised out of Nice, when a man with a livid scar down one cheek opened our cabin door. He reeked of smoke and declared he would be occupying the fourth berth. But Xanthe's cot was already on it, Richard's towel a crumpled wet heap on the floor, Tallulah's voice sang out from the bathroom to report on her experiments with the vacuum flush toilet. Richard quickly convinced the intruder that he would sleep better elsewhere.

Earrings and scars: Corsica was already living up to expectations, and there was still a whole night before we'd get there. Scarface turned out to be a France Telecom engineer from the Loire valley. He and Richard shared a table in the brasserie, the only diners.

Xanthe woke and I took her in my berth. I trundled through the night across the Mediterranean with a baby in my arms. We were in a cabin without a porthole, and it was too dark to see my watch, but I guessed it was about 5 a.m. We both drifted back to sleep, to be woken by a thud and the engine reversing and the tannoy announcing that we had docked in Bastia. It was 7 a.m. We flung our possessions into bags and hastily dismantled Xanthe's cot, and all the while Tallulah was sobbing because there was no breakfast on board and she'd been so looking forward to the cereals in mini-packets. When we shamefacedly found our Mob, the lorry drivers were steering round it, irritated at being held up.

Through the dark loomed a posse of blue, the national police. They were heavily armed. We'd been warned of a security crackdown in Corsica.

Dawn was breaking on a new island, a new country, a new world. It was immensely exciting. And the air was warm. I knew I was going to love Corsica, and that Tallulah would recover here.

We parked in the elegant nineteenth-century Place Saint Nicolas, in the French part of town, and made breakfast. Grey light began to reveal a fringe of palm trees, a bandstand, then the sea.

The great thing about Corsica was that it had had its moment of glory: fourteen years of independence, and not just any old independence, but independence led by a Corsican who devised an enlightened and democratic constitution years ahead of its time, with a national legislature elected by universal suffrage, its own currency, and its own flag. Between 1755 and 1769 the Corsicans managed to slough off their long-time rulers, the Genoese, and also those waiting in the wings, the French, to achieve a moment of self-respect that today still fuels their fight for self-determination, with demands ranging from support for Corsican culture to autonomy and even outright independence.

Corsica also spawned one of the world's greatest soldiers and statesmen, a source of a different sort of pride – not that he did much for the island of his birth, except to bind it tighter to France. Quite the opposite: he couldn't wait to escape. But it haunted him in his final days on St Helena – that scent of the maquis – as it would haunt so many exiles. Napoleon, absurdly attired as a semi-naked Roman emperor, sat near us on a plinth.

A few cafés were illuminated, a few *tabacs*. Steel shutters clanged open. I wandered the narrow streets. Evidence of Corse was non-existent: shop and road signs were in French, as were all newspapers. I knocked on the door of a bookshop, and the surly-looking owner reluctantly unlocked. I explained why we were here, and with a lot of effort forced him to thaw. His name was Jean-Patrice Marzocchi. This mixture of French and Italian was promising – but what lay in between? That was what we had come to find.

Marzocchi, a professional footballer turned historian and bibliophile, had founded Corsica's sole repository of second-hand books about the island, and I had stumbled on it. I spent a long time browsing. It was in Bastia that a reaction to the *françisation* of Corsica took hold during the mid-nineteenth century, and historians, poets, composers of traditional songs and photographers engendered a mini Corsican renaissance. From 1880 so-called 'Erudite Societies' collected works about the nature and history of Corsica, and Marzocchi was their heir. I sacrificed half our weekly budget on an anthropological tome, typically French in its analysis of every detail of Corsican culture. Despite his weary, frigid manner, I persisted. It was all very well stocking books about Corsica, but did he not have anything written in Corse? Yes, Marzocchi grudgingly admitted, he had two volumes of poetry in '*nuestru lingu*'.

I bought the poems.

'Where can I find this poet? Who's his publisher?'

'I am.'

The poet was a young teacher called Anghjulu Orati. He lived over the mountains, in San Fiurenzu. I called him from a phone box and spoke to his mother. Her accent was strange and she was unexpectedly welcoming. We would call again tomorrow.

By now the boules players were out in the Place, clacking in the sand.

We spent the day exploring Bastia. Above the more modern French part coiled the old Genoese city. It was a secret, mysterious place. Precipitous alleyways gave on to vertical coloured slices of fishing boats, sea, and sky, slashed by electric wires. Around the Vecchju Porto, eight- or ten-storey tenements backed against the cliff, towered over by the tremendous Baroque façade of the church of St John the Baptist, whose twin bell towers framed a perfect pediment and niches, which sprouted two curlicues, like ears. All was crumbling, honey-coloured render dropping off to reveal medieval stonework, peeling shutters swinging by a single hinge. Grass and moss – entire wildlife havens – sprouted from roof tiles. The tiles were not the usual Mediterranean terracotta, but slabs of stone. Ramshackle flats had been 'improved' with concrete boxes stuck on the back, suspended in mid-air, to provide balcony privies, but they looked as though they might become detached at any moment. Pipes and cables criss-crossed the façades and sagged with laundry. Flying buttresses wedged between buildings, traversing roads in mid-air, kept them upright.

In the old citadel – a medieval walled city of its own – a spidery matron shouted from her window down to a friend in the cobbled street. Her skin was dark, her clothes black. I heard what sounded like a harsh Italian, with the odd French word thrown in. I guessed it was Corse, and I longed to hear more. Outside a rough-looking bar (closed) hung the Corsican flag, the famous piratical Moor with his knotted bandanna. It looked as if the citadel, once the home of Genoese governors of Corsica, was now a Corsican core.

We picnicked in the fifteenth-century ramparts that dropped in terraces below the fort.

Throughout its history Corsica has been coveted – for safe harbours, timber, and its strategic site in the Mediterranean. Consequently it has been raided, fought over, exploited, bought, sold. Greeks, Carthaginians, Romans, Vandals, Ostrogoths, Lombards, Byzantines, Saracens: all these and more landed on the island and, in different ways, stamped it. Then in 1077 the Pope, titular sovereign of the island since the time of Charlemagne, gave the responsibility for its defence to the Bishopric of Pisa. The Pisans revived Christianity on the island and built exquisite Romanesque churches. But Pisan ownership was disputed by Genoa, so the island was given to Aragon, then wrested back by Genoa.

This opened a blacker period in Corsican history. Genoese and Corsicans loathed each other. Rebellion broke out in 1729 and sporadic fighting continued for the next forty years, with both sides aided and manipulated by foreign powers. From this turmoil emerged the brief independence fathered by Pascal Paoli, but in the end this came to nothing: the Genoese sold the island to France.

Some welcomed the French as an alternative to the Genoese, but there was no love lost between them and the islanders. During the French Revolution the Corsicans became more disenchanted than ever. Riots spread and Paoli, who had fled to England when the French annexed Corsica in 1769, was summoned back. In 1790, after twenty years of exile, he landed triumphantly in Bastia and declared Corsica independent once more. He appealed for British protection. This was eagerly given, since by now the Napoleonic Wars had broken out and the British had no naval base in the Mediterranean other than Gibraltar. Corsica dropped like a strategic fruit into the British hand, and George III not only offered protection, but went so far as to proclaim it an Anglo-Corsican kingdom. His envoy, Sir Gilbert Elliot, landed in 1794.

Over the following months British forces captured from the French San Fiurenzu, Bastia, then Calvi, where Nelson lost his eye.

Sir Gilbert was a delightful man. Educated in Paris, he spoke fluent French, and also Italian which would have made it easy for him to understand Corse. He was liberal, sociable, cultured. His wife (née Amyand) was lively, and liked to entertain with unprecedented flamboyance. They chose not to live in the gloomy old governor's palace, but down in the town in an elegant house with a garden running to the sea.

But there was uncertainty. A question remained: who was to be appointed Viceroy of the Anglo-Corsican kingdom – Elliot or Paoli? After nine months of growing tension, word came at last of Sir Gilbert's appointment. He was crowned in a suitably regal manner. Paoli was furious. His resentment festered. His supporters ignited revolt. At Elliot's urging, Paoli was eventually induced to return to England with a large pension, but his supporters had joined the small but growing number of pro-French Republicans. Meanwhile, Napoleon was advancing inexorably through Italy and, when Napoleon made an alliance with Spain, Sir Gilbert was ordered to evacuate Corsica. The last British troops left just as Napoleon's arrived, unopposed.

Sir Gilbert was distressed to abandon Corsica after only two years. When he was made Baron Minto he chose to include the Moor's head, proclaimed by Paoli as the official emblem of Corsica, in his coat of arms. He went on to be Governor-General of India; his great-great-grandson was Bertrand Russell, who taught Wittgenstein at Cambridge, who inspired Alf-Isak Keskitalo in Samiland, who inspired me.

I phoned Anghjulu Orati again. He was soft-spoken, gentle. I often felt like a hunter in pursuit of prey, and this time my quarry was close. We were invited to visit him in San Fiurenzu tomorrow.

Bastia and then the Cap Corse shrank. We wound up into mountainous scrub of lentisk, arbutus, myrtle, cistus, rosemary, lavender, thyme, and juniper. Its aromatic scent filled the Mob. Grey crags jutted like vertebrae: we were crossing the spine which runs almost the 114-mile length of the island, a granite protuberance of crests, chasms and promontories, harsh and wild. The island was like a bunched fist with its index finger pointing upwards, making a rude gesture at Genoa and France. It reminded me of Madagascar, the same shape, the same knuckles of mountains, the same streams running off the eastern escarpments, the same watery east coast. No wonder so many Corsicans felt comfortable as colonial administrators in Madagascar.

We drove west towards the gentler bumps of the Balagne. A red kite circled alongside, and we had the kite's eye view of ancient churches and villages that saddled the hills, then the striped vineyards of Patrimoniu.

Richard concentrated on the precipitous bends; Tallulah was deep in her latest passion (cutting things up); Xanthe was asleep; I took another look at Orati's poems. They were about bandits, special places in Corsica, Genoese towers, Pisan bridges, liberty. One praised the sweet muscat of Patrimoniu ('O ma chì dolce liquore / U vinu di Patrimoniu'); another was about famous men of Corsican history, 'Omi di a storia'. They were illustrated with photographs of old Corsica that had been collected by Marzocchi – mostly scenes of rugged stone-walled poverty and types Corses.

The language was another Romance, the Romans having been here for over six hundred years. After the fall of the Roman Empire Corse fragmented into the three main dialects, but Tuscan wormed its way in as the more prestigious language and influenced Corse itself. Even after incorporation into France, Italian continued as the language of culture for the Cosican elite. Today Corse looks close enough to Italian for an Italian speaker to pick up the sense – but with the substitution of 'u' for 'o', and the frequent use of 'ghj', as in San Ghjuvanni. Loan words from French are minimal. This is because since annexing Corsica the French have succeeded not in influencing the vernacular, but in virtually wiping it out.

This did not wipe out the Corsican sense of nationhood – far from it. Unlike Catalan, the Corsican sense of identity does not depend exclusively on the language: they have their island to define the extent of their culture. The Catalans have little but their language to mark their territory; the Corsicans have the sea. And there it was: a fjord-like bay of exceptional beauty, the Golfe de Florent, curving beneath us. The sea was a taut blue skin.

As agreed, we parked in the main square of San Fiurenzu, and phoned Anghjulu again. He sprang into the Mob, an enthusiastic man, a friendly Corsican at last. He commented on the beauty of our daughters, so I liked him at once. He looked older than thirty-two: his black hair was streaked grey, and his narrow intelligent face was furrowed, a bit anxious. He was dressed in a cowboy shirt and jeans and clean trainers.

His family home was a pleasant modern house set back from the sea in a garden filled with flowering fruit trees, dazzling mimosa and ripe clementines. Tallulah couldn't get over this, the fact that clementines didn't sprout mysteriously in supermarket trays but could actually be plucked from a tree. It was pruning time and the air was pungent with bonfire smoke.

Anghjulu's mother gave us a delighted welcome. Like her son, she cooed over the children. It transpired that she was not Corsican, but Italian, which explained things. Madame Orati was elegantly dressed, and the house immaculate. She gathered us in the marble-floored sitting room, and pressed us into velvet sofas. I became conscious of my big dirty boots, and of the fact that I would have to stay in my jacket as I had nothing on underneath; I had been unable to find a clean shirt. Monsieur Orati senior joined us, a gruffer Corsican, but still polite. Sweet muscat from Cap Corse was uncorked, and there were chocolates for the children. Anghjulu talked about the traditional Corsican music he played, and demonstrated his collection of flutes, some made of fig or boxwood, some of sheep's horn, but I was on red alert as Xanthe tottered around the room, the melted chocolate on her hands threatening to continue its voyage on to the furnishings.

Madame Orati kindly gathered the girls into the garden. I took reviving sips of muscat and let the quiet settle back in. Anghjulu smiled encouragingly. He was patient.

'I want to ask you about Corse. Why do you choose to write in Corse?'

He had a gentle face, and a soft voice. 'It's my passion.'

'But you are only half Corse yourself.'

He laughed. 'I know. Maybe that gives me a perspective. It makes me more aware of what we have to lose. I'm very aware of the traditions of this island, and I am desperate to keep the language alive.' It was not just dying, he said, it was being actively wiped out. He described the French as 'linguistic zealots'.

Françisation of the island took place rigorously from about 1870, accelerating when Jules Ferry introduced compulsory primary schooling in French into every village, and Francophone secondary schools into every town. Connections with Italy remained, particularly when Italian Republicans of the Risorgimento took refuge here, and during the 1930s when the radical anti-French element saw Mussolini as a way out of France and back into Italy. But the two world wars also reinforced a sense of Frenchness, particularly the Second World War when Corsica, unlike Ireland, fought valiantly for the Allies.

Anghjulu spoke both Corse and French at home, but Corse had long been banned in school, and even when he was a child it was not taught. In 1951 the Deixonne Law legalized the teaching of France's four minority languages – Basque, Breton, Catalan, and Occitan – but this law was not extended to Corse until 1974. Now there were eleven bilingual primary schools. Anghjulu taught at one of them. But it was very half-hearted, he added. A 1982 survey showed that of around 20,000 pre- and primary school children, only 4780 could speak Corse. Few spoke it at home. Lately, the government had encouraged Corse teaching, declaring the revival of the language as one of the ways of dragging the island out of its 'difficult social and economic situation'. Since 1987 teachers had been encouraged to teach Corse for one to three hours a week, but in reality the government was indifferent and provided little money. The government did not *enforce* language teaching, as demanded by both nationalists and the left. Without it being enforced, nationalists and the left argued, the bilingualism from infancy that was crucial for the survival of Corse would never take off.

Data is scant (which is significant in itself) but it seems that by the mid-1990s only half the population could hold a conversation in Corse, as opposed to 80 per cent in 1977. Only 10 per cent considered it their first language. It looked doomed.

There were the post-war problems that were becoming familiar: tourism, peasants selling useless coastal strips for development – although nothing like on the scale of Catalonia. There was the fossilization of agriculture, demographic haemorrhage, immigration, lack of local employment, loss of self-respect. There were the first generations off the land seeking the urban sophistication of French culture. The Corsicans seemed to resent French presence, while at the same time clamouring for more of it in the shape of better roads and other infrastructure. They hated the French for being there, and hated them for not being there enough; they hated them for taking the island, and then for neglecting it.

Then there was the problem of good old dialectical variation. Dog, for example, was *carne* in Bastia, but the completely unrelated *largaro* in the southern dialect of Sartè. The newly opened University of Corsica had produced a standardized spelling, but this was regretted in parts of the island, particularly in the south, because of a loss of local idioms. The pro-standardization lobby argued that people must recognize that languages change, and that standardization was necessary if young people were going to be able to communicate at university, to perform in touring musical or theatrical events, to make recordings, and to persuade the French to recognize Corse as a united, whole language of its own, not a fragmented collection of Italian dialects. In order to survive, Corse had to be seen to be of use.

At the eleventh hour Anghjulu was striving to retrieve what had not been irredeemably lost. Anghjulu had named one book of verse *E Strade di Altore. Altore* was Corse for lammergeyer, the rare bearded vulture that has developed the uniquely intelligent way of feeding whereby it picks up bones and smashes them on rocks so as to devour the marrow. His other book was *Á Passi di Muvra; Muvra* being Corse for mouflon, the curly-horned mountain goat. Both these creatures had been hunted almost to extinction, and survived now in tiny numbers only in the most remote mountainous regions of the island. Both were metaphors for the Corsican language.

Anghjulu began writing songs in 1989, then poems. He had founded a group called I Campagnoli, the countrymen, and if we waited, we would be able to attend a rehearsal. While other men were hunting or playing boules, he and his group were singing. They were mocked when they started – so old-fashioned and peculiar – but now they were quite famous. They'd performed at festivals and made a couple of CDs.

Thickset black-haired black-booted men arrived. They shook hands all round. They were in their early thirties. One was an ambulance driver, another a builder, there was a property developer and an accountant. What they had in common was their love of Corse, but I noticed that they spoke French amongst themselves. Anghjulu regretted this. They'd been seduced, he said. Most people didn't bother with Corse now because they were apathetic. It was easier – and until recently was seen as more refined, more sophisticated – to speak French.

Only a tiny minority, the so-called 'terrorists', sought independence from France.

'*Il faut être réaliste quand même,*' Anghjulu observed. Forty per cent of Corsica's income came directly from France; France paid the teachers' salaries, including Anghjulu's. What Anghjulu and his friends sought was recognition that they, as Corsicans, were a people apart. They were French citizens, but were not French.

Anghjulu denied that his writing was political, despite appearances to the contrary. He insisted it was cultural, but it seemed to me that Corsican culture was, by its very existence, a matter of politics. I think he was afraid of being classed as a terrorist. He was afraid of the French security service.

The girls returned from the garden clutching clementines. Tallulah stood beside me. 'Can I whisper something in your ear?'

'Go on.'

'The lady says it's springtime!'

We joined I Campagnoli in the attic, five men standing in front of the *Tête de More* with his piratical bandanna. The original crest is thought to have come from the crusades and would have been blindfolded; when Paoli adopted the image as the national emblem, he lifted the bandanna as a symbol of enlightenment.

They sang in unaccompanied harmony the traditional Corsican sung Mass that now exists in only a handful of churches up in the mountains, where a few Corse priests remain. It was strong and mournful, entirely in the minor key. Then they sang Corse wedding songs and a sad song for Easter week. Sometimes Anghjulu accompanied them on the nasal *cialamella*, or on the more sprightly sheep's horn, the *pivana*. They were instruments made by shepherds, made to play in the mountains to while away lonely days, lonely months. Many of the songs were shepherds' songs too, and had been inherited aurally over centuries. Traditions varied from village to village. Others were never handed down because at the time they had been improvised on the spot. Now I Campagnoli had become these songs' respository.

Tallulah sat on my lap, totally absorbed, while Xanthe tottered about, returning for cuddles then tottering off again. When Anghjulu put down his *pivana*, Xanthe wobbled her head and called 'More,' and the big dark men smiled. We were distracting them but Tallulah cried when we said it was time to go.

Tallulah recovered from her bronchitis. She was almost back to her old self. While Richard searched for gas, she helped me clean out our pipes. We found water in a garage and while I held high-pressure hoses over the plug holes in sink and shower, blasting out accumulated debris, she turned the tap on and off as instructed. She was thrilled to be of use, dancing about in the puddles we made.

Then we drove west across the Desert of Agriates. Rubble and rock poked through the maquis. It was not desert in that there was no sand, but it was a lonely place, deserted of people. There was the odd stone sheepfold, and shepherds' huts with turf roofs, but no sign of life. We were the only vehicle on the road. It ground tortuously up and over perilous scree. We were stopped by a road gang. The single-track road was being widened. It looked like jobs dreamed up to occupy the Corsicans all winter, before they could give themselves over to the summer onslaught when the island's population would multiply five times, from 250,000 to 1.75 million, mostly Germans and Italians.

As we neared the coast Richard took on an alert expression, his eyes darting towards gateways and unsurfaced tracks. The Agriates relaxed, broadened, then subsided into the sea. He stopped on the roadside and we scrabbled down rocks and (carrying the girls) waded waist-deep across a river to picnic on a white sand beach. It was a beautiful watery reedy place, not a building, not a person.

Tallulah said, 'Oh no!'

'What is it?'

'Oh no. Just don't look. You mustn't worry.'

I knew what she meant. Litter, a growing phobia. You could tell a country by its litter – France with paper tissues, Italy with water bottles, Greece with plastic bags. So I didn't look.

Seaweed rose in steep banks. Perhaps that was why the beach was so unspoilt: it's not glamorous to sunbathe topless on a thatched roof. The top layer was dry, but underneath it seethed with sandflies.

Richard left us to investigate further. I could see he had a plan. Then he reappeared on his bike on the other side of the river.

'I've found a sort of heaven,' he said.

Its name was Ostriconi. Richard helped us across the river, then led us along a path fringed with willows and hazels; catkins were sprouting. Then the secret reedy watery valley broadened into fields of grass and asphodel. The Mob was parked on a flat spot at the end of a riverside track.

'Is this it?' I asked Richard. 'Is this our dream spot? Is this what we've been looking for all this time?'

'Looks like.'

We danced around the Mob, whooping for joy.

'And we can stay as long as we like,' Richard said, 'or at least until we run out of food. There's unlimited water –' he waved in a patrician manner at the river – 'and unlimited wood.'

'And you brilliantly found it.'

Down here we had gentle deciduous trees, bramble hedges and the smells of animal dung where the sheep came down to the water's edge; beside us rose the crags of Agriate, dotted with prickly pear and cacti. We had the best of both: Mediterranean desert abutting English meadows. Looking east and south we counted eight successive tiers of mountain ranges climbing to the ridged and crested Niolo, the brooding uncharted hinterland.

There was no sound but the river rattling on its bed. Overhead red kites twisted forked russet tails.

Near the Mob was a wild boar's rootling. Richard scooped it out for the fireplace. From then on there was always water bubbling away. We revelled in the abundance. At night we sat by the fire watching the Milky Way. Owls and other nocturnal creatures made occasional noises, but otherwise there were only the flames that we huddled round.

We woke to grass white with frost. Our alarm call was the clang of sheep bells. A brown and white herd several hundred strong was followed by a fearsome bearded shepherd in a Mitsubishi pick-up. He wore square spectacles and looked like a modern King of the Bandits. A hint of warmth behind his glasses encouraged us to ask if it was all right to stay here, and he said he'd ask the driver. The driver had a walrus moustache. He gave us a dismissive wave. So now it really was perfect.

One man was the shepherd, the other the owner of the sheep. The Desert of Agriates was their winter pasture. We ate their cheese, pale slabs, mild but not too mild, and drank the last of our local *vin du table*.

On the riverbank Tallulah made a fairy house amongst the tree roots, then she jumped to an island and said she was an explorer. She used a long thin leaf to tie a broad leaf on to a stick to make a flag. Over the next few days she colonized her island. She built a fence around it, constructed a miniature Sami *kota*, and built a miniature fire on which she cooked her own miniature damper, turning it all the time so that the flour and water paste did not gloop off into the flames. She ate it dripping with butter.

It wasn't a long walk to the beach, through the asphodels into the dunes. Tallulah kept sighing, 'This is *bliss*.'

'Mmm.'

'No, it's not bliss. It's beyond bliss. There's no word for it. Oh dear, I've died. This must be paradise.'

She climbed a cypress and picked off balls of sap to join the berries in an old tuna tin she'd found, chatting all the time. Then, as we scrabbled over a rock, I almost stepped on a snake. It writhed from under my feet and paused in the undergrowth, before twisting away. It was as thick as Tallulah's wrist, a deep green with strong back markings. It made my legs throb, thinking how close we'd been. It was our first intimation of trouble in paradise.

As we reached the sea the wind smacked our ears and we sheltered in a cave while Richard fished. On the way home we rolled down the dunes. The sand was white velvet. Tallulah lay spreadeagled in a soft white coomb.

'Come on,' I said. 'Let's go home. I want my cup of tea.'

'I want to stay here, all calm and private, singing my song.'

But she came anyway, and collected spent cartridges, rattly colourful containers with copper bottoms to put her berries in. This was our second intimation.

Trouble arrived on Sunday. Attired ludicrously in full military regalia, Corsican Man bumped down the track in a jeep, guns bristling, dark glasses glinting. From that day, the air ricocheted with gunfire. They said they were after duck and *sanglier*, but one man had a belt hung with blackbirds and thrushes. Another fired at tiny finches. Two hunters parked beside our Mob, then crouched in neighbouring bushes, down on their haunches as if dodging fire in a war zone. Tallulah and Xanthe cowered indoors, hands over ears, crying. Then a dog pounced and there were two shots, close up, bang bang, and a hunter waved his prize – a rabbit.

The children were frightened, but we weren't in danger, we reassured ourselves. They weren't shooting at us. But when Richard was washing dishes in the river, he was rained with droplets of lead. The next day he found the children playing around a funny lumpy thing like a pine cone. It was an unexploded hand grenade, still with its pin intact. We fled.

If I felt like a hunter myself, sniffing out poets and musicians, now we were the hunted, chased away like Anghjulu's lammergeyer and mouflon, put to flight like the Corsican language.

The Corsicans have always had an urge for violence. It is an essentially Corsican characteristic, along with cunning and courage, a consequence of a thousand years of invasions. Until the 1950s it was expressed ritually through the vendetta. *Vendetta* is the one Corse word that has made its way into the outside world.

The vendetta began during Genoese times when it filled a primitive need for justice that was not supplied by the Genoese rulers. The Corsicans fell back on their own form of justice – a life for a life. It was brutal and thousands died, but it was still justice in the form of a strict social code, an unwritten series of laws. The duty was to avenge not just a murder, but any dishonour, including something as inconsequential as a donkey straying into a neighbour's garden, and certainly any form of disrespect to women. To exact revenge, the closest male relative of the victim would be charged to kill the offender or his next of kin. Women and children were not immune; in fear of vengeance children were sometimes kept from school, and women were incarcerated in their homes, the windows bricked up, for their entire lives. The family was ruthlessly welded together by hatred or fear. Each new generation was born into one of the two sides, and bore the burden of having to continue the battle until there was no one left to fight. The result was a climate of fear, and also puritan standards of morality.

A bearded man was a man who took on the role of avenger. Wild, lawless, he hid in the maquis from his enemies and the police until he seized his moment. It was amongst these rocks and maquis that Corsicans enacted their feuds. The bandit lived by moving secretly from house to house, surviving not by hunting so much as by planting himself on the population, mostly shepherds, who supported him willingly (as long as they were not related to his enemies). He was a '*bandit d'honneur*', respected and admired, all the more so if he had blood on his hands.

One of Anghjulu's poems, '*Banditu*', celebrated these fearsome outcasts. It was illustrated by a photograph of one of the most famous bandits, Antoine Bellacoscia, *Roi des Bandites Corses*. He sits at the base of a Corsican pine, gun resting in his lap, flask at his waist, black mortarboard-like cap wedged above snowy eyebrows, and a tremendous white beard curling down his chest. He looks flamboyant, handsome. No wonder English ladies took to visiting bandits; in Victorian times it was all the rage. His father had been an equally flamboyant character; Bellacoscia was a name given to him and it meant 'beautiful thighs'. It referred to his three concubines, sisters who bore him eighteen children.

So powerful and popular did Antoine Bellacoscia become that although he had been condemned to death more than four times, when he eventually gave himself up in 1892, the court in Bastia acquitted him in a storm of applause.

Vendetta was a phenomenon of poverty and it died its own natural death after the Second World War. Nowadays Corsicans are more interested in money than honour. They get respect for having a big jeep, not for shooting a neighbour.

We were stopped at a roadblock. Police demanded our papers and searched the Mob. They said it was a routine custom search, but they were fully armed.

We learnt that while we were in paradise, the nationalist FLNC (Front Liberation Nationaliste Corse) had carried out a *nuit bleu*. Following what they described as a wave of repression by the colonial army of occupation, the FLNC had exploded seventy-six bombs across the island, perfectly synchronized. No one had been killed, but they had destroyed post offices, French-owned holiday homes, and the odd hotel. We had seen and heard nothing. The *nuit bleu* was in response to the deportation of twenty-five militant nationalists to French mainland jails, and was to be the FLNC's proof to fellow Corsicans that the battle continued.

'*U Ribombu Di a Corsica Nazione*', a militant publication that I found later in a library in Corti, was headlined: '*Notre combat est encore légitime*'. It warned of continuing violence both in Corsica and Europe. '*Oui, le nationalisme corse est bien là pour porter son message, un message adulte, responsible . . .*' The publication included news of IRA activities, and of Basques, and Bretons.

The road south passed signs of nationalist activities – burnt buildings, and graffiti silhouettes of men with machine-guns daubed '*LIBERTA PE I PATRIOTTI*'.

This was Corsica's violence redirected, not against each other but against the state. It was still a question of honour, but with nationalist resonance. They were a small group but noisy. Like ETA and the IRA, they occasionally made pronouncements dressed in black and fully masked. They included gangsters, and demanded protection money. Unfortunately their cause was disintegrating into infighting; the previous summer rival groups in Bastia had bombed the old town and killed each other, although there were probably well-founded suspicions that this had been set up by the French Security Service to discredit the movement. The effect was to destroy tourism and to harden public opinion against the nationalists, but there was no active hostility, partly because they were dangerous, and partly because there was also sneaking support, especially for the destruction of French second homes. It was the politics of envy, the root of so much Corsican violence.

A group of women, traditionally vindictive harpy-like promoters of the vendetta because it endowed their men with honour, had recently made a volte-face and founded Manifest pour la Vie, a peace movement, but it looked as if, as in Northern Ireland, ancient hatreds would continue to tear the place apart.

South of Calvi the west coast grew rockier and more dramatic with each twist in the narrow road. Mile upon mile of untamed maquis plunged to the white-flecked sea. We'd driven all day and seen no buildings, just the occasional ruined watchtower. This was the coast attacked so frequently by pirates – many of them Corsican – that the beleaguered remnants of the population fled inland.

There was nowhere for us to stop. One side lay the sea, the other the maquis. The verges were too narrow. The children were hungry and fed up. I struggled into the back and, bracing myself against the fridge, managed to slice bread and make sandwiches as we careered around bends. We were desperate. Then Richard said, 'We're going to find somewhere now, I can feel it in my bones.' And we did: a flat track beside the Baie de Crovani, sheltered by a flurry of tamarisk, ringed by an amphitheatre of mountains, and overlooked by a ruined mansion on a crag.

It was a mysterious, deserted place. A collection of industrial buildings had once been part of the Argentella silver mine, but all was long gone, just a rabid-looking dog, and some washing hanging out. When the sun collapsed into the sea it turned the amphitheatre red.

Our road bent east, into mountains and a cloudless sky. We wound up valleys so steep that we could spit at the road we'd driven on an hour earlier. We shared the road with goats and soft hairy cattle who used it as an extended farmyard. The road was so little used that moss grew all over it. Waterfalls plunged and *villages perchés* grew out of granite crags, each one a fortress. There were no isolated manor houses, no chateaux; because of constant invasions no one dared live outside the confines of the village. Arab slave raids ended only in the 1830s when France conquered Algiers from where the slavers came: so at that time the French were seen as protectors.

The villages were stark, pared down to the minimum, without ornament except in the little shrine-like springs where we filled up with water. There was no room in that harsh rocky landscape, or in that harsh puritan social system, for frivolity.

There was also the fact that the Genoese crushed the nobility. One of the unexpected effects of this was that the Corsicans grew up without overlords; they are among the few European peoples to have avoided the oppression of feudalism. Like the Basques, they developed a system of collective democracy in the villages, which in turn became the basis for Paoli's constitutional advances. It engendered a sense of pride, a feeling that one man is as good as another and should be treated as such.

All this fledgling democracy was usually damaged by the vendetta, which tore villages apart, and locked them into a spiral of hatred that would take generations to wear out. There were not only personal hatreds, but political ones – who supported who.

The maquis grew denser and sweet chestnut woods grew up; in the rotting humus pigs rootled. Many looked as if they had crossed with wild boar. But for the pigs we were alone, hour after hour, in the silent enveloping darkness of the forests. Then the great chestnuts with their corkscrew bark evolved into majestic pines, as splendid as cedar trees with russet trunks, and the forests opened out. The pines thinned, and we drove into snow. Tallulah was on my lap, beside herself with excitement.

We stopped on the Col de Vergio, up at 1477 metres. A granite Virgin looked west to the sea, and east towards the great rock walls of the Niolo that imprisoned the heart of the island. It was getting late, but we were unsure of the wisdom of stopping on a snow-covered pass for the night. We decided to risk it, and Richard chocked up beside a decapitated pine, mutilated on this climactic front line. He changed the gas from butane to propane, which freezes at a lower temperature.

We climbed up into the last of the sun and built a snowman, and Richard waxed the underside of our bed extenders to turn them into toboggans. They were nothing more than flat boards with two strips of 1″ x 1″ screwed on, but we hurtled down the slopes, shrieking with exhilaration, until the sun set and the snow-melt froze and iced the slopes.

In the morning the snow was pocked with tiny paw prints – weasel, or maybe fox.

We plunged down the Golo Valley into a gorge that grew more barren with each turn, its walls red and savage. The road was merely an indentation in the serrated rock face, propped up on fragile stone bridges. For two days we'd seen only the odd shepherd. Then the land opened slightly, and there before us, nestling in a bowl at the base of a snow-clad massif, its citadel perched above it like a lammergeyer on a pinnacle, was Corti. Wood smoke drifted through the valley and with the smoke rose the cries of children, barking dogs, cocks crowing, the crack of guns. Steep houses were clamped to steep rock faces. Peaks loomed through clouds, great brooding heights, solemn, grand. Cloud shadows rode across the valley and up and over the foothills as if over the sea. Then the peaks would evanesce and I wondered if I had imagined them towering above us, if they were really only clouds after all.

We parked on the outskirts and cycled in. Close up, Corti was astonishingly rundown. Yellow stucco façades on the main street were crumbling; their back regions were little more than stacks of stones with plumbing tacked on. Many shops were boarded up. In the lower town flat blocks of East European squalor crawled across the plain.

For fourteen years, from 1755–69, Corti was capital of Paoli's independent Corsican nation. This was what remained of Corsica's triumph.

We drank beer in a bar where old men played cards or sat and talked politics and smoked. They'd been there all day: looked set to be there all night. The smoke was so thick we had to move outside. Sullen men with cropped hair loitered on corners. There was a feeling of suspension, of something waiting to happen. Walls were daubed with FLNC graffiti. One graffito announced that May '97 would be Independence Day: three months from now. But it had been crossed out.

I felt disorientated, and Richard felt the same. We had come looking for Corti, but it was still a surprise to reach a town in modern Europe so isolated, so wild, so imprisoned by harsh mountains with their hidden trails and chasms.

In 1981 Corsican pressure forced the French to open a university. It was Corti's triumph to have it sited not in the French-dominated administrative capital Ajaccio (Aiacciu in Corse) but in Corsica's heartland, on the site of Paoli's triumphs. It was no beauty – a mess of concrete boxes daubed with graffiti – but at least it was there. In fact, it was not new; Pascal Paoli had founded a university in Corti in 1765. Napoleon's father, Carlo Bonaparte, studied law here while acting as Paoli's private secretary. But the French shut it down only four years later. The Corsicans waited 212 years for it to reopen.

I trawled the Syndicat Culturel Universitaire for someone to talk to, and was advised to visit the curators of the Corsican Museum that was soon to open in the citadel on its rock spur.

I climbed through the old town, crossing little eighteenth-century squares, and a modest house with a plaque commemorating this as the birthplace of Napoleon's eldest brother, Joseph. The Bonapartes were right in there with the patriots, burning with enthusiasm for their rebel state. But after Genoa ceded Corsica to France and Paoli fled to England, the Bonapartes found it politic to switch their allegiance, especially when they were ennobled by the French government, and especially when their son Napoleon was offered an irresistible scholarship to a military academy on the mainland.

Twenty-one years later, when Paoli was summoned back and landed at Bastia in triumph in 1790, the Bonapartes were on the wrong side. When that same year Paoli was proclaimed Father of the Nation, his partisans took revenge on the turncoat Bonapartes and ransacked their home in Ajaccio, humiliating the family and sending them fleeing for their lives to the mainland.

It is thought that this early humiliation scarred Napoleon, and helps to explain his lack of interest in Corsica. His inflated Corsican pride had been offended. He returned home as infrequently as possible. Indeed, he not only neglected the island, he also imposed on it the loathed Military Governor General Morand, who was said to ensure the happiness of Corsicans by executing one man every day.

The museum curators were barricaded in the citadel, surrounded by scaffolding and looking down over the ramparts on to the dour slate rooftops of the town. Below the citadel the Tavignanu and the Restonica met in a thunderous collision of white water. This was Paoli's garrison, used by the French as a barracks until recent years. It was a truly Corsican construction, built at the end of the Middle

Ages by the people of Corti themselves during an earlier but doomed struggle against the Genoese.

Richard was away taking photographs with Xanthe on his back; I had Tallulah with me, bribed with sweets to stay quiet. She lay on the floor drawing and never uttered a word. The walls were tacked with plans and there was an exciting atmosphere of a new project taking shape, financed mostly by the EU. It was to house a collection of Corsican artefacts and vernacular objects from the lives of Corsican shepherds.

The woman had long dark hair and a nose like a witch. She looked hard, sharp. The man was bearded and softer. In her youth she had been more militant than him. She kept saying, 'This will no doubt shock you but . . .' I guessed she was using me to air her views that until then she had felt obliged to keep hidden. They were both Corsican, but employed by the French government, and I sensed they were being careful of what they said. 'This may shock you,' she said, 'but the Corsican language is not as important as people make out. Of course it's important if we want to read our own literature, but it isn't crucial to our survival as a people. You can't impose a language, it has to recover naturally, and if it isn't seen to be useful, no one uses it. But there are other things.'

'Such as?' I asked.

The woman mentioned the diaspora. 'When I was a student in Paris,' she said, 'I knew people in all walks of life who were Corse. It's like the Jews. We had this strong sense of being Corsican that made us feel different and drew us together.'

'And what is that Corsican thing? How can you define it?'

This was always difficult. They looked at each other and agreed that there were positives and negatives. On the positive side was the creative energy, the sense of potential. On the negative side was a lack of motivation and leadership. When they wanted to set up the museum, there was no one qualified to help them. Anyone with any sense of drive had traditionally gone to work in the French colonies, and now that few colonies remained they stayed on the mainland. The university might help to keep people on the island, but there was so little for them here, no industry, only tourism which was itself so destructive. The French had always underestimated Corsica, but the Corsicans, they agreed, had an inability to think of an aim, a future. After centuries of domination by others, they now found it hard to organize themselves – apart from the militant activists, who represented only a tiny minority. It seemed they felt impelled towards extremes: either to extreme action, or to extreme passivity, extreme fatalism.

'And what else? What makes you Corse?'

'There's the sense of community, the communal life.'

'Yes,' the man agreed. 'The village, the family, the clan. Their pull is still very strong. Even those who live abroad tend to come back every year – a huge number of tourists are Corsican exiles who can't rid themselves of their Corsican past however much they might want to. Some people long to escape the tight-knit village, the oppressiveness of an extended family, but they rarely succeed. You meet so many people who hate it here, who long to get away, but when they do they never find anywhere more beautiful.'

I expressed shock at the state of things in town. They were taken aback by my criticisms.

'That medieval look is very popular with visitors,' they cried. 'It looks so exotic.'

'I don't mean the citadel, I mean the main street.'

'They're nice inside.'

'I've just come from Catalonia,' I explained.

'Oh, Catalonia! Spain's California. We are nothing to France. Just a drain on their purse. Those properties on the main street all belong to the government. It's their responsibility. It's up to them to restore them. But they won't. We are marginalized, forgotten.' They sounded bitter. These days, the woman added, their orientation was increasingly back towards Tuscany, Sardinia, and the Balearics rather than towards Paris. They had more in common with these smaller peoples, and their languages were closer.

The next day it was down again, down towards Ajaccio through rocky gorges, down through pine woods that evolved into sweet chestnuts then into heather and evergreen oaks then into the maquis. Down past more *villages perchés*. We filled up with water from a little grotto-like spring beautifully walled with cobbles and a niche for a saint.

When we first arrived in Corsica I had picked up a brochure that mentioned Dorothy Carrington, 'the British author who became Corsican by adoption' after arriving on the island in the 1940s. It had been love at first sight, I read, and her last wish was to be buried in Bonifaziu: 'to gaze at the sea for all eternity'. So I had been surprised, in a bookshop, to discover that she was still alive, living in Ajaccio. The bookshop owner had said she was the best living writer on Corsica – quite some concession from a Frenchman. The best writer *in English*, the Corti museum curators frowningly corrected me.

She had arrived in Corsica soon after the last war with her husband, an Anglo-French Surrealist painter. They had befriended a Corsican waiter in London, and been invited to visit his family near Propriano. She intended to write a travel book, and move on. But she was captivated, and after toing and froing back to England, where her husband chose to remain until he died, she stayed on. Steeping herself in Corsican history, uncovering forgotten Pisan churches and Neolithic sculptures, she found a sense of permanency that until then she had lacked, which grounded her here. It would be nineteen years before her book, *Granite Island*, was finished.

It is a hugely well-informed book, based on original historical research, but what I most admired was its sensitivity to the dark mystery of Corsica, and to its beauty. She had followed *Granite Island* with an exploration of the prophets of death, *The Dream-Hunters of Corsica*. I couldn't wait to meet her.

The bookseller gave me her number. She sounded frail but enthusiastic. She looked forward to meeting my family and me. The girls envisaged someone like Granny, who would cuddle them and feed them cake. This prospect was held out to Tallulah like a carrot, as something tantalizing to look forward to. I imagined a fey old lady trailing bohemian scarves through light-drenched rooms overlooking the sea.

We found her in a basement off a busy thoroughfare. Richard dropped us off and went to find somewhere to park. We entered a granite doorway opposite Monoprix, picked through a ramshackle courtyard, and descended a gloomy staircase. A door at the bottom had a note stuck on saying 'Lady Dorothy Rose', which sounded like a gypsy fortune-teller, but which I assumed was her married name.

She was pale in her subterranean lair, as if it was years since she had made the journey up into the light. She had sandy-grey hair and a miniature hooked nose and a long wrinkled upper lip. She had a sharp, intelligent look, like a baby kestrel. Tallulah reached up to whisper that she was the oldest person she had ever seen.

The flat was decorated with hideous flower-power wallpaper, untouched since the 1970s, and stacks of books. Lots of Shakespeare, with markers at important pages sprouting like leaves. A frugal, intellectual woman, who in her day had revelled in the simple luxuries of Corsican hospitality, or in the voluptuous scent of the maquis, but eschewed more commonplace material comforts: it was an academic style that was almost aggressively cerebral and ugly. Or perhaps she was just poor.

An ancient typewriter in the centre of the room had a half-completed sheet in the roll: a Canadian had made mistakes in a piece about the vendetta, and Dorothy was taking the trouble to write a nine-page letter setting him straight. She was physically frail, it seemed, but not mentally: she had published *The Dream-Hunters of Corsica* only two years earlier, and chose to remain in Ajaccio rather than in her preferred Bastia because of her proximity here to the national archives where she did her research.

She grumbled that she couldn't see well, and appeared flustered and mistrustful of me. She had been visited by some other travel writer, some frightful American, she couldn't recall his name, who had written scurrilous things about her and had disliked her late husband's paintings. Browsing in a bookshop a few years later, I discovered this was Paul Theroux.

She had also spent the morning being interviewed for the radio about the latest political shenanigans, and this had unsettled her, made her anxious and apologetic. I could see that the girls unsettled her further, and this in turn disturbed them. It was all wrong. They wanted to play around the flat, but no: there were fragile objets d'art, they must stay in the sitting room. She sat me opposite her in her window, looking out on a light well with orange trees in tubs; Xanthe sat on my lap while Tallulah was allowed to sit at a table and leaf through a magazine with pictures of Corsican houses, but only if her hands were clean. Both were soon bored. Xanthe needed a nappy change and Tallulah wanted to do a drawing, but she didn't want a page from my notebook, she wanted plain paper, and she didn't want an ordinary pencil, she wanted one with a rubber on top, and then she began to cry. Dorothy supplied the rubber-topped pencil, but she was allowed it only if she *didn't* chew it, and *didn't* suck it (as if she would!). Clearly Dorothy had no children and did not like them.

Xanthe found a little game. She peeped through the bars of a chair at Tallulah and let off piercing shrieks. The terracotta-tiled floor doubled the volume, which seemed to please her. Dorothy sat back in her seat and flung up her hands. 'No, I can't go on, I simply can't. Not with that noise.'

Where was Richard?

I apologized. Xanthe seized a bottle of Tippex off a trolley and Dorothy squealed in alarm: that was her writer's trolley, everything had its correct place (including a neatly folded, half-eaten packet of crisps). I hauled Xanthe back on to my lap but she grabbed my pen, yodelled, then – worse – wanted me to yodel. She patted my mouth and made wobbling movements with her head. Tallulah scraped her chair back and forth over the tiles.

'No, I simply can't,' Dorothy cried.

Where was Richard?

I offered to leave and wait for him on the street. Dorothy dismissed that as hopeless, I would never find him. While we argued, Richard rang the bell. I had rarely been more pleased to see him. He had to remove the girls. While I held them out of view ('No no! Not in my kitchen!') Richard photographed Dorothy, then departed with them for the bars of Ajaccio.

Silence returned. She apologized again: she was a widow, unused to noise – though I could hear a child crying somewhere upstairs. I didn't blame her at all.

We talked for an hour. Corsica and its history were her passion – not in a blindly romantic sense, more of an addiction. Over the years since 1948 the island had become part of her. And she had become part of it: in 1991 the University of Corsica in Corti had awarded her an honorary doctorate, quite something for a non-Corsican.

We discussed the vendetta. Two bandits were still alive when she arrived in Corsica. One died soon after of cancer of the face – an irony since his vendetta had begun with a slap on the face. She had met the other, François Bornea. He had ruled central southern Corsica, extracting protection money from local firms and politicians, ordering champagne and the best guns from Ajaccio. He had become a bandit not because he had killed someone, but because he liked the adventure; only later did he murder a man, a random killing carried out to make him feel like a real bandit. After eventually serving five years in prison, he married and settled in Porti Vecchju, where the young Dorothy was taken to meet him. They drank wine and ate goat stew in a spartan stone house. He was not what she expected, she recalled. He was fragile-looking, with beautiful hands and a lovely voice, not an obviously outstanding personality. Once he'd left the maquis, all he wanted was a comfortable life and a car.

Now that violence had been channelled politically. Dorothy was critical of the separatists, but felt that as a foreigner it was not her place to judge, at least not on the radio. In the early days they did good things, she said. They encouraged Corsican culture. But now they had grown bitter, and were turning to racketeering and money laundering and fighting amongst themselves, quite apart from destroying public buildings like post offices, which were vital to ordinary Corsican village life. Yes, the post offices were instruments of the French state, but they were also where people got their money and pensions, their letters and essential medicines delivered by post. The separatists were not young firebrands, she said, but the middle-aged disenchanted. 'They want the French out,' she observed, 'but it's not as if they've been here two years, it's over *two hundred* years. They have the same rights as the French. They *are* integrated. And besides, eighty-one per cent of the population wants to remain French. They'd never be able to survive economically on their own. Anyway, the whole idea of independence is old-fashioned. One must think of Europe as a united people, made up of regions. I don't like the word nationalist. I've lived through two world wars. The nation state is a dangerous entity.'

Over the years, travelling by bus or on foot, she had seen pretty well the whole island. Many things had changed, but she concluded that she didn't think there was such a thing as progress. 'You simply change one set of disadvantages for another.' When she arrived people rode donkeys (or the men did, while their wives toiled behind); the roads were winding dirt tracks, the villages were isolated and riven with disputes. But at least people worked the land; they were not dependent on jobs or on the whims of others; they were hospitable. All those things had withered, largely because of the one and a half million tourists.

'Do you feel possessive about Corsica?' I asked her.

'Not really. But I hate it when things go wrong. If everyone put down their guns and got to work to ensure the prosperity of Corsica, that would lead to less dependency on the French state, which would make people calmer.'

'More tourism?'

'No. Tourism isn't the answer, because the Corsicans have a mis-directed resentment of serving foreign tourists. It's seen to be demeaning. Loss of face.'

They'd be better off redirecting their energies into building up Corsica, marketing local produce like mandarin jam, olive oil, marrons glacés and cheeses, all delicious, making what they could of the island. But there weren't enough experienced people; they'd gone to seek better jobs on the continent, to return only on retire-ment.

Our conversation veered off: we found mutual friends in London, the late artists Elisabeth and Cecil Collins. She'd known them all her life, as had I. But she didn't get back to England much now, she was too frail. Instead she spent the summer up in the mountains.

'Do you make much money from your books?' she asked suddenly.

'Not much. Do you?'

'Not really. Lots of good reviews, lots of publicity, not much cash.'

'I suppose that's better than the other way round.'

'Yes.'

'Well, maybe not.'

'No. Maybe not.'

I felt sad. Throughout our journey I had toyed with the idea of settling somewhere. Should we park the Mob in that wild open space and buy that ruined farmhouse? How about that cliff-top castle? Room for me to write, Richard to paint, the children to play – and cheap, so cheap. I had envied Dorothy her commitment to Corsica, her deep involvement with one place, unlike us, always passing through. But there she was, nearing the end of an exciting life of travel and research, an outsider, widowed, alone, apparently penniless. There's not much between leaving a country, I thought, and being cast off; there's only two letters between exit and exile. But she seemed happy, liked her apartment, had friends: this was just my own fear that imposed itself on her.

Richard returned. Dorothy seemed relieved that the interview was ending. She must have been exhausted. Or maybe she wanted to make a good final impression. Anyway, she expressed delight that Richard was a painter and took him into her bedroom to show him her late husband's work. There wasn't much, she warned, because most had sold. And, she added by way of a let-out, some people liked them, some people didn't. I couldn't look closely because Xanthe was squeaking and wanting to run about, but her wanting to show them to us touched me. She pointed out a small tree with three branches (the Trinity), leafless and pale. It was sensitively done, a gentle charming picture. She described it as a poignant portrait of old age.

We drove south to Filitosa in search of the statue-menhirs that Dorothy had helped to discover, and that put Corsica at the centre of a Neolithic culture (from the Greek *neos*, 'new', and *lithos*, 'stone') which invented portraiture over a thousand years before the Greeks.

We glided through an Arcadian land – gentle hillocks, smooth rocks, ancient olives, meandering streams, grazing lambs – and parked outside a farm. It belonged to the Cesari family. Dotted about the farm were standing stones, but with a difference. Unlike the menhirs of Brittany or Great Britain, these were not massive, but they were carved with rough-hewn faces, swords, daggers, even with ribs and shoulder blades and backbones. They were possibly portraits of real men, possibly phallic symbols, possibly symbols of power. Richard had seen something similar outside Patrimoniu in the Balagne, but that was alone: here there were twenty, some whole, some now in fragments, having been used by later inhabitants as building blocks.

On the left bank of the Taravu, we wandered among them. Their expressions were hard, remote. I tried to explain to Tallulah that actual hands had worked those actual stones, possibly five thousand years ago, at the same time as writing was being developed in the Fertile Crescent of south-west Asia. But it was hard to bring the barbaric faces to life. A group had been re-erected near their own quarry; a horse grazed amongst them imitating a David Jones painting. Slivers of sun shot through a black sky and briefly illuminated the faces, the shadows emphasizing the deep, unseeing eyes.

They were by no means the first anthropomorphic representations. A few highly schematic human figures adorn the walls of Lascaux, drawn 12,000 years earlier. The earliest portrait in stone is thought to be a round face found at Lepinski Vir in the Danube valley, dating from around 9000 BC – six thousand years before Filitosa. But the Filitosa megaliths are full-sized, and armed. They were contemporary with Avebury, with the Alta rock carvings, and about a thousand years older than Stonehenge. While the sculptors here were at work, proto-Basques were living in the cave mouth at Santimamiñe, decorating the walls with images of bison.

In 1948 Dorothy's Corsican waiter friend, Jean Cesari, had mentioned these great blocks of sculpted stone that lay strewn about his cousin's farm. Dorothy had persuaded him to take her there, and it was she who revealed to the owner their immense significance, proving that Corsica had been home to an ancient and sophisticated prehistoric culture. More than that, she saw the representation of individuals in stone as a foretaste of the Corsican belief in the power and pride of the individual, something that lies behind the vendetta, behind Paoli's democratic constitution, and ultimately behind the modern nationalist movement. She saw that individuality as intrinsic to Corsican identity, an individuality evident five thousand years ago.

It was Dorothy who took to Filitosa a French archaeologist who then made more exciting discoveries of dolmens, more menhirs, and, in the heart of the complex, two rounded *torre* surrounded by a cyclopean wall. Yet Dorothy is not mentioned in the Cesari booklet about Filitosa or in any of the museum displays; she is given no credit whatsoever. It may be that the Cesari family felt slighted by her portrayal of their peasant-like ignorance about the treasures over which they farmed and which they used to support gates and to sit on to eat lunch. Maybe it was a sign of that Corsican pride which stamped itself in stone on that same plot of land all those millennia earlier.

The air was a tumult of weather. Mist poured over the Bavella Pass behind us, then down into the valley in front. All colour was vaporized, reduced to black and white, the towering Corsican pines – as Tallulah pointed out – nothing more than black shadows against the white-out horizon. Then the mist abruptly cleared and, like a slide flashed up on a screen, we saw granite crags and pinnacles, perpendicular escarpments, and the trees were suddenly green again. Then the mist flooded in, and the world vanished.

The gusts literally took our breath away, sucking it out of us and sending us spinning. We sought a safe place to spend a few nights, but a fallen tree blocked the most sheltered spot; its roots were still raw, dangling fresh earth. We tucked into a cleft below the pass, above a collection of tin-roofed huts. One had had its roof blown off by the wind, revealing its Spartan interior. We discovered later that they were summer houses of a few families who once lived in the village of Conca, down towards the coast; most were now dispersed across what the Corsicans refer to as 'the continent', but they returned here each summer.

I crouched in the lee of a granite slab. Two weather systems collided on the uppermost peak, hurtling towards each other from west and east, causing a perpetual boiling of the clouds. The striations of the rocks hung like the folds of a gigantic curtain; other rocks were scoured by the weather until they were as hollow and fragile-looking as eggshells.

I had never seen a European landscape more majestic and alien. Again, I thought of Madagascar, of the impenetrable limestone *tsingy* escarpments of the north-west. Tallulah, looking out of the window, had other thoughts. She sighed wistfully: 'I wish I was in Stockwell.' Then Xanthe's naked body distracted her. 'Doodo's got silk feet underneath,' she cooed, stroking her. 'Never walked on ... too *touching*.'

The next morning there was ice inside the door. Richard heaved the bikes off the back of the Mob while I pushed the girls into snowsuits. It was bitter out of the sun, especially for the girls who were static in their bike seats, but it was lovely to enter the sunless forest and then climb on to a new ridge, and see before us new peaks, and more countless layers of mountain ridges, and an empty forested land rolling away below. We perched on logs in patches of snow, then lit a fire and roasted marshmallows. This was supposed to be a fun way of having elevenses, but as usual Richard and I ended up doing it all while the girls cried with the cold and complained that they preferred the marshmallows raw anyway.

It transpired that we were not alone. There was a solitary gîte owned by one of the Conca families and in it a half-Moroccan manager who had worked here, in solitude, for three years. Richard persuaded him to turn on the TV so that they could watch France v Wales; Richard was rewarded with a beer for reminding him about the match. We gave him a lift down into Zonza. He had black hair and fleshy lips.

'Aren't you afraid,' I asked, 'living here alone?'

He laughed at the idea.

'What about wild animals?'

'I shoot them.'

Everyone shoots, and after shooting what they like best is fighting. Everyone's related, he said, but they're always fighting. Constant battles. Recently there was an explosion in the gîte kitchen.

'Why?' I asked. 'Gas?'

'No! A bomb. It's always bombs.'

'Politics?'

'I don't know. It's not necessarily politics; it can be for any reason, but it's never against people, only buildings.'

Someone had recently blown up the *mairie* in Zonza; we saw it, a bulldozed site in the village centre. The Moroccan laughed. We passed a racetrack in the forest and he said: after *la chasse*, what people like best are horses. Everyone has a horse. They are all rich round here.

'They're all bosses,' he said, '*patrons*. They've all got restaurants and tourist businesses.' When his parents arrived forty years ago, it was different. They had long beards; they were savages, almost. Now they drove around in important *quatre-quatres*.

By evening we were parked on a promontory in Bonifaziu. After coming down off the Bavella Pass we had found nowhere suitable to stop, so had just kept on going until out of the maquis had risen this extraordinary isolated town. We stayed a few nights in the upper town, a craggy warren clinging to the cliff top sheer above the Straits of Sardinia. Here, as far as possible from continental France, there was a resurgence of nationalist feeling; the walls were covered in fresh FNLU graffiti – '*LIBERTA!*' scrawled over daubed Moors' heads and machine-guns.

Our orientation shifted: we overheard people speaking not only Corse, but also Sardinian, and Italian. We began to turn our backs on France and think about heading south.

We stocked up on final supplies of *fromage de Brébis*, local honey, chestnut purée, and found a cosy vaulted cellar in the ancient Pisan quarter where we dined on *brocciu* omelettes. The *patron*, a moustachioed bon viveur with yellow braces taut over his capacious belly, sat with a regular over balloons of brandy. The customer mentioned a certain *livre de poche* and the *patron* replied: oh yes, everyone's writing books these days.

Dorothy had chosen to end up here, in the cliff-top cemetery. It lay beyond a windswept plateau of abandoned barracks and windmills, overlooking the sea and Sardinia to one side and to the other the mysterious wastes of the maquis. It was a village of its own, not with tower blocks for the dead as in Barcelona, but with family houses – neoclassical façade here, baroque curlicue there. There were streets of them; you could almost imagine the dead heaving themselves out of their coffins each night to gossip over the garden fence, ghost children playing ball in the alleyways. Many had nice new front doors with frosted glass and wrought-iron grilles. Some were even furnished with porcelain books, forever open on a page saying, 'PPL [*priez pour lui*] from your wife and family.' An enclosure of Legionnaire graves had been freshly whitewashed. The most moving memorials were to the *mort pour la patrie*, especially poignant in Corsica where the ultimate sacrifice was, in effect, for a separate country. One father and son had died within five days of each other, just one month before the end of the First World War. Another boy, a neighbour in life as in death, had been killed the same day. It was as if the neoclassical grandeur that had been denied the fortress-like houses had been permitted here. The grandeur of the final resting place: it was the ultimate expression of the Corsican sense of family, and pride, and also of a Corsican fascination with death.

We embarked the next morning for the seven and a half mile crossing to Sardinia. We edged out of the almost completely enclosed harbour into choppy sea. Bonifaziu loomed behind us, white as an iceberg and weather-beaten, ringed by unscalable ramparts – both Genoese walls and the sandwiched striations of the natural cliffs. The houses teetered like guano-coated cormorants' nests over the void. The whole dramatic scenario was topped by the glimmer of a distant snow-clad peak – perhaps our very own Bavella.

Richard had rung Dorothy to say goodbye.

'I'm glad you liked Corsica,' she said. 'And send my love to your terrible children.'

ELEVEN

Bandit Country

We docked at a flat little port called Santa Teresa. Suddenly that high-pitched buzz of Vespas and three-wheeled Ape trucks; suddenly supermarkets with that familiar salty hammy smell mixed with floor polish. Italy! We stocked up on polenta and Sardinian *malloreddus* pasta that looked like albino woodlice, and Sardinian bread called *pistokku*, wafer-thin rectangles that broke your teeth. We were instructed to '*bagnare sfoglie prima della consumazione*', but this just made it sodden. The shepherds take it into the bony hills and live on it for weeks in their circular stone *pinnette* with thatched conical roofs, remnants of the Stone Age.

It was daunting to be so abruptly faced with two new languages – Italian and Sard, our nineteenth and twentieth.

We drove south-east. We were heading into a wild region called Barbágia, a name derived from the *Civitates Barbariae* which was how the Romans described areas they won but never tamed. Ridges rose to right and left, but the valleys were not confined and wooded like in Corsica but spacious and treeless. Sardinia had been almost completely deforested, its majestic oaks and pines chopped for charcoal to fuel the Piedmontese industrial revolution. Now it was shorn, and sheep swarmed on it like maggots over a sheep's knobbly carcass. The largest cargo on our ferry from Corsica had been timber.

On the map Cala Gonone, in the Gulf of Orosei, looked a good place to stay. It was on the road, but far from conurbations, and surrounded by dolmens. But it wasn't a good place to stay; it was a desolate off-season tourist development with a fake beach, cement mixers turning, and nowhere to park.

Then we noticed a sign to a beach. In desperation we followed a narrowing track over the cliff, up into the mountains for ten miles, higher and higher, ever more unlikely, then down the other side. Nothing was marked on the map. The track turned east. Richard followed it: he had no choice as we couldn't turn round. But instinct led him there too.

'I think it's going to be all right,' he said.

A gorge broadened into a valley of flowering euphorbia and gorse. A stream ran through it, down to a pristine cove. The stream petered out in a brackish pond and we parked between the pond, a willow grove, and the sea. We had food and drinking water to last a week, with washing-up water and wood in abundance. Richard, with his do-it-now energy, strung up the clothes line and lit a fire.

But then, as if scenting our arrival from afar, the police arrived. They remonstrated with Richard, tried to move us on. Richard pleaded that it was winter, we wouldn't cause trouble, and – yes, here they were – we had two *bambini*. It was so good here for the *bambini*. The police melted.

For a week our only visitors were cattle and sheep jangling their bells beside the stream. Sometimes they wandered on to the beach and drank from the pond. On the cliff stood a ramshackle hut; its owner had put planks over stumps for a table and benches, and laid out glasses as if expecting a party. He tended his broad beans and shooed the sheep away. On the tideline the white pads were not sanitary pads but cuttlefish. It was Homeric and lovely, like the Mediterranean had been for thousands of years, and no longer was anywhere but here. And it was ours, we had found it ourselves. We had the illusion of discovering treasure.

By day we lay on the white sand, sifting through layers of shells. Tallulah and I practised her reading. We would inscribe words in the sand, and between words she insisted on rolling down to the sea: the three Rs, reading, writing, and rolling. Richard entertained her by building boats from bits of polystyrene and sailing them across the pond. We explored the shore – to our left limestone pinnacles and rocks hollowed out by the iridescent sea, and to our right flowering cliffs of twisted cypress, holm oaks, myrtle and man-sized euphorbia. They were slightly unnerving cliffs, full of grottoes and white boulders; there were signs of human activity – cut branches, fireplaces – but it was too clean to be tourists. We suspected shepherds or hunters (the wild boar season was just ending). The cliffs amplified the wave sounds, and the eroded rocks at the waterline made mysterious slappings and gurglings. We tucked up in the maquis, drowning in the scent of tamarisk, lilies, and lavender, while I read Tallulah *The Little Prince*.

By night I joined Richard by the fire, gazing up at the Milky Way. Not a single sodium light dimmed its brightness, not even the orange glow of a distant town. The stars were more colourful than I'd ever known them; one was flashing blue and red and I was convinced it was a satellite until we took out Philips' Chart of the Stars and found it was Sirius, the brightest star in the middle heavens. Betelgeuse was a deep orange. We traced Orion and the Pleiades. We may not have known the name of our beach, or even where we were, but with Philips' Chart of the Stars at least we – like the Little Prince – could find our way through the solar system.

Our Mob was a speck of breathing life in the desolation of night.

When we finished our drinking water we wrenched ourselves away. Our first town was Dorgali. It was featureless grey granite, but after our solitude it seemed like a metropolis – a couple of bars, a bakery. It had an air of gentility. We shopped extravagantly on sweet Dorgali wine and pecorino cheese and prosciutto and a bewildering variety of pasta, every shape and size.

Older women in full-length black scurried nun-like through cobbled back streets. Their heads were shrouded in black shawls that fell to the ground. There was a strong Muslim element to the garb, perhaps a reminder of medieval Saracen invasions or, according to one local, to the supposed Turkish origins of the name – Turkali. They were sinister figures, but closer inspection revealed their weeds to be more luxurious than at first appeared; there were tassels, and embroidery, and glimpses of expensive shoes.

Dorgali's walls were papered with black and white notices announcing deaths, or anniversaries of deaths.

While Richard refilled the water tank, making nine journeys with the water container between town fountain and van, I took Tallulah to the library. It was a pink stucco building with damp-patched walls.

Tallulah gripped my hand shyly while I explained to the librarian that I was looking for someone to talk to about Sardinia. She summoned a reader, who emerged smiling and bespectacled from behind some stacks. He was an economics student. Between them they knew the perfect person, Tiziana Fancello, a friend of the librarian's sister. While the librarian made a phone call, the economics student found a book of Sardinian costumes, a dazzling array of dresses and shawls of bright, hard colours which were seen on the streets every day until at least the First World War. It was during that war that Sardinians first discovered the rest of the world, when they went off to join the Sassari Brigade to fight the Austrians. Many never returned, either because they were dead, or because they found a better life elsewhere. Now the costumes were seen only at festivals.

The librarian arranged a meeting for that afternoon, then handed round a tray of almond and aniseed *dolci Sardi*. Tallulah didn't dare try hers until I ate mine. She deposited sucked raisins discreetly on the desk.

Tiziana lived in Cala Gonone, the ugly resort. Dorgali people had developed it after a road was tunnelled through the mountains. Until then it would have been hemmed in between mountain and sea, cut off to all but fishermen. As we crested the mountains we realized that we were cresting a volcanic crater; that explained the fertility of the soil around the town, and the quantity of basalt on our beach.

We found Tiziana at La Pinetta bar. She was smart in a cream silk shirt and black trousers and blood-red lipstick, a world away from the shrouded crones of Dorgali. I think she had dressed for us, hoping for some fruitful outcome from our interview. She was twenty-six and looking for a job. She had black eyes and crooked teeth. She looked more Spanish than Italian: not surprising since Sardinia was part of Catalonia and then Spain for 400 years, until the eighteenth century. In a north-east corner people still speak Catalan. After the War of Spanish Succession, Sardinia passed from the Spanish Bourbons to the Austrian Hapsburgs. The Austrians then exchanged Sardinia for Sicily, with Sardinia becoming the so-called Kingdom of Sardinia, a remote and backward outpost of the Kingdom of Piedmont-Savoy.

Tiziana summoned beers and coffees from the big ugly barmaid, the librarian's sister. The bar was off-season empty, the mood intimate. She said that in Dorgali, or up in the mountains, you'd never see women in bars. In parts of Barbágia women never even went out after 7 p.m. Until recently in those places they seldom ventured out at all, but spent their lives as shadows flitting past shuttered windows.

Cala Gonone was different, what with all the tourists, and Tiziana herself had spent one year in Spain and another in the US, and also had a degree in political science. Yet it was that which made her desperate. She had assumed that her qualifications would lead easily to a decent job, but she was wrong: there was nothing. The most she could expect was guiding tourists during the two frantic summer months. Nearly half the population was unemployed, with industries closing all the time.

'The big problem is politics,' she said. 'The politicians don't want to change. The people want change, but the politicians are corrupt and self-interested.'

Hence the sprawl of Cala Gonone, built with complete disregard for planning laws.

'Everything's for a sister or a brother or a brother-in-law.'

'Why won't they change?' I asked her.

'I don't know. It's something in our blood.'

That apparently congenital southern corruption and nepotism lay behind the recent declaration of independence by 'Padania', a move by north Italian politicians to sever connections with the financially draining south – which included Sardinia.

'Padania would be a disaster for us,' Tiziana said.

'What about Sardinian independence?'

'There is an independence movement of sorts.'

We had seen the graffiti – 'SARDEGNA NATZIONE'.

'It's not violent like in Corsica. There's never been that sense of being a united country, conquered by another. But there's a historic resentment that this island has always been exploited, neglected.

Even now, most tourist income ends up not in Sardinia, but on the continent, or abroad.'

Like Corsica, Sardinia had always been besieged and dominated by foreign powers.

She went on: 'But most people see the continent as our only source of hope. Most people have more to think about than independence: they have to survive.'

'Do people emigrate?'

'Yes, to Rome or Milan, or to the United States. Sardinia's been drastically depopulated. But it's very difficult for us. We are close-knit, very rooted. We're very simple inside. We're different from the north Italians, very friendly, very warm. We have different priorities, such as friendships, family relations. We have a family reunion every weekend, and that kind of family support is really important now there's so much unemployment.'

Her mother tongue was Italian, not Sard. In her family, only her father spoke Sard, and she found it hard to understand the guttural 'c', like 'h', or the 's' like 'sh'. In fact Sard, another Romance language, is very similar to Italian. The Italian *cielo*, 'sky' (from the Latin *caelum*), is *kelu* in Sard; *canta*, 'sing' (*cantat* in Latin), is *cantat* in Sard; *acqua*, 'water' (*aqua* in Latin), is *abba* in Sard; *pietra*, 'stone' (*petra* in Latin), is *pedra* in Sard. A few pre-Roman words remain such as *cùccuru* (mountain peak) or the delightful *tilipirke* (grasshopper), but as the island was Roman for over six hundred years it is not surprising that Romance took over. The longevity of Roman occupation is testified by it being the only Romance language to retain the use of the hard 'c's of Latin before 'e', 'i', and 'y', as in *kelu*.

Tiziana faced the usual problem of the plethora of dialects. These go back to pre-history when the island was first inhabited around 6000 BC. People landing in the north were probably from Etruria on the Italian mainland; those in the centre from the Iberian penin-sular via the Balearics, and those in the south from Africa. So there was never one Sardinian tribe. They did come together linguistically to a degree, but were divided against each other politically, and over the next millennia experienced invasions by different peoples at different times who left different legacies of different words. As the Roman Empire collapsed the island was ravaged by Vandals and Muslim Berbers to such an extent that it was considered safer to divide the island into separate states responsible for their own self-defence, laws, and parliaments; these were exploited by different outside powers – Genoa, Pisa, Catalonia. Today there is no single Sardinian standard, although the dialect of the Logudoro region is used as a common form for songs.

In 1986 55 per cent of families still spoke Sard at home, but the number was dwindling rapidly, especially among women. At school Tiziana was taught in Italian. She was proud of her 'good' Italian, and boasted that because the Risorgimento was launched from Sardinia, the Sardinians were the first true Italians. Victor Emmanuel of Savoy, who was proclaimed the first king of a united Italy in 1861, was initially King of Sardinia. As early as 1827 legislation in Sardinian had been abolished for ever, which meant that Italian had much more scope to flourish at the expense of Sard. It also became a class thing. During the first half of the twentieth century it was accepted that the elite spoke Italian and the poor spoke Sard.

Since the early 1970s, the Partito d'Azione Sardo began to include the language issue in its political demands. A resolution adopted by the University of Cagliari in 1971 called upon national and regional authorities to recognize the Sardinian people as an ethnic and linguistic minority, and their language as the official language of the island. But nothing happened. In 1978 the Comitau Limba Sarda presented the Regional Council with a petition signed by 15,000 electors demanding official Sardinian–Italian bilingualism and protection of the Sardinian dialects, as well as of the Catalan spoken in Alghero. Yet still nothing has legally changed. Given the absence of an official policy, Sardinian is left to play a minimal role at every level of society.

'Would you ever wear the Sardinian costume?'

'No one under forty-five would dream of wearing it.'

But it wasn't just age. Like the language, it was a class thing: even during the nineteenth century to 'wear costume' was to be a peasant from some remote village, however lovely that costume may be. Tiziana was not a peasant girl.

'And when those women die,' she added, apparently without regret, 'it will be finished.'

She was interested in the costumes only in so far as they provided interest for the tourists.

In his curious 1923 travelogue *Sea and Sardinia*, much of which is preoccupied with the discomfort of the hotels, D. H. Lawrence rails against the disappearance of Sardinian uniqueness.

> I am glad that the era of love and oneness is over; hateful homogeneous world-oneness . . . I shall be glad when men hate their common, world-alike clothes, when they tear them up and clothe themselves fiercely for distinction, savage distinction, savage distinction against the rest of the creeping world . . . when men fiercely react against looking all alike, and being all alike, and betake themselves into vivid clan or nation-distinctions.

There is something ludicrous about Lawrence's panting 'distinction, savage distinction, savage distinction'. You can almost hear him dropping his drawers, his Sardinian audience running in fright. But he was right.

He went on:

> Men will set their bonnets at one another now, and fight themselves into separation and sharp distinction. The day of peace and oneness is over, the day of the great fight into multifarious-ness is at hand. Hasten the day, and save us from proletarian homogeneity and khaki-all-alikeness.

Of course the khaki-all-alikeness arrived (literally) sixteen years later when the Nazis tried to impose on Europe their 'hateful homogeneous world-oneness', and to wipe out all nation-distinctions except their own.

Tiziana for her part seemed torn between nostalgia for her culture (and pride in it), and a longing for sophistication. She saw herself not stranded in this backwater within a backwater, but strolling down Via del Corso, off to some important job in Rome. She longed to be *someone*, and she would never manage that hanging out in Cala Gonone. She was panicking about her future, but meanwhile she couldn't wait for the start of the tourist season. Not just for the work, but for the buzz. The population of Cala Gonone would burst from 1500 to 40,000. She loved to escape into the anonymous world of foreigners. It was a substitute for her real escape, for which she waited, and then for her eventual return, for which she also waited. Because for all her aspirations, she was also in the grip of a tribal feeling, a connection with the island which she could never break.

'Not many British come,' she commented. 'I think Sardinia gets a bad press in Britain. The kidnappings.'

'Does that still go on?'

'Oh yes! Two weeks ago a woman was kidnapped. She was dragged from her car. Her child was left sleeping on the back seat.'

That would have been just as we arrived. This news did not make me comfortable.

'Most people don't make a sound because they don't want to wake the child. If the child woke, the bandits would take the child too. Don't worry,' she added hastily as she noticed my expression, 'the bandits were waiting for her. They only go for people they know have money. It's a big problem for us. It's the shepherds.'

'What about the woman? Has there been any news?'

'No.'

Later I heard about kidnap victims who were imprisoned for months in a van like ours, buried under ground. I imagined the clods of earth rebounding on the van roof as it was buried; the darkness; the pipe that was the only source of air; the meagre food and water bottles that were dropped down it; the pipe outlet hidden in rocks.

In Italian kidnapping is known as 'Anonymous Sardinian Sequestration'. It was less to do with the Mafia than in Sicily, and less to do with the vendetta than in Corsica: it was more to do with the culture of *sos balentes*, the macho men, who shared bitter memories of exploitation going back hundreds of years. This was revenge of the poor on the rich, of the underdog. Above all, it was simple extortion.

Tiziana insisted on paying for the drinks, despite her poverty.

'We always pay for the guest.'

We spent the night on the cliffs. A herd of goats with kids rattled discordant bells like soldiers clanking mess tins. There was no sign of a shepherd, although I suspected one lurked out of sight. The goats nibbled the lowest branches of ancient olives whose trunks flowed over the rocks. As the sun plunged so did the temperature.

Beyond the Mob, and surveying the Gulf of Orosei, rose the Nuraghe Mannu. It was the remains of a conical Bronze Age fort and watchtower. The vaulted cone was built of massive blocks, some rough-hewn; the largest were over five metres high and had been immovable when other rocks were plundered to build Cala Gonone. *Mannu* is Sardinian for 'great', from the Latin *magnus*. I ducked under a vast lintel. It was dank inside, claustrophobic, like being in a drain.

Somehow, at some point, these blocks had been dragged here and laid stone upon stone. There was not a trace of mortar, yet this tower had stood upright for several thousand years.

Around 7000 of these nuraghi dot the Sardinian landscape, with two more within walking distance. The only building shape they resemble is a windmill, or towers I had seen in Ibiza (although they were whitewashed and inhabited).

I looked up to where the blocks, carefully placed one on top of the other, drew towards each other to form a dome, leaving a discoidal patch of sky, the same shape as the hole in the top of a Sami *kota*, left open to draw smoke upwards. Who built this? No one knows for sure. Since the nuraghe builders had no system of writing, no native historical records exist, but Greek sources portray a fabulous Sardinian golden age with intensive agriculture and building that flourished before the Carthaginians invaded. If there was ever a united and unique Sardinian culture (or to be more precise, Proto-Sardinian) it was this, the so-called Nuraghic civilization, which lasted for over a thousand years.

Sardinia's first permanent inhabitants, who arrived around 6000 BC, were probably cave-dwellers, but it was not long before Proto-Sardinians began to live a farming life in hut villages. This Sardinian

Copper Age culture was flourishing in the first half of the second millennium BC, and was transformed very slowly by the influences of Bronze Age civilizations that were already ancient in the near east. This oriental influence was absorbed by the local culture and made its own, reaching its peak in the eighth or seventh century BC. In a more or less degenerate form, it survived the Carthaginian invasion that began around 500 BC, until the Romans defeated the Carthaginians in 238 BC and began their own conquest of the island.

Archaeology has had a revival in Sardinia over the last twenty years. Many of the discoveries are brand new. Archaeologists had spent the last two years unearthing round huts around Nuraghe Mannu, and also foundations of a large rectangular temple. The tower might have been the main element of a fortress with a village and temple around it. Given its strategic cliff-top location, it probably served as a look-out post against invasion; it might also have guarded the boundaries of tribal territories. Alternatively, it may have been the residential castle of a chieftain that would have included storerooms, foundries, and a place of worship. In the museum in Cagliari we would see the exquisite bronze statuettes made by these people. Like the portrait megaliths of Filitosa, they featured daggers strapped to chests, but unlike the Filitosa statues these were only a few inches high. The miniature warriors, being of a later date, were also far more detailed, with cloaks and knotted sticks, and swords held over their shoulders. They wore short tunics and bare feet and had long thin noses and pursed lips.

For centuries Phoenicians had traded along the coast, establishing ports that hugely boosted Proto-Sardinian wealth. But after Carthage attained leadership of the western Phoenicians, the Carthaginians tried to exercise more control over the island, and began to conquer the most productive parts. This drove the proudest of the Proto-Sardinians to a fierce life in the mountains, something which was to shape the Sardinian character for ever.

This was an interesting time to be here. Sardinia's newly revealed ancient history was helping to shape its future. While archaeologists were unearthing Sardinia's thriving Nuraghic culture, so linguists and politicians, encouraged by this archaeological evidence of a truly

Sardinian culture, were devising ways of keeping its language alive. Nine months after we left, in January 1998, a new regional law would for the first time acknowledge Sardinian as having equal status with Italian. The law would approve the promotion of Sardinian language and culture, finance Sardinian teaching in schools and university, and for the first time allow Sardinian to be used alongside Italian in public administration. Original Sardinian toponyms would be reinstated. Italian national magazines demonstrated a growing sympathy towards minority languages by hailing the new law as 'the right to speak', and 'a cultural revolution'. Nevertheless, by 2001 Italy had still not ratified the European Charter for Regional and Minority Languages.

Tiziana said we should go to Orgósolo, though she had never been there herself. She'd heard about it, how wild it was.

The road jackknifed up out of rocks and olive groves and drystone walls and waterfalls of sheep and terraces being ploughed by oxen. It was a pagan landscape. And for years after the rest of Sardinia was Christian, it *was* pagan. During the sixth century the Barbágians even established an independent heathen domain. Only in the last few years have roads been built to take us there.

Grandiose gates with new concrete posts led to nothing but the meanest tin-roofed peasant hovel. It gave the landscape a crazy optimistic feel, as if these peasants were confident that one day their gates would lead to a correspondingly magnificent mansion.

And everywhere were walls. During the nineteenth century, a fatal piece of legislation imposed the *chiudende*, the enclosures. Anyone able to enclose land became its owner, so overnight people built walls, shouting '*Tancate*', raise the *tancas* – fences. But only the rich could afford the labour for more than an acre or two. Suddenly shepherds found that grazing grounds they had used for centuries were denied to them. It led to bitter resentments, privation, and lawlessness. Many people were forced to become vagrants, and turned to banditry to survive. In the wild Barbágia mountains this grew into warfare between villages on a major scale; in an attack on Tortoli in 1894, every man in the village was killed or wounded.

The sign to Orgósolo had been shot to bits.

We knew we were nearing the town when a bend in the road revealed a rock slab painted with a recumbent female. Orgósolo, Tiziana had heard, was covered in mad murals.

It straddled the hills of Barbágia like a jawbone of old teeth. The houses were half built, bristling with reinforcing rods, rough with exposed airbricks and breeze blocks. We stopped in the main piazza – such as it was. Just an open space overlooking the fields that rose to the plateau of Sopramonte: nothing more. There were no decent buildings, no benches, no fountains. Men loitered, but had nowhere to sit except on doorsteps, or propped against a bulge in a wall. They were rough-looking, with dark fierce eyes under cloth caps. Some had cropped hair and big boots and black stubbled chins. There were pinched, furtive faces, others tough and weather-beaten. They looked as if they were waiting to be hired as hitmen. They watched us, unsmiling, aloof. Their eyes were blank. They had a marvellous rebellious pride, but they made me feel uneasy. An African offered them carved nick-nacks from a sack, without success, then stared at us, scratching his groin. Cars clattered past, horns honking as if every driver in town was drunk. Richard asked the most respectable-looking of the men if he thought this a safe place to park, and he said no.

These were descendants of the Nuraghic brigands who escaped from the Carthaginians to the hills and who kept the Romans at bay.

We retreated to a lower piazza and parked outside the *polizia*. We informed the police of our presence, but I suspected they stayed barricaded in their police station and didn't dare venture on to the streets.

The noise and machismo intimidated me. And I couldn't forget the kidnapped woman with her child on the back seat. Feeding the girls gave me an excuse to stay in, leaving Richard to explore alone. With straggly beard and holes in his jeans and shoes he felt confident of not being a kidnap target.

He returned triumphant, having persuaded the denizens of the piazza to be photographed. Four were willing – eager even – to pose beneath a mural of a bandit, but two turned to the wall begging Richard to stop. They were afraid of being recognized. Someone had adorned the mural with a speech bubble emerging from the bandit's gun. Written in the bubble was the word 'bono'.

Richard had followed a splendid striding man in a three-piece velvet suit with breeches and knee-length boots. He had caught up with him beneath a mural of Gershwin's 'Summertime'. The man was a local landowner. He posed under the words: 'Summer's here, and the living is easy.' But black-draped women scurried off at Richard's approach.

Saturday night exploded with revelry. Shouting men, hooting, revving engines, barking dogs, crying children. All around Orgósolo the country was desolate, swathed in silence, empty but for a few lonely shepherds. The settlements on their hilltops were, in the words of Sardinian novelist Salvatore Satta, as remote from one another as are the stars. Yet close up this star was a burning supernova. It was almost demonic. Long after we were in bed a car revved beside us, and someone banged on our bonnet, then rattled the door. Bravely, in his underpants, Richard opened it and confronted two young *barbaricini*. I lay paralysed, expecting him to be knifed, for this to be the kidnapping I dreaded. But they wanted Richard to come drinking. They implored him with spirity breath. He wasn't in the mood.

I felt braver after that encounter. Perhaps my fears had been exaggerated. Richard hoisted Xanthe into the backpack and embarked on another photographic mission, while Tallulah and I explored the old town. Up shadowed labyrinths of uneven concrete, between DIY houses built of the cheapest materials, one stage up from a shanty town or gypsy camp. Urchin children running with sores scrabbled after a ball in a gutter. Street names were daubed in white paint directly on the concrete. People used their half-built upper storeys to hang hams. It transpired that the houses were so rough because of the Sardinian reluctance to pay tax on the finished building. They made Corsican villages seem havens of fabulous architecture.

The wall paintings were not formal murals so much as up-market graffiti, mostly political. Images borrowed from Picasso and Miró and Henry Moore were used as images of class struggle, or as statements on behalf of beleaguered minorities like the Palestinians. There were anti-war, anti-American, anti-fascist texts, while others simply advertised the wares in some hole-in-the-wall shop. One wall of the doctor's surgery portrayed Virus, Hunger, and Epidemic as an avenging sword-wielding devil, while Preventive Medicine in the form of women and children stood resolute to one side. It was basic propaganda.

The people of Orgósolo had found the perfect expression for their vibrant, volatile, humorous character. I was reminded of Christiania, the drug-dealing hippy enclave in Copenhagen. But this was less self-conscious, just a town gone wild.

As we penetrated deeper into the maze, we glimpsed immaculate interiors. For all the exterior squalor, many houses were beautifully finished inside. Their owners had come by money, somehow. Black-clothed crones scrubbed marble halls lined with pot plants. Suds poured down alleys reeking of detergent. In the heart of town we found ancient circular houses built of blocks of stone like nuraghi, possibly remnants of the primitive *fughiles*, the windowless houses with holes in the roof to let out the smoke – stone versions of the Sami *kota* – that we had seen dotting some more remote hillsides. Their presence in the town, surrounded by the makeshift houses of today, made me fear that we were witnessing the end of an era dating back to prehistory.

The main church opened for the children's service. We went in. The old church had been abandoned and this one built in the 1970s. After the meanness of the streets it was surprisingly spacious. It was painted pale blue and white and hung with Stations of the Cross. An altarpiece showed the Madonna ascending into heaven in Sardinian costume.

The church was packed. In the back rows old women huddled like crows. We sat amongst them, which gave me a chance to study their costume at close range. To my right a woman was swathed entirely in dark brown, from head to toe, apart from the moon of her kindly old face, and her knotted hands that plucked at her rosary. Man's hands, used to toil. Her outfit was more severe than in Dorgali, and the shawl worn not only over her head but also across her chin. At times she drew it secretively across her mouth. It was pinned at the throat with a simple broach. Her shawl was hemmed with a patterned brown band, from which fell tassels two feet long. She didn't bother with her service sheet, and I wondered if she was illiterate.

I thought of the novels of the other great Sardinian writer, Grazia Deledda, and her descriptions of the harshness and poverty of Barbágian life. It is in her novels that the secret past of Sardinia is revealed – and in many ways the secret present of Orgósolo. The darkness of the traditions, conformity, the Church, the black-hearted priests, the patriarchal shepherds, the violence, ancient feuds, taciturn passions, and above all the harshness of the land. The accursed Sardinian soil. How they hate the land.

Then there is the claustrophobia. Because for all the wide open spaces – the empty plateaux – the strict moral codes of these tight little communities, including the codes of the vendetta, are still strong enough to be suffocating. I could see it in the shrouded way the women dressed, the way they huddled together.

There were children everywhere, neat with brushed hair, and a choir of boys who filed into the apse where they wiggled their legs. The priest was young and fun, inviting the boys to speak into the microphone. It was busy and irreverent. When children came with bags for the collection, not many people put anything in. There seemed to be no shame in that. Our old lady put in 1000 lire so I did the same, realizing afterwards that this was only 40p.

A little girl in a frilly red dress and matching hairband sidled in beside Tallulah and stroked her leg. Tallulah was shy, but pleased too. I towered over the congregation. I felt like a giantess.

Outside, a gang of youths waited for the girls. It struck me that there had not been one man in church, apart from the priest.

Meanwhile Richard had been touring the bars. This was where the men were. They were looking around for something new, so Richard received a lot of smiling attention. However, it was the exquisite blonde Xanthe who was star attraction. From bar to bar

Richard was bought congratulatory beers, and when he staggered home he found Xanthe's pockets stuffed with bars of chocolate.

After the service, about thirty people remained contemplatively behind. Five men joined them and sat together on one side. Then they began to sing in plainsong harmony. It was mournful, like a lament, as if summoning memories of an ancient and less convenient time. It was very moving. This was the Sardinian equivalent of the polyphonic songs we had heard at Anghjulu Orati's house in Corsica, here sung not by a revivalist group but by the strong men of the town.

Outside the church, Orgósolo was a twirling frenzy; inside there was, suddenly, an ancient stillness. I felt as if we were in the epicentre of the island, that it was almost imploding. I couldn't wait to escape.

TWELVE

Macédoine

By mid-March we were on the quay in Otranto. We had explored Pompei, climbed Vesuvius to peer with trepidation into its sulphurous depths, and lingered in the heel of the Italian boot. For once Tallulah agreed that it was better than being stuck at a desk at school like her friends. Now we sought a ferry to Greece.

Suddenly two rusted gunboats commandeered from the Albanian navy roared into port, escorted by powerboats from Italian customs. A white T-shirt fluttered from the Albanian radio mast and refugees huddled on deck. Two Italian navy choppers circled overhead; Xanthe cowered in the backpack.

A financial scandal had propelled Albania into civil war. There would be no ferries across the Adriatic.

After four days the crisis abated slightly, and we found a ferry from Brindisi to Igoumenitsa. On deck Richard met an American missionary who described his escape from Albania, his panic-stricken drive to the nearest port only to find the ferry refusing to take passengers for fear of gunmen – there were three guns per person, he said, and ten rounds of ammunition per gun. Even the children were armed. He had spent last night hidden in the Albanian docks, surrounded by mad gunmen. A friend with him was hit in the head by a bullet fired into the air; it knocked her out and gashed the back of her neck. He was forced to give his truck to a stranger. He and his wounded friend were rescued by the Italian navy and transferred on to this ferry. He planned to wait in Greece until things calmed down, then go back to plant some more churches.

It seemed an appropriately Balkan start to our sojourn in Greece.

Wind-blown sleet lashed us into the Pindos Mountains. The sky hung bruised and heavy, rivers were in spate. The turbulent weather increased our apprehension about grappling with a new country and a new language that we could neither speak nor read. I hated the isolation this imposed. It wasn't for a week that we discovered we were in a new time zone. Fortunately road signs were in Greek *and* English. SLOW ICY ROAD; NARROW BRIDGE; PASS OPEN. Nevertheless, the tortuous E90 was punctuated by shrines to victims of road accidents. On the map the road wound like intestines, red and twisting. Lorry drivers had made propitiatory offerings to rusty shrines of saints, with plastic flowers and vials of holy water.

Much of the view was despoiled. EU-funded road widenings made scalpel cuts through the mountains. The verges were deep litter, bags flapping from branches. We rode through it like a ship, leaving a wash of plastic.

Tallulah said, 'You know, Mummy, I really like litter because that's what I'm *used* to. London is full of litter. That's what I'm *used* to.'

Thank you, Tallulah.

Other shrines were springs where we filled up with fresh water. Since ancient times the Greeks have made much of their springs, and several were sheltered by roofs like bus stops. But many were smashed up, daubed in graffiti, reeking of piss. I suppose Tallulah really liked that too, because that was what she was *used* to.

We were heading for Macedonia. Not the former Yugoslav Republic of, but the Province of, a swathe of mountains and plains that cross northern Greece along the southern frontiers of the former Yugoslavia and Bulgaria, home of Philip of Macedon and his son Alexander the Great. I was intrigued by the crisis provoked by the EU's recognition of the newly independent former Yugoslav Republic of Macedonia in 1992. Greece had been outraged. There had been riots. The Greeks felt so strongly that they were prepared to cut off their own route north into central Europe by closing the border between the two countries. Thus they isolated this fledgling republic between a chaotic Albania, a decidedly unsettled Bulgaria, and an increasingly volatile Kosovo, hardly a propitious start for a new country that relied for much of its survival on trade with Greece, and through Greece with the world.

That blockade had now been lifted, but tension between the countries remained high. Why did the Greeks react like this? Who are the Macedonians? It is this, the intractable Macedonian Question, that has baffled historians and politicians for the last 150 years.

The *Handbook for Travellers in Greece* that the publisher John Murray presented to my great-grandfather in 1896 contains a chapter on Macedonia, but as 'an almost uncharted region, *in no sense Hellenic*'. It consisted of portions of what is now Greece, Bulgaria, and the Former Yugoslavia, and was still part of the crumbling Ottoman Empire. 'Probably no single province in Europe can in ethnological variety and interest surpass Macedonia,' enthuses Murray's handbook, going on to list Orthodox Slavs, mostly Bulgarian but also Bosnian and Serb in north and north-east Macedonia; Muslim Albanians further south; Orthodox Greeks in the projecting trident of Halkidiki; swathes of Muslim Turks; a huge population of Sephardic Jews in Salonika; Polish Jews 'of a very inferior class'; Catholic Poles along the border with Thessaly descended from the Polish Legion employed by Turkey in the Crimean War; nomadic Orthodox and Muslim Wallachians (now known as Vlachs) around Kastoria; nomadic Turcomans in the plains around Salonika; and the largest concentration of gypsies on the Balkan peninsular. There is no mention of 'Macedonians'.

By contrast, we also had a modern Greek guidebook which implied that no one had ever inhabited this region except indomitable Greeks with their high morale, the genius of the nation hitherto oppressed by the evil Turk. No mention of Slavs, Bulgarians, Albanians, or Vlachs. Only because we had Murray's handbook, published before the province of Macedonia became part of Greece, was it possible to unravel who had once founded and inhabited the villages we travelled through.

When modern frontiers were drawn up at the end of the First World War a minority of Slav speakers found themselves on the Greek side. There were rumours of their mistreatment by the Greeks. But according to our Greek guidebook, no such people existed.

A little town like Siatista, huddled below the barren shale of Mount Askion, was by all accounts Greek: founded by refugees fleeing from the Turks on the plains around Salonika. It was our first pretty town in Greece, white houses with red-tiled roofs instead of the usual concrete and corrugated iron. We parked in the *chora*.

Here eighteenth-century merchants built *archontika*, mansions with carved enclosed balconies, their interior walls decorated by local craftsmen with patterns and flowers and stained glass. Hidden behind glazed balconies, girls had filled dowry chests with embroideries and weavings. The *archontika* were fortress-like, stone-built as protection against the Turks and, as the decaying Ottoman empire left a vacuum of authority, against marauding bands of Slavs and Albanians. The *archontika* were family strongholds, built with money and taste; but also with fear. As the British journalist H. N. Brailsford wrote of Macedonia in 1906, 'Fear is the dominant, the ever-present motive. It builds villages. It dictates migrations. It explains deceits. It has created the morals of a country.'

Tragically, each *archontika* was more decayed than the last. Some had trees sprouting from the roofs, abandonded by owners who had escaped from this backwater into the Greek diaspora. I climbed into the garden of the Nerantzopoulos mansion and tried to peer between broken shutter slats, but all was dark.

The owners of the *archontika* had Greek names (Poulko, Kanatsoulis, Manousis, Nerantzopoulos), so presumably considered themselves to be Greek.

The exquisite Greek Orthodox church of St Paraskiva stood beside its separate belfry. Smoke-blackened frescoes in the exonarthex promised treasures within, but it was locked. Then we saw a note with a phone number, and rang the number from a kiosk. A guardian arrived with a Siatista emigrant who was back on holiday from Australia. Inside it was cave-like, its frescoes so charred by candle smoke and age that it was hard to decipher the imagery. It smelled aromatic, of beeswax and incense. Splendidly carved throne-like seats lined the west wall of the naos, and the iconostasis rose as a jewelled screen. The men beckoned us behind the iconostasis into the inner sanctum. It was like penetrating the recesses of a shell. Here, they whispered furtively, was the school. For many years under Turkish rule this school had been held in secret; later more openly.

*

If Siatista was Greek then Kozani, provincial capital of West Macedonia, felt like eastern Europe. A dreary muddle of post-war flats,
Kozani was as bleak as any town in Romania. Window displays were
dusty, stacked unimaginatively with boxes or 1950s mannequins in
cheap clothes. Shop assistants responded as curtly as pre-1989 East
Europeans. We were frequently reminded that this was not the
Greece of the all-dancing ouzo-drinker of the sunny islands, but a
place more northern, more dour, more Balkan.

People spoke Greek, but I suspected they were Slavs who had
been Hellenized. This feeling was backed up by the Communist tone
of the museum – photographs of people in traditional costume posing
in meadows in front of concrete flat blocks; a painting of a peasant
woman 'distraught at the pollution of the environment'; a photograph of a bridge built not by a famous architect or engineer but
'by the apprentices of Kozani'. My suspicions were confirmed later
when I discovered that after the First World War, when Macedonia
was parcelled out at the Treaty of Neuilly and hundreds of thousands
of 'Slavophones' fled to Bulgaria or Serbia, many chose to remain
here. They had a hazy awareness of their identity, of whether or not
they were Greek. Contemporary Greek surveys suggest that around
half considered themselves Greek whatever their mother tongue,
while the rest considered themselves Bulgarian. New Greek-speaking
schools would have bolstered the number of Greeks.

We were woken on Independence Day by a church service amplified
from the village below. A priest's sonorous chanting droned on for
several hours. It was through the churches – and therefore the
schools – that nineteenth-century Macedonians struggled against
the Ottomans, and each other. Museum photographs of the two
Balkan Wars, the invasion of Anatolia, and the Second World War
always include pictures of Greek Orthodox priests, ferociously
bearded and armed. Even now, our Greek guidebook could speak
of the Orthodox faith as 'the weapon of Hellenism which armed the
hearts of the priests'.

I noticed that none of the museums made any mention of the
Greek civil war. It was clearly taboo. It *would* be taboo to remind

the population that many Greeks had fought for a Communist state of Macedonia, independent of Greece. Instead we were given the impression that the Greeks had always been united in Hellenic brotherhood.

The singing was mournful. It seemed to bemoan the horrors of trampling armies, exported populations, civil war. But the massiveness of the landscape, undulating over the horizon across the Balkans to Russia, dwarfed the conflicts of man, made the centuries of brutality and confusion seem puny.

From the plateau at Vergina we could see over the plain of the River Aliakmon to the sea: a perfect place for a palace. The palace was under our feet, just a plan in stone, dating from the fourth century BC. It belonged Alexander the Great when this was the famous Macedonian city of Aigai. Its grandeur was hinted at by the remains of a beautiful floor mosaic. From a central rosette sprang intertwining and spiralling shoots and tendrils, and in each corner the shoots sprouted a female demon. As I climbed over the knee-high walls (Xanthe in tow), I tried to imagine the Macedonian surveying his kingdom before setting off to conquer the East. It was easy. Polyphonic rivers of sound tumbled from the hills as goats flowed down a ravine, controlled by the whistle of a shepherd swathed in sheepskin and holding a crook.

Below the palace lay the remains of a theatre. It was grassy and dotted with olive trees that teetered on rooty islands above the lower excavated ground. Here in 336 BC King Philip of Macedon, Alexander's father, was celebrating the marriage of his daughter when he was assassinated. A peculiarly Macedonian form of death, as it turned out.

By the time of his assassination, Philip had extended the kingdom of the Macedonians as far as Byzantium, almost from the Adriatic to the Black Sea. A tiny ivory portrait of Philip that we would see in the Salonika museum showed a face not of brutish power but of touching humanity, with kindly crinkles at the corners of his eyes. Alexander extended his kingdom as far as northern India, where Kashmiris still claim their blue eyes are *his* legacy.

We had come here to find Macedonia's roots, which grew here like the olives. We were standing on remnants of the cradle of Macedonia's Hellenic civilization.

I had expected to champion the underdog, but instead I felt some sympathy with Greek outrage at a new country taking the name Macedonia, when Macedonia was clearly here, and in other remnants of Macedonian cities such as Dion and Pella that we would visit nearby. The language of Macedon was a dialect of Greek, and Philip and Alexander considered themselves to be the instruments of the spread of Hellenic culture throughout the East, standing as a bulwark against the barbarians. As Strabo wrote in his *Geographica*, book VII, 'Macedonia too is Greece'. The area that the Greeks now call FYROM, the Former Yugoslav Republic of Macedonia, roughly follows the edges of one of Philip's acquisitions called Paeonia. Although subject to Philip, and then to Alexander, this people maintained its language and its distinct identity with Scupi, today's Skopje, as its capital. They did not become Greek. The Slavs who arrived later, and who occupied much of this region, particularly concentrated in present-day FYROM, did not come until 800 years after Philip's assassination. However, to complicate matters, most of the region *had* been part of the Roman Empire's province of Macedonia.

Philip was buried down the hill. Murray's handbook knew nothing about this, nor the treasure trove inside it, since excavation of the Great Tumulus that swells above it did not begin until 1952, and Philip II's tomb was not discovered until 1977. Incredibly, it had never been plundered. A marble tunnel swept us down to the two-chambered tomb. It had a classical façade – not huge – with two Doric half-columns topped by a frieze depicting a hunt through trees of lions, bears, antelopes, and boars. It was beautiful, not overbearing. We were not allowed in. Beyond a glass shield in a temperature-controlled bubble, restorers were at work under lights; it seemed unreal, like a film. In the Salonika museum we would see grave objects the archaeologists had unearthed. They were of superb quality, including two gold chests emblazoned with a sixteen-rayed sun, an image repeated again and again, symbol of Macedonia.

The Greeks were disconcerted when the new Republic of Macedonia unveiled its flag, which was the Sun of Vergina.

Down into the plain, into market gardens, waste plots, service stations, industrial units, pitted roads, puddles, broken paving, spilling rubbish, stray dogs, electric cables, barracks, ruins, corrugated iron, advertising hoardings, half-built or half-ruined buildings, litter, EU-funded road building, superstores.

We spent weeks in Salonika, on and off. The central car park became our home – slashed by rain when we arrived, a boiling furnace by the time we left, and throughout a cruising place for gays. We chose it because Richard needed to be constantly in reach of a telephone. He had had bad news from England: his father was dangerously ill.

Once the second city of the Byzantine Empire, poised between Hellenic and Byzantine worlds with Vergina and Dion to the west, Mount Athos to the south-east, Salonika is now a dull provincial city scored through by parallel motorways. But it is dotted with gems – Roman and Byzantine ruins, and churches, museums, old markets, the waterfront. Murray's handbook provides a tantalizing description of the city in 1896:

Along the quay are large warehouses, cafés, and residential buildings . . . Further back are the tumbledown wooden houses of the Turkish quarters, divided in many places by pleasant shady orchards and gardens. Behind all comes the vast straggling city itself, with its tortuous streets, fine Roman remains, Frankish counting houses, stately mosques, Byzantine churches, cypresses, citadel and synagogues. More than half are Jews, who here wear a peculiarly handsome and picturesque dress . . . The Greeks form the chief commercial and seafaring population. The Turks are about twice as numerous and the remainder consists of Bulgarians, who form the rural and suburban population, with a large sprinkling of Albanians and Wallachs. As all of these different races retain their national costume, the general effect in the streets is gay and picturesque beyond description.

A hundred years later all has gone. National dress has dwindled to black trousers and platforms for girls, baggy trousers and trainers for boys, fur coats for women, suits for men. The Bulgarians and Turks were exported, and during the Second World War 60,000 Sephardic Jews, who arrived in 1492 to escape persecution in Spain, were transported to Auschwitz. Only one Jewish family returned to Salonika with all its immediate members alive.

Ruined nineteenth-century mansions in the town centre are memorials to those departures.

Another cause of dreariness was a succession of fires, the most devastating in 1917 when three hundred acres of the city were burnt. Venizelos's government took the opportunity to expropriate all the gutted areas and rebuild them in Greek style – i.e. neoclassical and Byzantine. Instead of the colourful hotchpotch, there was now a city of open squares, right angles, grids. Greeks were encouraged to move in. It was Hellenizing on a grand scale, on Greece's front line for the Great Idea of recapturing Constantinople and re-establishing the Byzantine Empire. It was also near the front line of the Great War. Modern Salonika – in all its dullness – is thus a Greek nationalist idea.

Murray's handbook describes the great churches of Salonika as mosques, each one appropriated by the Turks, their Byzantine frescoes and mosaics whitewashed over, daubed with Turkish inscriptions. With the close identification of Orthodox church and state, this was, of course, a political gesture as well as a religious one.

Off the Via Egnatia, the Roman highway that once joined Constantinople to the Adriatic, young people were trotting up the steps to the Byzantine church of Santa Sophia, buying beeswax candles, sticking them in sand trays, saying a prayer for loved ones living or dead.

The church had a flat yellow façade, a squat exterior, four-square, beside a stunted belfry. But inside it was broad and spacious beneath its dome, a small version of Santa Sophia in Istanbul, but a hundred years older. Despite being heavily restored, it maintained its sombre, enclosed atmosphere. We looked up into a dome that capped us with a glorious ninth-century mosaic of the twelve apostles and the Virgin, who circled Christ ascending into heaven sitting on an arc of light within a blue sphere, like a bubble. He was supported by two elegant angels with golden wings. Murray's handbook describes the upper half of the Christ figure defaced by a Turkish inscription and obliterated with whitewash. He said it had been irreparably damaged by fire, the leads were being stripped off the dome, the damp was getting in, the mosaics peeling off. It was hard to imagine in its present pristine, mausoleum-like state.

We bought postcards. The bag was decorated with Philip II's sunburst, and bore Strabo's slogan 'Macedonia is Greece!' It seemed an extraordinary political and aggressive statement to read on a bag used to sell postcards in a church.

On one peregrination about the city, Richard noticed the Institute of Balkan Studies. I was introduced to the short, rotund, balding form of Dr Spyridon Sfetas, a research fellow. He led me into his office, a cave of books. He had a conspiratorial air, a delightfully Balkan air of intrigue.

He was Greek, but his grandfather was Bulgarian, and he spoke Slavo-Macedonian, Bulgarian, Greek, German, and Russian: he was Balkan to the ends of his toes. So fluent was his Slavo-Macedonian that he had recently attended the elections in Skopje as a monitor. Because of his mixed background I hoped that Dr Sfetas' version of events would be as unbiased as I was likely to get in Greece.

I asked him why Greece had reacted so vehemently to the creation of the Republic of Macedonia. He replied that some journalists had written that Greece refused to recognize Macedonia because of the fear that the former Yugoslavs would try to create a Slav-dominated Greater Macedonia, which would include the Greek province of Macedonia and parts of Bulgaria. This Tito had attempted to do during the Second World War and the Greek civil war.

'That memory still haunts the Greeks,' Dr Sfetas said. 'But I do not share the opinion that the Skopje leadership have an expansionist policy towards Greece and Bulgaria.'

'Not when Greece has the support of Nato and the EU.'

'There is that. Besides, the Skopje leadership is essentially pro-Greece, because of the need to counterbalance the power of Serbia and Bulgaria.'

'What about the Slavo-Macedonians who remain in Greece?'

'Those Slavo-Macedonians who remain now,' said Dr Sfetas, 'want to live quietly in Greece. They chose to remain here when they could have gone to Bulgaria or Yugoslavia.'

'I've heard about discrimination against them,' I said. 'There have been reports by human rights groups of oppression, because of fear of militancy by pro-FYROM activists in Greece, sparked off by the Macedonia debacle.'

'Nonsense. There is no proof whatsoever. Most so-called Slavo-phones now speak Greek better than Slavo-Macedonian.'

'So they've been effectively assimilated?'

'Yes.'

'In other words denied the right to schooling in their own language, with place names Hellenized and so on.'

'These reports! I have read them all. You would be amazed by the misuse of material, the repeated quotes from unattributed sources, the lack of proof. These academics and journalists – several of them English and respected there, I believe – fail to comprehend the complexities of ethnicity in the Balkans. For example, in Greek the words "ethnic" and "national" are the same. We have another word, *katagogi*, meaning not only ethnic but geographical origin. If you ask someone in the Balkans what their identity is, you are likely to get a very confusing answer, difficult for translators. Ethnicity cannot be denoted purely by language, because languages change. It is also important not to simplify the situation into "evil state" (Greeks) versus "suppressed peasants" (Slavophones in Greece). It would be better for the so-called experts to do some genuine research in the field.'

'But assimilation *has* happened.'

'It did happen between the wars, as all over Europe. It happened under Metaxas's dictatorship. Non-Greek toponyms were changed because of the need to create a sense of unity in this new country. People complain that Greek-language schools were imposed on their villages, but in fact these schools were set up all over Greece. But you cannot use past events to colour the present. There *is* a political movement in Greece called the Rainbow movement, including some priests, who want a Macedonian Church, and recognition of the Slavo-Macedonian language, but they have very little support among the Slavophones. If they were a distinct minority, with national awareness, they would have demanded minority rights. But they haven't. Slavo-Macedonian has no official status and no public presence because the Slavo-Macedonians have not asked for this. Most consider themselves Greek and are happy to be so. They have a better life here than they would in FYROM or Bulgaria. Skopje is not an attractive prospect. It's the same with the Muslim minority, most of whom don't consider Turkey an attractive proposition. They are better off in Greece, within the EU.'

This was true. There was abundant evidence of the millions being spent by the EU in Greece. I was beginning to understand that this latest Macedonian question concerned far more than the rights of a small group of Hellenized Slavs. The question was not about them but about the dramatic swelling of nationalism in Greece and FYROM, and thus the stability of the whole of the southern Balkans.

"The Greeks' reason for objecting to Macedonia,' Dr Sfetas was saying, 'is above all historical pique. It's about the ideological use and misuse of history. So to answer your question I will have to go back over the entire known history of this region.'

For the next few hours this was what he did. I listened enthralled as we pored over maps, tracing population exchanges over thousands of years, as he burrowed into the complexity of nineteenth-century Bulgarian secret societies and assassinations of Balkan kings. It was a potent mix of intrigue and brutality. It boiled down to this: a region of mixed population that, having freed itself from the Ottoman yoke, was fought over by Serbs, Bulgarians, and Greeks, each struggling for control, and each assisted for strategic reasons by competing greater powers – Austro-Hungary, Germany, Russia, Great Britain, and France – who were jostling for spheres of influence in this crossroads of the Balkan peninsular, a strategically vital part of Europe.

There was one thing these disparate peoples shared, and that was a sense of grievance against each other and the opportunistic outside powers. They shared a sense of victimhood.

Having disintegrated after the death of Alexander the Great, Macedonia became a Roman province in 148 BC, whose borders included much of the present FYROM. The fourth and fifth centuries saw the arrival of plundering Goths, Huns, and Avars, and during the sixth and seventh centuries the Slavs. In the ninth century almost all Macedonia was conquered by the Bulgarians, an Asiatic people who carved their way into the area, and whose language became Slavicized (or was possibly replaced by a Slavic one). The famous Samuel (976–1014) became 'Tsar of all the Bulgars and Greeks' and ruler of a dynasty which extended over much of the Balkans. Samuel was chased out in 1018 by the Byzantine emperor Basil the Bulgar-Slayer, and all Samuel's lands, including Macedonia, returned to Byzantium.

Invasions never stopped: the Normans, the Latins of the Fourth crusade, reconquest by the Greeks, reconquest by the Bulgarians, then occupation of western Bulgaria and most of Macedonia by the fourteenth-century Serb Kral Stephan Dushan who was crowned in Skopje in 1346 as 'Tsar of the Serbs and Greeks'. Macedonia was then wrested back by Byzantium, which was itself torn apart by Byzantine imperial rivalries.

As the centre weakened, the entire region was conquered piecemeal by the Ottomans. The Ottomans did not call it Macedonia. There was no such administrative unit. Instead Macedonia was divided into *vilayets* or provinces, which by 1864 were the *vilayets* of Monastir (now Bitolj in FYROM), including parts of Albania, Salonika, and Kosovo, with its capital at Skopje.

Within these *vilayets*, the Ottomans organized different ethnic groups into *millets*, meaning 'nation' determined by religion. Albanians, Turks, Slavs and Greeks lived cheek by jowl but occupied separate *millets*, which often had their own markets, even their own judiciary. The situation was confused, however, by Orthodox Slavs becoming Muslim, Muslim Albanians becoming Greek Orthodox, and Jews becoming Muslim; identities were fluid, changing according to convenience, opportunity, expediency, or fear.

These *millets* co-existed, but were not necessarily bonded in love. There were huge differences even within each *millet*. The Orthodox *millet* – which comprised Greeks and Slavs, as well as Albanian converts – was by no means a united body, whatever our Greek guidebook would have us believe. Their Christianity did not unite them heroically against the Turks, any more than the Greeks would later unite against the Nazis. They were riven by far more complex social, linguistic, regional and ultimately ideological differences.

Since the Sultan – in cahoots with the Greek Orthodox heirarchy – banned the Serb and Bulgarian patriarchates in 1766 and 1777, Greek had resumed its importance as the language of the Church. This was crucial because the Church was the only institution in the Orthodox *millet* that taught reading and writing. After 1777 all Orthodox, whether Greek, Slav or Albanian, would be taught in Greek, and therefore would speak Greek, and would possibly come to think of themselves as Greek. Indeed, all Orthodox Christians had long been referred to by Western Europeans as Greeks, whether they spoke Greek or not.

Greeks were not only churchmen, but merchants, shippers and traders, the educated elite who could afford to build *archontika*, while Slav-speakers tended to be the peasants. Greek became the language of both the Church and Levantine commerce. Greek also became the language adopted by upwardly mobile Slavs. This growth of Greek-medium education coincided with the outpouring of texts by mainly British, French and German scholars, who by the middle of the eighteenth century had performed the indomitable feat of translating and making available the great body of the Greek classics, not just for their own audiences but for the Greeks themselves. Greek-speaking intellectuals found that a heroic Hellenic past was suddenly accessible. Through schools and books, by the late nineteenth century even the Bulgarian bourgeoisie, the *chorbadjii*, had become Hellenophiles who despised the peasant culture of their fellow Slavs. At home they spoke Greek. Their language defined their social staus.

In 1830 the region that is now southern Greece won its independence from the Ottomans and became the first new nation state to be born since the French Revolution. Nationalist feelings inevitably seethed throughout the rest of the Ottoman Empire. Who were these burgeoning tribes? At this stage 'Bulgarians' were assumed to be the same Slavic people as Serbs and Croats, but between 1800–1850 native scholars undertook the prodigious task of distinguishing between the three languages of the northern Balkans: Slovene, Serbo-Croat, and Bulgarian. Now these Bulgarians sought a state independent of the Ottomans. But what was that state to consist of? It had always been a Bulgarian article of faith that it should include Macedonia. But were the Macedonians Bulgarian? And did they want to be part of a putative Bulgaria?

National or political consciousness barely existed amongst the uneducated of Macedonia. But under pressure from Russia in 1870 the Porte allowed an autochthonous Bulgarian exarchate to be established. The Bulgarian Church proved an immensely useful tool for awakening that consciousness. Plebiscites were held in disputed areas for people to decide whether to belong to the Greek or Bulgarian church. They tended to ally themselves to whoever offered the best deal. A hitherto Greek community, for example, would be tempted to switch to the Bulgarian exarchate by being offered a teacher at a cheaper rate; the community would henceforth be taught in Bulgarian, and would speak Bulgarian, and whatever its racial or linguistic origins would come to think of itself as Bulgarian. Meanwhile the Serbs, who also had a stake in Macedonia, were forging a nationalism of their own. By 1900 the Greeks had 927 schools in Macedonia, the Bulgarians had 785, and Serbians 178.

The 1878 Congress of Berlin saw the foundation of a small Bulgarian principality backed by Russia, while Serbia became an independent state backed by Austro-Hungary. The Ottoman Empire was deprived of all other territories except Albania, Macedonia, and Thrace. Of these, Macedonia was in the worst condition. Albanian and Turkish soldiers and mercenaries fleeing south from Serbian and

Montenegrin expansion plundered and razed villages in their path. There was also a succession of disastrous harvests. Homeless Greek, Albanian, Turkish, and Slav villagers fled for safety to the nearest towns.

In the early 1890s desperate Macedonian refugees poured into Sofia. They came burning with anti-Ottoman and revolutionary zeal.

Those who converged on the outskirts of Salonika – Murray's 'rural and suburban' Bulgarians – were in touch with nationalists in Sofia, and were also stirred up with anger at the appalling conditions they suffered. Excluded from Salonika's Greek- and Sephardic-controlled industrial boom, these Slavs turned instead to politics and education. A group of them formed a committee, which in 1905 became known as VMRO, the Internal Macedonian Revolutionary Organization, with its slogan, 'Freedom or Death'. In a climate of fear, violence and intrigue became their weapons.

It was acknowledged that the Ottomans would lose Macedonia some time soon. VMRO called for a Balkan federation with Macedonia for the Macedonians. But who were these Macedonians? The Bulgarians claimed the majority Slav population of Macedonia as Bulgarian because most spoke a language almost identical to Bulgarian. The Slavs in Macedonia had also instinctively veered towards the non-Greek Bulgarian Church, with its use of Church Slavonic. The Serbs on the other hand claimed that the Slavo-Macedonians were *not* Bulgars, as they retained certain Serb traits such as the *slava*, the feast of the ancestors, common to all Serbs but non-existent in Bulgaria. Slavo-Macedonians were therefore only superficially Bulgarianized Southern Serbs and should be incorporated into a Greater Serbia that would resurrect the glorious medieval kingdom of Tsar Dushan. Greek nationalists claimed that the few hundred thousand 'Slavophones' they acknowledged to be in Macedonia were attracted by the superiority of Greek culture and considered themselves to be Greek, so therefore Macedonia should be allowed to restore its ancient links with the Hellenic world.

Violent guerrilla bands from all three groups press-ganged villagers into joining them.

But the Macedonian Slavs did not call themselves Bulgarians,

Serbs, or Greeks, they called themselves Macedonians. This did not mean that they were not other nationalities too; it simply meant that they shared a sense of belonging in the geographical entity of Macedonia.

The crisis, and the birth of the central myth behind the formation of FYROM, came on St Elijah's Day, 1903. Encouraged by Bulgaria, VMRO (or IMRO as it then was) attacked Turkish forces near Bitolj, expecting help from Sofia. This never came, and after heroic successes the uprising was ruthlessly quashed. According to Bulgarian sources, 105 Slavo-Macedonian villages were razed, and 60,953 civilians made homeless. Slavo-Macedonians had found themselves fighting alone, and punished alone. What became known as the Ilinden Uprising fuelled a sense of themselves as a separate people.

By 1912 uprisings, intrigues, and terrorism, backed on all sides by the Great Powers (today's 'International Community'), escalated into the first Balkan War. Ottoman tyranny was finally thrown off, but the following year war erupted again, with Serbs and Greeks turning on Bulgarians in an exceptionally bloody fight over the spoils. This ended with Greece being granted the southern half of Macedonia. It was a war of intense nationalistic hatreds that still persist.

These wars caused upheavals on appalling scale: 100,000 Turks fled or were transported back to Turkey; pro-Bulgarians fled to Bulgaria; Greeks in Yugoslavia and Bulgaria fled south into the new Greece.

Hard on the heels of their success, the Greeks – with the backing of Lloyd George – made the disastrous decision to invade Anatolia. This was the Great Idea, to re-conquer Constantinople and, with British encouragement, control the Near East. The result was an inferno of bloodshed. (One of the victims from Smyrna, who managed to escape with his family, was Aristotle Onassis.) At the 1923 Treaty of Lausanne it was agreed that the solution would be to 'ethnically cleanse' the entire region. Huge swathes of population were exchanged: 800,000 Muslims were sent east to Anatolia, and 1.3 million Pontic Greeks – or adherents of Greek Orthodoxy – were sent west, most to be settled in newly vacated land in the new Greek province of Macedonia. It was an upheaval on an appalling scale. In many cases people had dwelt in these lands for thousands of years, and were now uprooted, forced to abandon everything to begin new lives in lands where they spoke a different dialect, had different customs, and were resented as incomers.

The effect of this population exchange on the Greek province of Macedonia was to Hellenize it. Greek schools opened, and they and the Orthodox Church were used to unite these disparate peoples into one coherent state. They held not only Byzantium in common, based as it was in the monasteries of Mount Athos. They also shared the ancient heritage of Hellenic Macedonia, reinforced almost daily by astonishing archaeological discoveries such as we had seen in Vergina.

Thus the Greeks felt that their historic right to 'Macedonia' had been usurped.

Dr Sfetas said, 'It's a question of compromise. The Greeks suggested they call themselves "Slavo-Macedonia", but they can't accept that because of their huge Albanian minority.'

The Albanians had already suffered for nearly a century from being denied existence by the name of their country – Yugoslavia.

'The Former Yugoslav Republic of Macedonia is the present compromise, the only name the Greeks will accept. But they don't like that either.'

'If the Greeks are so worried about this tiny defenceless country, doesn't it show that they themselves are unsure of their own identity?'

'Yes. Because those identities have always been so changeable. The latest situation is that if we accept some compromise with Skopje, Skopje will renounce territorial claims to northern Greece, and not raise the question of minorities.'

Then he added, 'The crucial thing is that FYROM survives, because if it is divided between Bulgaria and Albania, that will change the balance of power in the Balkans. Skopje needs Greece, and Greece needs Skopje because through Skopje we have access to Belgrade and Bucharest and Sophia.'

When we began to speak of more personal matters, he leaned forward conspiratorially. 'Now I find I have to improve my English, to realize our plans.'

'And what are those plans?' I whispered, anticipating a political movement, or the launch of some Balkan project.

'Oh, to get a better job at this university.'

We both laughed at the mundanity.

Richard learnt that his father was dying, and he would have to fly back to England. We decided that I should stay in Greece with the girls, and take care of the Mob. Following repeated (Greek) warnings of roaming (Albanian) robbers we didn't dare leave it.

It was a moment I'd been dreading. After a year on the road, Richard and I had come to rely on each other utterly. In the airport Tallulah gripped Richard's clothes with her teeth to stop him going, a desperate screaming thing.

The Mob seemed larger than ever as I manoeuvred out of the airport. I had barely ever driven it. I headed south-west. I needed somewhere secure, with access to a telephone, shops, and water, but I also wanted privacy. I kept driving, largely because I wasn't sure where to stop. Site-hunting with Richard was fun and easy: he seemed to anticipate a good spot before we'd even seen it. But I noticed suitable tracks only after we'd passed them. It was hard to go back to them as I also didn't know how to stop, or reverse.

I stalled when I could go no further, at the end of the road that disappeared into the forbidden Holy Mountain. I was on the outskirts of Ouranopolis, the Last Resort. Ahead of us rose a barbed-wire fence and a fierce NO ENTRY sign. Entry to Mount Athos was forbidden to all females – a ban that until recently included all female animals of any sort, even hens. I had reached the stronghold of the Orthodox monastic tradition, but could not enter it. I didn't know what impelled me to come here. Having explored Vergina, I think I wanted to be as close as possible to the other, Byzantine, root of Macedonia.

We overlooked the parallel prong of Halkidiki, islands, boats, the sun subsiding into the sea. It was beautiful but without Richard I felt disorientated, exposed.

Ouranopolis was a forlorn rainswept off-season resort. Tavernas were being repainted. A blackboard menu offered the following delicacies: Lamp on Red Sauce; Chicken Spit; Roast Beer; File Sterk; Select Kitchen; and (worrying for Tibetan visitors) Lama Chops.

The days seemed long without Richard, lonely and hard. Xanthe, now nineteen months, still needed hauling around, in and out of her screw-on table seat, in and out of her car seat, in and out of her cot, in and out of the backpack. Morning and evening I built and dismantled bed and table. I'd always appreciated how much Richard did, but only now did I understand how much he *thought* about practicalities. It was always him who remembered that we needed to fill up with water or buy gas. Without mentioning it, he would look out for a spring or a suitable shop. He bore these things in mind, but lightly. I worried about them constantly.

When it sleeted, we sheltered indoors all day, turning Xanthe's cot into a puppet theatre, or baking a cake in honour of Granny's birthday, far away. At night the Hale Bop comet burned, a poignant link with home.

Women came by with bags, foraging for edible leaves in the hedgerows. I knew what strict moral codes they lived by, despite the veneer of liberality brought by television and tourism, and they seemed to look at me askance, like a fallen woman. I longed to speak to them but could not. Partly because of tourism, the second language was German, but I didn't speak that either. For all my rejoicing in the diversity of Europe's languages, here I was faced with the reality of their exclusiveness. They rendered me frustrated, alienated, confused, physically handicapped. Not that this was the language's fault; it was my own.

When the sun reappeared two women sat with their children on a bench near our Mob. Friends! Playmates! Fellow mothers! We went out with slices of cake. They took it gingerly. They clearly thought we were mad. They never came back.

We were returning from the phone box when a Greek man grasped my arm. Where was Papa? He spoke a German–English hybrid. He too was living in a caravan, and he insisted that we should share his site. He had water, he said, and I would be much safer. His name was Angelo. I was grateful for his offer of friendship and security, and I decided to trust him.

I packed up the Mob and transferred to his patch of ground. It was a junkyard of wrecked machinery and other people's cast-offs, but it was private, and it overlooked the sea.

His only stipulation was that none of us would ever, not even once, look inside his van.

My loneliness vanished, and so did the physical arduousness of life alone. Now I didn't have to carry Xanthe and push Tallulah the half-mile to the phone box: Angelo buzzed us back and forth on his moped. And he showed us where the sweetest water fountain was, the freshest bread. He made life fun. Sometimes we went into Ouran- opolis and ate sardines with his friend Costa – Angelo was life and soul of every party, fingers in every pie – but mostly we spent evenings in the Mob, drinking retsina and soda and eating mussels.

Angelo said he was a rich Greek businessman with a clothing factory in Salonika and outlets throughout Europe. But eighteen months ago he closed his factory, locked the Mercedes in the garage, bought this tiny plot, and now lived like a hippy without even a telephone.

'I arrive in Salonika and my partner say, "Hey, Angelo, what you doing here? You meant to be in Germany." And I say, "You go slave in Germany. Here's the factory keys. I'm off to Ouranopolis." '

He said he was building a holiday village nearby in Nea Roda, one of many developments that would soon spoil this lovely coast, and that he co-owned a boat with Costa that would ferry tourists round Mount Athos when the season began. I didn't know how much to believe.

He was fifty-four, and marvellously ravaged-looking, with a hooked nose and a scar down his cheek, but he had a smoker's cough and was out of shape. Tallulah privately called him Mr Blubber Belly. He talked a lot about his wife, who had left him fourteen years earlier. He had never got over it. He was lonely and depressed. He vowed never to spend another winter alone.

'You tell me when to leave,' he would say, as I stifled a yawn. 'But come, have another drink! The night is young!'

For all his renunciation of worldly goods, he was obsessed by money. How much you pay for this? How much you pay for that? He was scornful if I'd paid too much, and equally scornful if I'd paid too little.

'Everybody have money in Ouranopolis,' he said, rubbing finger and thumb together, a gleam in his eye. 'The man with chicken and goats have money. The olive make money. Tourist make money.' Then his face fell. 'But in winter this place is death. You lucky if you see one person in the street.' He longed to sing and dance on the tables and watch girls go by: he was so very Greek.

He showed me photographs of himself with different women. He was always leering over their shoulders. He said they were his 'secretaries'. He encouraged me to take showers under his hose in the garden and gave me a bikini that was three sizes too small. I wondered when he would make a pass at me, and what I would do.

Then news came. Richard's father had died. After the funeral he would return to Salonika, where we were to meet him.

'Bye-bye, lady.' Angelo peered through the window as I reversed out of his garden. 'Come back and see Angelo.'

'I will. I promise.'

He escorted us out of town on his moped, tooting his horn, our outrider.

It was wonderful to have Richard back. Although sad about his father, he was eager to get going again. We took the straight road north to FYROM.

The route led over rolling plains through Kilkis, which in June 1913 saw one of the fiercest battles of the second Balkan War, and where only five years later the Bulgarians (with the Germans) were again defeated in the battle of Skra-Ravine. A monument to fallen Greeks stood on a hill. The road was dotted with pillboxes and Nissen huts. An eagle swooped in front of the Mob, trying to prise a hedgehog off the tarmac.

Hoardings in hedgeless expanses of wheat announced: 'INTER-AMERICAN' or 'BE YOU, BE COOPER'.

It was our first serious frontier. We crossed a stretch of no-man's-land, heavily fenced, and drove through a basin of pink disinfectant, like a sheep dip. But we had no green card. For a heart-sinking moment we feared the Macedonians wouldn't let us in. Then they said it would cost £150. We didn't have £150 to spare. So the nice bank clerk locked his office, vanished on to the phone, and returned to explain that he was new to the job and had got it wrong, and instead it would be only £40. The inhabitants of FYROM – call it what you will – turned out to be the friendliest in Europe.

We reached Lake Dojran during a May Day festival. Rows of tin-pot Ladas and Yugos had parked on the shore and the air was filled with the scent of barbecuing sausages. Families and groups of young people picnicked on the ground or around plastic tables, Serbian pop music thudding. Young footballers secretly made the sign of the cross before each shot.

Mountains fell gracefully to striped fields of wheat, vines, and plough, which ran down to the water's reedy edge. Greece had one shore, FYROM the rest. The Greek shore was dotted with watchtowers. I was reading Stratis Myrivilis's epistolary novel *Life in the Tomb*, with its brutally honest descriptions of trench warfare on the Macedonian front in 1917–18, and I was looking at the very mountains and the very border that he fought over. Later, during Communist times, the two communities would gaze at each other, inexorably divided. Some on the Greek side spoke Slavo-Macedonian, while many Greeks who had fought for the Communists during the Greek civil war were exiled here in FYROM.

We whiled away the week in a lakeside bar, drinking good Skopje beer. A seven-piece gypsy brass band played wild exotic melodies. The leader had gold and silver teeth, the rest were young and smiley, though with funny upper lips swollen from playing. They blasted directly into our ears, drachmas posted between the notes and behind their ears. A man sat alone at another table, and he and Richard raised their glasses.

'It's a good cure for deafness,' he commented as he joined us. His name was Todor. Like many Macedonians – but unlike the Greeks – he spoke good English. He said the music was Serbian, not Macedonian. Macedonian music was traditional shepherds' music played on a bagpipe of sheep's hide.

'Is there such a thing as "Macedonian"?' I enquired, and he insisted there was, that his father and grandfather always thought of themselves as Macedonian, which was why Macedonia seemed an obvious name for the country.

Among its list of different nationalities in Macedonia, Murray's handbook makes no mention of Slavs other than Bulgarians, Serbs, and Bosnians. There was not thought to be such a nationality as 'Macedonian'. There was thought to be no such people, no such tribe. But from the 1880s the Serbs began to encourage the idea of 'Slavo-Macedonianism' to counterbalance the power of Bulgaria in the region, although the aim was eventually to Serbianize it. As the Bulgarian-born agitator Misirkov wrote in 1903, when campaigning for an independent Macedonia within the framework of the Ottoman Empire: 'What does not exist can be created, if the historical circumstances call for it.' When Tito failed to create a Greater Macedonia, he continued the Macedonianization of the region to counterbalance not only Bulgaria, but also Serbia. A literary language was created, history was rewritten, and – crucial in the Balkans – in 1967 an autocephalous Macedonian Church was founded, although this is still not recognized in Constantinople.

Yet Todor maintained that this 'Macedonian' ethnicity was not a cynical creation of politicians, but one which genuinely existed. In *Life in the Tomb* Stratis Myrivilis has his alter ego, the Greek Sergeant Kostoulas, billeted in a village called Velusino, west of Dojran along the 1918 front line. It is a happy interlude in horror. Kostoulas describes his simple, generous hosts speaking a branch of Slavic, with many Turkish and Greek elements. To him it sounds virile, bracing, the soft femininity of vowels drowned in burly consonants. Both Serbs and Bulgarians understood it. His hosts' sons were fighting for the Bulgarians – Kostoulas's enemies – and hated the Serbs who tyrannized them; but they also hated the Bulgarians, who had conscripted their sons into the army. As for the Greeks, his hostess's elderly father-in-law recalled the bishop (presumably from Ohrid) making circuits of this region during Turkish times for tax collecting. He came in his velvet-lined brougham, but instead of horses in the traces there were peasants, lashed by the coachman's whip. They accepted the Greeks, nevertheless, because of their reverence for the ecumenical Patriarch, and because of the Greek writing in their Bibles and on the icons. All they knew was that they wanted to be neither Bulgarian, Serb, nor Greek.

Modern FYROM's claim to nationhood depends heavily on claims to a separate language. In fact the South Slav languages are all close, and can be hard to distinguish from vernaculars in Serbia or Bulgaria. The Macedonian literary standard is based on dialects of the Bitolj region, close to western Bulgaria, while the Bulgarian literary standard is based on dialects of eastern Bulgaria, allowing both to be sufficiently distinct to claim to exist alone.

Greeks, Serbs, and Bulgarians may claim that the Macedonian people do not exist as an ethnic group in their own right. But looking at Todor I thought what does it matter? Different peoples form all the time, as people migrate or form new allegiances or intermarry. They may not have any genetic tribal distinction, any specific blood group, but they think of themselves as one people. The Ulster Protestants are among the most distinctive and tribal people in Europe, yet until they went to Northern Ireland they were simply Scottish or English Protestants like any other. Their tribe was created by their journey. The question of whether or not theirs or the Macedonians' are false nations is not appropriate. What matters is the fact that a substantial number of people believes there is a fraternity, some commonality of purpose, which binds them together. As the Catalan leader Jordi Pujol put it, a tribe can be a historic fact, and a spiritual ethnicity, but it is also an act of will.

After Tito's death Greece feared war would erupt on its doorstep between Serbia and Bulgaria over the Yugoslav Republic of Macedonia. But by then 'Macedonianization', whether spurious or not, had been so successful that the people declared themselves to be neither Bulgarian nor Serb, but truly Macedonian. They didn't feel themselves to be part of any other state.

Of course the problem for the Macedonians is that they have now created a nation state that does not bear solely that Macedonian consciousness, since it includes the Albanians.

It occurred to me that here was a country with a population of a mere two million that had achieved what the Basques wanted, and it was a frightening sight. Macedonia's existence was precarious, relying on its own agriculture, but more so on foreign investors taking advantage of absurdly low wages, and on US aid. It was threatened on all sides, and also within. What it lacked was the comforting umbrella of the EU. This was the crucial difference. EU membership, in FYROM, was the great hope. And that relied on repairing relations with Greece. Todor bemoaned the economic effects of the Greek blockade, but said relations were improving.

'What about the Slavo-Macedonians in Greece: is there discrimination against them?'

'No,' he admitted. 'I think not.'

Todor had a narrow face with a long lugubrious nose and he nursed a single glass of ouzo. He had a bad stomach, which cursed him every spring. He worked in the local casino, one of the few wealthy Macedonians. He would finish work at 6 a.m., sleep until 1 p.m., wander down to the bar to drink and play backgammon. He had grey curly hair and kind chestnut eyes.

He recalled his pride and relief when FYROM's president appeared on TV to announce that Macedonian soldiers would not participate in war against Slovenia or Croatia. The mainly Serb Yugoslav army was ordered out of FYROM. They trashed all barracks and immovable military equipment before going. It was exciting and frightening becoming a new country: no one knew what the future held. The current problems were internal, the fear that the disruption in Albania and Kosovo would spread to the Albanian minority here.

'This country is treading a tightrope,' he said. 'We have to be incredibly careful not to destabilize it.'

As the days passed, he admitted that for all his patriotism, he longed to escape. He felt humiliated by European visa restrictions. He dreamed of Italy. He kept glancing down the street. He explained that he was waiting for his wife, who he was expecting from Greece. In his car.

'Is it something special?' Richard asked on cue.

Todor hesitated. 'A Maserati.'

Richard was impressed. Todor had bought it new in Rome a few months ago. It had a white leather interior. He had flown it to Skopje at a total cost of £100,000. It was the most expensive and special thing he would ever own in his life. Now his wife had taken it to Athens for a service, but she had not returned. She was several days late.

His eleven-year-old daughter Isabella, a serious bespectacled girl who spoke English, befriended Tallulah – although like all these girls she was really more interested in baby Xanthe. Tallulah fell in love with her, calling her 'my little friend'. It made my heart bleed to see Tallulah, so slender and pretty in her red Easter dress, enjoying Isabella's company but with the knowledge that we would soon part.

'What I want,' Tallulah sighed with yearning, 'is someone to be *naughty* with.'

To fill the void she drew pictures of imaginary friends. One was of a woman throwing back her head with laughter, displaying tongue and dangling uvula.

'What's she laughing at?' I asked.

'At someone showing off their arse.'

Isabella seemed even lonelier than Tallulah. She was an only child, and Mama no call, Mama no come. She wanted clothes from Greece, but Mama no show. She was a week late now. Maybe she had had an accident; maybe she had decided that freedom in Greece without her husband and daughter, financed by the Maserati, was better than being stuck in Dojran.

We woke to overcast sky, the mountains deep blue and vaporous, wind ruffling the lake, a strange pre-storm light. The party was over. Two pigs rooted through litter. Under a plane tree two men in tracksuits snored on a rug, sheltered behind a strip of cardboard. Tallulah put on her prettiest dress, special tights and (as always) trousers too, but Isabella never came.

Everyone in Macedonia seemed to be waiting, yearning, hoping.

*

We had driven through the centre of Skopje before realizing that the concrete suburb was the city itself, capital of FYROM. We spent several nights in a city parking lot. Beside it, overlooking a sea of metal, an old lady tended her apricot and plum trees, currants and roses. She lent us her hose to fill up with water, we gave her cucumbers, she gave us wallflowers. She also served us coffee in her garden. She was bent-backed but her narrow face was still refined and pretty. Her single-storey house was once in streets of similar, but an earthquake flattened most of Skopje in 1963. She'd seen neighbours vanish beneath a cloud of dust. Three hundred had died, but she and her family were unharmed.

'Thank God,' she said, pointing at the heavens.

'Yes, thank God.'

She looked at me eagerly. 'Are you Catholic?'

'Anglican. But it's nearly the same.'

She nodded thoughtfully. As a Catholic here she must have felt ostracized; the Orthodox hierarchy mistrust the Catholics almost as much as the Muslims, if not more. She was from Mostar in Herzegovina; her brother lived in Sarajevo. 'It's been terrible,' she whispered. 'But all my family are OK.'

The new town was dominated by a stupendously ugly shopping centre built of stained concrete and bereft of anything faintly delicious or interesting. It was poignant to recall Todor and Isabella's pride – Oh Skopje, it's as good as any European town, you can get anything you like there. It edged a cobbled piazza, made tolerable only by the chestnut trees, now laden with candles. We sat in Bull's Hamburgers eating chips and feeling startled by the sight of enormous black American UN peacekeepers sauntering in camouflage down the street.

On the bridge over the Vardar, gypsy babies, some horribly deformed, lay beside open hats, so still and alone that I guessed they were drugged. Passers-by tossed in money, but no one seemed concerned.

Then the bazaar unravelled. It was how I imagined old Salonika: a warren of tiny shops and workshops making buckets and watering cans and leather holsters, wedding dresses, white pantaloons with gold embroidered jackets, hallal meat. There were no cars, only rickshaw-like trolleys pushed from stores to shops, teetering with stuff. The alleyways were packed with men in skullcaps and women in headscarves and long drab coats with padded shoulders and low-heeled shoes; beneath the headscarves their faces had an unhealthy pallor. We lunched beside a fountain in the shade of a plane tree with two mad men. One was a raving bearded tramp who ducked his head in the fountain between haranguing passers-by. The other sat in white shirt and socks and khaki shorts. He had a severe blond haircut. He ordered beer and before drinking he crossed himself, then stood, lifted the glass as though lifting a chalice, intoned a prayer, and drank. He had a provocative fascistic look. The Albanian waiter exchanged glances with us, and shrugged as if to say: he's nuts.

The town was ethnically divided, but other than this peculiar incident, we encountered no obvious hostility. However, a few weeks earlier a hunger strike had taken place here. Albanian students had sought permission to study at the teacher training college in Albanian, in order to be able to teach Albanian children; the Macedonian students launched a hunger strike in protest. So here lay the problem of a minority within a minority.

I dressed Xanthe after her sleep, her honey curls fluffed up. Tallulah leapt on her with overenthusiasm, so I said, why don't you go and see the old lady? Later I found her seated gravely at a table in the centre of the tiny damp sitting room in front of the TV, a glass of water on the plastic tablecloth and the old lady's son seated opposite in his longjohns, smoking. Slobodan had worked in a radiator factory in Rotterdam and longed to go back there.

'Ah, Holland,' he'd sigh, cupping his heart. But there were new visa restrictions. He was divorced and unemployed, father of three, scratching a living from smuggling cut-price perfumes and cigarettes. A cabinet was stacked with empty whisky bottles and religious nick-nacks and a plastic dolly that Xanthe loved. He had a mouth like an earthquake city, one tooth heroically upright amidst the rubble.

He wasn't refined like his mother. A sofa bed was covered with a rumpled blanket: Tallulah must have interrupted his siesta.

I was woken on my birthday – my second in the Mob – by Xanthe calling 'Appy appy appy!' Richard draped the cupboards in tinsel, and the table groaned with popcorn, sandwiches, and an enormous cake he had found in the shopping centre. Tallulah was thrilled; no matter that the cake was smothered in an inedible cream resembling brown shaving foam. She carried slabs of it into the widow's house; in return Slobodan pressed on me a large bottle of perfume – it's your birthday, you must accept, no, not *one* bottle, *two* bottles. He was distraught that we were leaving before he and Richard had been fishing together on the Vardar.

'Please say goodbye to your mother.'

'No, wait!'

He dragged her from her siesta, and we all embraced.

We despaired of finding a place for the night. Every green patch south-west of Skopje was cultivated, every field busy with men in embroidered caps waving at us. Villages were strung out, one melting into the next, with lots of new buildings. It was the heart of the Albanian region: martial-looking minarets thrust up like silver-plated rockets, elegant but violent. We entered the hills, up and up, and at last found a flat area of beaten earth below the school in a village called Vranjovce. A football game halted as every eye turned to us in astonishment, and crowds of eager children gathered round. Tallulah and Xanthe were an instant hit with the girls, while Richard was pulled into the game and promptly scored a goal, which raised excitement levels even higher.

Although Muslim, the girls were provocatively dressed in tight T-shirts and absurdly high platforms. Most were fair or redheaded, and all were different from each other: I could see no defining racial characteristic. There were children everywhere: up trees, on the pitch, in our Mob, babies on hips, poking into our cupboards, fascinated by every detail.

A doctor formally welcomed us to Vranjovce: it was a great opportunity for the village to have us here. So far as he knew, it was the first time any foreigner had been here. He shooed the children away and locked the door behind him. He sat on our pink velour sofa with his broad face beaming out his loneliness. He had spent four years training in Zurich and spoke French. He yearned to go back there, and bitterly envied our opportunities – not just material, he insisted, but cultural and social. Now it was almost impossible for him to get a visa. Tallulah promptly got a nosebleed, and we invited him to display his medical knowledge, but he was more interested in talking to us. His name was Kamberi.

Our conversation was accompanied by the call to prayer, the pre-recorded muezzin wailing his mournful, haunting, un-European sound.

Kamberi said the Albanian minority was either 40 per cent of FYROM's population or 22 per cent, depending on who's talking. The government's lower figure did not include refugees from Kosovo, who in May 1997 were already streaming in to escape gangs of armed Serbs and KLA. This influx threatened the balance of power within Macedonia. There was also fear that KLA demands for an independent Kosovo would encourage the Macedonian Albanians to break away from FYROM and join the Kosovo Albanians to create a new nation within the boundaries of the old Ottoman *vilayet* of Kosovo, which had its capital at Skopje. Worse for FYROM was the threat of both groups uniting with Albania to form a Greater Albania. Two years later the 'International Community' would watch as Serb aggression and NATO airstrikes propelled a biblical exodus of Kosovo Albanians into FYROM; the world would also hurl criticism at FYROM for refusing to admit enough of them. This was because they did not understand the fragility of FYROM's balance of power.

Kamberi saw himself not as Macedonian or Albanian, but as an Albanian from Macedonia. That was why he felt so at home in Switzerland where it was OK to be German Swiss or French Swiss. There was no ethnic violence here yet, but relations were cold. There was an Orthodox village four hundred yards away, but there were no relations between the two.

We were woken by a woodpecker drilling into a telegraph pole, and a cuckoo calling, and a man gathering firewood from a heap near our window.

'*Gut morgen*,' he cried, and reappeared at the window with two cups of Turkish coffee.

It was a beautiful spring day, a great oak shading the football pitch, snow peaks glinting in the distance. At 7.30 a.m. school started. The big history teacher gave us an ebullient greeting, while another teacher named Mezi, a thinner, more refined man, called the children into line; then he suddenly noticed Xanthe at the Mob window, and rushed over to say hello.

Off the narrow lane lay secret family compounds enclosed by high walls and secured behind metal gates; further up the hill the houses were simpler, built of unfaced mud bricks. From the poorer part of the village came Kamberi, bearing breakfast. He unpacked pastries stuffed with cheese and meat, a bucket of yoghurt, and an Albanian–French dictionary. He was concerned about our night: had we slept well? Were the bikes still there? He peered round the Mob: was nothing missing? He had even come past at midnight to check all was well.

Between lessons Mezi invited us to view the school. There were two classrooms, one for 6–8 year olds, another for 8–13 year olds. They were chanting by rote – in Albanian; there were few books. Tallulah sat down to do some colouring-in in someone's workbook. She longed to go to school. She should have been in the reception year by now. Outside they were playing football again; a teenage girl in platforms stood in goal.

A lot of us squeezed into a Yugo – the men were energetic and handsome, many with good clothes, sharp haircuts, and unlike in Dojran not a shellsuit to be seen. Several had worked in Germany and Rome, and were kicking their heels, dreaming of escape. We stopped in a flowering meadow overlooking wooded hills, mountains, minarets. Tallulah held hands with one of the handsome men, who led her through wildflowers as tall as her.

A shambolic figure waded towards us, belly swinging, skullcap at a jaunty angle. His house was turquoise, with a vine-covered balcony and courtyard and the finest view over the hazy Vardar valley. He had been a baker in Bosnia and fled home when war started. He seemed happy to be back. 'All this is mine,' he announced, waving at the meadows.

'Is it good living here?'

'Yes, very good, very beautiful.'

'What about these?' I asked, pointing to the holes in his trousers.

'Oh, that's the best bit – *la mode*.' And turning round added, 'You just need a split round the bum too.'

Everybody shouted with laughter. He bowed to Tallulah and gave her a bag of apples.

The most handsome of the handsome men put on Italian shoes and announced that his mother was cooking our lunch. His three brothers arrived with bowls, cutlery, a saucepan of chicken soup, and barbecued chicken and rice. I was overwhelmed by kindness and generosity, not sure how to repay it, confused by their evident poverty. It was a feast, but difficult to eat with crowds of children leaping at the Mob windows, banging at the door, shouting at the girls to stick their heads out and giving their cheeks a squeeze.

The next day school closed for the history teacher to plough his field. Two horses dragged the metal plough, scything off a narrow chunk of turf, one man leading, another steering, staggering along with one foot on the turf, the other in the fresh soil, the skinny nags staggering too and mercilessly whipped. What took five hours would have taken one with a tractor, but Kamberi said people preferred to use horses, even if they could afford a tractor, because they did the job better. The whole village cheered on the ploughmen. Little girls in dresses sat Renoir-esque under a blossoming apple tree; behind them a boy ruminatively picked his nose.

Kamberi was excited: the history teacher's nephew had arrived. He said the teacher had been so ashamed of his lack of English that he had summoned his English-speaking nephew from the town of Gostivar. He was an artist who had shown in New York. They had gathered in what was once the village bar – now closed, its owners having escaped to Switzerland.

Reshat Ahmeti was our age. He had a squat neck and a broad

face burrowed into by two black furnace eyes. I noticed how tiny his hands were, like a child's.

'My uncle apologizes that the bar was closed during your stay. He wanted to make it nice for you, put on the lights and so on.'

'We didn't mind. We didn't need a bar.'

'Oh well, he wants to tell you that anyway.'

His uncle was not only a teacher, but president of the commune, a member of the Albanian Party, and a passionate nationalist. Reshat's uncle brought us glasses of orange juice while Reshat held court. Reshat was a city boy, a sophisticate in jacket and tie. He and Richard exchanged photographs of their paintings. He taught in the teacher training college in Skopje that had recently been embroiled in the hunger strike. The Albanians studied half their courses in Albanian, half in Macedonian. They wanted to be taught entirely in their mother tongue, as the Macedonians were. So they boycotted the Macedonian professors.

'I said to them, "Why are you so stupid? You need to behave like pedagogues, not like crazy people. You won't finish the course." And they say, "So what if it takes ten years? That's what we want." So the Macedonian students went on hunger strike – two weeks' starvation! It became a cause célèbre. They even brought in Macedonian children to join the agitators, waving banners of Goce Delcev [the Anti-Turkish VMRO hero killed at the Ilinden uprising, a potent symbol as the Ottomans had used Albanian irregular troops]. Well, of course it was a political set-up, divide and rule. They appeal to our basest instincts. But it's ridiculous,' he added. 'Why shouldn't I teach and study in my own language?'

Why indeed.

For the Albanians, more than anyone in the Balkans, language was the thread that bound them. There are dialectical differences between the northern Ghegs and southern Tosks, but they are mutually intelligible. Albanian is the only survivor of its particular Indo-European subgroup. Albanians had always been divided by religion and geography, with many long-established Catholic communities in southern Italy and northern Albania, and Orthodox communities in southern Greece. The Ottomans had insisted that they were kept administratively within their separate religious *millets* and forbade them from teaching in their own tongue, and this fuelled Albanian resentment and nationalism.

Reshat complained not of racial hatred, but of minor discriminations: the best jobs in the police, the post office, the government always going to Macedonians, or Albanians paid less for doing the same jobs. Reshat revealed that years after the end of Communism he was still questioned by the secret police. 'They phone, say, "Hi, hear you're going abroad, why not tell us about it when you get back?" They're paranoid about Greater Albania, that I'm going to stir up trouble. They're crazy if they think we want a Greater Albania. We want to love FYROM, if only they will let us. They portray us as bandits, blood feuders, breed like rabbits, we came in with the Turks and don't belong here, fundamentalists. Rubbish. The blood feud stopped years ago, and in fact we were here before the Slavs. We converted to the Muslim faith because for us it was the only way to survive. Lots of Albanians are Orthodox. Many are ethnically Slavs. And we are not extremist; we only have one wife.'

Kamberi was unable to understand the English. I felt sorry for him. He had been sidelined by this more glamorous man. I felt his despair as he fell silent beside me. Reshat had managed to escape: he had exhibitions abroad, in that promised land, while Kamberi faced being stuck here for ever.

Reshat sat up front like a king as we waved goodbye to the entire village and sailed in our galleon down the lane.

Reshat's studio was in the Gostivar family compound, in a barn above metal prison-like gates. Abstract oils were propped on easels and against the walls. They were predominantly dark, the surface scumbled, but patches of light and geometric forms flickered through, suggesting some astronomical explosion, a primal act of creation or destruction. He said they were about space, seeking some mental or spiritual space, perhaps in this country, or in his small-town world, or in the mentality of his people.

He said he was the best-known Albanian painter in FYROM, but even he struggled to sell work.

Tallulah grew bored. She had noticed children outside the gate, so

I suggested she played with them. Bravely, she trotted off. Some time later we heard banging on the metal gates and sobbing. She had followed the children into their courtyard, but they had turned on this stranger and pushed her out. She had fought back, unable to believe after Vranjovce that she was not welcome, and determined to get into the lovely garden. My heart ached – it was my fault – but I was proud of her: she had got into her first fight and survived.

Reshat wanted to show us something. It was a new café-gallery in Gostivar. He was thrilled by the cultural progress this signified. We sat there drinking beer, pretending we were in New York. Really it was a pizzeria in a one-horse town with Reshat's works on the walls, in light too dim to see them. Nevertheless it was a start. They had music at night, a clubby atmosphere, Reshat's passion and energy. Maybe one day Gostivar would be at the front line, not of tribal warfare but of the avant-garde. That was Reshat's dream.

We drove south to Ohrid, the spiritual capital of FYROM, and formerly of the whole of this region. It straddled the north shore of a beautiful lake. Breezes wrinkled its epidermis. We hired a boat and drifted past churches. Dimitri, our captain, produced a bottle of home-made brandy, and invited Richard to help himself. The sun on snow was metallic, and reflected in still waters. Albania stood on the opposite shore, war-torn but lifeless.

Murray's handbook ignored Ohrid's greatest church, presumably because in 1896 it was a mosque, and had been for four hundred years. Its frescoes had been plastered over and whitewashed, its dome demolished, iconostasis destroyed, apse opened, sanctuary gone, and in their place a mihrab and a minaret erected. It was the church of Santa Sophia, once the cathedral of the Archbishopric of Ohrid, a patriarchate so vast that it stretched from the Danube to the Adriatic via the bay of Salonika. It included our little furriers' town, Siatista.

This was the episcopy of the peasant-whipping, tax-collecting bishop described to Myrivilis's Sergeant Kostoulas.

It stood like a barn in the old town, hairy with weeds, terracotta tiles crumbling, tiny Byzantine bricks pitted with age and abuse. Boys played football in the narthex, banging against the doors. There was no money to rescue it properly. It was built not in the conventional Byzantine cross-in-square, but long like a Latin church, a shape derived from Graeco-Roman temples, with a nave and two aisles, a transept and galleries. It was built soon after the Slavs were converted to Christianity in the ninth century by the missionary saints from Salonika, Methodius and Cyril (hence 'Cyrillic'). Here the saints' disciples translated the Greek ecclesiastical texts into Church Slavonic.

I had it to myself, just me and a grave, sad guardian who loved his church. We spent an hour crawling over ruined timbers above the narthex, studying the frescoes up close.

He said that the plaster and lime had begun to be removed thirty years ago, disclosing one of the largest complexes of eleventh-century Byzantine frescoes in the world. They were painted during an artistic flourish in this region following its reconquest by the Byzantine emperor Basil II, the Bulgar-Slayer. The guide pointed out patriarchs, bishops, writers, Latin popes, Old Testament prefigurations of the sacrifice of Christ and the Eucharist, the Virgin and archangels. The presence of popes surely dated these frescoes to before the Schism of 1054 that sundered Christendom into two halves, dividing Europe for ever.

'Look at the classical faces of these angels,' the guide pointed out. 'Look at the classical handling of their hair and drapery.'

'They look almost like Italian Renaissance frescoes.'

'That's the exciting thing. When they were first uncovered, after the Turks abandoned it in 1912, art historians thought the Italian Renaissance inspired many of the figures. But then it was discovered that these were earlier than they thought. These were instead the missing link between classical and renaissance worlds. The Dark Ages were not as dark as people think. Certain forms of classicism never disappeared, they were maintained in places like this.'

He said that by covering the frescoes the Turks had helped to preserve their colour and that now they were exposed to UV light they would fade. But many had also been destroyed by being hacked into to create a surface to which the plaster could adhere.

Here in Ohrid in 1958 the ancient Patriarchate was revived when the Macedonian Church separated from the Serbian Church. Nine years later it was declared autocephalous. But the Macedonian Church has not been recognized by any other Orthodox branches. In the Balkans, not recognizing a church is tantamount to not recognizing a state.

When he finished showing me round, we sat in his little cubicle near the door and talked of Macedonian history. After a while we got confused. Everyone I thought of as Bulgarian – Tsar Samuel for example – he claimed was Macedonian.

'But Basil II was the Bulgar-Slayer. He slew Bulgarians, not Macedonians. There was no such thing.'

'No,' the guard contradicted. 'That is not correct. There was always a separate Macedonian consciousness. We had a separate language. And now we have a separate church. It is only the chauvinism of the Greeks that prevents it from being recognized. Why shouldn't we have a Macedonian Church?'

'Because the Greeks say there is no such thing as "Macedonian". They say the Church was artificially created as a political act by an atheist regime.'

'It's more than that. They are bullies.'

We drove into the mountains. Signs warned of bends, steep gradients, bad road surfaces. As Lake Ohrid shrank and clouds appeared alongside us, we feared the worst – that we would reach the end of the road and have to reverse back down. But it never happened. We crossed a pass, then descended through a beech forest to another vast mountain-ringed lake, Prespa. It was more secret than Ohrid, with just a few villages dotting the shore. Albania had one shore, FYROM another, Greece the third. It felt like the middle of nowhere and at the same time the centre of the world.

It was silent, no birds, no boats, no animals, the only sound my daughters splashing. I washed our clothes on the beach, and Richard built boats. The hulls were plastic flotsam bottles filled with sand, the masts and spars were bamboo, the sails were sheets of paper towel. Off they sailed, straight to Albania, one bearing a message saying 'Hello from England', the other a story by Tallulah.

At night the shore villages twinkled, evenly spaced apart, between the parallel mysterious blackness of mountain and lake. Now we could hear dogs and frogs, and inhale gusts of damp grass. It was one of the most beautiful places I had ever seen.

Then we were back over the border into Greece, swinging the girls in a playground in Florina, and wondering why the Greek Macedonians are so unattractive, so dour. No one smiled; no one asked where we were from. I approached two people and asked if they spoke English and was curtly dismissed; in FYROM we would all have attempted some other language. Maybe memories, resentments, bitterness, confusion had soured these people. Perhaps they were disgruntled Slavo-Macedonians. It was hard to tell, as they were so uncommunicative.

In Florina the Slavo-Macedonian Rainbow Party office had recently been ransacked by people from the town. Rather than the mob being prosecuted, it was four members of the Rainbow Party who were being tried for inciting citizens to commit acts of violence. They had supposedly achieved this by having the gall to set up their Florina office with the name in both Greek and Slavo-Macedonian. This bilingual sign had caused such outrage, and aroused such bitter memories of the appalling acts of the pro-Yugoslav agents during the Second World War, that a mob led by the mayor of Florina had sacked the offices. No political party or media condemned the sacking.

We agreed that even if I couldn't go to Mount Athos, Richard should. I could experience it vicariously. And now that I knew Angelo, being alone again did not seem such a dreadful prospect. Richard fixed up his Athos permits in Salonika and by mid-May we were back in Ouranopolis. Buzzing out of the Jetoil station on his moped, as if coming to greet us, was Angelo. He wasn't surprised. He said our parking spot awaited us. At first Richard was repelled by his bloodshot eyes, and suspicious of the sexual undercurrent, but he was won over. He named him 'Guardian Angelo'.

Ouranopolis was transformed. Restaurants were open, umbrellas sprouting on beaches, broom and poppies flowering like yellow and red flames.

Richard waved from the deck until he vanished. Angelo called me an Athos widow. He pointed out a grizzled old monk and declared, 'That's Richard in thirty years.' A few years ago, Angelo added gleefully, five German men left behind five German women; two of the men never returned. Another German, wife of a professor, had been stranded in Ouranopolis for six months. At least I felt at home here now, and had Angelo to look after us, although there remained the lingering anxiety about his motives. Tallulah sobbed on the pier. Angelo produced a stray puppy to cheer her up, but Xanthe was terrified as it romped towards her, so now both were crying. I felt like crying too.

Angelo had erected a table in the shade of his solitary tree and put wild flowers in a rusty soda can. The heat was suffocating. I felt drowsy with retsina, and Tallulah and I tried to take siestas but were too hot to sleep. By late afternoon it was still 95 degrees inside the Mob. Xanthe woke smelling of wet cat fur.

Xanthe was frightened of Angelo, and he called her 'the Demon' because she was after me all the time. 'Mummy, Mummy, Mummy,' he chattered at her, while she twisted away from him. Richard's departure and Angelo's sudden presence confused her. He sat Tallulah on his lap and called her his angel. One day he brought a tub of ice cream and rubbed some round her belly button and she squirmed with a mixture of pleasure and revulsion and fear. It worried me. I oscillated between mistrust of him and relief in his big male presence; sometimes the alternatives seemed to be being alone and unprotected, or with him and unprotected. On balance it was preferable to stay, but I kept watch on the girls constantly.

When they were in bed, Angelo and I sat under his tree trying to get cool, playing the Greek lottery and listening to the sea lapping and sighing, gulls crying, dogs barking, people chatting in a far-away house, the rhythmic chug of an invisible motor.

'How long time you living?' he would ask rhetorically. 'Maybe one year, one month, one second – who know? So why spend all day working for others? I like Angelo. I love Angelo. And then I love others. I am a wolf – you know – wolf hound?'

'Lone wolf?'

'Yes. I am Lone Wolf. I look after *me*. I think "What do I like?" I take from the nature, I have water, honey, fish, octopus, wine. What do I need? Nothing. I know the plants for aspirin, rheumatism. Why go in the pharmacy when you can have it from the nature? This is my philosophy. What do you need for the living? One: Air. Two: Water. Three: Food. Four: a nice place.'

'Friends?'

'Yes,' he agreed, but with a dismissive wave. He was much less maudlin now that there were 'bikinis' to admire on the beach.

He recalled his commando days in Cyprus, how he bayoneted a man, and his dreams of bombing Turkey.

'If there is war with Turkey, I go at once,' he declared. 'Like a shot.'

'What about FYROM?'

'They took our name, Macedonia. But they are nothing. Bah! It is Turkey the enemy. Constantinople is ours!'

Ouranopolis had been formed in the 1920s by refugees from Anatolia. The same went for Nea Roda – and many villages scattered throughout Macedonia with 'Nea', New, in their names, recalling the villages the refugees had left. Angelo said the Turks had tortured many of them. Old people in Ouranopolis told him the Turks had put spikes through their tongues. He was full of the atrocities of the Turks, but was ignorant of the murder and pillage by the Greeks during the Anatolia campaign. The noble and heroic Greeks were only victims. I suspected he was a Pontic Greek himself. He stood up. 'Lady, I'm tired. Goodnight.'

I pushed the buggy – Tallulah in the seat with Xanthe on her lap – over a sandy path to the road entrance to Mount Athos.

'Wave to Daddy!'

A party of Albanian builders was admitted through the barbed wire; they were part of a massive EU- and Greek-funded restoration programme, which required new roads to be built all over Mount Athos, destroying its ancient peace.

Angelo arranged for us to take a trip on the boat he co-owned with Costa to the tip of Mount Athos and back. Steep scrubby mountains led to the dramatic triple-peaked mountain of Athos itself, but it was a long time before there was sign of a monastery. First we saw a ruined *scete*, a hermitage, just a pile of stones tucked in a valley. Then the great monasteries and *scetes* began to rise from the cliffs, holy fortresses with projecting upper balconies that resembled – on massive scale – the *archontika* of Siatista. Some were like fantasy cities, self-contained within their walls, turreted and balconied, with belfries and onion domes. The monastery of Pantelimon was surrounded by barracks which once housed Russian pilgrims in their thousands, but now lay ruined and gloomy. But from their midst rose the vivid mint-green domes of the church. A black-robed monk strolled along a beach.

Not being able to land was tantalizing beyond belief. Richard was in there somewhere, walking between monasteries over ancient paths, pondering the mysteries of *hesychasm*, spiritual oneness with God.

Angelo's friends would sit under his tree and drink. They cast me knowing looks. They thought I was a 'secretary', but I was determined not to care. There was Elias, a sunburnt, unshaven peasant; Angelo would make him welcome, drink wine with him, then turn to me and mutter: 'This is politics for me. I must be nice to these people. He gives me baskets of vegetables.' There was a policeman from the Athos border who was copiously wined. 'It's politics,' Angelo muttered. 'It's not legal to live so close to the sea, I should be sixty metres back. So I keep in with the police.' Actually he enjoyed their company. If he were to live here two to three years, the state would give him a parcel of land. 'Of course! This is Greece!' Sometimes Costa came by and Costa's father, a fisherman. No women ever came; the Greek women still didn't even go to the *kafeneion*.

Angelo liked his friends to see me. We were on the beach when Mike went past in a boat, so he quickly snuggled up to impress Mike. When Mike came closer, Angelo was delighted.

'The trouble with Mike,' he said, 'is his egoism. If I catch one octopus, he's always caught three bigger ones. If I get a big fish, his from the previous night was always *huge*. One hundred per cent he'll come round here to have a look at you. Yes, there's nothing like the egoism of Mike.'

Elias announced he had killed a poisonous snake. Angelo roared off to fetch it, and dangled it in front of the girls, who recoiled in fascinated horror. It was a metre long, with black and white zigzags down its back, its guts hanging out. Angelo said he protected himself from snake bite by catching a snake between the prongs of a stick, forcing its head over a cup, squirting in venom, then letting the snake go. He would then drink one drop of venom in water. The next day two drops, then three, until at ten drops he would vomit. Then he went down to nine drops, eight drops, until he reached zero, and stopped. This built up his antibodies. He also beat the grass with a stick, and in eighteen months had never yet been bitten.

We cooked for each other. He was disgusted by the aubergine pâté I produced. 'That is in a pot from Italy; this is from Angelo!' he thundered, banging down plates of piquant marinated sardines, and his tasty sausage, peppers, and egg dish.

'I know what I eat, because mostly I catch it and cook it for myself. I know what I drink because I have seen the grapes growing here, beside my home.'

He made a fish soup called *kakavia*, a Greek bouillabaisse. He bought a fisherman's entire catch, and we washed and gutted them on the beach. One fish – already dead – ripped open Angelo's hand with its teeth; he refused a plaster and insisted on unwrapping a cigarette and laying on a wad of tobacco instead. The fish had another fish caught in its gullet. Tallulah was appalled and had to sit inside, pale and drawn. That night she had a nightmare of us driving into a cave and me having to slaughter a monster with the bread knife, and over the next few months she made drawing after drawing of fish with gargantuan jaws with other fish inside them. We boiled the fish for five minutes in half seawater, half fresh, then added coarsely chopped vegetables, then boiled again, removed fish bones and skin, mashed the potatoes, then boiled with the lid off for five hours. ('Use any fish,' Angelo said, 'the uglier the better. The ugly ones seem to have firmer flesh.') We used up most of my gas, but it was worth it.

Another day he came back waggling an octopus, a gift from Costa's 85-year-old father who had spent the night fishing off Athos. Angelo sliced it, then boiled it for half an hour, poured off half the water and added red wine, peppercorns, onions, bay leaves, and olive oil. This was boiled again with the lid off until tender and the juice almost caramelized. It lasted for days.

Sometimes Angelo's dominating maleness got too much. But when I got tired of being ordered around, I reminded myself of his generosity and thoughtfulness – fetching water from the village, putting a rake across the path so other mopeds wouldn't come too close and wake the babies, bringing flowers. He never stayed still.

He strictly enforced the rule that none of us were to enter his van. Was he Bluebeard? Was it a corpse? Pornography? Was I Pandora, to be tempted to open a forbidden box? There was a tap near his door where we washed the dishes. One day he saw me there, looked round sharply and demanded, 'Where's Tallulah?'

'In our Mob, I think,' I replied nonchalantly, pretending not to know what he implied.

I never did find out.

There were always jokes about telegrams from Athos saying Richard would be staying another year, but one day the ferry passed and I discerned a waving arm. Tallulah grabbed the binoculars. Angelo sat her on the moped and phutted down to the port and brought Richard back to us, on his birthday.

I was longing to be alone with Richard and hear about Mount Athos, but instead we embarked on another major cooking event. Richard was bursting to tell me, but it was only late that night that we were able to talk. He described the crumbling monasteries with jewel-like churches enclosed within courtyards, the monks he had sat with in refectories, discussing the Orthodox principle of *hesychasm*. But he also expressed dismay at the noisy parties of Greek men who had come in groups from work, apparently on Iron John-type holidays. They found it hard to remember they were in a spiritual retreat on a holy mountain. They charged about in minibuses. In walking from monastery to monastery in the traditional way, Richard was considered almost an anachronism; nobody bothered with the old paths any more. They had served for over a thousand years, but weren't needed any more, not when the monks (in dark glasses, murmuring into mobile phones) had four-wheel drive 'Unimogs' to whizz about in. Thanks to an injection of cash from the Greek government and the EU, the Athos monasteries were rebuilding their churches, restoring their ancient frescoes. In order to transport building materials across the peninsular, roads were built. In return for the cash, the abbots had been persuaded to expose their most precious treasures for the first time ever at a forthcoming exhibition in Salonika. The world had entered Mount Athos, and it could never be the same.

Over dinner Angelo became formal in Richard's presence: no more spraying us with hoses, no more flirtation, and it was awkward because he couldn't understand our English. It wasn't a celebration for him because now that Richard was back, we would leave. But I guessed he would soon forget us and move on to the next stray secretary.

THIRTEEN

South Tyrol and the Ladin

We were driving up Italy's leg to the South Tyrol. Although it was early June, we'd had ten days of rain. Gridlocked traffic on the E45 to the Brenner Pass forced Richard to reverse illegally down a slip road, then turn off to Bozen. Suddenly the rain didn't matter any more: we were in a land of fairy-tale castles, Turneresque gorges. A road north ducked in and out of tunnels, nineteen in all, which was scary as most were unlit and single lane. Then it unfolded into flowering meadows at Sarnthein, an exquisite Alpine town.

We sought somewhere to stay, but could find nowhere that was not either cultivated or vertical. Richard risked an unmarked turn-off beside a sawmill. As it writhed up a valley, it became ever more remote, the farmhouses ever more primitive, fields ever more perpendicular, the views ever more beautiful. With our ascent grew an exhilaration that was breathtaking, literally. I felt like spreading my arms wide, opening my chest, filling my lungs with mountain air.

Tarmac dwindled to gravel, and we feared it would wither away altogether in some farmer's yard, when we reached a new bridge over the Tanzbach that tumbled down the valley. Bridge builders had chiselled a workplace out of the mountainside, sheltered and private on one side, open to the river on the other. They'd left it strewn with rocks and timber: rocks to build our fireplace, timber for our fire. It was what we'd been looking for.

Below us tumbled iridescent meadows so soft that I wanted to stroke my cheek against them. They rose to foothills covered in forest, mainly spruce, whose darkness was enlivened by the fluffy spheres of birches and poplars. A breeze flicked up their silvery undersides.

Edging a meadow was a chalet, its wooden roof mirroring the upturned 'v' of the Alps and spruces. I had supposed the roof line was practical, to let snow and rain slide off, but now I saw it was aesthetic. Any other shape would have jarred. And not just aesthetic but spiritual: the up-thrusting peaks, the pointed trees and roofs and church spires were part of a verticality that for these Tyroleans thrust upwards to God.

In the evening sun Tallulah and I strolled up an ancient stone-lined path. It branched off beside a crucifix adorned with flowers, one of several stations of the cross that lined this road, with sculpted Christ figures dripping with blood. They were lovingly tended. Watering cans stood by. They led to a pilgrimage chapel high in the mountains. Our path ended in a meadow. We fell on grass, except there was no grass, only clover, harebells, wild geraniums, stitch-worts, violets, cowslips, thrift, campions, daisies, lillies, orchids, wild peas, pansies, huge buttercups, sorrel, scabius, strawberries. We were drunk with the scent. The only sounds were crickets and the river, and the startling shriek of a peacock.

I returned in triumph with a Chicken of the Woods. It was fan-shaped with a skin lumpy and wrinkled but soft as suede, the straw colour of cooked chicken. I'd found it growing in tiers on an oak stump. We sliced it and fried it with bacon. It smelled very fungusy, but tasted surprisingly like chicken, and had the crumbly texture of overcooked breast.

We made this idyll our home. We washed clothes in the river, built a fire, and hung our latest acquisition, a hammock. Tallulah swung above moss-clad stones on the riverbank, singing to herself, water flitting from pool to pool.

We had failed to buy bread, but Richard was undaunted. He found rocks the right shape, cemented them together with mud, and built an oven. He kneaded flour and water and baking powder, placed his dough ball on the base of the oven (we had no bread tin) and sealed the holes with pebbles. The whole contraption was lifted on the fire. Out came a delicious steaming scone.

A man arrived with huge forearms and a blue apron. He had sawdust on his chest. All this loveliness, and now we were to be moved on. But he accepted a whisky, and sat down beside Richard on a log. He was blond and taciturn, but he came alive when he spoke of the salmon and the ceps and the deer and eagles. He lived in the chalet below our bridge and worked as a forester. His name was Luis and he asked if we'd like some milk.

Richard returned hours later. He and Luis had been boozing in Luis' kitchen with Anna, his mother, and his brother Hans. By 9.15 Anna and Luis were yawning, but Luis still insisted Richard stay for yet another beer.

The following evening we took them a gift of marmalade, made by Richard from oranges he had picked in the heel of Italy. Anna welcomed us into her neat kitchen. She wore a flowered apron and her hair plaited round her head. She exuded warmth and goodness. She seemed to embody thrift, hard work, piety, but she was also full of laughs. Luis sat at the table beside another (livelier) son who worked as a carpenter in Sarnthein – two of Anna's eight children. She poured us coffee and cut slices of bread which was flat like a nan, but baked with caraway seeds. (Tallulah spat hers into my hand when no one was looking.) Hans peered in, ducking his head shyly. He ventured into the kitchen to help himself to a bowl of curds; through the window we watched him eating supper on the grass, gazing at the view.

Anna and her sons could speak fluent Italian, but amongst themselves spoke German. This was because until the First World War the South Tyrol was part of Austria. But as a bribe to persuade Italy to enter the war on the side of the Allies against the Central Powers, Italy was granted this entire region up to the Brenner Pass. Thus in 1918 Italy was rewarded, and the southern half of the Tyrol found itself cut off from its capital, Innsbruck, and from relatives or lands that were now the wrong side of the border. Anna's parents suddenly found themselves part of a German-speaking minority in Italy. The family continued to speak German not just because it was how they had always communicated, but because it was the badge of their identity. More than anything else, it made them who they were. As far as the South Tyroleans were concerned, I speak therefore I am.

Anna described how in 1930 Mussolini decreed that all teaching should be in Italian. Even private German lessons were banned. This was part of Mussolini's attempt to Italianize the region. Italian became the only official language. In this way all minorities would be actively assimilated.

This power battle between Germanic and Latin worlds was nothing new. The Tyrolean passes had always been vital links between north and south, east and west. Although the Tyrol had been Austrian since the 1815 Congress of Vienna, it had also been Roman, Frankish, Bavarian and Italian. It had been invaded by the French and divided up by the Great Powers. It had even been an independent state of its own, briefly in the Middle Ages and even more briefly – for only a few months – in 1805.

Italians had always settled the lower region around Trent, and the two languages had always coexisted. But towards the end of the nineteenth century, as ideas of nationalism flourished, so disputes with the Trentinos grew increasingly radical. The Trentinos were then a minority in Austria.

By the early twentieth century the two communities had polarized. One Ettore Tolomei, who founded a newspaper called *La Nazione Italiana* in 1890 which claimed everything south of the Brenner was Italian, set out to translate every toponym into Italian. When Mussolini took power in 1922 his fascist aims were well supported by Tolomei's useful *Handbook of Names and Places in the South Tyrol*. This involved either direct translation or simply adding an Italian suffix to a name – Brenner becoming Brennero, for example – or, even more simply, plucking a name randomly from the Italian hat. Sarnthein became Sarentino. The Italian versions became the official ones. In 1936 Tolomei went further and published *La Restituzione del Cognome Atesino*, a list of 5000 Austrian surnames translated into Italian. This too was useful for Mussolini. It caused outrage amongst the German speakers, who claimed that the Tyrol with its toponyms and its people and their names had been German for 1200 years.

Meanwhile Mussolini deliberately altered the population balance by importing Italians from the deprived south into factories he set up for this purpose around the hitherto German bulwark of Bozen, and into the civil service. In 1921 there were 21,000 Italians to 230,000 Austrians; by the 1940s there were over 100,000 Italians to 155,000 Austrians. The new Italians occupied the cities while the Austrians remained mostly in the countryside. Italian became the language of bureaucracy, the police, and local government – in fact, anywhere other than in the home. The indigenous population received the immigrants with hostility, particularly as the incomers had access to all the best jobs. The two groups tried to avoid each other, but the German speakers were soon dependent on the Italians. Every farmer had at some point to deal with the state; every male had to do military service. The German speakers felt discriminated against and bitterly resentful.

I couldn't see Anna disliking anyone: she was too good. She didn't speak about the Italians; I got the impression that she didn't know much about them. There was an innocence up here that I loved. At times, she said, the narrowness of the valley could feel just that – narrow – even claustrophobic (her carpenter son nodded thoughtfully), but she loved it so much. It was hard to imagine her as a Nazi. But almost everyone was. Not only did they support the Nazis, they even had their own home-grown brand as early as 1933, the South Tyrol People's Front (VKS), which campaigned enthusiastically for the Third Reich, and looked to Hitler to liberate the South Tyrol from Italian occupation.

In March 1938 that moment seemed to have arrived. When Germany annexed Austria many South Tyrolese saw it as the opportunity to join their 'compatriots' over the border. The Nazi programme for German minorities abroad was to annex their lands or to resettle them within the borders of the now expanded Reich. But Hitler was Mussolini's ally, and therefore faced a diplomatic problem. During his first state visit to Rome the following May, he disappointed his South Tyrolean supporters by making a pact with Mussolini to guarantee the Italian border on the Alps' watershed at the Brenner pass. But Hitler also offered a radical alternative. German speakers would be given the option: to stay as second-rate citizens in fascist Italy, or to leave their homeland, their farms and narrow valleys, and emigrate voluntarily into the Reich. Hitler thought the South Tyroleans would make useful colonizers in the Crimea.

The South Tyroleans were tormented. Ever since their state had come into existence in the thirteenth century, both urban and rural communities had been obliged to defend their *Land*, an obligation that was codified in 1511. This had increased their sense of *Landesbewußtsein*, their identification with their *Land*, which was why the severing of their *Land* and occupation by the Italians wounded them so deeply. Now they were being invited to abandon it. Some argued that if they all chose to go, the whole thing would be impossible and would be abandoned. The Italian government encouraged them to go, offering to buy their land. The powerful Church was divided: the conservative high clergy advised the people to go, while the low clergy, who seemed to have woken up to the Nazis' anticlericalism, advised them to stay. Most enthusiastic were the urban poor, and rural younger sons deprived by primogeniture. Others such as VKS members welcomed the Anschluss and fully supported Nazi aims.

After stormy meetings a massive majority – 86 per cent – voted to emigrate to the Fatherland. The fact that only 74,824 people achieved it was due not to any change of heart, but to the vicissitudes of war.

When Italy surrendered in 1943 the South Tyrol at last came under German control, but ironically life under the Nazis turned out to be far worse than under the Italian fascists. Between 1943 and 1945 there were more victims than there had been during twenty years of Italian repression.

Those who emigrated were not considered traitors by those who remained. This struck me as odd. There was no sense of collective shame in having supported the perpetrators of the Holocaust, no moral transgression. Everything was justified by the threat to Tyrolean identity. After the war, when the Gruber–De Gasperi Agreement of 1946 guaranteed South Tyroleans equal rights for German and Italian speakers, safeguards to their ethnic character and culture, schooling in the mother tongue, bilingual topographic naming, and an autonomous legislative and executive regional power, many *Optanten* were welcomed home.

But despite Gruber–De Gasperi all was not well. The German population was depleted, particularly in the towns, which were now almost entirely Italian. Young rural Germans were still forced to emigrate in search of work. The provisions for autonomy were not fully implemented. Employment in any government institution, whether the postal service, railways, or civil service, was impossible for German speakers, and subsidized housing was reserved mostly for Italians. Military and police presence on the streets became oppressive. Frustration and anger grew amongst the Germans until they exploded in a terrorist campaign during the 1960s that left nineteen dead and hundreds injured. Hydroelectric power lines were blown up, plunging Northern Italy into darkness. Hundreds of people were arrested and tried, some tortured. But the bombings continued. Extremists from Austria and Germany infiltrated the South Tyrolean groups. But, disgusted by the escalating violence, local support for the terrorists waned, and eventually a new legislative package was agreed.

This included a quota system for jobs, but ironically led to new tensions: now the Italians felt discriminated against and set up their own neo-fascist party and began their own bombing campaign, this time of cable cars in ski resorts, the source of the South Tyrol's burgeoning wealth. At the end of the 1980s this was echoed by German nationalists campaigning for the return of South Tyrol to Tyrol, but they received little support, and evaporated when two 'freedom fighters' killed themselves with their own bomb.

Hans took us past the old bread oven – a detached stone-walled shingle-roofed building, now used for storage – into the barn. Its eaves sheltered the family wood supply; little carved figures of a man with a scythe and a woman in a peasant skirt were visible against the walls of the upper storey. Inside he kept four cows, a calf and two yearlings. Like Basque cows, they never went out because it was too wet and they would destroy the hay and need to be fenced in. Hans seemed comfortable in here with his beasts. He didn't say much.

The next morning we braved the road down to Sarnthein for Sunday Mass at 9.30 a.m. We missed Anna and family: they had been to the 6 a.m. service and were already back doing chores around the farm.

Outside the parish church a mountain bike event collided with the faithful, a collision of costumes: fluorescent lycra for the bikers, traditional Tyrolean dress for the churchgoers.

Such was the isolation of these Alpine valleys that each developed its own unique costume. These women of the Sarntal wore black blouses and calf-length black skirts, covered by silk aprons of blue, silver, or gold. A flowered, black-fringed shawl was worn with a V hanging down the back, and was drawn over their heads in the rain. It resembled costumes we had seen thousands of miles north, in the Åland Islands. Their hair was neatly plaited and rolled around the head, held in place with a black hairband or hairnet.

The men wore black felt hats with a red or green band stuck with feathers or flowers. Then came a collarless white shirt, a dark waistcoat of dense wool, and a leather belt six inches deep embroidered with white and red flowers and animals. These belts explained the unlikely presence of the peacock up our valley: they were *federke-ilsticken*, embroidered with peacock quills that had been split into long strands.

Short wide black trousers with a coloured strip down each outside leg fell to black shoes, some with rosettes on the toe. Leather straps over the men's shoulders supported a stamped and embroidered leather bib, almost like a cuirass; these gave them a military appearance, and indeed they were the uniforms of the rifle brigade to which each of these men belonged. It was hard to imagine them defending anyone – they didn't even have rifles – but that was not the point. What they defended were their traditions, their rights and their pride.

They milled about, meeting and greeting, entirely unselfconscious. There was nobody to watch them in this rain, except us. The point was that their uniform, like their language, was a badge of the tribe.

People removed their hats and bowed to pay respects in the graveyard. It was divided into strict rows of wrought-iron memorials with identical-sized plots divided by identical stone walls. Photographs of the departed were black and white, and oval – Alois Burger, Anton

Hofer, Filomena Moser – their names and dates in Gothic script. We were in Italy, but there was no presence of Italy whatsoever.

Many of the dead sported Hitlerian moustaches, and we saw several on the faces of the living.

The church was full. I was beginning to see that the Tyrol was a bastion of fervent Catholicism. This was the country that spearheaded the Counter-Reformation; whose brief nineteenth-century rebellion saw their leader and hero Andreas Hofer persecuting the Jews, abandoning the ideas of the Enlightenment, and closing down the university at Innsbruck for being too liberal; and the country whose main political conflict during the mid-nineteenth century was whether or not to admit Protestants.

The congregation had no other children. We sat together at the back and soon realized our blunder: the women were on the left, the men on the right. The service was in German with a full choir. Despite a flow of sweets Xanthe started squeaking, so we had to leave. We wandered into the adjacent chapel. It was a war memorial, with a long list of dead from both world wars, an array of flowers and freshly lit candles, and on the altar two German helmets adorned with the eagle of the Third Reich. Young men came in to pay homage.

We sought shelter from the rain in the nearest tavern. It was a cosy dive with panelled walls and wooden tables and benches. Almost every person – all male except the waitress – was in traditional dress. They smoked pipes and played cards. We drank beer. Rain smeared the windows, and a smoky fug soon built up. (We had committed our second blunder: the women filed through to a room at the back.)

I felt ambivalent about it all. It was charming, and I respected their traditions, but I was repelled by the conservatism. I sympathized with them as underdogs but I couldn't get used to the Nazi connection. I found it hard to draw a line between their cultural pride – their patriotism – and a nationalism that was altogether more objectionable.

The people themselves were ambivalent, not so much about their past which they seemed comfortable with, but about their present and future. The quota system, for example, relied on each decade's census in which every individual had to declare to which language group they belonged, with jobs apportioned accordingly. This was not as simple as it seemed. Many had intermarried, so their children may have been bilingual, and attended schools that taught in both languages. What was their identity? Were they German speakers or Italian? Also, fashions were changing, and younger Germans were more attracted by pasta than liverwurst, and by Italian style, while uprooted Italians envied the Germans' sense of belonging. Most people are now bi- if not trilingual. Tyrolean German is littered with Italian loan words, particularly the language of bureaucracy. Now there is the threat of English/American, thanks to tourism and the media, so the fear amongst older Tyroleans is not of deliberate Italianization but of a more subtle cultural erosion, a more general European homogenization.

It was dark as evening when we emerged, thick clouds blanketing the valley. As we climbed back to our spot, the rain became a deluge. Then, to our shock, we found that in just two and a half hours our tumbling river had become a brown churning torrent, swollen to twice its width. It had risen over three feet. The transformation was terrifying. I stood on the bridge, gripping the handrail, looking down on boiling waterfalls of thunderous raw power. Boulders were tossed like pebbles. Our beach, once six feet above the waterline, was now flooded, and rivulets eddied round our wheels. Rain streaming down fresh cuts into the mountain made by the bridge-builders created the danger of landslides from above. There was no way we could stay here. We crossed the bridge to higher ground and tucked under trees on the verge.

I was joined on the bridge by Luis. With great kindness, he had come to check we were all right. He had also come to gape.

'Is it normal in June?' I shouted.

'It can happen all year,' he shouted back. 'Whenever there's heavy rain.'

'Do your fields get flooded?'

'Yes, once or twice a year.'

He seemed as much in awe of the power of this river as I was.

A shrine on the bridge marked the spot where Valentin Burger Mitersohn (God help him) drowned in this *wildbach* thirty-one years earlier. It was easy to see how it happened: you wouldn't last a minute in that maelstrom. He had drowned on 8 June – this very day. The coincidence fuelled our unease.

Luis must have known the drowned man. Perhaps it was his father.

The river was surprisingly sensitive. As soon as the rain stopped, the level dropped. Then as soon as it began again, it rose. By evening the rain had stopped long enough to allow us to risk returning to our place. Two boys from a chalet up the road even came to fish; they had country faces and shy smiles. Tallulah wanted to make friends, but Anna had warned that all the valley children had some red rashy disease, possibly chicken pox, and I didn't want Xanthe catching that. They inspired Richard to get out his rod and to his delight he caught a trout. He grilled it on his fire, and we ate it with his latest loaf.

From then on the sun emerged intermittently, occasionally revealing ever-higher green slopes, ever-steeper fields that I had not even guessed at. Many farms, like Anna's, were occupied by widows; this was because farming here was so hazardous. If they weren't drowning in *wildbächer*, they were falling off mountains. It was one of the main causes of death.

Anna and Luis continued to visit us, sitting in our window seat, smiling in fascination at our little cupboards. They never came empty-handed. There was always a lettuce from the garden, a bottle of milk or beer.

One day they caught Richard sliding his dough into his Stone Age oven, and they were delighted when Richard gave them the loaf. They responded with a bag of ceps that Luis had picked the previous autumn and frozen. They were lovely people.

Breadmaking came to absorb Richard. He perfected his oven, and moved the fireplace to the ideal spot. One day I cycled down to Sarnthein (twenty minutes there, two hours back) and bought yeast and organic Bozen flour so now he could perfect his loaves too. It was as if Richard had unconsciously picked up on the passion for bread that was another Tyrolean characteristic, although we didn't discover this until later. Bread and the culture around it – ploughing, sowing, and harvesting the rye, threshing and winnowing and then baking – were what shaped the lives of these Alpine farmers. Because winnowing and threshing and even batch baking in the great bake houses were done communally, bread also lay at the heart of communal life. The baking was a tremendous event, taking place only a couple of times a year, the men plunging their bare arms into vats of dough, the women laying out patties of dough on planks covered with sacking, then sliding them on paddles into the wood-fired furnace. Each valley, even each village or each family, had their own traditional ingredients and shapes. Loaves were stored on wooden racks, like plate drainers or shelves, and kept for months.

Bread shaped the daily calendar but also the religious one – throughout the year there were services in honour of different saints connected with the production of bread. There were even services to which people took piles of flat loaves to be blessed. Bread meant life. And bread meant the body of Christ.

Bread also became another tribal badge, a way of distinguishing Austrians from Italians. Italians did not eat rye bread; they ate wheat bread. Rye suited the thin mountain soil; wheat did not. Because bread meant so much, this distinction was far greater than a matter of taste. It was a fundamental cultural gulf. During the 1920s and '30s some Italian immigrants hated the Tyrolean bread so much that they fled back south. Those that stayed had to import their own wheat and set up their own bakeries.

Anna had tears in her eyes when we said goodbye, and so did I. Richard was happier to leave: he had become fatigued by the sense of danger – the temperamental river, the threat of landslips, the perilous journey up and down. And once we had gone, I realized how deafened I had been by the river, and how exhausted by its constant roar.

Friends in southern Italy had given us an introduction to Count Johannes Trapp von Matsch, Herr und Landmann in Tyrol, and his wife Cecily, distant cousins of the Von Trapps and their governess Maria Augusta, the singing nun. They lived in Churburg, a thirteenth-century fortress above Schluderns in the Vinschgau valley. It rose white and crenellated from the hill with heraldic 'W's painted on every shutter. In the visitors' car park we changed into our 'best' clothes and climbed nineteen cobbled steps to the keep that was clamped shut with massive bolts. The doorbell made a plaintive bleat in some inner sanctum.

The caretaker admitted us to a beautiful Renaissance courtyard that rose three storeys, enclosed by painted arcades.

We were shown into a panelled salon and introduced to Johannes, a long man with a grey streaked beard and a long medieval face of immense gentleness and seriousness. His wife Cecily was his opposite, small and round and blonde and relaxed. We sat in arm-chairs and drank wine, overlooked by Johannes' elongated ancestors, then retired to the panelled dining room for lunch. Even the ceiling was wooden – inlaid with chestnut, Johannes explained, to keep the spiders away. It was like being in a box, looking down over the needle-sharp spires of Schluderns and along the sweep of the valley as it curved towards Switzerland and up towards the majestic snow-patched Alps.

A maid bustled. I was on tenterhooks that the girls would misbe-have – they were not used to such refinement. But they loved it all. When they chased each other round the table, Cecily didn't mind. Johannes kept glancing at his watch: they had just arrived from their main home in Innsbruck in the North Tyrol, and Johannes had an appointment that afternoon in his armoury. We joined him there in his huge iron wardrobe, mostly Milanese armour of the very finest. Cecily observed that one complete suit – and one for the horse – cost the equivalent of a house today.

Pasted to the keep walls were press cuttings from a visit last March by the Queen of the Netherlands.

Cecily said, 'I hate all this, it's showing off.'

Johannes replied, 'Oh, you have to do it, people love it.'

They'd forgotten to ask her to sign the visitors' book, so they'd left a space and would forge it later. They loved their castle, and maintained it beautifully, but they were irreverent about it too.

Tallulah was longing to play in the Churburg garden and pick wild strawberries, but Cecily and Johannes wanted to have tea in our Mob. Unlikely though it seemed, they had spent holidays in vans themselves and felt nostalgic. Johannes was splendidly aristocratic, speaking to all he met with noble courtesy, inclining his head from his astonishing height – he must have been over six foot seven; it was hard to imagine him behind the wheel, changing the gas, emptying the loo, trundling off to the supermarket. I couldn't even imagine him doing something as mundane as working in a bank, which was his day job.

'If you want to eat breakfast with me, come at eight-thirty tomorrow,' Johannes announced before extricating his legs from under our Mob table. Tallulah grinned: she was in love with both of them. She assumed they were prince and princess, despite the regrettable absence of crowns.

'Oh no,' gasped Cecily. 'I won't be having breakfast until nine.'

So at nine we rang and rang, but no one came.

'What will we have for breakfast? What do princes and princesses eat?' Tallulah asked anxiously, hopping from foot to foot outside the massive gates.

'Toads, I expect,' Richard said.

Her mouth opened wide, tears spurted forth. 'I don't want toads. I want Rice Krispies.'

'Don't worry, he's only joking.'

We tried other gates in other walls. Suddenly Cecily's head popped out of a turret.

'Oh, there you are. We were just about to come and wake you.' She unbolted the doors and turned to Tallulah. 'Would you like a mouse for breakfast?'

Tallulah looked alarmed. This sounded nearly as bad as toads. But on the plates were mouse-shaped buns with raisin eyes, which had been bought specially that morning. Xanthe said 'Nyam nyam,' and poked her finger in the butter. We ate the mice with delicious apricot jam made from local fruit – not their own, but from back down the valley. What *they* had was tons of organic apples which they exported to Russia.

Cecily and Johannes postponed their return to Innsbruck. Tallulah was so happy.

'We want to show you Glurns,' Johannes announced.

It was a walled town whose long-standing mayor (the baker) had enlightened views on preserving old buildings. This was something close to Johannes' heart; his father had been an art historian, and Johannes himself was highly knowledgeable. Glurns was like a living Aigues Mortes, surrounded by rough-hewn battlements and towers. They encircled hulking farmhouses with working barns reeking of hay and dung, tractors roaring in and out. Cecily explained that farms were kept within walls to protect them from siege. We wandered into one farmyard that, like most local properties, once belonged to the Trapps. A toothless man, with a basket suspended from two shoulder straps like a basket rucksack, greeted us with a broad vista of gum.

Cecily whispered, 'I'll tell him you're English, in case he thinks you're Italian.'

'Would he resent us if we were Italian?'

'Oh yes, because he's from the older generation. The younger ones don't remember.'

As the Trapps' homeland had been sundered, and as their other family home now lay the other side of an international frontier, I thought Cecily would be interested in North and South Tyrol reuniting. But she dismissed it out of hand. It would never happen. There was no need. Money was pouring in to the South Tyrol from Italy, Austria, and the EU, quite apart from the tourists. Younger people had every reason to feel happy. They had, in effect, been bought off. And now that the EU was dismantling its internal borders, crossing between the two countries as the Trapps did most weekends was no more complicated than going from, say, London to Sussex.

Cecily seemed calm and serene, but Johannes went at top speed, his long legs striding boyishly through arcades, in and out of churches and museums. He rushed off to a neighbouring village to pay a carpenter who had restored the statue of St George in Churburg's courtyard. Typical of the South Tyrol, these villages were full of high-class craftsmen, generation after generation. It gave the altarpieces and ecclesiastical statues a special resonance, knowing that all the crucifixions and angels and pietàs and saints had been carved nearby, by people whose descendants were still in the business. The Church was still their main employer, which reinforced the sense of strong religious fervour in those valleys. That evening in Schluderns the bells tolled for evensong, and the next morning, a Sunday, we were deafened by bells, ringing out along the Vinschgau.

A full-sized Calvary, each contorted torso dribbling red blood, loomed over the valley.

There was a Tyrolean gathering at Schloss Tyrol, in the castle that gave the region its name. The castle was impressive on its promontory, and the gathering was of locals in Tyrolean dress dancing to their oom-pah-pah band, their felt hats resting on rose bushes. It was picturesque, and although the town of Dorf Tyrol was swarming with parties of fat German tourists, none of them found their way here. On the grass in the castle courtyard they did thigh-slapping dances that made us smile: it was so chaste and buxom and unsexy. They gossiped over sausages and beer. They felt ashamed of their chaotic Italian government, of the bureaucracy and the Mafia and of the corruption of the south; they were a thousand miles from all that. There was nothing Latin about these people at all.

My eye was caught by a blond curly-haired man. He was the best of the young dancers, throwing his partners higher, slapping his thighs with more vigour. He smilingly explained that he was a maths teacher in Meran. He came here once a year not to celebrate anything particular, just for fun.

We also noticed someone looking on fondly but from a sophisticated distance, dressed like an international art dealer. He wasn't big and blond like the Tyroleans, but small, refined, more stylish. We suspected that this was Dr Siegfried W. de Rachewiltz, and we were right. He was Director of Schloss Tyrol, and owner of the neighbouring Brunnenburg Castle. He was a friend of the Trapps, and they had given us an introduction to him. He was also Ezra Pound's grandson.

We visited him the next afternoon. Today as he shuttled past on his moped between his own castle and Schloss Tyrol, he seemed less intimidatingly glamorous. He shouted that he would see us at Brunnenburg and puttered on.

Brunnenburg was a mass of medieval walls with a mini turret sticking out below like a supernumerary toe. Siegfried W. de Rache-wiltz met us at the door to his family's private tower – the rest of Brunnenburg was occupied by his collection of agricultural implements, by Pound memorabilia, by his mother (Pound's daughter), and by American students who came to study art history and anthropology. Siegfried was thin, sensitive. He had a narrow nose and fine, well-formed lips. He looked tired. I guessed he was in his late forties. He guided us up a spiral staircase to a panelled study. It was comfortable and strewn with treasures – bronzes and drawings by Gaudier-Brzeska, portraits of Pound, signed first editions.

The girls flung themselves around and sucked excitedly on Sprites, banging their glasses down on a glass table. I had brought a picnic but they needed more space to eat it, away from objets d'art, so we moved on to a roof terrace. It opened off the kitchen where the wooden floor was bulging, having been soaked during the recent tempest that had forced its way through massive wooden window frames and double-glazing. Siegfried blamed the castle's exposure on its crag; the windward westerly side had been clad in concrete, but even that had not solved the problem.

Siegfried explained that Brunnenburg had been a ruin for three or four hundred years, until the turn of the twentieth century when it was bought by a mysterious character from the Rhineland who restored it in the 'medieval' style. During the First World War his funds ran out and in the 1920s it was confiscated by the Italian government, by which time it was ruined again. Siegfried's parents, aged eighteen and nineteen, his mother expecting Siegfried, came upon this ruin and bought it. The money was sent by Ezra Pound from America. Pound was in a mental asylum, having been deemed unfit to stand trial for treason for his pro-fascist wartime broadcasts from Italy. Nevertheless, he was fit enough to send not only money but useful and interesting paying guests, and also to write to his grandson wonderful letters about birds and nature. Although he was absent, Siegfried grew up with his massive presence. Then after twelve years of incarceration, Pound was eventually released in 1958, and arrived at Brunnenburg on a festive high. Siegfried remembered him as a man of volcanic energy.

'He sat on our sofa in the room where you were sitting just now, and he'd read the *Cantos* aloud.'

'Did you understand them?'

'No, I didn't even speak much English. I was ten or eleven. Then he'd read from *Uncle Rhemus*. Again, I wouldn't understand, but he had this great ability to do voices, the southern slang. I loved it.'

Pound was passionate about organic farming, years before his time, and took his grandson with him on walks, teaching him about the natural world. He was mad about birds.

But after six months his volcanic high burnt out, and Pound slumped into depression. He was seventy-four, the world had moved on and his friends were dead; he had a physical and moral collapse. After another six months in a mental institution, Siegfried's grandmother, a violinist, took Pound to Venice where she kept him going for ten years.

Siegfried's collection of Tyrolean tools began as a collection of words, recording before it was too late the names of things that were central to Tyrolean culture but were being abandoned. It was not Pound's collection, but the idea was sparked off by Pound, who loved not only farming and folk life and poetry, but language itself; he had studied Romance philology at university. When it became hard to explain what the words meant, Siegfried brought the tools up here too. He was fascinated by the manual intelligence that had enabled these mountain people, over centuries, to control their dangerous and difficult environment. Men like Luis and Hans were not given to flights of eloquence but they had a practical intelligence that had resolved problems of farming on almost vertical slopes in all weathers, using both craft and craftiness. Siegfried had collected scythes and ploughs and winnowing machines and sledges and threshers and linen-making machinery – like those tossed aside in Anna's barn.

'Is this the end of an era?'

'Yes. I believe it is. The pace of change since the fifties has accelerated enormously. When I was a child Dorf Tyrol was just a few farmers, then in the 1960s it exploded with tourists. Now it's almost saturated, and people are starting to realize they are losing their quality of life, and that the tourists won't like it here any more.'

'Will it get worse?'

'Yes, I think so. Take the farmers higher up. They're campaigning to put in a road. They don't need this – they have a funicular and walking paths, and they all have houses in Dorf Tyrol and work in tourism. It isn't a matter of survival. Farming is now just something they do as a pastime, like a hobby. But they want a road because other people have roads. But a road will bring traffic, and will cause geological and environmental damage. I see it as a demonic thing, as if these clever old peasants are little Fausts who think they can sign a deal, build a chairlift, open hotels, and still maintain their old way of life, their Tyrolean identity. They can't.'

It struck me that Siegfried had not a drop of Tyrolean blood. He was Tyrolean only by birth. Yet he had adopted a culture that was exceptionally rooted in its place. And he had steeped himself in the most rooted aspect of that culture – not only its dress and its literature, but the very means by which the people tilled the soil. It was as if he sought to belong not just to the present but to the past, not just to a rooted culture, but to the earth in which it grew. Siegfried smiled, and said he was like all converts. I wondered if his passion came from a need to belong, or if as an outsider he was more aware of what was at stake than those who took it for granted, or if he had some need to prove himself to his neighbours. Perhaps all those things, he replied.

'I'm even a *Bildungsoffizier* in our local *Schützen*, our rifle brigade.'

'How come?'

'I joined after spending ten years in the US. It was a way of keeping in touch with the people I grew up with.'

But there was more to it than that. A cultural leader from one of these groups had recently shot a politician, so the authorities had turned against the *Schützen*, fearing them as paramilitary groups. As a leading figure in Tyrolean culture, who had studied in the US and had a liberal international persona, Siegfried was asked to appear on television to defend them against charges of gun-toting Nazism. Siegfried was then invited to take this cultural leader's place.

'Of course these groups do attract those with a less than peaceful attitude to their fellow human beings, which was another reason why I accepted. To keep them out.'

'It's a very conservative culture.'

'If you mean conservative as in bigoted, then I disagree. The priests have a hard time keeping the lid on their congregations' vitality. The most devout Catholics are often the most pagan. There's a religious respect for nature, for its power, and the force of the mountains, and this is a strong bond here, the kernel of their character. If they go up the mountain they are still confronted by a sense that technology can't solve it all. If they experience a storm, they are reminded that the power of nature is still all-present. The vast views up there still give the people a sense of pride, and that pride is good, because it makes people stay.'

The return of Siegfried's wife reminded us how late it was – we had been talking for over three hours. She had been to Meran with their son to buy a coffin. It was for a wounded bird he had found. The boy was still in mourning, his bird covered with a white sheet. He asked Siegfried where he should bury it, and Siegfried, who understood his son's grief, gently advised him to go off with a trowel somewhere in the grounds of Brunnenburg.

Tour buses hurtled towards us, guides mouthing into microphones. Between rain-swathed mountains streaked linear developments of hotels and health complexes and solaria and supermarkets selling hideous carvings. Richard noted in his diary: 'Busy wipers squeaking on the windscreen, children complaining, wife feeling sick.' This was the Grödner Valley in the Dolomites. The famous Grödner Pass was scarred by ski lift terminals, pylons, roads, and motorway-sized channels cut through the woods for ski runs and lifts. They were revealed by the absence of snow in all their environmental desecration.

There was one exciting feature. Suddenly public notices and toponyms were no longer bilingual, but trilingual. The Grödner Valley was not only the Val Gardena, but also 'Gherdëina'. The new script lacked the Gothic curlicues of German; it looked more like Italian, but with German elements thrown in. There were un-Italian accents – umlauts, circumflexes, acutes, and graves – indeed, French elements too. It was Ladin.

We'd been looking for the Ladins – and they were hard to find since there were only 30,000 of them in the Dolomites – but the devastated Gherdëina was not what we'd had in mind.

We pored over the map and found one minor road that branched off the Val Badia, passed a village called Wengen/La Valle/La Val, and petered out in the mountains. There was not a ski lift to be seen.

From what we could see through the rain, it looked promising. The vernacular architecture was little different from Anna's farm, but the way barns and chalets and bread ovens were concentrated in small inward-looking clusters – *viles* – was typically Ladin.

We parked between a raging stream and a sawmill, beneath fir trees. Brindled cows munched on flowers and jangled vast bells which, I noticed as a sad sign of the times, were padlocked on. Rain dripped through the vents, mostly on to Tallulah's bed – lovely weather for the end of June. Richard struggled up on to the roof with his sealant gun. He was wearing three layers of clothing, as much as in the Basque Country in December, and needed a strong whisky to revive. The chill seeped into our lives.

In a rain break we wandered down hill amongst houses and meadows. Every wooden balcony was festooned in geraniums, everything neat and immaculate. A man in a barn worked with a lathe, making a wooden statue for sale in one of the carving marts down below. We sat on stone slabs in a chapel porch while Tallulah and Xanthe ate their elevenses, and a little girl in pink hair bows cycled past, back and forth, longing to make friends but too shy. She was the wood-carver's daughter. So, I thought, tourism had killed the lower valleys, but at least it kept these upper reaches alive.

And tourism had impoverished the land but enriched the Ladins: such were their profits that despite their tiny number they had managed to wangle extra powers in local government, even forcing the authorities to include Ladin in official communications.

In the lower fields haymaking had already started. Men and women were forking the grass up on to long trellises to dry; the only other place I had seen this system was in Samiland, thousand of miles north.

Above the pine foothills loomed a crenellated wall of limestone and magnesium streaked with snow, the Sas dles Diesc, up at 3023 metres. In the changing light it was sometimes grey, sometimes pink, sometimes golden, sometimes lost altogether behind massing cloud. Under the moon it grew more majestic and turned a metallic colour, creased by jagged shadows.

We walked in the mountains and sprawled in Dolomitic meadows. Richard, impatient with the girls' snail pace, would stride ahead while we lay on a log pile in a heathery plateau. Tallulah crawled over me, stroking me with hairy leaves.

'Mummy?'

'Yes?'

'Why do Ratty and Mole and everyone talk about "luncheon"?'

'It's the real word for lunch. We just say lunch for short.'

'Oh good. I've been wondering about that for a long time.'

Rubble, disturbed by us or by some hidden creature, clattered down the fissures of the Sas dles Diesc and littered the snow. We were in shaly, inhospitable terrain. Some devout mountaineer had scaled each peak, carrying cement and tools, and fixed crucifixes to the summits of every one.

On the way up we had met an old man with an egg-spattered beard. He wore the regulation blue apron and carried a man-high spade. He was going to dig gravel out of the stream. He lived down below – a good two miles' walk.

'Giovanni Ploner,' he announced, holding out his hand. '*Contadino.*'

He had hummocky gums and watery blue eyes that sometimes focused far away. One dreamy moment was broken by the announcement that he was ninety-two. We spoke Italian together, but he spoke better German because he had been at school when this valley was still Austrian. He was thirteen at the end of the First World War. We stood for some time while he murmured, '*Ja, ja, ja, ja, ja, ja,*' farting all the time. Yet he posed for a photograph like a lord, standing still and straight as if waiting for the slow shutter release of the cameras of his youth.

On the descent we found cracks in a bridge filled with the gravel. He was now forking fir branches into a pile. He gave a dignified wave.

We were home drinking tea when he came by. Richard invited him in, and offered him cakes and a cup of tea, which he drank with quantities of sugar. He sat at our window table, his *contadino*'s hands cracked with use. Xanthe was eating yoghurt with her fingers and making a horrible mess beside him. Giovanni picked up a spoon and courteously presented it to her; normally she would have flung it on the floor in disgust, but she accepted it gracefully and said, 'Poon. Blabberlabber poon.' Spoon. Tallulah's spoon. Giovanni nodded sagely.

I asked him to write his name in my notebook. His script was shaky but full of beautiful curlicues. It was not something I'd ever asked anyone to do, but it transpired that his handwriting was his greatest source of pride.

He leafed through a book about the Val Badia, studying the old photographs.

'That's my aunt!' he cried, pointing out a nineteenth-century woman with a butter churn. She was pretty, with her plaited hair neatly wrapped around her head; to her left stood another girl wearing an extraordinary woollen hat like an inflated turban. Those hats were bright blue. You don't see them now, he said.

He had books he could show us, better books. He invited us to visit him the next day, '*dopo pranzo*'.

Richard cycled to the 9 a.m. Sunday Mass. The church was so crowded it was standing room only. Mass was in Ladin (the prayer and hymn books were translated into Ladin only in 1984). The women were in front, the men at the back, all in traditional dress that was much the same as in Sarnthein. And as in Sarnthein, after the service people filed into the graveyard to pause over different graves, looking down and praying and remembering. (I had praised this ritual to Cecily Trapp, who had scoffed, 'They only do it because they are afraid of what the neighbours will say if they don't. I used to visit graves with my grandmother, and she spent most of the time wondering if her neighbour had pinched her flowers.')

No one answered the bell, just a dog barking ferociously. Then Signor Ploner appeared, hatless and in holey carpet slippers. We escaped from the rain into a broad hall that ran the length of the house, stepping over a dog that sprawled rug-like at the foot of the stairs. He yawned and Tallulah and Xanthe leapt in terror into my arms, but he only wanted a sniff.

A door of old pine with a handsome wrought-iron handle opened on to the smiling form of Signora Ploner. She was twenty years younger than her husband, a spritely seventy-two, with her hair plaited in the traditional way. Like Anna, she wore a floral cotton apron over a floral cotton dress; it matched the flowers on her windowsills and balconies, and in the meadows. She seated us at a table in the right-hand corner, near the heater which was blasting away although this was midsummer.

Now I could take in the room. It had panelled ceiling and walls, with a burnt stencil running round the dado and door frames. At one end squatted a huge cylindrical oven like a boiler, and over it a raised bed: this was where they slept in winter. Another single bed now stood where Signora Ploner once kept shelves for the dozens of loaves she used to bake once or twice a year. Like the Germans, the Ladin made rye bread, which never went stale. She didn't bake any more, she said, it was too much effort, and there was no one left in the village who remembered how to do it. It was so much easier to walk to DeSpar and buy a loaf. That, she explained, was why the fields were full of flowers: because nobody grew rye or wheat any more.

Signora Ploner fetched plates of biscuits and sweet raisin bread, jugs of juice, spinach pasties, potato and spinach croquettes. She had baked them at midday – traditional Sunday specials. Xanthe gouged out the filling and dropped it on the floor; when I picked it up, I found I'd picked up a mouse dropping too. Signor Ploner ate at the far end of the table, too deaf to join in much.

'Why not get out the trains?'

Signor Ploner looked up from his tea.

'The trains!' his wife shouted, laughing.

They kept them for their grandchildren. Tallulah got wildly excited, shooting the old-fashioned tin trains across the floor, rolling about and shrieking. It was her new wild manner that took hold of her when we went to other people's houses – a sort of hysteria induced by our boring conversations in a language she didn't understand. I wondered how much longer we could keep up this way of life. Inevitably a train broke. I was cross, but Richard said it was already broken, and he and Giovanni had a friendly time trying to mend it. Giovanni proved very dextrous, and set to with string.

Their daughter appeared; she wore a traditional lacy blouse and flowered apron. She had sweets for the girls, and when she left Signora Ploner shook her head and cast up her eyes. 'Thirty! And still not married!' It was hard to find a mate when so few people spoke their language; those who did were divided into separate valleys that even now were self-contained, inward-looking. To get from one valley to another did not mean nipping over the hill, but long journeys down one valley and up another, with mountain ranges towering between. If they did get to another valley, they found the dialect quite different.

Another problem was that the Ladin valleys were not contiguous, but were dotted about in south-eastern Switzerland, the Dolomites, and in Friuli between the Alps and the Adriatic. As the Frisians are divided by water, so the Ladin are divided by mountains; and like the Frisians have never belonged to a single cultural, administrative or linguistic unit. The language is sometimes called Rhaeto-Romance and thought to stem from the original pre-Indo-European Rhaetian spoken here since at least the fifth century BC. 'Rhaeti' was how Strabo characterized the powerful and warlike peoples of the Alps.

In classical manuscripts, Rhaetia appears as a province of the Roman Empire, bounded on the west by the Helvetii, on the east by Noricum, on the north by Vindelicia, and on the south by Cisalpine Gaul – parts of today's Switzerland, Lombardy, and Tyrol. Little is known about the Rhaeti, although Livy believed they were of Etruscan origin. They lived by cattle breeding and cutting timber – much as Giovanni did today – while some fertile valleys produced wine and corn.

But they may in fact have been several different tribes, with languages evolving with different pre-Latin substratum, and different linguistic superstratum. These days linguists believe that only the language in Switzerland can properly be called Rhaeto-Romance (or Grishun as the people themselves call it); the language of Friuli can be called Eastern Ladin or Furlan; and that of the Dolomites should be called Ladin.

By the time the Romans arrived, the Celts, pouring in from the north, had already pushed the Ladin up into these narrow valleys and settled among them. The valleys also served as refuges for other peoples driven here by war; they too stayed and settled, leaving behind their genetic and linguistic imprints. The Romans obviously left their Latin tongue, but they never settled here as enthusiastically as in the south; to them this was more important as a through-way, a route between Gallia Transalpina and other possessions to north and west.

These Alpine provinces were the first to fall before the devastating onslaught of the Germanic tribes of Alemanni and Bavarians that from the fifth century AD came in swathes from the north. Had they been better organized, with a common goal, then all this area might have become German speaking. Likewise, if the speakers of Rhaeto-Romance and Ladin had been better organized, they too might have formed a coherent political whole and produced a separate standard Romance language. But they did not.

As German and Italian spread, so Ladin retreated. It is still retreating. Innsbruck did not become wholly German speaking until the thirteenth century, and there were Romance villages in the Vinschgau even into the nineteenth century. But Ladin could not withstand the power and prestige of what were to become national languages.

Today Grishun has the best prospects. It is not despised but cherished and cultivated, and since 1938 has been Switzerland's fourth official language. But these last remaining Dolomitic valleys, facing the threat of German and Italian media and bureaucracy, combined with the need to search wider than the immediate valley for a spouse, would be lucky to survive. Yet with Alpine resilience Giovanni and his family had managed to do just that – so far.

Their son had escaped from the valley by becoming a champion cyclist. Now he was back to run the farm, and had recently married the daughter of a rich factory owner, which explained the new house being built alongside. The carpenters were raising high the roof beams. His silver trophies stood in pride of place on a little shrine that was tucked into the corner above our heads. It bore a statue of Christ – not the Madonna, for Madonna worship was an *Italian* thing.

Giovanni carried in some of his books about the Ladin, many with photographs of the old days, of people ploughing with horses, hauling logs on sleds over the snow, carrying preposterous loads of hay on their shoulders.

'They were good days,' sighed Signora Ploner, 'but life was hard, too hard.'

'Did Giovanni do this, and this, and this?' I asked, pointing at the pictures.

'Oh yes!'

'Hauled entire tree trunks down the mountain by hand?'

'Yes. But not for the last two years.'

Not since he turned ninety.

'There were no cars then, of course. We walked to Mass. In winter there would sometimes be only three men there, all the women and the rest of the men had stayed at home.'

But recently there had been warm dry winters without much snow. It was a pity really, she said.

There were Ladin family portraits, and the Ploners recognized most of them. This one was dead, that one ill, that one had thirteen children, that one had fourteen children, all still living in La Val.

Many men married several times as the mortality rate for women in childbirth was high; Giovanni's own mother had died when he was six and his father had remarried; his two half-sisters, now in their eighties, still lived in the valley. Signora Ploner's mother had died when she was seventeen. Both deaths were mentioned sotto voce, as if still painful, even though Giovanni's mother had died eighty-six years earlier. She told me this to explain the hugeness of the houses. Many, including this one, were small mansions, three storeys high. The building material grew all around.

Tallulah and Xanthe came for cuddles, and when Signora Ploner uttered endearments, her language sounded like a harsh cross between German and Italian. She said the words were easy because they resembled other Romance languages, but the pronunciation was difficult.

She handed me a poem.

> *Bun dé y bun ann*
> *Por l'ann nü dan man*
> *Che al vesportes sanité*
> *En pü de rí y incontenté*
> *L'amur, la pêsc, la sinzirité*
> *Daite y defora.*
> *En ann tira a fin*
> *É stlü jö so destin*
> *Metü man ligherziu*
> *Dan da püch dër jonil*
> *Gnü teniade atompé*
> *Tan debota che döt é 'ndô passé!*

Good day and good year
For the year that's coming
That brings health
A little laughter and contentment
Love, peace, truth,
Here and elsewhere.
The year draws to an end
And reaches its destiny . . .

Here our combined powers of translation ran out.

'This is no good! Hansi, why don't you fetch your notebooks? You wait till you see his notebooks.'

Giovanni opened his desk and carried out a pile of exercise books. He unloosed a red ribbon and handed us each a book in which he had transcribed his favourite poems and proverbs. I admired his beautiful handwriting, and Signora Ploner agreed that it was lovely, and proudly opened four more notebooks filled with verses and texts.

'He sits here all winter, writing away. Not just in the evenings, but all day, when he can't go out.' She lowered her voice, and looked fondly at her husband. 'He was the best in his class!'

I noticed that although many were in Ladin, some were also in German.

'He was at school when this was Austria, so he is better at German,' Signora Ploner explained. In those days there had been no schooling in Ladin. 'I was at school when this was Italy, so I don't speak much German.' The cut-off date was 1930, the very year Signora Ploner started school. Suddenly all the classes were switched from German to Italian, which caused utter confusion. The Ploners' children had studied mainly in Italian, but they had also had a couple of years in Ladin at nursery school and in the first year of primary, something that had been stipulated in the Autonomy Statute of 1972 even though there was no teacher training in Ladin.

'Do you feel closer to the German speakers or Italians?'

'Our language is more like Italian, but our culture is more Germanic. Our way of life is very little different from the German-speaking South Tyroleans. We are not hot-blooded like the Italians; we don't gesticulate like them or shout. We are Alpine people.'

Mussolini denied the existence of a Ladin ethnic group, and claimed that Ladin was nothing more than an Italian dialect, so when given the choice in 1939 many Ladins opted to leave their land and join their Tyrolean brethren in Nazi Germany. Two thousand actually emigrated, but more would have done so had the war gone a different way.

The Ladin cause followed a familiar pattern. The nineteenth-century development of a written language; publication of grammars; and towards the end of the century the flowering of Romantic ideas of nationalism. In 1905 a 'Uniun Ladina' was founded in Innsbruck, which aimed to bring together all the Ladin of the Tyrol, unite the dialects and scripts of the different valleys, publish newspapers and almanacs, and generally raise Ladin consciousness. But, as usual, the two world wars put paid to any aspirations to self-determination. They never dreamt of independence, but after 1918 they sided with the non-Italian Tyroleans in demanding autonomy for the region. Since the Second World War they have ridden on the back of German activism and campaigned to be recognized as a distinct linguistic group, on a par with German and Italian. They have had moderate success. Some valleys are able to receive a daily radio broadcast in Ladin, and since 1988 a brief twice-weekly TV broadcast. In the mid-1970s two Ladin cultural institutes with libraries and archives were set up, and since 1989 the provincial authorities in Bolzano/ Bozen/Balsan have had to use Ladin in administration, as well as German and Italian. There is one weekly newspaper. However, all this does not amount to much; it is only better than nothing.

Giovanni wanted to show us the rest of his library. He led us up the broad staircase. The layout of the upper storeys mirrored the lower – one long panelled corridor with substantial rooms opening off it. The corridor was walled with coffee-table books in Italian and German, tomes about art and culture, a complete Dante, crumbling Bibles from the 1840s and earlier, books about the Second World War in which he served. The corridor ended in a glazed balcony where he read in summer; an ancient manual typewriter sat on a table. He had a genuine love of poetry that had survived into his nineties, and all the proceeds from his mill and his farm had been spent on books.

'Have his children inherited his love of books?' I asked Signora Ploner.

'No. And his parents weren't like him either.' She smiled at him fondly. 'He's unique.'

The next morning, when the rain stopped, they took us into their mill. Although corn milling had been abandoned, the water still powered a generator making electricity for the house. Great wheels turned, pistons fired. Flour still coated the old milling rooms. The Ploners showed us how everything worked, how they used to tip the corn in here, collect the flour here. Every tool was wooden and beautifully made – wooden pails, wooden shovels, huge wooden screws; Signor Ploner showed us how he used to twist those great screws, and how he controlled the mill races. But no one came here any more. His office was untouched since the day he stopped milling, twenty years earlier. On the panelled walls, festooned with cobwebs, hung his official documents from the 1920s entitling him to act as miller, and between them and a list of safety rules from the 1930s was a carved crucifixion. Everything was rotting away. Maybe their son would dust it down and get the mill going again, but these days there wasn't much call for mills like this.

FOURTEEN

The World Bitch

We'd been driving north-west. The rain never stopped. It was impossible to leave the Mob without full waterproofs that then streamed on to the carpet. Through the North Tyrol, across the Black Forest, over the Rhine to France.

We stopped at last, south of Rennes on a bank of the Vilaine, the most beautiful river we had yet seen. On the opposite bank woods bent to the water; below their eaves a heron stood in aristocratic solitude. A family of otters frolicked in the shallows. Towards evening they would glide up and down, the river coagulating like mercury on their glistening backs. They would raise their snouts, then twist sinewy bodies to plunge into water lilies, thrashing around in search of fish, honking or barking a harsh nasal 'whaah'. The sun came back. We lay in the hammock, the river sliding below. I swam too, gliding downstream beneath clouds of mosquito hatchlings. Everyone was happy.

But this was not what we were looking for. We were looking for Brittany, and we were in Haute Bretagne where Breton had never been spoken. All the place names were French. Haute Bretagne had been incorporated into Brittany only in the ninth century, just the other day in Breton terms. Besides, the landscape was too gentle to be truly Breton, not raw enough or windswept. So we headed west again.

Surely the great alignments of standing stones at Carnac, their parallel avenues over a thousand metres long, would reveal something about Breton identity. The very word *menhir* is Breton, *men* meaning 'stone', *hir* meaning 'long'; *dolmen* is also from the Breton *taol-ven*, meaning 'stone table'.

It was a dusty day. The menhirs stood in sand, the feet of millions of tourists having worn away their surrounding vegetation and even earth to such an extent that it was feared they would topple over. Now tourists were banned; we could view the stones close-to only with a guided tour.

Any lingering romance was withered by the guide's typically French intellectual attention to detail – 1169 stones, average width between the lines 100m, lines 1167m long. Even the words *menhir* and *dolmen* turned out not to be proof of ancient Breton connection with the stones, but neologisms coined by eighteenth-century archaeologists: the Bretons call the menhirs *peulvan*, 'stone pillar'.

Richard and I returned at night. Now orange lights illuminated the stones, and buried at the roots of some of the more impressive slabs were violet or green lights that turned on and off for interesting effect. There was music in the air but not the pipes of yore; it was disco music from neighbouring campsites. A security guard drove up. He spent eight hours a night alone with the stones; his job was to prevent drunken campers from vandalizing them. Mostly he sat in the car but he was busy in July and August, he said.

Only when we escaped from the coloured lights at the far end of the alignments was it possible to feel any connection with the past. We stood alone, dwarfed by the stones' massive, rough-hewn, licheny, venerable bulk. No one knows for certain their origin or purpose, and one can only assume they have masculine, fertility, and celestial connotations. The marvel is that these stones have stood here for seven thousand years. Their mystery only adds to their allure.

Once it was assumed that these were Celtic monuments. At that time it was thought that European history was the result of successive waves of migration, and that the Celts, redheaded and fiery, invaded as a marauding horde from the east, bringing with them their culture, religion, and language, wiping out all they encountered. They were at once warlike, yet simultaneously the mystical morbid romantics of the Celtic Twilight so beloved of nineteenth-century English literati, like Matthew Arnold. But the master race theory has been challenged by archaeological finds, many being unearthed as I write – our most vibrant history is our most ancient – and thanks to carbon-14 and genetics those finds are being revealed as far older than was previously thought. These days the orthodox view is of indigenous development *combined* with imported developments, rather than superimposed – imperialist – change. It is now thought that Celtic language and culture were brought to Gaul and thence to Britain in the last millennium BC by small groups of migrants who culturally dominated the indigenous peoples they found living there, but that some features hitherto considered specifically Celtic, such as respect for women or druidic rituals, could now be attributed to their predecessors, the semi-nomadic dolmen and menhir-raisers of the second millennium BC.

The Celts, who arrived over succeeding millennia, made this their heartland, and incorporated the stones into their own rituals. Where did they come from? Their language had to be Indo-European. Why else would 'young' be *juvenis* in Latin, *yaouank* in Breton, *ieuanc* in Welsh, and *yuvan-* in Sanskrit? Why else would 'three' be *tres* in Latin, *tri* in Breton and Welsh, and *trayas* in Sanskrit? When the Romans conquered Gaul they would not have realized that their barbarian enemy spoke a language that evolved from the same buried roots as their own.

The language that the Celts introduced to Gaul spread to Britain in around 600 BC. This became known as Gallo-Brittonic, the ancestor of Breton, Welsh, and Cornish, as opposed to Goidelic, which dominated Ireland and later Scotland and the Isle of Man.

The term 'Celt' was first used in 500 BC by the Greeks, and referred to a people who dominated much of Iron Age Europe. This was a culture confident enough to conquer Rome in 390 BC, and dominant enough to leave its mark on place names throughout Europe: the rivers Rhone, Rhine, and Danube, the cities Paris and Vienna. By 300 BC the Celts had become the most powerful people in northern Europe. Celtic territory extended from modern-day Turkey to Ireland. The town of Bala, a Celtic word meaning 'outflow from a lake' was built on the shores of a lake in Anatolia several centuries before a small and very Welsh town called Y Bala was built at the edge of a lake in north Wales.

This may be ancient history, but it is crucial to modern Bretons keen to stress their non-French identity, and their connections with the non-French, pan-Celtic world.

After being conquered by Julius Caesar in 56 BC, the westernmost outpost of Gaul became a Celtic refuge. The Romans called this region Gallia Armorica from the Celtic *ar*, 'on', and *mor*, 'sea', and turned it into a Roman province. But they never got very far here: they built few towns, and left the population only superficially Romanized; in the countryside the people continued to speak Celtic, and Christianity made little headway.

Four centuries later the Roman Empire had collapsed and Salian Franks filled the void in most of northern Gaul, along with the Rhineland Franks or Ripuarians who inhabited the banks of the Rhine. The Franks were quickly absorbed into Gallo-Roman society, converted to Christianity, and although they added new words and forms of pronunciation to the Romance already spoken, they abandoned their native tongue. Thus began the Frankish Empire, which reached its zenith under Charlemagne (AD 768–814).

For all their success, the Franks never made it to that remote north-west peninsular of rugged cliffs and plateaux. Instead there was an invasion of a very different sort. Meagre sources suggest that between the fourth and seventh centuries Celts from the British Isles, particularly Wales and Cornwall, took flight from the Anglo-Saxons and climbed into not very seaworthy craft to make perilous journeys across the channel in search of refuge. They also came in search of land. Fracan, cousin of a Brittonic king, landed in about AD 460 with his wife Gwen (White), his sons Weithnoc and Jacut, and followers. They pitched their tents a few miles from where they landed on the north Breton coast, and there founded the first Breton *plou* or civil settlement, today known as Ploufragan.

These Britons, who brought with them their priests and monks, their *sancti*, found a place in which Christianity, where it existed at all, had become seriously corrupted. They set about ousting the Druid priesthood, building monasteries and hermitages, and evangelizing among the people.

Others who came were missionaries obeying a divine order made known in a dream. St Malo, one of the great Breton bishops (Maclou in Breton) came from Wales. St Brioc (or Brieuc), a famous Christian healer, sailed in AD 485 with 168 monks in a large barque from Northumberland. St David – Dewi Sant, patron saint of Wales – fled here with his mother Non in 547, possibly to escape the Yellow Plague. Non died here. St Ronan, Brittany's most popular saint, was in Ireland when he heard God summoning him to Cornouaille; he was soon spotted by Breton fishermen bobbing over the waves on a huge stone. The missionaries spoke a language the Armoricans could understand, so they were welcomed. Thus an already Celtic country was re-colonized by Celts. The languages grew closer. Armorica became Little Britain, or Breizh.

Welsh and Cornish missionaries were aghast at the Breton attachment to their stones, tainted with ancestral paganism and still potent. They tore them down, mutilated or buried them. But the more pragmatic or sensitive among them understood how deeply the stones were embedded in the Breton psyche, and instead of destroying them, they assimilated them. They Christianized them, either by placing a crucifix on top or carving them with Christian symbols, or by moving them into a consecrated enclosure. They coated them with a Christian veneer. When St Samson left Wales for Brittany, he crossed Cornwall where he found the locals dancing round a standing stone. He was outraged, and had the stone destroyed. But once he reached Brittany his horror mellowed. The massive menhir near the monastery he established at Dol was left untouched.

We followed Celtic migration to its westernmost outpost on the continent, to the place where we could go no further, to the *finis terrae*. The rocky peninsular of Finistère, Pen ar Bed, 'world's end', thrust its finger into the Atlantic.

A road dropped to one of the few stretches of accessible but unspoilt coast on the Bay of Audierne. Now the toponyms looked distinctly Cornish – Penhors, Pouldreuzic, Treguennec, Kervinou. Suddenly our orientation changed: now towns were twinned with Welsh or Cornish towns. We felt as if we were coming home. We were in Cornouaille, *kornaoueg* a Breton word for 'west', Brittany's own Cornwall.

We parked on pebbles beside tufts of windswept grass. The low tide offered up its secrets like innards: weed, glutinous pimply anemones, stranded crabs leaving husks of claws and bodies, mysterious pools. Tallulah leapt about in the shallows, her slender naked body stretching and loving it. Xanthe prodded the rocks.

'Dat?'

'Sea anemone.'

'No!'

'Jelly?'

'Arright. Delly. Baby delly.'

Men with buckets prowled over the barnacles hunting edible molluscs. We tried winkles, rubbery little things. We had mussels too, prised off clefts, shorn of beards and cooked in cider; they were small and nutty but tastier than the flabby things we bought in the market. Then there were crab feasts – we even bothered with spider crabs that had nothing in their bodies but were fun to poke out with skewers, the sort of food that appeals to people who enjoy picking their toes. One evening an aproned woman came with a plastic bag and peered into the tufty grasses in search of snails, but they were too huge for us to tackle.

We were here because of Pierre-Jakez Hélias. He was a Breton peasant who had become professor of Celtic at Rennes University, and in 1975 had written *Le Cheval d'Orgueil* (*The Horse of Pride*), a marvellous sweeping description of life in a Breton village during the first half of the twentieth century. The largest village in the neighbourhood, where his father was born, was just inland from our beach. Its name was Plozévet.

Le Cheval d'Orgueil was written in Breton and translated by Hélias himself into French. It was a wonderfully honest account of his hoodlum childhood, fighting rival gangs, playing marbles and ninepins, exchanging obscene insults. But it was also an intimate social history, and an ethnographic study. He described the family cottage with its floor of beaten clay known as toad-mud, and the box bed that he shared with his grandfather, a bolster of oats keeping them apart. He described the nagging hunger, the insufficient bowls of gruel, the round of unremitting toil in the fields, the grinding poverty. There was the hard earth of the moorland, the *landes*, to clear for cultivation, the long distances to walk, the remorseless Atlantic winds, the cruelty of teachers and priests, the early deaths. One misfortune – a disease, a bad harvest, a harsh employer – was enough to pitch the family into destitution, into head-to-head combat with the 'World Bitch'.

Yet Hélias and his family were fortified by pride, dignity, honest labour, and by the warmth of their relationships. There were stories round the fire, laughter in the box beds, rites of passage celebrated with as much lavishness as the family could afford. His mother considered it a matter of honour to be spotlessly attired, crowned at all times except harvest by her towering *coiffe*. Over the earliest years of the twentieth century these *coiffes* had grown until they were more than thirty centimetres tall. Women wore them even when during the 1950s they began to take the unusual step of going for a swim. The lace peak protruded from the waves like a swan's neck. Without fail Hélias's mother would arise before dawn to devote half an hour to combs and hairpins in order to sally forth with her head held high.

Hélias described a period following the apogee of Breton life, when the Breton population had increased until the First World War, especially in the countryside – in other words, especially amongst Breton speakers. His life spanned that heyday, and its subsequent decline.

This was Hélias's territory, that part of Cornouaille known since the start of the twentieth century as the Pays Bigouden from *beg*, the word for the original *coiffe* point. It was also said to be one of the last hideouts of Breton. If one in five Bretons spoke their mother tongue, as the statistics claimed, this was where we would find them.

In a damp misty morning Plozévet was deserted, but then we found everyone pushing trolleys in Ecomarché, one of the familiar metal hangars despoiling the edge of town. I had a haircut. The hairdresser, though local, spoke not a word of Breton, '*hélas*', and knew no one who did. I asked her the meaning of the BZH stickers I had seen on a few cars.

'I don't know. Gaston, do you know the meaning of BZH?'

The other hairdresser dumbly shook his head. An old woman looked up from under the helmet of her dryer. 'Brittany. Breizh,' she muttered. The autonomy movement. The hairdressers clucked with disapproval.

A main road ran through town. It had become a dull place. We wandered into the church. Its gloomy bulk was relieved by a lovely barrel-vaulted roof painted sky blue, and beside the porch an ancient well. Fountains and springs like this were worshipped by the Celts for their magic properties; like the stones, many were maintained after the arrival of Christianity, and had chapels or shrines built over them. In this church Hélias's uncle Alain was punished as a boy for not learning his catechism. He was made to stand alone in the dark church for many hours. Dismissed at last, he was running the three miles home when he beheld a ghastly vision of a cloaked man setting light to the ground. His father led him back there later and found no evidence of burning, and it was agreed that he had been a victim of one of the cruel priest's well-known magic spells. This was in 1900.

In a niche stood a sixteenth-century statue of a Breton saint, Alar. He held the amputated leg of a horse, with the three-legged horse beside him. He was one of thousands of such saints worshipped only by the Bretons. Over centuries, miracles performed by the Brittonic missionaries had been told and retold, and their fame spread until they were canonized. The bishop of Kemper has counted more than 7500 saints within his diocese, of which only three are recognized by Rome. The saints acquired powers once attributed to stones and sacred fountains and the Celtic pantheon: some cured, some protected, each did something different. I supposed that Saint Alar was one of many veterinary saints, turned to in desperation when an equine injury could mean, literally, destitution. The World Bitch.

In a cemetery beside the church was Plozévet's only other objects of interest, a menhir and a war memorial. The latter was unusually dignified and un-martial. It said simply, 'We died for love of France 1914–1918.' Several Le Goffs were listed; Le Goff was the maiden name of Hélias's mother. Hélias described his own father going off to war. The only thing he gained from it was a good trench coat and some khaki trousers that were cut down for his son. A quarter of a million Bretons were killed.

But the First World War killed more than those young men. It was the beginning of the end for Brittany. It was that same old story of nineteenth-century revival cut off in its prime. A world war opened this hermetic country to a patriotism greater than to their immediate *pays*, a patriotism to *La France*.

On a more intimate level it saw young men sharing trenches for four years at the front with soldiers from the rest of France; thus the Bretons discovered an outside world, and another language, one they were forced to learn not only so as to communicate with their fellow conscripts, but to understand orders. After the war, many of these Breton men found work alongside their new friends in more productive parts of France like the Dordogne or in Paris. Their understanding of 'Frenchness' expanded, while they also learnt of the perceived backwardness of Bretons, stubborn and conservative. Many never came home. Those that returned to visit lorded it over their bumpkin relatives who had stayed behind and not learned French, the language of success; the emigrants were despised in return.

During the Second World War Breton bravery was repeated, and resistance to German occupation was stronger here than in much of France. Near the Vilaine River we had found a moving memorial to resistance fighters who in 1944, during the German retreat from the Americans, had been tortured and massacred by the Germans. But this was not the whole story. There were also Breton autonomists, members of Breiz Atao, Brittany Forever, who during the 1930s praised Nazi Germany. They wanted a pure Celtic state purged of Jews, Arabs, Negroes, and Latins (including Occitans). Attempts were made to ship arms from Ireland to help construct a Breton state and sabotage French war efforts. Resistance veterans and Communists even claim that when France was occupied, BA members donned German uniforms in 1943 and actively hunted them down. After the war many Breton autonomists sought refuge first in Germany, then in Ireland. This has been played up by the French, partly to discredit the autonomy movement, but also to avoid their own guilt for their own collaboration. It's easier to blame a minority.

Completing our tour of Plozévet was someone's front room converted into a museum. It was as Hélias described, with the box bed hidden behind its sliding doors and studded with polished brass, a pretty room but lifeless. The old lady who lived here had been brought up in that bed but wouldn't dream of sleeping in it now; she displayed it for the likes of me.

'And not only you. Also for Breton people who want to see how their grandparents lived.'

'What's their reaction?'

'They are curious. And maybe nostalgic. Everyone wants what they don't have, or what they don't have any more.'

'If they like it, why don't they install box beds of their own?'

'Because those days are gone.'

Fields reached the cliff edge, the very fields that Hélias and his family tilled, piling up lumps of granite to make stone walls, grubbing up gorse, ploughing, planting, hoeing, scything. They grew wheat, barley, and millet, which were eaten as pancakes, bread, or gruel. This was little different from the diet of the megalith builders of Carnac. But after seven thousand years traditions have changed. Now they grow EU-subsidized maize, Day-Glo rape, and linseed, not for local consumption but for oil.

Dotting the fields and increasingly encroaching on them were the slate-roofed Breton houses Hélias described with whitewashed walls and granite corners. They were picturesque, always in keeping with the traditional style. But their random placing, and the untended gardens, and the size of the cars and boats in the driveways gave away that they were not 'real' houses but holiday cottages.

How much of Hélias's world remained? We had been in Brittany for several weeks and seen not a single *coiffe*. We had heard not a word of Breton. I was beginning to suspect that Hélias – now dead himself – had written a monument to a dead culture.

Certainly today's Bretons were proud of their folkloric past. Brittany seemed to have shouldered the mantle of folk capital of the world. The streets were adorned with posters advertising *Festoù* of both *noz* and *deiz*, night and day, either local Bigouden, or provincial Cornouaille, or pan-Celtic. Plozévet was going one step further, and the following week would be hosting a Folklore Festival of the World. We decided to stay on for it.

Meanwhile all over Cornouaille were Pardons, religious pilgrimages. We chose the one most appropriate to us, dedicated to Notre-Dame de Bon Voyage. We drove through windswept fishing villages towards the Pointe du Raz, and found an eighteenth-century chapel above cliffs near Plogoff. It was surrounded on two sides by sea and on the others by bracken and gorse. It was a bright washed day. Women were erecting trestles.

'We're waiting for the Pardon cakes.'

Cars gathered in the field. Most people were old, in traditional Breton dress of knee-length skirt, white cardy, and comfy shoes. Anyone with a *coiffe* was off parading at a rival festival, the popular Fête des Brodeuses in Pont L'Abbé, a major tourist fest. But perhaps it was better this way; perhaps this would be a festival which people actually believed in, not staged for tourists.

The chapel had a blue wooden roof painted with stars and anchors, and on biers, waiting to be processed, were model boats, votive offerings given by survivors of shipwrecks and other maritime adventures. There were votive plaques on the walls; indeed, the whole chapel was a votive offering, built in 1798 as thanks to God by someone rescued from drowning at sea.

Mass, disappointingly, was in French. This was another blow to Breton. During Hélias's childhood, catechism had been in Breton and Mass in Latin. This had caused some confusion for the Bretons who assumed that Latin was a different dialect of Breton. The *Kyrie eleison* was sung fervently but with some puzzlement because the congregation thought they were singing *Kirri eleiz 'so*, meaning 'there are lots of wagons'. But they knew what the service was about; it didn't matter if they missed the details.

Throughout the early twentieth century it was debated whether or not to use French in church and school, and French eventually prevailed. Church schools continued to teach in Breton long after state schools insisted on French. It was Reds versus Whites, Republicans versus Royalists. In Hélias's world the divisions were so strong they determined which gang you were in, on which side of the street you lived. Hélias and his family were Reds. Traditionally Breton, like Basque, was associated with clericalism, and anti-Republicanism, the Whites.

The service lacked charm, but the priest was eloquent about the Bon Voyage as a metaphor for Notre Dame making her voyage amongst us. She accompanied us on our voyage through life, he said. A Pardon, he said, meant reconciliation, a return to Notre Dame after absence.

Most went home for lunch, taking boxes of Pardon cakes – apple pastries and custardy cakes with pink icing. A bar had been set up. I asked the middle-aged barman why Mass had been in French.

'Because nobody speaks Breton now,' he grunted without looking up. 'We all speak French.' He was rinsing glasses.

'Are you Breton?' I persisted.

He looked up and put his hands firmly on the bar top. 'Me, I'm Breton, I live here in Plogoff, but I speak French. My wife is not Breton. Our children don't speak Breton. They don't understand a word.'

'The Breton hymn this morning was the only one sung with enthusiasm.'

He shrugged. 'Oh, a few songs, that's all they know. Breton – it's gone. *C'est du folklore.*' He turned back to pouring rosé.

I walked away, near to tears with disappointment at his indifference. *Ah bah*, as Xanthe would say. All gone.

Now everyone had left except us and a man in a lemon-coloured jacket and his lady friend who picnicked at a folding table. We lay in the lee of the wind against the Mob and listened to them chatting. How the French do talk, I thought, jabber, jabber, never draw breath. Then the man peered round the Mob, offering *crêpes* and Pardon cakes. I felt guilty. The old lady had made the *crêpes*; she invited us over, so now I could join in the chatter and be grateful for it.

This man was passionately pro-Breton. He and his lady friend were from Quimper, Kemper in Breton, and often came out to little Pardons like this. The irony was that the bourgeoisie from towns, who traditionally spoke French and sneered at the clodhopping Breton-speaking peasants, were now the ones seeking their Breton roots, while the rural dwellers like the barman, the ex-peasants, couldn't wait to be French.

He had also been disappointed by the lack of Breton in the Mass.

'It's not only the language that's going.' He shook his head in despair. 'It's our whole way of life.'

'What's the cause?'

'The French state, obsessed about centralizing.'

Brittany was always isolated. Independence almost ended when Francis I in 1532 bound Brittany to France, but local liberties were guaranteed. Thus provincial autonomy survived, and local patriotism opposed Bourbon attempts at centralization. This remained the state of play until the French Revolution, when Brittany was incorporated fully into France, only to stagnate as another poor province on the outer perimeter of the country.

The nineteenth century saw a revival of folk tales and language. Myths were woven around Brittany's origins. Arthur, it transpired, was not Welsh or Cornish but King of Brittany, married to Gueni-èvre, the most beautiful woman in Brittany, while Merlin lived in the Breton forest of Brocéliande. Arthur, apparently, travelled back and forth between Great and Little Britain, ridding Mont St Michel of a terrorizing giant and performing other heroic deeds. Arthur fought a great battle on the island of Aval off the Breton coast against the joint forces of Saxons, Picts, Scots, Norwegians, Normans, and Danes, but he was mortally wounded. He lay down on the island and slept for fifteen centuries, waiting for the hour to come when Brittany shall call upon him once more. At least, according to the *Barzaz Breiz, Chants Popular De La Bretagne* ('Breton Bardic Poems: Popular Songs of Brittany'). Of course, the Barzaz Breiz was a nineteenth-century fake, written as part of the Celtic twilight, and the Saxons and other enemies were metaphors for nineteenth-century Republicans. This was important because for the first time it showed links being sought by Bretons with the Welsh and Cornish, and being cut with France.

'What else threatens the Breton way of life?' I asked the man in the lemon jacket.

'Conscription. You know we had military service in France since the late eighteenth century, long before any other European country? Then public education, compulsory since the 1880s. Mass culture.'

'Benetton.'

'Bah. We're all becoming the same.'

Breton faces the usual problem of different dialects, although since the nineteenth century it has been progressively standardized, and intrusive French words removed from the dictionary to be replaced with the closest Breton equivalents that could be found, which were Welsh.

I discovered another intriguing reason for the decline of Breton. During the Second World War the Vichy regime introduced optional Breton language study and financed the private schools. By the time war was over both had become tarnished, associated in Breton thinking with the Occupation and the threat to France.

But times had changed. Feelings about Breton, the oppressed minority tongue, had swung round to the radical left, the Reds. What had been dismissed as reactionary was now embraced, while the right wing, traditionally White, veered towards supporting French and centralization.

This man had realized about nine years earlier that they were about to lose everything when the old people died, taking with them living Breton encyclopedias, living dictionaries. Then something wonderful happened. Young people throughout Brittany realized the same thing. They woke up.

'They grasped the old ones by the hand before it was too late.'

'Was it not too late for Breton?'

'Normally I'm a pessimist but I must say I'm astonished by our young people and what they've achieved.'

Festivals were revived, traditional Breton instruments were brought out of attics and dusted down, young musicians listened to the old accordion and *biniou* players and wrote down their songs, music was imported from Scotland and Ireland. It wasn't only music, but politics. Separatist groups proliferated. The man himself opposed militant activism, and few really want autonomy, but he was prepared to campaign to save the language.

'The two languages are quite different,' he said. 'Not just in the obvious sense but in what they can express. French is the language of the spirit, of the head. Breton is the language of the heart.' He sighed sentimentally. I didn't speak Breton, but I would have thought it was the language of fields and fishing boats.

When he was at school, French was seen as liberating, from both the Church and the squirearchy. The poor wanted their children taught in French: it was the same throughout France. Because the Bretons had always expressed themselves orally, they were particularly sensitive to dialect, accent, and languages. Those that did not learn French felt humiliated every time they had to go to town or deal with bureaucracy, because it was always in French. After the Second World War they were made aware that the peasant existence was not a valued one, and that to get on in the world required a good (French) education and a good (French) accent.

The *instituteurs* were progressive, devoted to the emancipation of the poor through French. It was the same in Wales and Scotland. Finlay J. Macdonald's descriptions of growing up before and after the Second World War in the Outer Hebrides almost exactly mirror those of *Le Cheval d'Orgueil*, with a teacher encouraging the one bright pupil to learn the majority language, to get on and get away, leaving him severed from his roots and always with a lingering regret. One of my own Welsh great-great-grandfathers, John Edmunds, was just such an educationalist, a teacher and Chairman of the School Boards in Caernarfon. In 1868 he founded a ragged school of his own. When his Welsh-speaking niece came from the heart of Wales to study with him, John Edmunds formed a scheme whereby if anyone spoke Welsh at table, they lost a mark, and if Father or Mother lost more marks than the children, they would give the children a penny to divide between them. Hélias describes the use of *La Vache*, the pottery cow that was used to humiliate Breton speakers in school, as in Provence. The extent of this is disputed, as is the use of the Welsh Not, but its existence was enough to cause outrage. Besides, Breton activists need to believe it was widespread in order to sustain their unity in the face of opposition, as something to fight against, and against which they could define their Breton identity. Those *instituteurs* are now looked back on not as liberators but oppressors, as agents of a determinedly centralizing state, of cultural imperialism. The lady from Kemper said her grandson was a Breton activist; he called it cultural genocide.

'Take the place names,' the man said, his eyes kindling. 'It's so important to us, because the names actually mean something. The French Frenchified them. Their versions have no meaning. And we were here first! Those Franks came later. Charlemagne never conquered us.'

He referred to events of the ninth century as if they happened last week. It might have sounded absurd, but it *mattered*. It mattered to him, as it mattered to almost every tribe we had visited. It mattered to whoever felt they had rightful claim to a land from which they felt they were being ousted, and it mattered to those who sought to justify their sense of separateness.

I asked him whether the EU would help Brittany – Brittany had certainly been supplied with plenty of EU cash – but he went off on a rant against 'gigantism'. How the real enemy wasn't Brussels but the USA. 'Their terrible culture, their words, their Clinton. If all they can offer is that ghastly food, what's it called, McDonald's, then that's pretty pathetic.'

Throughout our conversation the old woman grimaced at me through her gap teeth, raising her eyebrows at the man behind his back. She agreed with him when asked but was amused and embarrassed by him too.

They assumed we were from Cornwall. Why else would we be there? He stressed the connections with the Cornish saints. The old woman chuckled. 'He knows more than you do. Or thinks he does,' she added. I think they wanted us to be Cornish, or Welsh, so that they wouldn't feel we were the enemy, the imperialist equivalent to the French. They both envied the Welsh. When she went on a bus trip to Wales, she couldn't believe the bilingual road signs and the Welsh-medium state schools, and the fact that with the Welsh Language Act Welsh was actively encouraged by the government in

England. She complained of the lack of Breton-language radio – a maximum of fourteen hours per week transmitted by Radio France as opposed to 126 hours a week transmitted in Welsh by BBC Radio Cymru. It was pitiful, she said. Radio was crucial for communication, education, to broadcast Breton music and literature and comedy. It was the only way to prevent Breton artists from disappearing to Paris, and to keep people together, to forge a common identity. But the money wasn't there.

'Do you two speak Breton?'

'We do,' they chorused.

'Yet you were speaking French amongst yourselves.'

They looked almost shamefaced. It was what they'd got used to. The old woman gathered up their bags. Pardon-goers were returning. It was time for the second Mass.

Plogoff, this humble stretch of cliff, was as vital to the Breton movement as the Alta Dam was to the Sami. In 1980 the French government proposed building a nuclear power station here. There was fierce opposition, but what might elsewhere have been an anti-nuclear protest became a Breton one. The Bretons felt victimized, that this nuclear plant was being dumped here because no one cared about Brittany. It became a focus for opposition to everything French and bourgeois. Thousands of militants occupied the site, fought riot police, were arrested and beaten. It became a cause célèbre, and gave a huge boost to the Breton movement.

It may also have been another reason why the barman was so unenthusiastic about Breton. Maybe he hadn't enjoyed having all those militants camped on his doorstep.

Kemper was buzzing. Every corner revealed a busker playing music from somewhere in the Celtic fringe. I found a Celtic bookshop, and at last heard Breton being spoken. It was a strange harsh clipped sound with every letter pronounced right up to the end, lots of 'z's and 'k's and 'ch's. I bought a dictionary full of wonderful no-nonsense words like *gwinkal*, 'to kick', *gortoz*, 'to wait for', *didamall*, 'blameless', *trimiziad*, 'quarter'. It looked blunt and humorous. It sounded not sophisticated like French or intellectual like German, but ancient, peasant-like. It wore sabots. But there were other words like *neoazh*, 'yet', or *yac'h*, 'good health', and *youc'h*, 'yell', that gave it a more breathy, airy feel, the language of Celtic fantasy.

The shop assistant, a tall man with wispy hair, said that the future for Breton was improving, but terribly, terribly slowly. It was like a patient in an intensive-care ward. Not quite dead, not quite coma-tose, but hovering between those states of silence and a tentative recovery.

'It is very difficult for us. The French are so sensitive about the loss of French speakers when their language is already under threat from English.'

But progress was far greater today then he could have envisaged ten years ago, helped by a growing awareness of Celtic links with the British Isles. Where Welsh had forged ahead, assisted by legis-lation, Breton could follow. I complained of the lack of Breton in Plozévet, and he said it was probably because people are still ashamed, or because it is a private thing, spoken only with others 'in the know'.

This conversation took place sotto voce. The assistant was nervous, his eyes flitting to the door. I couldn't believe that he was afraid of discussing the status of his mother tongue, but he said the French security service was everywhere, and to be feared. He didn't want any trouble. Particularly at the moment, as there had just been a trial in Paris of fifteen Basques accused of ETA member-ship, and of five Bretons who had given them shelter. The French security service feared links between the two, but those links had long existed. During the trial Herri Batasuna had toured Europe to present its view of the Basque situation, and had been officially received in Kemper town hall.

The shop assistant revealed that although the autonomy movement was very small scale and divided, it had an enormous amount of publicity. He gave me a pamphlet, published by the Celtic League, which included an article by POBL, Parti pour L'Organisation d'une Bretagne Libre. This was founded in 1982 by, amongst others, Yann Fouéré, an activist working before the Second World War who fled to Ireland to escape being accused of collaborating with the

Germans. POBL described itself as a party campaigning to stop the language being steamrollered out of existence, and to escape the 'economic mismanagement' of Paris. The article cited countries that during the twentieth century had managed to achieve independence – Norway, Finland, Iceland, Ireland, and so on – and wanted to add Brittany to the list. Ideally, Brittany would form part of a federation of Celtic countries within the framework of a federal Europe.

The Folk Festival of the World began in a hangar-like community hall on the edge of Plozévet. I cycled there one evening to see a Breton band called EV. Young people milled around beer stalls. They were calm, unthreatening. I noticed a young woman who had been playing accordion in Plozévet's main square that morning. She was eighteen, with thick brown hair that curled in a wedge to her neck. I introduced myself, explained why I was here. She seemed pleased. She was passionate about Breton music, and had been playing at *Festoù noz*, 'night festivals', since she was thirteen, usually alone, sometimes accompanied by a tambourine or drum, sometimes a *biniou* or bagpipes.

'Why does no one speak Breton here?' I asked her. We were strolling around the stalls.

'But they do!' she exclaimed. 'Lots of my friends go to Breton schools. You must know about Diwan, the association of Breton schools? Most are just nursery schools; some – or at least one – is up to baccalaureate level. Lots of my friends teach there.'

'Are you militant?'

She laughed. 'Oh yes.'

'Is language at the core of your militancy?'

'Of course. You can't be a Breton militant if you don't speak Breton.'

'What if you can play Breton instruments or dance?'

'No. Not even if you blew up Versailles. You couldn't be taken seriously unless you spoke Breton.'

I asked her to write down her name. Delphine Rodriguez. I peered at her, and she smiled.

'Yes, I'm not Breton. My father was a *pied noir*, from Spain.'

Another outsider, wanting to belong.

I found myself sitting next to a man with beer breath and a tropical shirt. He whispered something about a Breton Mafia, but this was only an excuse to get his arm round me.

'My wife's jealous,' he leered.

She sat, huge and dyed blonde, like a dolmen across two seats, and took no notice. He put his arms round us both and introduced us and told her how nice I was. To deflect him I took out my notebook, but he leaned over to watch me write, and told me more about the Mafia, then got aggressive when he thought I was going to write what he said and get him in trouble. I fled.

The music was terrible, French heavy metal. The French language was too soft and sophisticated, and the shaggy-blond bare-nippled singer too pretty despite his attempts to look mean. The band wore black and white kilts, a reference both to their Celtic connection with Scotland, and to the Gwenn ar du, the black and white Breton flag. The look was too contrived, the sound a mess. I went outside and milled around the chips and beer stalls, and later rejoined the younger people standing in front. Not many were dancing. Then the singer announced (in French) that they would now sing in Breton, and the place erupted with a new energy. Everyone began to dance; even the bourgeoisie in their seats seemed roused. I looked round and saw that even the megalithic blonde looked animated.

The synthesizer player emerged playing the accordion, lumbering like a pregnant woman. He became master of ceremonies, whooping up the crowd. I saw him as L'Ankou, agent of death, his shadow cavorting across the back wall. His was thunderous Last Judgement-like music, or perhaps he invoked the beginning rather than the end, with the bare-chested singer as primitive caveman. Now the bassist was playing a *biniou*, its sound narrow and hard like him.

I didn't know how much the audience understood, but the fact of Breton excited them. This evening they could tap into a language that was the repository of their collective memory. I envied them that shared identity and shared purpose, and the secret subversive glamour of their ancient tongue.

I cycled back around midnight, exhilarated, downhill all the way without lights. I was high, my ears still throbbing. I wanted to carry on feeling raw. I went down to the sea and shouted at the waves.

We missed the Mass for peace, but arrived in Plozévet in time for the processions. The main street was lined with spectators, and we stood at the widest place where performers paused and danced. They were led by weird clay-covered stilt men. Tallulah and Xanthe cried with fear. Then along came dance troupes from Ethiopia, Russia, Mongolia, the Andes. Fear was replaced by joy. They were followed by pipe bands from local towns, each sporting their banner, the dancers in Breton costumes, including their absurd skyscraper *coiffes* and pearl-beaded aprons over black skirts. All the dance troupes were fake, no more connected with the real life of their countries than Morris dancers. But nevertheless I was moved to tears. It was the sight of small peoples, like those we had met all over Europe, fighting to be allowed to exist in the modern world, and brought together in insignificant Plozévet with such good will.

Tallulah, sitting on the road holding Xanthe's hand, gazed up, her eyes shining.

'It's the loveliest festival of my whole life.'

It continued for several more days. There were feasts of *crêpes* and cider, and a *Fest-noz* with Breton bands to which everyone joined in shuffly line and circle dancing in a courtyard. I sat alone in the dark over a glass of beer. The dancers knew the steps, recognized the music, spoke the language, shared their common feeling of Bretonness. I didn't mind being excluded; I enjoyed watching the way their dance created and expressed a fraternity, a sense of themselves as a community that had been – and perhaps no longer was – on the brink of extinction.

I was struck by the irony of our journey. We had spent nearly eighteen months studying peoples whom history had rooted in one place, and whose characters had been shaped by – and had shaped – those landscapes. But we were nomads, always passing through. We were watching but were invisible ourselves, exploring other peoples' identities while remaining nonentities. The people we met knew little about us and cared less. Until now, being a nobody had given me an almost vertiginous sense of freedom. I had loved the lightness of not being, I had enjoyed my transient invisibility and lack of connection. But over the last few days I had noticed that many of the Breton revellers had narrow features and pointed chins and dark hair. The members of EV, the Kemper bookshop assistant, the man in the lemon jacket at Plogoff: they were a Celtic type. I realized that I looked the same. It gave me a sort of thrill, as if I too had a stake in this Celtic fringe. But I was only half-Celtic. Being a typically British hybrid, I could never belong anywhere. Perhaps it is that hybrid quality that gives the British – or at least the English – a natural dislike of homegeneity. Nevertheless, in trying to make this Celtic connection, I realized that for the first time in our journey – and I could hardly bear to admit this – I wanted to belong somewhere.

Our journey was ending. The longer we stayed in Brittany, the more clear that became. We had had our *bon voyage*, and it had been blessed, but it was the logic of the route: our next destination lay over the Channel, which happened to be home.

What had I learnt? Throughout Europe a pattern of shared histories had emerged, beginning with the decline of Latin and breakdown of Christendom, and the rise of largely spontaneous popular nationalisms in the eighteenth and nineteenth centuries. These had been spread by liberal intelligentsias who had inspired – and had been inspired by – lexicographical revolutions; the gathering up of language, folklore and myth. There were the *Félibrige* of Provence; the 'Erudite Societies' in Corsica; the Basque *Berpizkundea* and Catalan *Renaixença*; the *Atlas linguistique* and Prince L. L. Bonaparte's dialect map; the outpouring of forgotten Greek classical texts by European scholars; the distinctions formed between Slav dialects into Bulgarian, Serbo-Croat and Macedonian; and the gathering together of folk tales to create Finland's national text, the *Kalevala*. There was the secessionist movement in the Ålands, and the National Awakening in North Frisia. Some of the new nationalisms welded themselves to older political structures, such as monarchies and empires, and together prompted the spread of state-national languages and customs, largely through schools. But despite the efforts of the lexicographers, where the vernaculars did not fit the geo-political space of the new/old state, they were squeezed out.

Then during the twentieth century the empires around the world broke up, giving rise to the realization of a thousand new dreams of independence. Throughout the world, nations were born. Despite being all but killed off by the two world wars, today the smallest nations or tribes are rediscovering themselves and breaking out, dreaming of becoming independent or autonomous states in their own right.

In Europe their success rates have varied considerably. Macedonia, a sort of infant Belgium, achieved political independence but without the internal stability, cash or friends to support it. The Catalans, on the other hand, eschewed independence, to more or less run Spain themselves. They are the envy of the smaller peoples of Western Europe. Up there with the Catalans are the Swedish-speaking Ålanders, then the Welsh and South Tyroleans, and close behind – for all their whingeing – the Basques, and then the Frisians. At the other extreme lie the poor non-French regions of France – the Pays Basque, Occitania, Brittany, Corsica and Alsace. Their future self-determination looks unlikely. Somewhere in the middle lies Samiland. Of all Western Europe's peoples, the loss of a multitude of languages spoken by the Sami is the most distressing, because along with the languages goes a unique and remarkable way of life.

Over the last hundred years the politics of nationalism has veered from right to left. While the League of Nations was taking shape after the First World War, in liberal and left-wing circles the word 'nation' became a dirty one. During the Russian civil war, the Bolsheviks planned to subsume all disparate Russian peoples into a great proletarian universality. In *Dr Zhivago*, Boris Pasternak has Lara bemoaning the cultural differences of the Jews, which only leaves them open to victimization by the Russians. She wants them to shake off their national distinctions, for their own sake. After the Second World War a different sort of homogeneous world-oneness, a liberal melding of differences, was thought to be the solution to world peace. Then towards the late 1960s radical debate changed.

From having been concerned with internationalism and class struggle, left-wing politics now incorporated other forms of struggle: the struggle of colony versus imperialist, of periphery against centre, of region against centralizing state. Nationalism swung from being a right-wing reactionary force to one that preoccupied the left.

The languages revitalized in the nineteenth century became badges of the tribes. There were other forms of kinship, but again and again people cited language as the core of their community. Only those whose language is under threat fully comprehend that to lose one's mother tongue is like losing a part of oneself. The sense of alienation is frightening. And you cannot alienate yourself from your own language and culture without damaging your own personality.

Not all tribal feeling depends on language. Many Bretons feel Breton without speaking the language. However, fervent nationalists such as Delphine Rodriguez claim that you can't be a convincing Breton without knowledge of Breton. It is the same in Wales. Many Welsh people think of themselves as Welsh even though they have never spoken the language, but the Welsh poet and Anglican priest R. S. Thomas argued that those who have forgotten their ancient tongue have no right to claim to be Welsh, and he accused them of betraying the land of their fathers. 'I imagine Wales,' he wrote, 'beautiful at all times, deserted and betrayed by so many who should have remained faithful to her.' He warned of the subtle assimilations, and the impending loss of some of the world's great literature. After all, the written word has value only if someone is able to read it.

When we began our journey I shared the general fear of such nationalism or tribalism, linking it with xenophobia and hatred. In the name of nationalism, the Balkans were tearing themselves apart. I passionately supported peoples' struggles against centralization, and their right to defend their homes and culture and languages, but if what D. H. Lawrence dismissed as 'proletarian homogeneity' was the price of avoiding Balkan-style bloodshed, was it not worth paying?

I had come to understand that there are different forms of nationalism, and the answer lies in distinguishing between them. There is popular nationalism and state nationalism. The word 'nation' has always been notoriously hard to define. The Sami and Frisians are divided territorially and by languages, with no political centre, nevertheless many of them think of themselves as one people, as a nation. The sense of many people belonging to a distinct cultural tradition seems so real that it has become so. The Macedonians may have no historical legitimacy as a nation, but they have created (amongst the Macedonians, if not the Albanians) the consciousness of nationality. It is that consciousness of community that defines the word 'nation', and also 'tribe'. The OED defines 'tribe' as a group of people sharing a common ancestry, but it also gives an alternative definition of 'tribe' as a fraternity, and this is the definition I go by. The danger lies not in nationalism or tribalism per se, but in popular nationalist revolutionaries taking control of the state, and using the power of the state – the propaganda machinery, schools, communications, armies, and so on – to pursue other more aggressive or defensive aims, often with the help of self-interested 'greater powers'. This was what we had seen in the Balkans. There is also the danger of nationalism being taken up as a cause by fundamentalist bullies and criminals.

However, on the whole we had encountered not hatred or xenophobia, but their opposite, a passionate love. Nils-Aslak Valkeapää's compositions and books, Alf-Isak Keskitalo's philosophical articles, Chillida's sculpture, Atxaga's novels, Llimós's paintings, Orati's poetry and singing, Ferdinand L'Antoine's lyric verses, Siegfried de Rachewiltz's museum, Delphine Rodriguez's accordion playing: all of these expressed love for a culture, for a place. Not one of them generated negative feelings of any sort. Indeed, the very words for the tribe – the motherland, *vaterland*, *patria*, *patrie*, or home, *heimat* – for most people conjure up something warm, lovable, natural, familiar. Annie L'Antoine had felt that her love for Provence was what made her Provençal. That sort of love is dangerous only when it gets exploited.

Again and again we had seen the inclusive nature of this sort of popular tribalism, not its aggressive xenophobia. I thought of Siegfried de Rachewiltz in the South Tyrol who was half American, half Bulgarian-Italian, Anghjulu Orati in Corsica who was half-

Italian, the 'Breton' accordionist Delphine Rodriguez who was half-Spanish. It was a thread running through our journey. There had been a man running a Ladin museum who turned out to be Italian, and the head of the nationalist PNV in Bilbao who was only half-Basque.

As I sat in the dark watching the Breton dancers, all in jeans, all young, I thought how easy it was for us. We could return to a country where we could read and enjoy our own literature, share a culture and history, speak our mother tongue. Why shouldn't these peoples do the same? The *coiffes* have gone, along with the traditional way of life – and many said good riddance to that – but have the mentalities changed so much that the languages we had heard and puzzled over from the Arctic to the Mediterranean will inevitably be extinguished too? Is the price of escaping from the clutches of the World Bitch necessarily an impoverishment of culture?

What these languages will never survive is indifference. Funds raised from the Plozévet festival were being used to support a young Plozévetienne who had set up a school in Tibet to help Tibetans learn to read and write in their own language before it was exterminated by the Chinese. It was a worthy cause. But what about the Plozévetienne's own language? Was that not also facing extinction? The plight of the exotic Tibetans had blinded the burghers of Plozévet to an equally endangered language right under their very noses.

Increasingly, I feared not so much the loss of the ability of people to speak their languages, but the loss of the languages themselves. I saw these mother tongues not as social tools, but as living organisms, pulsating, mutating, sensitive, sometimes shy, sometimes bombastic, sometimes belligerent, sometimes fighting for self-preservation, sometimes going underground, sometimes popping up unexpectedly somewhere else. Languages can be excluding, divisive, alienating. But we can also take pleasure in their diversity, in the sounds of them, their appearance, their grammatical foibles, the aesthetic sensation they create, what George Orwell called 'the joy of mere words'. Our languages are the greatest achievement of our intelligence, an intelligence uniquely human, and at the same time mysterious.

The speakers of these languages have choices: they can choose passive assimilation, allowing their culture and language to die; they can stand by and yawn; or they can fight to save it. But there is a third way. It is adaptability, assimilating a different culture but without surrendering to it. Many people are content to have two selves – Breton *and* French, Welsh *and* British, Frisian *and* German. Most (except extremists) see a value in this. The route is bilingual education.

If Europe's peoples could be brought up bilingual, their languages could be saved. In the Frisian school in Risum children were taught alongside each other in Frisian, Danish, and German. They all performed equally well. In Sleat primary school in Skye children are taught in Gaelic and English, and it appears that the Gaelic-medium children are doing as well as their English-medium peers, if not better. Far from hindering a child, bilingualism can stimulate a greater facility for handling all aspects of thought. The Gaelic-medium pupils' maths improved noticeably, possibly because bilingualism helped to develop their ability to think in abstract terms. They seemed more open to the possibility that there might be alternative views, alternative ways of expressing things.

Some linguists argue that bilingualism in one generation often ends up with monolingualism in the next. Obviously the more dominant language wins. It is possible to see a few pupils emerging from Sleat primary school bilingual in Gaelic and English, but it is hard to see this being maintained over generations if English continues to dominate. Thanks to the English-dominated British media, even in Welsh-medium secondary schools where every family has Welsh as its mother tongue, the language of the playground is still English. And there is little possibility of bilingualism working the other way, with English-speaking children being required to learn Welsh or Gaelic, Fenno-Scandian children required to learn Sami, German children required to learn North Frisian, Spanish children required to learn Basque or Catalan. There just isn't seen to be the need. The majority of Dutch people are bilingual, but they are bilingual with the useful English, not with the 'useless' language of their own country, Frisian.

Nevertheless, I believe it is worth the huge effort to maintain schools in which people study in their mother tongue. Eventually the language is seen to be of use. Gradually it seeps back into ordinary life. Its status goes up. Slowly people are reminded that they once spoke this marvellous language, and can retrieve their pride in it, and rescue it before it is too late.

The other solution for Europe's lesser-used languages is, paradoxically, that bastion of homogeneity, the EU. The EU was set up to prevent war between European states; by curtailing the power of those states, it allows the smaller peoples within them to flourish and coexist beneath its benevolent umbrella. When we set out, I assumed that the devolutionary virus attacking the big political units in Europe would inevitably kill their hosts, as in the Soviet Union and Yugoslavia, but within the EU I came to see it as a dynamic force, both centrifugal and centripetal. Anyone can see that variety brings enrichment. The EU could financially support the mass of different cultural interests, the different regions defined by their common cultures, and prove that it *is* possible to have D. H. Lawrence's 'distinction, savage distinction, savage distinction', without bloodshed. And in the future, when nation states may eventually wither away, these tribes will doubtless continue to exist, and even flourish and mutate.

The difficulty would be keeping a lid on them all. I could foresee a time when each class, each village, each family, would assert its right to independence as a separate tribe. Where would it ever end?

Damp seeped into my legs as I watched those dancers. Summer was ending, and with it our journey. The mournful Breton *biniou* expressed my sadness. But now that the end was almost in sight, Tallulah was chafing to get home to her friends, and to playgrounds where children spoke *her* language. She yearned to be part of a community of people who she may not know, but with whom she could assume a shared culture, a shared future. There was also the question of school. Tallulah had already missed the first year. The autumn term began in three weeks.

Richard, too, yearned for the space of a house, for stability and privacy. He had a hundred seeds of paintings germinating in his head, and he wanted to plant them on canvas: he had been nomad, now he wanted to be farmer.

For my part, in many ways I dreaded the end of our roving life. I didn't want to live fixed in one place, sharing a party wall, smelling our neighbours' cooking. I didn't want to sink into the dull routine of school runs. I also dreaded being sucked back into a telecommunicating world. I'd enjoyed our isolation; and the girls had spent eighteen months living in their own imaginations, with time to get bored and dream, a rarity in the world we would return to. I hated to break up our own little tribe.

But the moment had come to take our seventeenth ferry and fulfil Tallulah's dreams. Reluctantly, we packed the Mob. We spent our last evening on Cherbourg docks. When we disembarked here Xanthe had been a suckling babe in arms, unable even to sit. Now she was an exquisite brown-eyed child of nearly two, a blonde angel who could dance and talk. Tallulah lay in her top bunk, twirling her legs and drawing, while Richard was washing up. Xanthe reclined on my lap. Richard blew kisses at her across the Mob. Xanthe gazed at him, pursed her lips and said, 'Bum hole.'

Select Bibliography

General

Anderson, Benedict, *Imagined Communities*, Verso, London, 1983
Ascherson, Neal, *Black Sea*, Jonathan Cape, London, 1995
Burgess, Anthony, *A Mouthful of Air: Language and Languages, Especially English*, Hutchinson, London, 1992
Davies, Janet, *The Welsh language*, University Press of Wales, Cardiff, 1999
Fernández-Armesto, Felipe (ed.), *The Times Guide to the Peoples of Europe*, Times Books, London, 1994
Morris, Jan, *The Matter of Wales: Epic Views of a Small Country*, Penguin, Harmonsworth, 1986
— *Fifty Years of Europe*, Penguin, London, 1998
Pinker, Steven, *The Language Instinct*, Allen Lane, London, 1994
Thomas, R. S., *Cymru or Wales?*, Gomer Press, Llandysul, 1992

ONE Prouvènço, ma Patrio

Daudet, Alphonse, *Letters from my Windmill*, first published France, 1866, translated from French by Frederick Davies, Penguin, London, 1978
Pagnol, Marcel, *Jean de Florette & Manon of the Springs*, first published France, 1962, translated from French by W. E. van Heyningen, Picador, London, 1988
Posner, Rebecca, *The Romance Languages*, Cambridge University Press, Cambridge and New York, 1996

TWO War-torn Borderlands

Ungerer, Tomi, *Tomi*, Roberts Rhinehart, USA, 1998

THREE The Åland Islands

Kalevala the Land of Heroes, first published Finland, 1849, translated from Finnish by W. F. Kirby, J. M. Dent & Co., London, 1907

Lagerkvist, Pär, *Evening Land*, first published Sweden, 1953, translated from Swedish by W. H. Auden and Leif Sjöberg, Souvenir Press, London, 1977

FOUR Samiland

Chapman, Olive Murray, *Across Lapland with Sledge and Reindeer*, John Lane, London, 1932

Haetta, Odd-Mathis, *The Sami*, translated from Norwegian by Ole Petter Gurholt, Davvi Girji, 1996

Linnaeus, Carl, *Lachesis Lapponica*, first published Sweden, 1732, translated from Swedish, London, 1811

Rae, Edward, *The Land of the North Wind or, Travels among the Laplanders and the Samoyeds*, London, 1871

Schefferus, Johannes, *Lapponia*, first published Sweden, 1673, translated from Latin, Oxford, 1674

Sutherland, Halliday, *Lapland Journey*, Geoffrey Bles, London, 1938

Valkeapää, Nils-Aslak, *Greetings from Lappland*, first published Finland, 1971, translated from Norwegian by Beverley Wahl, Zed Press, London, 1982

Vorren, Ornulv, and Manker, Ernst, *Lapp Life and Customs*, first published Norway, 1961, translated from Norwegian by Kathless McFarlane, Oxford University Press, London, 1962

FIVE Friesland

Childers, Erskine, *The Riddle of the Sands*, first published London, 1903; with foreword by Erskine Hamilton Childers, Sidgwick & Jackson, London, 1975

Storm, Theodore, *The Dykemaster*, translated from German by Denis Jackson, Angel Classics, London, 1996

— *Immensee and Journey to a Hallig*, translated from German by Denis Jackson and Anja Nauck, Angel Classics, London, 1999

Watson, Alan, *The Germans: Who Are They Now?*, Methuen, London, 1992

SEVEN Flemish v. Walloon

Santé, Luc, *The Factory of Facts*, Granta, London, 1998

Conscience, Hendryk, *The Lion of Flanders or, The Battle of the Golden Spurs*, first published Belgium, 1838, Burns and Oates, London, 1881

EIGHT Who is Bernardo Atxaga?

Atxaga, Bernardo, *Obabakoak*, first published Spain, 1990, translated from Spanish by Margaret Jull Costa, Hutchinson, London, 1992

— *The Lone Man*, first published Spain, 1994, translated from Spanish by Margaret Jull Costa, Harvill, London, 1996

Collins, Roger, *The Basques*, Blackwell, Oxford, 1994

Sullivan, John, *ETA and Basque Nationalism, the fight for Euskadi 1890–1986*, Routledge, London, 1988

Trask, R. L., *The History of Basque*, Routledge, London, 1997

NINE A Time of Inconvenience, at an Inconvenient Time

Conversi, Daniele, *The Basques, the Catalans and Spain: Alternative Routes to Nationalist Mobilisation*, C. Hurst, London, 1997

Hughes, Robert, *Barcelona*, Harvill, London, 1999

Morris, Jan, *Spain*, Penguin, London, 1982

Orwell, George, *Homage to Catalonia*, Penguin, London, 1989

Tóibín, Colm, *Homage to Barcelona*, Simon & Schuster, London, 1990

TEN Vendetta

Carrington, Dorothy, *Granite Island*, Penguin, Harmondsworth, 1984

— *The Dream-Hunters of Corsica*, Phoenix, London, 1996

ELEVEN Bandit Country

Deledda, Grazia, *La Madre (The Woman and the Priest)*, first published Italy, 1920, translated from Italian by M. G. Seegman, Dedalus European Classics, London, 1987

Lawrence, D. H., *Sea and Sardinia*, Olive Press, London, 1989

Satta, Salvatore, *The Day of Judgement*, first published Italy, 1979, translated from Italian by Patrick Creagh, Collins Harvill, London, 1988

TWELVE Macédoine

Gage, Nicholas, *Eleni*, Harvill, London, 1989

Glenny, Misha, *The Balkans*, Granta, London, 1999

Hetherington, Paul, *Byzantine and Medieval Greece*, John Murray, London, 1991

Leigh Fermor, Patrick, *Roumeli*, Penguin, London, 1983

Myrivilis, Stratis, *Life in the Tomb*, translated from Greek by Peter Bien, with an introduction by Peter Levi, Quartet, London, 1987

West, Rebecca, *Black Lamb and Grey Falcon*, Macmillan, London, 1942

SELECT BIBLIOGRAPHY

THIRTEEN South Tyrol and the Ladin

Goethe, J. W., *Italian Journey 1786–1788*, translated by W. H.
  Auden and Elizabeth Mayer, Penguin, London, 1982

FOURTEEN The World Bitch

Galliou, Patrick, and Jones, Michael, *The Bretons*, Blackwell,
  Oxford, 1991
Hélias, Pierre-Jakez, *The Horse of Pride*, translated by June
  Guicharnaud, foreword by Laurence Wylie, Yale, New Haven
  and London, 1978
McDonald, Maryon, *'We are not French'*, Routledge, London,
  1989

OTHER PAN BOOKS

AVAILABLE FROM PAN MACMILLAN

WILL FIENNES
THE SNOW GEESE   0 330 37578 4   £14.99

JEREMY SEAL
THE SNAKEBITE SURVIVORS' CLUB   0 330 34834 5   £6.99

ALEXANDRA FULLER
DON'T LET'S GO
TO THE DOGS TONIGHT   0 330 49023 0   £15.99

LAURA BLUMENFELD
REVENGE   0 330 49361 2   £10.99

All Pan Macmillan titles can be ordered from our website,
www.panmacmillan.com, or from your local bookshop
and are also available by post from:

Bookpost, PO Box 29, Douglas, Isle of Man IM99 1BQ
Credit cards accepted. For details:
Telephone: 01624 836000
Fax: 01624 670923
E-mail: bookpost@enterprise.net
www.bookpost.co.uk

Free postage and packing in the United Kingdom

Prices shown above were correct at the time of going to press.
Pan Macmillan reserve the right to show new retail prices on covers
which may differ from those previously advertised in the text
or elsewhere.